Articles on Cryptography and Cryptanalysis

U.S. Signal Corps

Contents

\pagenumbering{{roman}}

\newpage Nimble Books LLC: The AI Lab for Book-Lovers

~ Fred Zimmerman, Editor ~

Humans and AI making books richer, more diverse, and more surprising.

Publishing Information

(c) 2024 Nimble Books LLC

ISBN: 978-1-60888-319-6

Publisher's Notes

This annotated edition illustrates the capabilities of the AI Lab for Book-Lovers to add context and ease-of-use to manuscripts. It includes several types of abstracts, building from simplest to more complex: TLDR (one word), ELI5, TLDR (vanilla), Scientific Style, and Action Items; essays to increase viewpoint diversity, such as Grounds for Dissent, Red Team Critique, and MAGA Perspective; and Notable Passages and Nutshell Summaries for each page. # Bibliographic Keywords

Code section of the general staff, French Army; Cryptograms analysis methods; Radio communication during World War I; International Radio Convention; Cipher devices during World War I; Polyalphabetic encipherment; Telegraph and Radio Conferences; Signal communication in World War I; Military communication systems; Cryptogram decryption techniques;

TLDR (three words)

Codes, ciphers, secrets.

ELI5

This book is about secret codes and how people try to crack them. It's like a puzzle book for spies! Imagine you're sending messages to your friends, but you don't want anyone else to read them. You could use a code to hide the real words, like replacing "cat" with "dog." But other people might try to figure out your code and read your messages. This book tells you about the different ways people make secret codes, how people try to break them, and what happens when people make mistakes with their codes.

Historiographical Abstract

This collection of articles, originally published in the Signal Corps Bulletin, offers a glimpse into the evolving world of cryptography and cryptanalysis during the early 20th century. It primarily focuses on the experiences of World War I, showcasing both the successes and failures of code-making and code-breaking efforts. The authors, primarily military signal officers, emphasize the practical realities of using codes in the field, highlighting the dangers of carelessness and the need for well-trained personnel.

The work is notable for its historical perspective, offering valuable insights into the development of cryptographic techniques, the evolution of codes and ciphers in response to wartime demands, and the emergence of cryptanalysis as a vital tool for military intelligence. However, the book is limited by its focus on military applications and its occasional tendency to romanticize the role of cryptography. Nevertheless, it provides a fascinating account of the early stages of modern cryptography and its impact on warfare.

Summaries of Each Article

1. Cryptanalysis (Bulletin No. 30, June 1925)

This article presents a real-life cryptogram from the 18th century used in diplomatic correspondence. It challenges readers to decipher the message, which is encoded using a simple substitution cipher. The article highlights the importance of cryptanalysis in understanding historical events and emphasizes that even seemingly simple ciphers can be challenging to break.

2. Problems of Code (Bulletin No. 33, March 1926)

This article, translated from a French publication by Colonel Givierge, discusses the crucial role of code and cipher in World War I. Givierge argues that the Germans' success at Tannenberg was partly due to their ability to decrypt Russian communications. He highlights the dangers of carelessness and indiscretion in handling cryptographic materials, using numerous anecdotes from the war to illustrate his points. The article stresses the need for trained personnel, emphasizing the importance of cryptographic expertise within military staffs.

3. Problems of Code (Continued) (Bulletin No. 34, May 1926)

This is the second part of Colonel Givierge's article. It continues to examine the importance of code and cipher in warfare, focusing on the dangers of stereotyped formulas and the necessity of concealing repetitions within messages. Givierge advocates for the use of superencipherment (enciphering a code dispatch) to further enhance security. He also discusses the potential use of cryptographic machines to improve the reliability and security of communications, but recognizes the practical challenges of implementing such machines in military settings.

4. The New Regulations Governing Code Language in International Communications (Bulletin No. 47, March 1929)

This article by Major William F. Friedman, a renowned cryptanalyst, delves into the history of code language in international telecommunications. He traces the evolution of regulations governing code words, from their initial use of bona fide dictionary words to the introduction of artificial words and the complexities of the "pronounceability rule." Friedman describes the International Telegraph Conference of Brussels (1928) which led to new regulations aimed at standardizing code language and addressing the issues of cost and accuracy. He concludes by posing questions about the effectiveness of these new rules and the challenges they pose for communication agencies.

5. Tannenberg - A Study in Faulty Signal Communication (Bulletin No. 49, July-August 1929)

This article by Major H. C. Ingles examines the disastrous Battle of Tannenberg in 1914, focusing on the role of faulty signal communication in the Russian defeat. Ingles analyzes the organizational structure of Russian signal units, highlighting their lack of adequate equipment and training. He describes the failure of Russian commanders to establish effective communication between their armies and to coordinate their movements, leading to a widening gap between the Russian First and Second Armies and exposing the Second Army to a devastating German attack.

6. Cryptogram (Bulletin No. 56, September-October 1930)

This article presents a cryptogram for readers to solve. The message is in a simple substitution cipher.

7. Solution to Cryptogram in Proceeding Bulletin (Bulletin No. 57, November-December 1930)

This article provides the solution to the cryptogram presented in the previous Bulletin.

8. The International Telecommunication Convention (Bulletin No. 76, January-February 1934)

This article by Major William F. Friedman, discusses the historic background and significance of the International Telecommunication Convention (1932), which sought to unify regulations governing international communication by wire, telephone, and radio. Friedman contrasts the evolution of telegraph and radio conventions, explaining the reasons behind the United States' reluctance to join the International Telegraph Union. He outlines the key provisions of the new convention, emphasizing its importance for international cooperation and its impact on the development of communication technologies.

9. Secret Causes of German Successes on the Eastern Front (Bulletin No. 91, July-August 1936)

This article by Colonel A. M. Nikolaieff explores the role of cryptanalysis in the German military successes on the Eastern Front in World War I. Nikolaieff argues that the German victories were not solely due to superior artillery, aircraft, or strategy. He reveals how the Austrian intelligence service successfully intercepted and decrypted Russian radio messages, providing the Germans with vital information about Russian troop movements and strategic plans. Nikolaieff concludes by discussing the lessons learned from the Russian failures, emphasizing the need for robust cryptographic security and the dangers of careless radio communication.

10. Powers and Limitations of Radio Communication Within a Modern Field Army (Bulletin No. 91, July-August 1936)

This article by Major R. B. Moran, examines the role of radio in modern warfare, particularly in the context of a mechanized field army. Moran analyzes the technical factors influencing radio transmission, including frequency bands, interference, and transmission distance. He also discusses the strengths and limitations of radio compared to other forms of communication, such as wire lines, visual signals, and messengers. Moran draws on historical examples from

World War I to illustrate the challenges of maintaining reliable radio communication in combat situations. He concludes by emphasizing the importance of careful frequency assignment, maintaining radio discipline, and developing robust cryptographic systems to ensure communication security.

11. Powers and Limitations of Radio Communication Within a Modern Field Army (Continued) (Bulletin No. 92, September-October 1936)

This is the second part of Major Moran's article. It delves deeper into the threats posed to radio communications, including enemy interception and jamming, and the countermeasures that can be employed to mitigate these threats. Moran explores the use of radio goniometry, intercept, and camouflage techniques. He concludes by reiterating the importance of careful planning, training, and discipline in maximizing the effectiveness of radio communication while minimizing its risks.

12. Cipher Busting in the Seventh Corps Area A. A. R. S. (Bulletin No. 97, July-September 1937)

This article by Colonel Stanley L. James, describes the efforts to promote cryptanalysis within the Army Amateur Radio System (AARS) in the Seventh Corps Area. James discusses the introduction of single transposition ciphers to supplement the traditional substitution ciphers, fostering greater interest and participation in cryptanalytic activities. He highlights the use of Cipher Buster Certificates as a motivational tool and the importance of sharing knowledge and techniques among AARS members.

13. Analysis Versus the Probable Word (Bulletin No. 97, July-September 1937)

This article by Howell C. Brown, a cryptanalyst with the Ninth Corps Area AARS, explores two common methods of cryptanalysis: the "probable word" method and the analytical method. Brown argues that while the "probable word" method can be quicker, it is also riskier, as a wrong guess can waste considerable time. He advocates for a more balanced approach that combines both methods, using analysis to confirm or refute initial guesses. He also introduces the Bazeries-Efsee method, a technique for quickly identifying potential key words within a cipher text.

14. Edgar Allan Poe, Cryptographer (Bulletin No. 97, July-September 1937)

This article by Lieutenant Colonel William F. Friedman examines Edgar Allan Poe's reputation as a cryptographer. Friedman analyzes Poe's cryptographic writings, concluding that Poe was more of a dabbler in the field than a true expert. He criticizes Poe's tendency to exaggerate his abilities and his inaccurate statements about the complexity of certain cryptographic methods. Friedman also discusses a letter written by Poe to Richard Bolton, a reader who claimed to have solved Poe's challenge cryptogram. The article casts doubt on Poe's claims about Bolton's solution and reveals Poe's insecurity and tendency to downplay his rivals' accomplishments.

15. Edgar Allan Poe, Cryptographer (Addendum) (Bulletin No. 98, October-December 1937)

This is an addendum to the previous article on Poe. It provides further details about Poe's cryptographic writings and highlights his misconceptions about the complexity of certain ciphers. Friedman critiques Poe's explanation of a cipher alphabet based on the key phrase "le gouvernement provisoire," demonstrating its impracticality and highlighting Poe's lack of understanding of basic cryptanalytic principles. He also includes the two cryptograms Poe claimed to have solved, challenging readers to try their hand at solving them.

16. Jefferson's Cipher Device (Bulletin No. 99, January-March 1938)

This article focuses on Thomas Jefferson's invention of a cipher device, known as the "wheel cipher." The article reprints Jefferson's original description of the device, which he wrote in 1795. The article also discusses the historical significance of Jefferson's invention, highlighting its resemblance to modern cipher devices and its early use of polyalphabetic encryption.

17. The Use of Codes and Ciphers in the World War and Lessons to Be Learned Therefrom (Bulletin No. 101, July-September 1938)

This article by Lieutenant Colonel William F. Friedman provides a comprehensive overview of the use of codes and ciphers in World War I. He discusses the challenges faced by the various belligerents in developing and maintaining secure communication systems. Friedman analyzes the technical aspects of code and cipher systems, highlighting the importance of proper design, secure handling, and trained personnel. He also emphasizes the need for a balanced approach to cryptography, recognizing the limitations of both code books and cipher devices. The article concludes by outlining important lessons learned from the wartime experiences, underscoring the need for a robust cryptographic security program that encompasses careful message drafting, secure handling of cryptographic materials, and adherence to strict procedures for transmission.

18. The Cryptanalyst Accepts a Challenge (Bulletin No. 103, January-March 1939)

This article by Lieutenant Colonel William F. Friedman presents a series of cryptographic challenges taken from historical works on cryptography. He challenges readers to solve these ciphers, offering to publish the solutions and methods employed by successful decipherers.

19. One Method of Solution of the Schooling ("Absolutely Undecipherable") Cryptogram (Bulletin No. 104, April-June 1939)

This article by Major General J. 0. Mauborgne, the Chief Signal Officer, presents a detailed analysis of a cryptogram by John Holt Schooling, who claimed it to be "absolutely undecipherable." Mauborgne breaks down the cipher system, demonstrating the importance of frequency analysis and applying the probable word method to identify potential key words. Through a step-by-step process, he successfully solves the cryptogram, proving that Schooling's claim was false.

20. Solutions to "Challenge Messages" (Bulletin No. 104, April-June 1939)

This article provides the solutions to the "challenge messages" presented in the previous Bulletin.

21. The Continental Code (Bulletin No. 104, April-June 1939)

This article by Captain T. T. Teague discusses the Continental Telegraph Code, which is a modification of the Morse Code. Teague examines the historical development of the Morse Code and the reasons for the adoption of the Continental Code by many countries. He explains the structural differences between the two codes and evaluates their relative advantages in terms of speed, clarity, and flexibility. He concludes by tracing the adoption of the Continental Code by the U.S. Navy and Army and its continued use in telegraphy and radio communications.

22. Solutions to Ciphers (Bulletin No. 105, July-September 1939)

This article provides a brief summary of the solutions submitted by readers to the "challenge messages" published in the previous Bulletin.

23. The Earliest Solution of a Multiple Alphabet Cipher Written With the Use of a Key (Bulletin No. 106, October-December 1939)

This article by Charles J. Mendelsohn, a historian and former military intelligence officer, discusses the work of the Renaissance cryptographer Giovanni Battista Porta. Mendelsohn refutes the common belief that Porta's work only dealt with single-alphabet ciphers. He examines Porta's writings on multiple alphabet ciphers, particularly his discussion of disk ciphers and his claim to have solved a cipher using a proverb as a key. Mendelsohn concludes that Porta's work represents an early, albeit imperfect, attempt to address the challenges of deciphering multiple alphabet ciphers, thus challenging the traditional view of Kasiski as the first to address this problem.

24. Jules Verne as Cryptographer (Bulletin No. 108, April-June 1940)

This article by Lieutenant Colonel William F. Friedman examines the use of cryptography in the works of Jules Verne. Friedman analyzes three of Verne's novels that feature ciphers: A Journey to the Center of the Earth, The Giant Raft, and Mathias Sandorf. He critiques Verne's methods for solving these ciphers, highlighting the author's reliance on simplistic and often inaccurate techniques. He demonstrates how Verne's solutions rely on "trick" methods rather than genuine cryptanalytic skill.

25. The Crypt Bug (Bulletin No. 109, July-December 1940)

This is a humorous poem by Master Sergeant Charles Murray about a cryptanalyst who struggles with a cipher problem. The poem highlights the dedication and perseverance required for cryptanalytic work, while also poking fun at the frustrations and challenges of the profession.

These summaries highlight the diversity of topics covered in the book. The articles range from historical accounts to technical discussions of cryptanalytic methods, emphasizing the critical importance of cryptography for military and diplomatic security throughout the 20th century.

Striking Passages

1. **From "Cryptanalysis" (Bulletin No. 30, June 1925):**

   "In several respects this is a peculiarly interesting and valuable problem. At first glance it will appear to be somewhat simple; then it will look as if dynamite or T. N. T. will be necessary to crack it; then when you will almost have given up the ghost you will probably find a tiny place for your chisel, and will soon" knock it for a gool." It can be done, but you will need some patience."

This passage captures the allure and challenge of cryptanalysis, comparing the process to a thrilling, intricate puzzle. It highlights the often frustrating, but ultimately rewarding, nature of deciphering codes.

2. **From "Problems of Code" (Bulletin No. 33, March 1926):**

   "With regard to code in our armies, the officers employed in the staffs were more or less familiar with information designated as special, which came from a similar source. It is known that the French decrypting service has obtained much information from German code telegrams. With regard, however, to this subject, which it was endeavored to keep secret during the war, legends have arisen."

This passage emphasizes the vital role of cryptanalysis in gathering intelligence during wartime, but also points to the secrecy surrounding such activities. It underscores the tension between the need for information and the imperative to protect intelligence sources.

3. **From "The New Regulations Governing Code Language in International Communications" (Bulletin No. 47, March 1929):**

   "The large users had discovered a way of making code words so that they could send two or more at the cost of only one, a procedure which, of course, was highly useful to the users, and detrimental to the operating agencies."

This passage highlights the constant battle between code users and the agencies that provide communication services, revealing the challenges of balancing efficiency and security. It also shows how creative users can find ways to circumvent rules, a recurring theme in cryptography.

4. **From "Tannenberg - A Study in Faulty Signal Communication" (Bulletin No. 49, July-August 1929):**

   "The closest liaison must be maintained between the First and Second Armies. a sufficient screen being placed in front of the lake position."

This passage underscores the importance of clear and consistent communication, especially in complex military operations. It highlights the dangers of faulty signal communication, which can lead to miscommunication, missed opportunities, and even disastrous defeats.

5. **From "The International Telecommunication Convention" (Bulletin No. 76, January-February 1934):**

   "The only ones conspicuous by their failure to sign were the United States, Canada, and Mexico."

This passage reveals the unique position of the United States in international telecommunications, as the country's private ownership of communication facilities prevented its participation in the International Telegraph Union.

WAR DEPARTMENT

OFFICE OF THE CHIEF SIGNAL OFFICER
WASHINGTON

ARTICLES

ON

CRYPTOGRAPHY AND
Reprinted from
CRYPTANALYSIS

William F. Fre[...]
Washington
1942
3

Umol-huun   tah-tiyal

William   Frederick
yetel
Elizebeth   Smith   Friedman

Lay   ca-hunnil   kubenbil   tech   same.
This our book we entrusted you a while-ago.
Ti   manaan   apaclam-tz'a   lo   toon
It not-being you-return-give it us,
Epahal   ca-baat   tumen   ah-men.
Is-being-sharpened our-axe by the expert.

Declassified on 5 May 1950
W.F.F.

~~Restricted~~

WAR DEPARTMENT
OFFICE OF THE CHIEF SIGNAL OFFICER
WASHINGTON

ARTICLES

ON

CRYPTOGRAPHY AND CRYPTANALYSIS

Reprinted from
THE SIGNAL CORPS BULLETIN

was declassified on 5 May 1950. W.F.F.

Prepared under the direction of the
CHIEF SIGNAL OFFICER

UNITED STATES
GOVERNMENT PRINTING OFFICE
WASHINGTON : 1942

30 April 1959

Paul S. Willard
Colonel,   AGC
Adjutant General

FOREWORD

With a view to providing useful collateral literature for students interested in cryptography and cryptanalysis, the articles on these subjects which, with one exception, have appeared from time to time in the various issues of the *Signal Corps Bulletin*, have here been collected and reprinted in a single publication. The exception referred to concerns Yves Gyldén's *The Contribution of the Cryptographic Bureaus in the World War*, which appeared in seven installments in the *Bulletin* (Nos. 75 to 81, inclusive) and was reprinted in 1935 as a separate publication under the title indicated.

For technical reasons it was difficult to change the format of the original articles with respect to page and footnote references. The reader should, however, find no difficulty in locating references in case he desires to do so.

WILLIAM F. FRIEDMAN,
Head Cryptanalyst.

OFFICE OF THE CHIEF SIGNAL OFFICER,
Washington,
August 1, 1942.

TABLE OF CONTENTS

v

Cryptanalysis *

The following is an actual example of the type of cryptogram employed in diplomatic correspondence by European foreign offices during the early part of the eighteenth century. When found recently, in spite of the fact that the recipient wrote the translation in the exact interlinear manner given below, historians had some difficulty in proving the accuracy and, in fact, the authenticity of the translation. Can you do it?

As given below, a certain number of the " 1's " are underscored. In the original they were crossed out by a diagonal line the direction of which was opposite to that of a similar oblique line which seems to separate the figures into groups. Several errors in the original have been corrected. The lines have been numbered for future reference; they were, of course, not numbered in the original.

*(No. 30, June, 1925)

Whitehall 5th Febry 1747/8

Sir,

1	the King being informed that
2	1717818271 382 / 7265912
3	the Swedish Secretary here has received Orders
4	18, 8 / 31881 81, 96, 41 323232 / 1136621913
5	from His Court to present a Memorial the
6	9455, 26019 / 9871865 / 95415301227 / 778
7	purport of which is to desire your immediate
8	0006, 2 / 9471243 / 668 / 870 / 865 / 1398 /
9	479984
10	Recal, and as a compliance there with upon
11	14, 93771366 / 203 / 255 / 3041 2571 745 / 40811
12	such a representation would not be consistent
13	3, 658819, 2750 / 3014 / 11268954543 / 1887
14	with His Majesty's dignity, I have His Majesty
15	Com-
16	11536 / 249117585538706, 3474115188 -
17	-mands to direct you upon the receipt of this
18	6093, 292412, 4259 / 6091311, 2334 / 865
19	letter to leave Stockhom as soon as
20	8424, 1919, 2388 / 2681840 / 2, 142454741
21	12437873, 48615 / 3, 475717, 5 / 255 / 97321515
22	possible and to return into His Majesty's
23	presence acqu-
24	355, 2035814 / 5, 68, 66093, 2954, 777925 4614
25	-ainting However the Ministers of His
26	Swedish
27	3881 927870 / 5681 553 / 243 / 60918, 93,
28	221794, 91
29	Majesty before you depart, that the frequent
30	indig-
31	379 / 81, 8778260 / 835 / 659 / 6168 / 259 249
32	611661
33	Indignitys, which have been of late offered to
34	the
35	24 31974 / 339 / 592584 / 119446684, 19 / 249 / 5,
36	12
37	caracter you bear from the King, and for which
38	827 / 2031 83866184, 9259 / 5362, 29201640119,
39	8
40	you have not found any inclination in the
41	Court of
42	Stockholm, to make you redress, Notwith-
43	standing the
44	1 91877, 5 / 865 / 17, 2 / 4, 91 / 278 / 438 / 492 /
45	227 / 954592896
46	many Memorials presented by You in pur-
47	suance of Your Orders from time to time have
48	determ-
49	411, 99, 80006, 2979 4086319 / 4, 99455,
50	269758114
51	-ined the King to recall you, from your present
52	6197 / 2593985689, 81592 / 827 / 865 /
53	366832411, 91

54 residence: at the Same time I have t
55   pleasure
56 5, 24, 91954 / 26118 / 55312, 114293 /
57   984528202984 /
58 of acquainting you that the King is entirely
59 11543 / 388 / 370 / 697 / 2, 4 / 259 / 778 / 353 /
60   243 / 771792115
61 Satisfyed with your Conduct and with
62 4, 918, 81827 / 8701 6661 6971 268 / 7, 4 /
63   49751921
64 your Zealous and diligent endeavours during
65 5884, 19863 9365188 41, 19 / 9, 99843097431
66 the whole Course of your Ministry at Stockholm
67 2013 / 829 / 6166980 / 356 / 5531 1632 / 778 /
68   785 / 9874, 9
69   624633611594, 65437, 151.
70 I am, Sir, Your most obedient humble Servant

                    CHESTERFIELD.

   P. S. I have just received your letter of the
   15th past.

*   *   *   *   *   *   *

In several respects this is a peculiarly interesting and valuable problem. At first glance it will appear to be somewhat simple; then it will look as if dynamite or T. N. T. will be necessary to crack it; then when you will almost have given up the ghost you will probably find a tiny place for your chisel, and will soon " knock it for a gool." It can be done, but you will need some patience. Solution will be given in a subsequent issue of the Bulletin.—[Editor's note.]

*   *   *   *   *   *   *

After having wrestled with the above problem, here is a simple one while waiting for dinner:

ARLC) EIBNU (P
EIBNU

(Compliments of A. S. Marthens, second lieutenant, Sig-Res.)

PROBLEMS OF CODE *

[Translation of an article by Colonel Givierge, chief of the code section of the general staff, French Army]

[FOREWORD.—This interesting and important article, which appeared in the June and July, 1924, numbers of the Revue Militaire Française, was called to the attention of the office of the Chief Signal Officer by Maj. Karl Truesdell, Signal Corps. The translation was made by the translation section of the military intelligence division, General Staff, and edited, with notes, by W. F. Friedman, cryptanalyst, O. C. S. O. It is believed that the entire article is worthy of close study by all Signal Corps personnel having to deal with the problems of maintaining secrecy of communication. The article has been divided up into two parts. The second part will appear in the next number of this BULLETIN.]

In the first number of the Revue Militaire Française General Dupont stated in a few lines the importance of code during the World War. One of the elements of the Tannenberg victory, he said, was the understanding by the Germans of the Russian cipher. All the orders of our allies transmitted by wireless telegraph were translated in the staff of Ludendorff and sent each day to the general, who did not draw up the program for the next day until he had taken note of them, and who showed a certain impatience when these documents were not brought to him at the regular hour.

With regard to code in our armies, the officers employed in the staffs were more or less familiar with information designated as special, which came from a similar source. It is known that the French *decrypting* [1] service has obtained much information from German code telegrams. With regard, however, to this subject, which it was endeavored to keep secret during the war, legends have arisen. They have aided in supporting, in the study of questions relative to the employment of code, arguments the significance of which they singularly distort. Therefore, we have concluded that there were more advantages than disadvantages in settling the rôle

---

[1] One is said to decode a document of which he has the official key, a document addressed to him, for example. Specialists decrypt cryptograms the key to which they have found without the knowledge possessed by the enemy, generally by their skill.

[The French have coined the words "décrypt," "décrypteur," "décryptement," etc. (equivalent to the words proposed by me—cryptanalyze, cryptanalyst, etc.), to cover the special case of solution by analysis. The latter terms will be used in this translation as the equivalents of the French terminology. It may also be added that in the original the French term "chiffre" is used without distinction to apply to either code text or cipher text; where, from other information, the author really has special reference to cipher, I have translated the word "chiffre" as "cipher," but where special reference is to code, I have translated the same word, as "code."—W. F. F.]

*(No. 33, March, 1926)

4

of code at certain moments during operations and to deduce from it, if possible, conclusions applicable to future operations. The secrets which we might be reproached with violating are no longer such for those who follow these questions closely. The newspapers have made, and still make, innumerable allusions to the results of the work carried on in connection with code; the Matin of March 7, 1924, in connection with the arrest of a celebrated woman spy, mentions the part played by telegrams sent from Madrid to Berlin, and translated by the code section, in the investigation started in regard to her. Neither has the former chief of the code service in the Ministry of War seen anything improper in giving, in the review, Radio-Electricité, and in the April number of Science Moderne, information which we here merely summarize without much exceeding its scope.

The code section of the Ministry of War, established in 1912, was at first attached to the cabinet of the minister, for various reasons, of which some were of a very substantial kind, such as the necessity of encoding and decoding the current correspondence of the ministry. This work was previously intrusted to the officer on duty in the cabinet, and documents addressed to the official telegraph service or coming from this establishment were passed on by various methods, the only convenient liaison point of which was the building located at 14 rue St. Dominique. The section had only two officer specialists, Major Cartier and the writer of this article. A few other officers, included in organizations of troops and not exempt from any service there, formed a commission of military cryptography, certain members of which composed the nucleus of a decoding bureau provided for war time. The studies of this military commission, the secretary of which since 1903 had been Captain Cartier, had been directed to cryptographic methods in general, and to those which might be assumed to be prescribed by foreign regulations in particular. They had ended, on the one hand, in the adoption into service in our army of code books and word-for-word systems; on the other, in the printing of a series of confidential notes meant to supply new cryptanalysts with the materials for study necessary to enable them to undertake, without groping their way, researches with respect to certain already complicated systems.

Although it was attached to the cabinet of the minister, the code section worked in intimate liaison with the army staff. An experiment relating to the organization of the decoding service in war time was made during the trip of the army staff, directed by General Joffre, from April 28 to May 2, 1914. Another trip of the staff, from the 25th to the 29th of May, gave an opportunity to study the encoding service, then intrusted to all the staff officers, and its relations with the transmission service, especially by radiotelegraphy. Let us take note that the chief of the code section, being the chief of

6

the Central Bureau of Wireless Telegraphy, and as such charged with numerous studies regarding the operation of national and international radiotelegraphy, was interested primarily in problems relative to our military wireless telegraph system. Moreover, the regulations as to the employment of special radiotelegraphic stations (listening, interference, radiogoniometry), approved by the chief of the general staff, placed these stations, in time of war under the direction of the officer in charge of decoding at general headquarters. In fact, only one officer was provided to represent the code service in the armies, and this officer was assigned to *G–2*, of general headquarters.

Although the order which settled this last point was dated July 28, 1914, the commander in chief gave orders, on mobilization, for the establishment of a large code service at general headquarters, where code correspondence had to be exclusively intrusted to specialists. Arriving alone at Vitry-le-François, the ex-assistant of Major Cartier in the code section, now become chief of the code service at general headquarters, and soon, in fact, chief of the code service of the armies, had six collaborators less than a week afterwards. That was not too much for an intensive day and night service.

Just as the preparations for the code organization had proved insufficient, so the equipment for the study of enemy radios proved to be too small. The decoding bureau, which remained at Paris, was supplied with radiograms intercepted by stations established in time of peace in the great fortifications of the east. These stations prior to mobilization had only very rarely furnished to the commission of cryptography documents regarding German transmissions. Moreover, the nature thereof did not appear to correspond with the indications which the secret services had obtained regarding German methods and which had served as a basis for very complete studies. The decoding bureau then awaited with confidence and curiosity the first documents concerning the war. At first these were rare, the Germans still being in their territory, where there existed a system of wire communications. But after the passage of the frontier they soon became very numerous. Unfortunately, the personnel of the listening posts was not accustomed to such an abundance of documents nor to the method of transmission of field stations, and the text of a message collected by different posts reached the cryptanalysts in versions often very different and rarely similar. The attempt was made to have recourse, while awaiting the multiplication of fixed stations, to the collaboration of mobile wireless telegraph stations of the armies, in order to have more numerous versions, which permitted of establishing "on a majority basis" the most probable text. This organization did not, for lack of preparation, give a desirable result; but it was soon seen, nevertheless, that the

Germans had entirely given up one of the relatively simple methods, which we know were used in their army, and peculiarities unexplained at that time gave rise to doubts as to the use of the complicated method employed in time of peace conjointly with the former.

Fortunately, the difficulties encountered by our listening personnel were also encountered by the German radiotelegraphers. Many telegrams were full of errors, which gave rise to questions and repetitions, and soon, intoxicated perhaps by their progress, disdaining precautions, and exasperated by the difficulties which they encountered in the use of cipher correspondence, the Germans, especially on the marching flank, where the cavalry was, transmitted their messages in clear. That was the time of the Marwitz telegrams, which the officers of the *G-2s* still remember.

These dispatches in clear were the source of errors profitable to the cipher specialists. In view of the lowering of the barriers which prohibit the use of clear text for radio, even the units which still transmitted cryptograms allowed discipline to relax. It is known that in Germany telegrams were then enciphered and deciphered by the radiotelegraph officer; the text in clear was at the wireless telegraph station. When difficulties in decipherment occurred, request in clear was made for information regarding the words which could not be deciphered, and the latter were transmitted in clear. Moreover, the examination of the messages in clear familiarized our specialists with the formulas and the abbreviations of the German correspondence; these abbreviations and the letters of no significance used for punctuation explained the technical anomalies noted in the first texts. And soon the code section, which had been transported to Bordeaux, every day sent to general headquarters the translations of a few radiotelegrams. But these translations were made one by one by makeshift methods. What was sought were keys which would enable every officer of *G-2* to translate all the cryptograms.

The first key was not found until the 1st of October.[2] In view of the miracles of ingenuity displayed under the direction of Major Cartier, by Major Olivari, and the interpreters Freyss and Schwab, who accomplished this work, we can only deplore the incomprehensible delay in arriving at general headquarters of certain documents which might have facilitated the researches and would probably have brought them to a conclusion sooner. If, in fact, the papers relative to cipher, which had not been destroyed by the crew of the Zeppelin that fell on August 21 at Celles, documents of a limited interest, however, reached general headquarters by the 22d

---

[2] It seems clear, in view of the preceding paragraph, that certain cryptograms had been solved prior to Oct. 1, 1914, but that these solved dispatches had no bearing upon the tactics of the Battle of the Marne seems also very clear, in view of the statements made by Colonel Givierge in the fifth paragraph following this one.—W. F. F.

and the ministry by the 23d, it was because they had been sent immediately to the assistant chief of staff of the Twenty-first Corps, Lieutenant Colonel Thévenin, a member of the commission of military cryptography. A notebook containing reference to keys previously used, found at Fontenoy-la-Joute, near Baccarat, only reached general headquarters on September 22, and a still more interesting notebook found on the 20th, containing a rough diagram of encipherment based on an obsolete key, which already figured in the document of Fontenoy and verified the latter, did not reach Bordeaux until the 28th. Lastly, in studying later the records of the listening stations of the east it was seen that they contained many intercepted telegrams which, doubtless, owing to errors in the address or in translation, had not arrived in time to be of use in the deciphering bureau.

The key thus discovered was communicated to the armies, with strict orders to keep this source of information secret; but, by the 3d of October, it was necessary to try to stop, by means of a circular from general headquarters, the innumerable abuses of the preceding day, when the telephone lines had been congested with conversations regarding the messages which had been deciphered. On the 21st, in sending a new key, the general in chief wrote: "I have been informed that during the period when the previous key was in use, the most elementary precautions were neglected in certain staffs. The decipherment of German cryptograms had become a kind of game there. The existence of the key, the exact or supposed contents of telegrams, became the subject of conversations even among the soldiers of regiments or service units." The effect of this note was very small, as, toward the 10th of December, a new circular treats of the same subject: "Some officers speak in front of orderlies, sometimes among unknown civilians, about the German key. One of them even recently asked in a loud voice, in the vestibule of headquarters, whether the key had been found again. Allusions have been made before the troops as to the results of special information and have even reached the press (see Figaro of Dec. 2). In order to preserve secrecy in regard to such a question, it is necessary that a minimum number of persons be intrusted with it, and that these persons always bear discretion in mind."

This last circular was based on an important incident. The first key had been found on the 1st of October. On the 17th the radiograms became untranslatable, but an examination of them showed that the system of encipherment had not changed, and the new key was communicated on the 21st to the armies. A new change at the beginning of November left the staffs three days in suspense; one of the succeeding keys was discovered on the same day that it was put into use. Then, on the 18th of November, the telegrams once more became enigmas, and the technical changes showed that the system of encipherment had been modified.[3]

The contrary would have been astonishing, with all the carelessness to which we have alluded and which affected not only the zone of the armies but the entourage of the Minister of War and even certain civilian circles of Bordeaux The indiscretions had even worried the chief of cabinet of the minister to such an extent that the transfer of the decoding bureau to general headquarters was for a time considered.

For studying the new system there were available no data other than the cryptograms themselves, which, moreover, had become relatively few. The former members of the commission of cryptography, now with the armies—Captain Paulier and Captain Latreille and Lieutenant Colonel Thévenin—set to work to aid their comrades attached to the centers for cryptanalytic studies. *Carelessness of encipherers, skillfully turned to advantage, put the specialists on the track,*[4] and, thanks to the pooling of certain results, Lieutenant Colonel Thévenin, then assistant chief of staff of an army corps at Noeux-les-Mines, discovered, on the 10th of December, the new system and the new key. It was in communicating this information that the circular of the 11th, referred to above, was sent out, and, instead of familiarizing all the armies with the key, the information was restricted to those who were then conducting active operations.

We shall not dwell on the discovery of successive keys of the new system and its variants, nor on the work, of historical interest, which consisted in recovering the first keys, prior to October 1, and in translating telegrams captured since the beginning of the war. It was in this way that knowledge was first gained regarding the correspondence exchanged at the time of the Battle of the Marne and that *G–2* could begin a research of the reasons, now well known, but then still somewhat mysterious, which caused the German flank armies to turn off to the east of Paris. If this information had a historical interest, the solved messages presented at the same time an immediate interest. They were highly appreciated by the army commanders, especially during that period which has been called the race to the sea. General Maunoury said that he had found in the knowledge of German orders a confidence which was invaluable to him. The commander in chief wrote to the minister: "I have been able to appreciate, like all the army commanders, in the last few days the value of the services rendered by the code section of your cabinet.

---

[3] It thus appears that the basic cipher system employed by the Germans was unchanged from Aug. 6 to Nov. 18, 1914, and that the specific key was changed only twice a month. At the end of the war they changed keys for their important tactical cipher every two or three days, and this cipher system was exceedingly more complicated than the one first used.—W. F. F.

[4] Italics mine —W. F. F.

I would be obliged to you if you would express to Major Cartier and his personnel the thanks of all."

We can already deduce from the preceding statement useful lessons as to the rules which should govern the use of code. Even before it was possible to solve messages, the Marwitz radiograms in clear had already given the *G–2s* definite information of an interesting character. These radiograms, moreover, as well as the explanations in clear regarding the incomprehensible words, developed little by little, as we have said, the experience of the Bordeaux cryptanalysts. Lastly, the documents found on the field supplied the latter, as Major Cartier wrote at the time, with valuable information. Now, these unenciphered messages, these conversations in clear regarding service between stations, the possession by an officer on duty at the front of documents capable of being used by the enemy, were things strictly forbidden by regulations of both belligerents. Who would venture to affirm, however, at the present time, that all our officers are convinced of the importance of the precautions to be taken in this matter? In 1914 many recommendations in regard thereto had been made; yet the examination of a wagon retaken from the Germans led to the discovery in the straw, with which it was strewn, of French documents comparable to the Fontenoy-le-Joute notebook. With respect to carelessness in regard to radiotelegraphy, the trip of the staff from May 27 to 29, 1914, had revealed such carelessness as to service regulations for wireless telegraphy and encipherment that a summary report had been presented to the chief of the general staff. Certain addresses of radio circulars, drawn up in clear without call letters, gave the complete order of battle of the army and the location of headquarters. The cryptograms enciphered by staff officers, who, however, received each month from the code section an exercise in encipherment, violated the most elementary rules. It was, moreover, for that reason that as early as the 6th of August the chief of staff signed a circular reviewing the rules for cipher correspondence, and making the use of wireless telegraphy an exceptional method of communication, to be used only when there should be no communication by wire. The command was therefore obliged to insure safety by measures which resulted, in fact, in depriving it of a convenient means of communication.

Without these precautions the enemy, perhaps, would have no reason to envy us with respect to special information, although we have every reason to believe that perhaps owing to lack of data he did not translate our correspondence during the first part of the war. We shall see, moreover, that also the Germans soon decreased the activity of their wireless systems. We had simply anticipated them with respect to measures of this kind.

It was nevertheless necessary to face the possibility of having recourse to radiotelegraphy in case of an advance, and for this it was necessary to establish confidence in the security of cipher. As the enciphered correspondence by wire showed ignorance or gross carelessness with respect to the rules for this security, it was decided to intrust the cipher work to technicians, who would at the same time be the instructors of the officers with whom they would have official relations. It was on September 17 that, under the pressure of the realities of war, there was put into execution this measure, already demanded in time of peace, by the chief of the service, who on that occasion had had himself treated in a friendly manner as a "cipher nut."

A code officer, trained by the section of the general headquarters or, preferably, recruited among officers who before the war had followed various courses developed by the code section, was assigned to each army staff. The necessity of insuring a day and night service led the chiefs of staff either to order for the night an alternation of duties between officers of $G-2$ and the single code officer or to request of general headquarters two assistants for the latter.

Some chiefs of staff did not, however, at once appreciate the new establishment and placed the code officer in the courier service, under the pretext that coding of correspondence was in no way under the jurisdiction of $G-2$. This was not in accordance with the views of the chief of the general staff, who wished to make these officers the representatives of code work at the office from which orders issue in order to prevent documents useful to the cryptanalysts from being neglected by their handlers who would not know the importance of them. Soon, however, the discovery of German keys and orders designed to limit the personnel employed in deciphering caused formal orders to be issued by general headquarters for the delegating of code work to $G-2$.

It was therefore experience again which, at the beginning of the war, was to settle a question sometimes debated in our time; and while at the time of the establishment of the transmission service it was possible, in view of the $G-2s$ being now convinced as to the requirements of the code section by a long cooperation, to contemplate the attachment of the code officer to the new service, the reasons which in 1914 militated for a close union of the code section with $G-2$ will be applicable in case of a new war. We will add that the separation, sometimes contemplated, of the cryptanalytic functions from the cryptographic functions is not a new thing; this system exists in several ministerial departments. It was that of the Ministry of War before the establishment of the code section. It always leads to the same results—the cryptanalysts who do not encipher are ignorant of certain "tricks" of encipherers and are lost when con-

478603 O - 42 - 2

fronted with details of methods which they would have no difficulty in undertaking if they had frequently performed the troublesome work of enciphering. Encipherers who know nothing about cryptanalysis are unaware of the necessity of special precautions and of the exploitation of their faults by the cryptanalysts; they grow careless, and when it is necessary to give proof of initiative they often fail to meet the test. There remains, lastly, the question of compiling codes and originating systems of encipherment, which it is necessary to have actually handled in order to be able to create new ones that will be practical, and which it is necessary to make up while bearing in mind the weak points of the previous methods, which are perceived in analysis. There are many examples of complications theoretically admirable which have proved to be especially advantageous for cryptanalysts. The second system of the German campaign is one of them; they substituted a method which could be solved by means of a single telegram for the preceding system, for the solution of which we needed to find at least two telegrams fulfilling certain conditions.

The appointment of officers showed that the condition of this service in certain staffs was even worse than the higher officers had considered it. Exercises were then prescribed, which consisted in enciphering several of the papers brought by the liaison officers. Scarcely had the armies, as the result of correct exercises, noted that the instruction in cipher appeared to be perfected than a series of incidents showed that in many staffs only one officer had performed the work, and that in his absence the telegrams remained untranslatable. In one single Army staff three officers of subordinate units appeared successively, complaining of having received telegrams improperly composed. The text received by the first had resisted all attempts to decipher it; the forgetting of one letter by the decipherer was the cause. The second, assisted by his comrades, was unsuccessful on account of failure to distinguish a line directed toward the right from a line directed toward the left. As to the third, who complained that an incomplete order had been sent to him, his attention was drawn to the fact that he had skipped several groups of his telegram. In view of this situation, the commander in chief ordered in January, 1915, that for about a month the exercises would be daily and that each officer would perform four or five. "It will be said," we read in the correspondence, "that in the brigades, the division, and in the cavalry units the liaisons are made by auto, never by wireless telegraph, and that the necessity for encipherment never appears; but it is not known into what situation we shall be brought by the course of operations, and at the beginning of 1914 the cavalry corps operating in Belgium gave the lie to this theory, as well as an example of dangerous radiotelegrams."

We see here the difficulties which have been encountered in maintaining code instruction during the campaign. These difficulties were judged to be such that for a very long time the chief of service of general headquarters refused to change the regulation method of encipherment, although he was convinced, after a period in which the enemy had been able to inform himself as to our methods of encipherment, either by the documents which fell into his hands at the beginning of September, or by his secret service, that a modification was very necessary. The code dictionary employed in the armies was changed three times between August 1, 1914, and January 15, 1915, but for three years no one dared to interfere with the literal enciphering system.

It is therefore a great advantage, especially at the beginning of a war, to have a personnel of instructors and a trained personnel as numerous as possible. This is one of the reasons which, when circumstances had in 1918 led the staffs, even in the subordinate units, to specialize one of their officers in the Code Service, brought under consideration the measure, left pending at the close of the war, to assign to each of them a code office directed by an officer specialist.[5]

We have set forth hitherto the measures taken to maintain in the French armies regularity of encipherment and, by uniformity, the security of the cipher. We have mentioned the results quickly obtained in 1914–15 in the attack on enemy field messages at a period when the German radiotelegraphic correspondence was abundant and when we were intercepting the communications of the high command. The situation with respect to this point was about to be modified. The result of the indiscretions pointed out above in our army was not only to cause the enemy to abandon the system of encipherment adopted in August, 1914; it had also resulted, at least very probably, in restricting the use of radiotelegraphy among the Germans. Perhaps stabilization was one of the reasons for the use of a ground system. But, in view of the methodical nature of our adversaries, it is permissible to ask whether, in case they had felt no uneasiness with regard to their ciphers, they would have abandoned this simple, elegant, cheap, and very modern means of transmission constituted by the wireless telegraph. In this case, if our solving service had remained equal to its task, we see how much better our generals would have been equipped to conduct operations. The harm done inconsiderately by

---

[5] There is a great deal of truth in Colonel Givierge's contention that the cryptographic and the cryptanalytic functions should be combined under one section in order to preserve the secrecy of communications However, the working out of the details of such organization involves great practical difficulties. In the U. S. Army encoding, enciphering, decoding, and deciphering are performed exclusively by message center personnel; the preparation of efficient codes and ciphers, under the direction of the Chief Signal Officer, is supervised by competent cryptanalysts, who work in close liaison with the cryptanalytic section of G–2; and the latter exercises careful supervision and control of cryptographic communications in order to preserve their secrecy.—W. F. F.

14

these gossips is often much more serious than the harm done by spys who have been shot.

The German communications delivered to our specialists continued then to decrease in number and, it may be said, in interest. The higher staffs during a long period ceased almost entirely corresponding by wireless, and, toward the second quarter of 1916, the field radiograms intercepted (which, however, always resulted in studies on the part of one of the sections of the cipher bureau of the ministry, while the others profited by this forced leisure to extend studies to other subjects) were only conversations exchanged through local systems, sometimes limited to an army corps and to its constituent units.

From the cryptographic point of view this was a very interesting period. The systems employed varied from one communication net to another, and certain ones proved to be very simple, although frequently varied. We may assume that they emanated from cryptologists evidently possessing technical knowledge but without much practical experience. We would point out in this connection that the question of cryptographic systems appears very different when it is a matter of safeguarding a few communications between two cipher experts in offices and when it is attempted to furnish a common method to hundreds of officers who are not cryptologists and are obliged to use ciphers at posts which are not very comfortable. It is a point of view that appears to have escaped certain inventors, who curse the routine of official services because the latter have not compensated them for certain systems, no doubt ingenious, but requiring either delicate apparatus or a secrecy based on a principle incompatible with military use, in which the method must be capable of being taught in broad daylight, only an agreement or key being kept secret.[6]

The study of these various systems was the occasion of great successes for a new member of the cipher bureau, the reserve lieutenant of artillery, Painvin, professor of paleontology at l'Ecole des Mines, who, having worked since the end of 1914 on the staff of an army with Captain Paulier, had been called to the ministry and had perfected his rare talents by taking an active part in the work directed by Major Olivari. Our cryptanalysts employed in the armies and those of our allies, whose service, which began to rival ours, possessed means and materials on a much larger scale, to the great benefit of working facilities, showed themselves equally perspicacious; and very frequently in the course of a few hours, too short to report whose was the first discovery, general headquarters received from

---

[6] This is one of the requirements almost invariably overlooked by would-be "cipher inventors."—W. F. F.

two or three different sources the solution of a cryptographic problem just posed by our adversaries.

However, a new element was to make its appearance in the cryptographic war. It was a consequence of the development of wireless telegraphy in the front-line units. We mean the code notebooks.[7]

Those notebooks were introduced with us to facilitate secrecy of telephonic communications. It had taken a long time, despite the cautions of experts, to comprehend that the telephone was not a safe means of communication; but after a few cruel experiences, in which it was evident that the enemy had been advised of a relief or a surprise attack by an intercepted telephone message, a means was sought to conceal the meaning of the messages. There had been placed in service in our army, for the sole purpose of permitting the encoding of important words in telephone messages leaflets containing in essence tables serving to replace letters by groups of two figures, by selecting now one table and now another. These notebooks showed for 50 common words the way to encode them in a single group of three figures. When the communications by wireless telegraphy between small units developed, the use of these notebooks was authorized, by way of exception, to add to the signals which the posts were to employ—as a rule, a few encoded words. There was developed later the table of words in addition to the tables for encoding by letter. Then the idea of making this notebook a document for encoding, especially letter by letter, was abandoned, and it was made into a small dictionary of words and syllables. For the large units, documents more voluminous than the notebook designed for troop units were prepared, and they were called codes. Both of them, at the end of the war, were based on the same principle as the code book of the general staffs but on a smaller scale.

With the Germans, a similar evolution had been seen. The small units had at first used encoding tables, in which the most usual sentences were represented by groups of letters or figures. Some of these, Befehlstafel (command tables) or Geheimtafel (secret tables), were captured in surprise attacks. In order to modify the encoding work, certain of these tables were of a circular form, the words to be encoded being written on the radii, at uniform distances from each other, of a large circle, while the groups were on the radius of a small concentric circle. The latter was movable, and by changing the position of it the correspondence of the groups to the words was varied. Others of the documents were in the form of a notebook with variable pagination. Then, without these transformations

---

[7] The original French reads "carnets de chiffre," literally, "cipher notebooks." These are merely short lists of code equivalents for letters, syllables, and a few common words.—W. F. F.

succeeding each other according to a precise chronological order our enemies adopted notebooks nearly similar to ours. Was this merely one example among many which might be found in the history of cryptography, a science in which each guards his secrets, of those "ideas which are in the air"? Was it the result of information given by documents found on the field? It matters little. In any case, in June, 1917, the system had become general.

In our Army the study of cryptography was intrusted to an office directed by Captain Painvin. This officer, whose expertness had been demonstrated in the course of remarkable work relating to systems employed both on the French front and in certain theaters of operations in other countries, established a technique of cryptanalysis which yielded remarkable results. The most intimate collaboration was established between the ministry and the various organs for code work in the armies, the commanders of which came to Paris to take courses in study. The code service then had about 15 officers at general headquarters, 3 in each staff of a major unit, and a total a little less than that of the armies at the ministry, where the code section had many functions relating to interallied communications. In this number there were about 10 cryptanalysts working, according to the same method, on the translations of which we are speaking. A system of absolutely safe communications permitted the rapid transmissions of all the total or partial results obtained in any one of the offices. We had, in fact, to deal with radiograms emanating from small units relating to the life of these small units; and often the cryptanalyst, placed at the front where they operated, found hypothetical data which were valuable in learning of the events on that front. In this way a detailed work was performed which the ministry could not have done alone under favorable circumstances.

The result of this solving work was very considerable. It made possible very many identifications of units. If we open the archives at random we find that from the 5th to the 15th of December, 1917, four division movements were discovered by special information before any other means were used, and soon verified by examination of prisoners; 32 regiments, the situation of which was known, were identified anew; a radiogram of December 10 reports the presence of an "Eingriff (counterattack) division" to the north of St. Quentin. Another, of the 10th, reports the presence at a point on the front of General von Erp, commanding the Three hundred and forty-second Division. A message of December 15 gives warning of a German surprise attack at the Abia farm; our troops, being warned, repulsed the enemy. A communication of the 5th mentions a change of call letters of the German wireless telegraph stations and gives the equivalents of the new ones and the old ones. The mechanism of these identifications by the radiograms is shown by the following

examples: "May 13, 1918 * * * Infantry regiments 97, 137, and 265. Fire with gas will take place on the 14th of May, from 6 to 8 o'clock in the morning." "May 23. C. R. to the brigade * * * Liaison with 9/122 and 4/128. Losses: One man killed, five injured. (Signed) Regt. 479 * * *." Information concerning entraining, preparations for revictualing, etc., was carried by these methods to units much higher than the echelon regiments.

The Germans in time perfected their notebooks. From about 2,000 words they brought them to 4,000. These notebooks ("Satzbuch") were distributed to army or army detachment, and when, as about the 25th of December, 1917, for example, the 10 codes in service at the time were changed altogether the work of recompiling was considerable. Division codes, or "Schluesselheft" (key books), of 1,000 words were ordinarily used conjointly with the "Satzbuch"; the latter corresponded to our codes, the "Schluesselheft" to the small notebook.[8]

To conclude this statement of technical methods, we must note that, at the time of the successful German attacks, in 1918, the general staffs, not having any ground system in the conquered territory, again employed the wireless telegraph, but with a complicated system, strengthening the cipher, and appearing in theory extremely safe. Errors in the method of its use permitted Painvin and his crew to penetrate the meaning of a few of these telegrams. It was among them that, by a lucky chance, there was found this message, dated June 1, deciphered on the 3d, sent by a station near Roye: "Munitioniering beschleunigen, soweit nicht eingesehen auch bei tag" (Expedite supplies of ammunition, if not observed, even by day)—which, as it gave notice of an approaching action, constituted the alarm for the Humbert army, and permitted of preparing the means of action employed on June 11 at Mary-Courcelles by General Mangin to stop the attack launched on the night from the 9th to the 10th to the east of Montdidier.[9]

In view of this reconstitution of more than 30 German code books, one question will arise. Did the Germans translate our communications from the front?

---

[8] The French "carnet de chiffre" and the German "Schluesselheft" (literally, "key book") correspond to our "Emergency Code List," a single-page leaflet used for front-line messages; the French "code" and the German "Satzbuch" (literally, "sentence book") correspond to our field or trench codes designated by the names of American rivers and lakes. Toward the end of the war these names for the American Expeditionary Forces codes were abandoned and the codes were numbered serially, "Field Code No. 1" being the first.—W. F. F.

[9] The author here has reference not to code messages but to cipher messages in a rather ingenious system, designated by the Allies as the ADFGVX cipher, because the messages consisted only of these six letters. While it is true that errors in the method of its use in several cases permitted of solution, nevertheless, in the majority of instances these solutions were made possible by entirely overlooked (by the Germans) circumstances peculiar to the system itself when used for considerable traffic.—W. F. F.

[To be concluded]

PROBLEMS OF CODE [1] *

By Colonel GIVIERGE, French Army

In concluding the preceding article we raised the question as to the result of enemy studies of our correspondence encoded by means of the small code notebooks. The Germans seem to have failed in solving all the other systems employed in our armies during the war. Did they succeed with respect to the one based upon the use to small books placed in the hands of a numerous and inexperienced personnel?

The reply is in the affirmative. Many bits of information, reports of German intelligence services, which fell into our hands, for example, prove that the Germans had succeeded in breaking into our messages, when we had adopted the code books, or a portion of them. They always gave credit to our services by mentioning the rapidity with which our code books were changed when they had carried away a copy of them as the result of a surprise attack. It should be noted, in fact, that many documents were lost, that many losses were ignored when they were not concealed to avoid penalties, and that the enemy was thus able to translate telegrams, often, doubtless, less interesting if only a retrospective study was involved, but one which permitted of recognizing the turn of expression and style of our messages.

Now, it is very much to the interest of the cryptanalysts to learn the personal habits of the encoders. A division in the Chemin des Dames sector, in 1918, made it a practice to require of the regiments in the line a brief report every morning. Frequently the report was drawn up in this form: "Night calm, nothing to report." When the code book was changed, the routine practices did not change, and the same text was the subject of numerous messages, which could be classified, thanks to their being encoded in exactly the same way. The capture of even an obsolete code book enabled the

---

[1] This is the second and concluding installment of an article which appeared in the March BULLETIN.—Ed.
*(No. 34, May, 1926)

18

enemy to read cryptograms belonging to this daily series which were repeated, and even if these were dated some time back, this helped the specialists to make a hypothesis as to the meaning of groups in messages of a similar style, transmitted under similar conditions, and encoded with the new code book. Now almost always the great difficulty in studying code is the identification of a few first groups. This is what is called finding an entrance or getting a start. With an entrance effected, and a thousand groups, a number quickly acquired on the front during the last war, the cryptanalysts are full of hope in the success of their task. We have not found any statistics as to the number of telegrams in code collected in one day, but the days at the beginning of the war or during the attacks of 1918, when the posts of the major units furnished us 60 messages are not rare, and many of these telegrams have more than 20 groups. What is to be said then of the transmissions of the small units?

The repetitions of formulas composed of the same words, placed in the texts at places known to cryptanalysts is therefore expecially favorable for the latter in case the code book is changed. These are the formulas which have been called "stereotyped." We must include therein the forms: "I have the honor to ......"; short telegrams acknowledging receipt of communications or requesting repetition of untranslatable telegrams; references such as "in continuation of telegram," "in reply to," "to follow"; too numerous indications of punctuation such as "Paragraph 2," "Paragraph 3," "end of message"; grammatical indications such as "three large (plural) man (plural)," etc. We have taken here as the subject of the article only field cryptograms, but it is known that the code section has always had good success in decoding diplomatic matter, in which, among others, distinction was achieved by Captain Bassières, a member of the military commission of cryptography, seriously wounded in August, 1914, and long a prisoner in Germany, which deprived the code section of a valuable collaborator at the beginning of the war; and the reserve interpreter Déjardin, who died while acting as French consul in the Tokyo disaster. The studies in this branch were especially aided at the beginning by long service designations at the head of telegrams, and by final formulas indicating the office of origin. The numbering was the basis of hypotheses which made possible the long-sought "entrance" into the first German code reconstructed—that for communications with submarines; and alternations of numbers in clear and numbers in code, assumed to be such because the text had no number in clear at that time, served as a point of departure of another code. We can not insist too much on the danger of stereotyped formulas. This is a principle which it is the hardest to make dispatchers of military telegrams understand, who can not help including complicated

REF ID:A484988

references with dates and numbers, and who insist absolutely on making conspicuous, even in their telegrams, the honor which the fact of addressing their correspondent constitutes for them.

It is therefore very important to eliminate the stereotyped formulas or to conceal them. We might attempt to instruct encoders, or, better, the writers of telegrams, and to accustom them to write in a telegraphic style without making any digression which is not urgently necessary. It is also possible to represent by a single group in the codes each of the stereotyped formulas, which are not made so valuable in this way as when they are encoded word by word, and when they make series of groups repeated from one cryptogram to the other. This is the method most often employed in certain recent codes and it offers good safeguards. But with small dictionaries we can also have recourse to superencipherment.' We shall revert to this later.

Just as we have pointed out that in September, 1914, official service messages gave clear-text fragments of enciphered text, likewise these imprudences eventually gave to cryptanalysts the meaning of code telegrams. It will be easily understood that the comparison of text in clear (where a certain word, for example, is repeated three times), with its crytographic equivalent (where one group occurs three times in places corresponding practically to those occupied by the word) permits of originating a hypothesis as to the identity of the word and the group. The names which do not appear in a code, and which it is necessary to encode by syllables, give series of two or three groups which reappear at each repetition of the name, and permit of most far-reaching hypotheses. It is therefore imperatively necessary to prevent the enemy from identifying a text in clear with a cryptogram. If we bear in mind the possibility of surprise attacks and espionage, we shall, therefore, avoid writing on a sheet which may be captured by the enemy the translation under each of the groups sent by telegraph, or pinning a paper bearing a text with that on which the translation appears, or even keeping a useless crytogram after it is translated since the service designations permit of comparing it with the clear text left in the correspondence files. The examination of this file alone, with the numbers, hours and dates, will readily permit of investigations with a view to identifying the translations of the file with the radiograms that it may have been possible to intercept, and still more easily if something distinguishes them from the papers received through other channels (the inscriptions "translation of code telegram," for example). Now, during the whole campaign, inspections made in the general headquarters and command posts evacuated both by our forces and by

---

' By superencipherment is meant enciphering a code dispatch. Our term for the final product is "enciphered code."—W. F. F.

the enemy, resulted in numerous discoveries of data for study of these categories, which, unfortunately, were almost never reported as a subject of study to their authors, or transmitted to the code section for utilization, with sufficient rapidity. Many other sources yield to the cryptanalysts the plain language of code radiograms. Without mentioning telephonic communications, (which, under pretext of confirmation or warning orders, pass these texts along lines which, however, do not appear to be considered as safe, since in the region through which they pass telegrams are not transmitted in clear text but are encoded) accidents connected with utilization sometimes supply the specialists with unhoped for data. Thus in 1914, the German station at Norddeich transmitted meteorological telegrams in which, in the midst of encoded information, there was a list of forces and directions of winds in the form which is common in these communications and is considered as clear test—that is, in groups of five figures. The station installed at Bruges took charge of a part of these meteorological messages and encoded the numbers left in clear by Norddeich. The comparison of the two series of radiograms provided a check as to the preparatory hypotheses for breaking into the code and permitted assumptions as to the meaning of the other code words in these special communications.

If we extended this article to the subject of diplomacy we would mention the importance which press communications or parlimentary debates, in which telegraphed articles are made the subject of allusions and sometimes of citation, have frequently had for the reconstruction of diplomatic codes. Without doubt, even here we could, by a strict education of the personnel, eliminate the majority of fears to be harbored in this respect. It is possible to retain and especially to make public nothing but edited translations, that is paraphrased versions, of decoded messages. It appears expedient, however, to seek a method which makes it more difficult to compare a clear text with code text. The method adopted during the war was superencipherment. We shall point out, before discussing this subject, a third danger which threatens the code, and for which superencipherment seems to constitute a remedy.

We have shown the danger of sterotyped formulas. Without using any formula of this kind, however, the text of telegrams contains numerous repetitions. We are not speaking only of frequent words, prepositions, or auxiliary verbs, for which various equivalents may be assigned in the code book, enabling us to employ now one group and now another, but of names of places, of units, etc., which in the course of an action will recur frequently in the dispatches. Encoded ordinarily by words or by syllables, these terms given rise to repetitions of groups which attract the attention of the cryptanalyst.

The latter compares these series of groups of names on which it is possible to build hypotheses. In many cases, he secures in this way means of cross reference—for example, syllables common to several names appear in each series of groups. He then possesses an entering wedge. It is therefore well to conceal repetitions. Several means to accomplish this purpose are recommended to encoders— breaking a word into groups of letters differing from one time to another; employment of groups without meaning (nulls) which are so inserted between the groups of a series that the same groups are not seen to follow each other, and the series is not noticed, etc. For encoders of little experience, however, these means are complications frequently forgotten. Moreover, when a certain number of encoders are working on texts in which the same words recur, as is the case on a sector of the front at the time of an operation at a given point, each of them encodes in the best way, and perhaps his cryptograms alone would not offer any weak point; but comparison of the juxtaposed work of these encoders, who are unaware of each other's code versions, may supply an excellent basis for study to the bureau which centralizes the intercepts of the region.

The method which it has been considered necessary to employ to diminish as much as possible repetitions attendant upon the use of codes and notebooks is again superencipherment.

What is superencipherment then? It is a method (and there are infinite numbers of them) by means of which the groups taken from the code book, or furnished by a literal system, when they give rise to the danger that the repetition of a clear-text word may result in a repetition in the cryptogram, are disfigured in such a way that this repetition in the cryptogram will not occur again. For example, the succession of figures of the cryptograms will be so changed according to a known law, that the different figures of a group will be dispersed. Or else, variable numbers will be added with each figure so that the repetition in groups formed by the totals will not be found again. Or again, the figures of the groups will be replaced by other figures or by letters, according to a given law, etc.

For the reasons given above, superencipherment appeared to be indispensable in the course of the war. Let us see what use was made of it, chiefly with respect to the study of which we are treating.

In France we had long considered our types of code books used for the staffs as affording a quite adequate security. In fact, theoretically, codes sufficiently extensive, in which the groups consist of five figures, seem to afford full security. But the circumstances of employment, especially in war time, make the reconstitution of a code by a cryptanalytic bureau well served by secret services and well informed as to diplomatic questions a very different thing from the study of cryptograms by an isolated investigator. Therefore although our codes have been changed very frequently, the fears which might result from their being printed in an establishment employing a great number of officials and their transportation under conditions where their security might be endangered without the fact being noticed by a too confident carrier led the general headquarters to give instructions for superencipherment as early as 1915. The codes established by the central administration, as well as the field codes in general, printed by the armies, received also a superenciphering table on a separate sheet so that it might be modified while the code was kept in service. Lastly, it was frequently directed that the field codes, containing also a simple superenciphering table, were not to be employed unless this system were used; at least this was to be the case for radiotelegraphic messages. That is, however, an idea that the experts have not succeeded in imposing on the encoders in small units, the neglect of which certainly facilitated the enemy researches.

On the part of the Germans, superencipherment was also used in certain communications between high authorities. We shall give a sketch of certain means which permit of discovering such artifices. The code of the submarines, to which we have alluded, contained several groups of three letters of a special form, with regard to which the hypothesis was advanced that they referred to proper names, and which occurred much more frequently than the others. On a certain day all the groups were changed, and at the end of a certain period, in revising the new texts it is perceived that the repetitions of several groups are more numerous than those of others. One is led to suspect a superencipherment which consists in the replacing each of the letters of the groups taken from a code book (original groups which are not known, since they have been seen only when superenciphered) by another letter of the alphabet according to a conventional table. The identity of the group which occurs most frequently in the superenciphered texts of the first series with that which occurs most frequently in the second series of texts, is taken as a basis of research, and the hypothesis is set up of the equivalence of three letters of series 1, with three letters of series 2. In replacing these three letters in the radiograms of series 1 every time that they appear in any group, we see by their correspondence groups of series 1 which have been transformed into groups of series 2, that are already known. The hypothesis appeared to be verified. Attention had then been drawn to other groups, only two letters of which had been transformed. It was assumed that the third letter of the new group corresponded to the third one of the old group, and, gradually the whole process of superencipherment was reconstructed. In this way the various forms which a group assumed after superencipherment were reduced to a single one, which permitted of a successful study.

But the consideration of stereotyped formulas especially was, during the war, the basis of work connected with superencipherment. The practical certainty that the ciphers concealed by a new process were those which it was customary to find in a certain place, guided the researches, and it was that consideration which made it possible to analyze the superencipherment keys for radiograms in the "Satzbuch" of the German front. Moreover, the system of superencipherment did not present any great complication, or much security, and the superenciphering tables (Geheim-Klappe) often involved the change of only two letters out of the three which constituted the groups of the code.

The enemy gave us much more troublesome researches by multiplying in his latest editions the equivalents for hours, numbers and syllables; by frequently employing nulls, meanings for which were long sought, and by making considerable use of code names (Decknamen), to represent geographical points and localities.[3] These arbitrary names sometimes changed several times in a day, at hours agreed upon, and it became very difficult to identify them. Even in case of repetitions they did not yield very useful information, as the fact that one expects to find "Paris" in a text will cause him to search for the letters and syllables in "Paris," and not that of the code name which replaces "Paris." These modifications in the original arrangements of the code books gave new problems for our cryptanalysts to solve. It should be noted in this connection, however, that the discovery on the field of several examples of codes, unfortunately usually obsolete, permitted of completing the first results obtained by the cryptanalysts, or furnished clues as to the nature of these documents. We must also take note of the fact that it usually is sufficient to make sure of the translation of a quite limited number of groups in order to grasp the sense of the majority of messages. It is a matter of experience that the encoders who use a code are often required to encode texts written without regard to the resources of the code, in words and expressions, and that they do not modify these texts. It is, as a consequence, nearly useless in practice to overload the codes with ready-made expressions, and with very complete lists which are little used and, therefore, the number of groups which appear in the majority of messages encoded by not very expert personnel and the meaning of which is essential for the translation is not very great.

Another measure which was an indirect cause of trouble for our cryptanalysts, in 1918, was the adoption of daily change in the call

---

[3] This applies only to the "Satzbuch." The form and contents of the "Schlusselheft," which was a "one-part" code, underwent very little change.—W. F. F.

letters of the German stations. As the reader knows, a wireless
telegraph station receives as its call sign a name or a call symbol,
generally a group of two or three letters or figures, and a radiotelegram commences with the call signs of the station of designation and
of the station of origin. When there are several codes in use at the
same time it is essential not to mix the researches, as a group has one
meaning in one code and another meaning in another code, and
nothing would be accomplished if one worked on the two codes at
the same time in the belief that one was working on a single code
only. In order, therefore, to assemble a file of the cryptograms of
the same language, if we may apply this expression to those made
up with the same code book, one relies upon the composition of the
nets formed by stations which are conversing with each other, and
which are known by means of their call signs. The existence of the
net is ascertained by studying for several days the relations of the
stations, and it is noted that VA, PK, and RT, talk with each other
without addressing DU, DT, and DM, which form another group of
correspondents. If one has the proper facilities, one introduces radiogoniometry, which gives the positions of stations and which shows,
for example, that VA is at Mourmelon, PL at Suippes, and RT at
La Pompelle. When the call signs change every day it is no longer
known whether the station VA of yesterday is not DU for to-day, or
whether it is using the same code. One must constantly have recourse
to radiogoniometry to locate the stations and must have a report
every day as to what those of Mourmelon, La Pompelle and Suippes
are called. With a system in which one speaks only in case of absolute
necessity, and in which one transmits only short messages, it is quite
possible that the enemy does not get bearings on all transmitting
stations every day, especially if his goniometric system is not closely
knit.

The difficulty which this measure adds to cryptograms should be
particularly noted in addition to all the difficulties which it necessarily created for the *G–2s* with regard to the employment of radiogoniometry. Now, in our army, a measure of the same kind had
been taken, but it appears that many staffs have not grasped the
importance of it, as, for instance, witness the order which directed
that every morning at a given hour all stations should give a call,
always in the same order, to the division station. That was the
equivalent of the stereotyped formulas which we criticized above.
Equally dangerous in connection with the hypothesis of changes of
call signs, are the practices and the habits of operators who may
cause the stations to be recognized; such as, for example, the message
in clear text from telegraph operator to telegraph operator, "Good
morning, friends," which occurs with terrible regularity in reports of
messages received. If we examine the weekly report under date of

July 9, 1918, of the chief of intelligence section of the Seventh German Army, which fell into our hands, we read at the beginning: "The Tenth French Army was identified by the name of a radio officer; the Sixth by its transmissions without change from the meteorological post of Trilport." And we read further on: "Toward the end of the week, the calls of the Third American Division with fragments of clear English text, have no longer been heard except in the terrain to the east of Chateau-Thierry." One sees by these examples the effect of carelessness with respect to the identification of stations, and we have tried to make clear the effects of this identification on cryptographic researches.

The observations which have been successively presented in this study show how much carelessness was committed by both sides in the World War, and we have emphasized the advantage which the cryptanalysts were able to derive from some of them. This explains much of the success of the cryptanalytic services. Whatever the author of "General Headquarters, Section I," seems to say about it, and whatever may be the legends broadcast by those who were not actively engaged in the recent war regarding the rôle of "second sight," there exists of necessity no relation between sorcery and code work. Perhaps a cryptanalyst needs a certain amount of intuition in order to proceed boldly along the lines of hypotheses but usually he follows a method well known in the sciences—he makes observations in order to find a basis for hypothesis, and tries to verify them by experimentation and observation. In order to observe well he needs to be methodical in the classification of his files, where there must be no mixing of the wheat and the chaff; it is therefore well for him that previous knowledge regarding many cryptographic systems should facilitate the recognition of the chaff and the wheat in the midst of mixtures of grains; especially should he learn their peculiarities from the sample itself by examining the points in common, and the differences, in the documents which are submitted to him. He must also have the rapidity and the precision of the good observer, who sees important things and discovers analogies, which a less astute observer is unable to perceive. He needs also great perseverance, certain researches lasting for years, and certain hypotheses not being proven false until after the study of hundreds of texts. The hypothesis relating to the system under examination having once been formulated, he must either apply the methods known, if there are any, to solve the problem which it presents, which necessitates advanced technical training, or he must invent one by analogy. All this requires an education therefore in cryptanalysis; a good cryptanalyst does not become so without training, and if, during the war, we found individuals who, although ignorant of cryptography in 1914, accomplished very remarkable results, it must be noted that the one who has been most frequently cited did not fully show his ability until the beginning of 1916, after having worked for more than a year under the direction of two of our best cryptanalysts. And it should be said that the feat of translating as promptly as it was possible the German cryptograms, and of following the successive complications was an infinitely less difficult task than the study of the systems such as they used in 1918 would have been without this preceding experience. To cite an example, the code of the submarines was found at a period when the keys were changed every month. We would probably have met with a check by beginning this study later, at the time when the key was changing every day.

If we desire then, in case of war, to have a group work in cooperation upon encoded enemy correspondence it is necessary to train crypt-analysts and give them a very thorough course of study. We will express our regret, en passant, that cryptological literature, well developed 30 years ago, appears to be actually scorned by authors and editors.[4]

If we have enough cryptanalysts to be able to detach part of them for code service in the armies, they will have, among other missions, that of teaching the encoders of subordinate units the precepts necessary for encoding well. We have stated and demon-strated that often the origin of a cryptanalytic success if found in the lack of skill of an encoder. When the encoders are legion, however, blunders are hard to avoid. In such case a relative security may be sought in a very strict discipline. The German order re-garding liaisons of January 22, 1918, gives in this respect a hint which appears to be extremely wise:

It must be borne in mind,

it says,

that the enemy is methodically watching our communications. By the minute comparison of our shortest and apparently most insignificant messages he obtains results from which he draws the most important conclusions regarding our order of battle and our intentions. Our counter measures must tend to limit as much as possible the enemy's facilities for observation:

1. By the reduction to a minimum of messages liable to be intercepted;

2. ------------------------------------

That is an idea which it is most important to spread. We must not employ means of communication giving rise to the danger of interception, except where there is no other. We must then make use of them, but with such rapidity and such discretion as to furnish

---

[4] It is very doubtful whether the paucity of the literature of cryptography and cryptanalysis is due to lack of interest on the part of authors and editors. For the most part, the policy of silence, on the part of those really qualified to write such treatises has been dictated by interests of national security and domestic tranquillity.—W. F. F.

as few data as possible for enemy intercepts and goniometrics. The German regulations as shown by *G–S* of French General Headquarters deliberately sacrifices simplicity and therefore ease of operation to the rigorous maintenance of secrecy. Without going far into the matter we will not hesitate to say that, in certain cases, when the technical faults of a badly instructed personnel multiply the dangers to secrecy, when, for example, bad encoding or bad transmission give rise to repetitions or to endless explanations full of dangers for the code, we must consider the suspension of the dangerous method of communication and deprive the delinquent unit of it until it has learned how to use it in a sensible way. Again, from this point of view, we shall see the advantage of serious instruction regarding the use of facilities so dangerous as code correspondence may be, and hence the necessity of training instructors. It is only on this condition that we can avoid imposing on our field stations the silence which they maintained in 1914, without the risk of making illusory the precautions taken to preserve the secrecy of our wireless telegraph correspondence.

It is a question which may be faced at present. Since code instruction in certain units appears difficult at present by reason of the multiplicity of occupations of the troops and since it is shown all through this article that a certain complication is necessary in order to have reliable systems, would it not be possible, as has been done in other fields, to make up for the inadequacy of man by means of machinery? There are, in fact, machines for enciphering, and the question being to the point, we shall say a few words about it.

The large wireless telegraph companies, being desirous of concealing from indiscreet persons the meaning of messages entrusted to them, and wishing to offer to their clients the same security as that assured by the telegraph offices, owing to their communications by wire known only to agents bound to professional secrecy, have begun to adopt in their equipment automatic cryptographic machines. The principle of one of these machines is as follows: It is well known that one method of cryptography consists in replacing each letter of the clear text by another letter, according to a list of equivalents agreed on with the addressee. If we always replace a given letter by another given letter, always the same, the system does not present any security, for, taking as a basis the fact that in French the letter "E" occurs in the text more frequently than any other it will very soon be discovered that the letter which, being the most frequent in the cryptogram, replaces the "E" in the clear text, and the other letters will gradually be discovered. An improvement is effected when, having adopted a first series for replacing the letters of the clear text, by others in the cryptogram, as has been said, several others of the same kind are established, and it is agreed to replace the first letter of the text by means of the first series, the second by the second, etc., changing the series for each letter of the clear text. The letter "E" is represented by a different letter in each series and it is impossible to apply the method of research indicated above. It will be seen, on the other hand, that we might write on a dial the letters of the alphabet and place on a movable dial concentric to the former the series of the letters for substitution in the cryptogram, the substituted letter being located, for a given position of the dial opposite to the letter of the clear text. If the movable dial is displaced, the equivalent of each letter of the clear text is changed and we have another series of equivalents.

In this way an apparatus has been constructed which supplies a series of lists which permits of enciphering the letters according to the place which they occupy in the clear text (first, second, etc.) with different equivalents.

There is a standard method for analyzing the text composed upon this system. It is based on the following observation: If I use only two different series always in the same order: 1, 2, 1, 2, the first, the third, the fifth, etc., letters will be enciphered with the same series; the "E" will be represented there by the same letter, and it will be possible for me to search for the most frequent letter, which, very probably will be the one which replaces "E" of the clear text. If I use three series in the same order, the first, the fourth, and the seventh letters will give rise to the same observation. If I use n lists, without, however, forming any hypothesis as to the fact that several among them may be identical, and have the same equivalent for the same letter, the first, the $n+1th$, the $2n+1th$ letters will be encoded with the same series. Now, there is a means, when we have a cryptogram to deal with, of formulating hypotheses on the value of n and of verifying them, and, this being done, we can apply the search for the "E," on the one hand, to the first, $n+1th$, $Kn+1th$ letters, and on the other, to the second, $n+2th$, $Kn+2th$, etc. It is seen at once that if n is very large, it is possible that there is no $2n+1th$ letter in the cryptogram, and then it will be extremely difficult to find "E," as we shall have for this research only two letters, the first, and the $n+1th$, none of which perhaps represents "E." It is therefore important in enciphering to take a very large n, that is, to use the series of equivalents in a long and complicated order for a large number of letters before terminating a period in this order, and to recommence in the same order with the first series, then the second, etc.

When a long complicated order of this kind is taken with dials the operator runs great risk of making errors. He would risk none, if, for example, he so moved the dials as to advance the corresponding positions by a single letter every time that he enciphered a letter of the text, but after 26 movements he would take up the sequence again. By advancing by two letters each time the period would be a factor of 26—2 or 13. By adopting irregular movements we have much longer periods. If the operator runs the risk of making a mistake by forgetting the complicated movements made or to be made, a cogwheel gearing with teeth so arranged as to produce the variable movement desired at each complete turn of a certain crank, for example, would not make a mistake, and in this way we could have long periods and cryptograms presenting great difficulties to the specialists. It has been attempted to print the cryptograms with a typewriter when the letters of the clear text are struck. Let us suppose that a connection is formed for each position of the dials, between the letter of the large one and that of the small one (for example, two contact pieces each belonging to one of the dials giving passage to an electric current), so that the letter of the large dial is connected with the key of the keyboard, that of the small one with the letter printed, and it will be seen that by striking the same key, a letter which will depend on the relative position of the two dials will be printed. By means of devices multiplying the action of the pair of dials which we have considered by that of the similar pairs, moved by different cogwheel gears, so that the letter printed will depend on the different laws of change represented by these cogwheel gears, we shall have periods of several millions of letters—that is, for one sentence of the clear text to be repeated or represented the second time by the same cryptogram as the first, it will be necessary for millions of letters to separate the two repetitions. Otherwise the cryptogram will be different, and the repetition will not appear. From the point of view of crytography the method offers a quite considerable security.

An arrangement permits of automatic decoding.

Such machines do not require, it would appear, technical ability in the persons using them. A secretary typewrites the clear text; it is the cryptogram which is automatically printed. Perhaps, as a matter of fact, the cryptanalysts will find some clues in studying the blunders, the errors, the texts enciphered from the same position of the dials, etc. At any rate, with respect to the employment which concerns us—their use in the armies—the present machines are cumbersome and expensive and the models which have been presented as military models, do not appear to be perfected.

It will therefore still be necessary to work with the present methods, code books and cipher systems. We have shown that in time of war a certain number of systems have been broken down. It appears that the publicity raised concerning these questions, after the armistice, led those who employ the wireless telegraph in transmitting cryptographic dispatches, to complicate their systems and to entrust the service to a select personnel who know how to avoid gross errors, and know well the resources placed at their disposition, so that the security of communications is greatly increased thereby. We must seek to profit by the same advantages for war time. In concluding, we shall repeat once more, that a good encoder, and, in another branch, a good cryptanalyst, is not selfmade; that code work is a technical service, in which it is well to follow the advice of experts; that if the personnel charged with the work is not capable of encoding well, we must place at their disposal simple signals on which there is no cryptographic operation to perform, it being possible to compile signal tables of this kind at any desired time, for almost all needs; and, in conclusion, we shall set down the sentence often repeated by one of the chiefs of the code service to the armies:

Encode well or do not encode at all. In transmitting clear text, you give only a piece of information to the enemy, and you know what it is; in encoding badly, you permit him to read all your correspondence and that of your friends.

THE NEW REGULATIONS GOVERNING CODE LANGUAGE IN INTERNATIONAL COMMUNICATIONS *

By Maj. WILLIAM F. FRIEDMAN, Sig-Res., Secretary and Technical Adviser of the American Delegation to the International Telegraph Conference of BRUSSELS

In the latter part of September, 1928, the International Telegraph Union held its twelfth conference at Brussels, Belgium. Contrary to all precedent, this conference was called to deal with but one of

*(No. 47. March, 1929)

the many matters connected with international communication, namely, the rules governing the drafting of international correspondence in code language, a subject which has been a source of difficulty ever since the founding of the Telegraph Union in 1865. While the United States, for reasons which fall outside the scope of this article, is not a member of the Telegraph Union and therefore is not a signatory to the International Telegraph Convention, nevertheless an invitation is usually extended this country to send a nonvoting delegation to participate in the deliberations of the telegraph conferences that are held about every five years, political conditions permitting. In the case of the Brussels conference the United States was in the position of a more or less powerless but vitally interested spectator.

A knowledge of the historic background of the matter that the Brussels conference was called upon to study is essential to an appreciation of the very serious problem with which it was confronted, and for which it had to find some solution. Only a very cursory survey of this background can here be indicated. For those interested in details, reference is made to a paper prepared by the present writer, in connection with the International Radiotelegraph Conference of Washington.[1] Suffice it here to indicate that although it is certain that codes were employed from the very birth of electric telegraphy, in about the year 1840, and although the first international telegraph conference took place in 1865, it was only at the 1872 conference that even so much as a definition of plain language was incorporated in the regulations, to say nothing of a definition of code language. For a long time code words were treated in the same manner as plain-language words, for practically all code words were merely bona fide dictionary words to which arbitrary or code meanings had been assigned. By cipher language was meant only groups of figures, which were charged for at the rate of five figures per word. Code words, on the other hand, were charged for as single words up to 15 letters in length, and, at one time, up to seven syllables in length. Moreover, it was permissible to use words taken from any or all of the 50 or more languages authorized for international telegraph correspondence. Such a generous regulation, coupled with the fact that code language words were charged for as though they were plain language words, was bound to lead to abuses and difficulties. Also, the multiplicity of languages permitted, the technical inade-

---

[1] An official report entitled "The history of codes and code language, the international telegraph regulations pertaining thereto, and the bearing of this history on the Cortina report." It may be procured from the Superintendent of Documents, Government Printing Office, Washington, D. C., at 20 cents per copy. A limited number of copies is available for distribution for official use and may be obtained upon request from the office of the Chief Signal Officer.

quacies of dictionary words when used as code words, the errors in transmission due to the unfamiliarity of telegraph operators with the many languages employed, and so on, all combined to produce serious delays and difficulties in the exchange of international communications.

Attempts were made by the conferences of 1885, 1890, 1896, and 1903 to establish an official vocabulary of dictionary words that could be used as code words, and to make the use of this vocabulary obligatory. Naturally there was great opposition to such a project on the part of the large users of the telegraph facilities, even though this might have standardized code words and reduced their difficulties. Their principal objection, however, nobody brought clearly to light, perhaps because none of the official delegations understood the matter, perhaps because none of them dared state it openly. It was this: The large users had discovered a way of making code words so that they could send two or more at the cost of only one, a procedure which, of course, was highly useful to the users, and detrimental to the operating agencies. The method was to employ a code book in which figure groups (from 00001 to 99999, for example) were used as code groups, and then to substitute pairs of letters for the numbers. Thus, the two code groups 17529 43072 might be transformed into the code word AFLOZUCORE, which might pass as a dictionary word in one of the 50 languages, and thus be charged for as a single word. By similar procedure one might send three or more code words in a single chargeable word. But aside from this, such artificial words, as they soon came to be called, had other advantages. Operators found them to be easier to handle than many bona fide dictionary words belonging to foreign languages with which they were not familiar, words such as AANGEHAARD, AANGELIJKT, etc. Users also found them easier to correct if mutilated in transmission and much more flexible and economical than dictionary words. It was not long before the use of artificial words, despite the fact that they were not legalized and constituted evasions of rules winked at or tolerated on account of competition, became deeply rooted in the telegraph industry and their eradication could hardly be effected. Finally, in 1903 the use of artificial words was legalized by the introduction of a rule, which, unfortunately, was soon to lead to even greater difficulties. This was the famous " pronounceability rule," which read as follows:

> Code words, whether real or artificial, must be composed of syllables which can be pronounced according to the usage of one of the following languages: German, English, Spanish, French, Dutch, Italian, Portuguese, or Latin.

At the same time, the provision that code words could be of a maximum of 10 letters (adopted in 1875) was retained. Whether or not the members of the 1903 conference saw the large loophole that was thus left in the regulations is not clear, but code compilers and code users were quick to find it. Since code words merely had to be composed of syllables pronounceable according to the usage of 1 or more of 8 languages, and since these words could be of a maximum of 10 letters, there seemed to be no reason why codes should not be based upon 5-letter words and why every 2 such 5-letter words in a message should not be regularly joined in pairs forming 10-letter, singly-charged-for words. Thus, of course, the cost of every code message could be cut in half. The new idea spread like wildfire. At first these codes contained only about 30,000 code words which could be regarded as fairly pronounceable, words such as FORAB, LUFFA, FREAN, etc. They also incorporated a principle termed the "2-letter difference," that is, each code word in the book differed from every other code word in the same book by at least two letters. This principle was absolutely essential for safety in transmission and ease in correction of errors, but it greatly reduced the possibilities for the construction of euphonic words. Naturally, when code books began to increase in their extensiveness and the total number of code words in a single code grew from 30,000 to 60,000, then 70,000 and more, all with a 2-letter difference, the code words became less and less pronounceable. Such outlandish assemblages of vowels and consonants as EYYHOGORGT, BEEUHDWEWF, and ZAQROUARSC became common and, moreover, if even trained linguists and phoneticists could not dispute their "pronounceability" according to the definition adopted, what could be expected of the poor telegraph clerks? For the condition known as pronounceability can not be defined with precision, and even the significance of the simple word "syllable" taxes the knowledge of experts. The 1903 rules were simply impossible to interpret and enforce.

If the 1908 telegraph conference of London had any idea of being able to stamp out these artificial words and of eradicating a practice which grew out of an oversight on the part of the 1903 conference, such an idea was speedily dispelled. The fact that the 1903 conference had had absolutely no intention of authorizing any procedure that would permit of joining two code words and passing them off as single, 10-letter words was clearly emphasized, but the 1908 conference was powerless to change the situation. The argument was that although the 10-letter code words might not conform to the *spirit* of the rule established in 1903, they most certainly did conform to the *letter* of that rule; it was merely unfortunate that the rule was not made more specific. But even the attempts of the 1908 conference to add precision to the definition of code words, and to set up a code control committee were without any practical effect, and the situation grew from bad to worse. A conference was to be held in 1915 but had to be postponed on account of the World War.

Immediately after the war there was a tremendous increase in international telegraphy and a corresponding increase in the number and size of codes, and code words lost practically all semblance of pronounceability. Finally, in 1925 a conference was held in Paris. But the question of code language was impossible of solution by that conference, which appointed a special committee to study the whole matter and report its findings to the next international conference, whether radiotelegraph or telegraph. This committee met in 1926 at Cortina d'Ampezzo, Italy, and tried to present its report for decision of the Washington Radiotelegraph Conference in 1927. But the latter decided it had no jurisdiction in the case, and on account of the urgency of the matter it recommended that the next international telegraph conference, which had been scheduled to take place at Brussels in 1930, be advanced to 1928. This recommendation was acted upon, with the proviso that the sole subject to be discussed should be that of the rules governing code language.

Realizing the importance of the question to American commerce and industry the Secretary of State, upon receipt of an invitation extended this country to participate, recommended to the President that a careful and detailed study should be made, and that a delegation of experts be sent to represent the United States at the Brussels conference. The experts of this delegation made an intensive study of the report of the Cortina committee referred to above, and of the financial effects which the carrying out of its recommendations would have upon American business. In a nutshell, what the Cortina committee proposed was that all restrictions upon the construction of code words be removed and that code words merely be required to be not longer than five letters. But if 10-letter code words are cut in half, then what adjustment should be made in the rates for the new 5-letter words? Should the new rate be 50, 60, 70, or 75 per cent of the old rate? On this point the committee could come to no definite agreement, and, of course, therein lay a source of great difficulty. It is impossible here to go into the mathematical calculations and considerations the Cortina committee presented. There was no desire and no attempt to increase the receipts of the operating agencies, but all the adjustments proposed seemed to mean a material increase in the costs of overseas communication for code-language users, with a corresponding decrease in costs to plain-language users. Now the fact is that the code-language users are the business concerns, whose traffic forms about 88 per cent of the overseas business of the communication companies, and that the plain-language users are the private individuals, the total of whose traffic forms 12 per cent of the overseas business of the communication companies. The latter class of users is unorganized and not particularly interested in these matters, whereas the former is vitally interested, fairly well organized and can make its wishes known. In fact, at the Brussels conference the large users of the telegraph, cable and radio facilities were represented by an official delegation from the International Chamber of Commerce, and this delegation made strenuous objection to any decrease in rates to the small users at the expense of the large users, the large business interests. One may conjecture what would have happened if there had also been present an official delegation representing the small users, the millions of private individuals scattered over the whole world.

What did happen, however, was that after an apparent deadlock that lasted throughout half the conference a compromise was finally reached in an attempt to satisfy all interests involved. The following outline of the protocol finally adopted was drawn up by the writer to show the most important features of the new regulations.

TYPES OF LANGUAGE

PLAIN LANGUAGE

Plain language is that which presents an intelligible meaning in one or more of the languages authorized for international telegraph correspondence, each word and each expression having the meaning which is normally attributed to it in the language to which each belongs.

Requirements and conditions.—(*a*) Maximum length of word, 15 letters.

(*b*) Must present intelligible meaning; each word and expression must have meaning normally attributed to it in the language to which each belongs.

(*c*) Telegrams of this class must be wholly in plain language, but presence of bona fide commercial marks or commercial abbreviations in current use, registered addresses, or check words in banking telegrams are permitted.

(*d*) Unions of plain-language words prohibited.

Tariff.—Same as at present, at rate of 15 letters per word or authorized compound word. (Check word in banking telegrams must not exceed 10 characters in length.)

SECRET LANGUAGE

CODE LANGUAGE (DEFINITION)

That which is composed of (*a*) artificial words, or (*b*) bona fide words not having the meaning normally attributed to them in the language to which they belong and accordingly not forming comprehensible phrases in one or more of the languages authorized for telegraphic correspondence in plain language, or (c) a mixture of bona fide words thus defined and artificial words.

CODE LANGUAGE (CATEGORY A: THE 10-LETTER SYSTEM)

Requirements and conditions.—(a) Maximum length of word, 10 letters.

(b) Words of 5 letters must contain at least 1 vowel. Words of 6, 7, or 8 letters must contain a minimum of 2 vowels; at least 1 vowel must appear in first 5 letters, and at least 1 in remainder of word. Words of 9 or 10 letters must contain a minimum of 3 vowels; at least 1 vowel must appear in first 5 letters and at least 2 vowels in remainder of word, or vice versa, at least 2 vowels must appear in first 5 letters and at least 1 vowel in remainder of word. The vowels are A, E, I, O, U, Y; code words can not contain the accented letters ä, á, å, é, ñ, ö, ü, and the combinations œ, æ, aa, ao, ue, ch are each counted as two letters.

(c) Mixture of plain, code, and cipher language words permitted.

(d) Unions of plain-language words prohibited.

(e) Code book must be shown, if requested by authorized offices.

Tariff.—Same as at present, at rate of 10 letters per code word. Plain-language words inserted in code text at rate of 10 letters per word. Cipher-language words inserted in code text at rate of 5 characters per word.

CODE LANGUAGE (CATEGORY B: THE 5-LETTER SYSTEM)

Requirements and conditions.—(a) Maximum length of word, 5 letters.

(b) No conditions or restrictions as to construction of words, except that they can not contain the accented letters ä, á, å, é, ñ, ö, ü, and the combination œ, æ, aa, ao, ue, ch are each counted as two letters.

(c) Unions of plain-language words not prohibited.

(d) Mixture of only plain and code language words permitted; figures or groups of figures, except bona fide commercial marks, prohibited.

Tariff.—Word count at the rate of five letters per word, charged for at two-thirds the full rate in extra-European régime, and at three-fourths the full rate in European régime. (Telegrams from the United States to all other countries, except Canada and Mexico, belong to the extra-European régime or system.) A minimum charge for four words compulsorily collected. Plain-language words inserted in code text counted at rate of five letters per word.

CIPHER LANGUAGE

This consists of (*a*) Arabic figures, groups, or series of Arabic figures having a secret meaning, or (*b*) words, names, expressions, or combinations of letters not fulfilling the conditions of plain language or code language.

Requirements and conditions.—(*a*) No fixed maximum length of word or group.

(*b*) No conditions or restrictions as to construction of groups.

(*c*) Mixture of plain and cipher language words permitted.

(*d*) Unions of plain-language words prohibited.

Tariff.—Same as at present, at rate of five figures or letters per word, charged for at full rate. Plain-language words inserted in cipher text counted at rate of 15 letters per word.

No change is made in the present method of counting and charging for words in the address and signature. As to taxation, a code-language telegram can not be considered as belonging partly to category A and partly to category B. From this standpoint it must be classified in one of the two categories, the other being excluded.

*　　*　　*　　*　　*　　*　　*

Whether these new regulations, which go into effect on October 1, 1929, will be more practicable and more satisfactory than the old ones remains to be seen. It is to be feared that the examination of code telegrams of category A to see whether all the words conform to the vowel requirements will be difficult in practice. There are many codes in use to-day, especially the large codes, which have an appreciable number of 5-letter code words that contain only one vowel. When two such words are joined together to form a single 10-letter word there will be but two vowels. Such words will have to be charged for at the rate of five letters per word, and will therefore count as two words. The examination of thousands of cablegrams and radiograms filed daily within a short period, usually toward the close of the day's business, will be a serious matter for the communication agencies, and even now serious doubts as to the practicability of enforcing the vowel requirements for words of this class are being expressed. Again, under category B, since any group of five letters whatsoever is permissible, is the union or running together of plain-language words chopped up into 5-letter groups going to be tolerated? The new regulations specifically prohibit this practice under category A but are silent in this respect under category B. Will some of the companies and administrations permit the practice while others resist it? Will old codes be revised so as strictly to conform to the vowel requirements of category A? Will new and much larger codes be compiled to take advantage of the possibility of using category B? Will the 5-letter words prove themselves to be superior to the 10-letter ones on account of their shorter length? Will the vowel requirements of words of category A reduce the errors and make the 10-letter words easier to handle by telegraph personnel? On this point grave doubts may be expressed. If, as seems to be the belief of the majority of the principal delegates at the Brussels conference, the presence of vowels aids in accuracy and ease of handling code messages, what was gained in this respect by the decision taken?

According to statistics presented to the Cortina committee, the average number of vowels in the present-day, 10-letter code words is 4,322. The new regulations will require the presence of only three vowels. Does this then not represent a loss rather than a gain? Furthermore, the present-day large codes contain approximately 100,000 code words, of which over 50 percent are of difficult or doubtful pronounceability and for that reason are considered to have brought on the serious situation in which code communication finds itself today, according to the Cortina committee. Will the new regulations reduce the number of code words that can be employed? On the contrary, the number will be greatly increased, for the theoretical maximum number [1] of 5-letter code words with a 2-letter difference, each containing at least two vowels, is 150,480. This will practically increase the present capacity of codes by 50%. What then has been gained, aside from the elimination of disputes concerning prounceability—which for all practical purposes had already been allowed to die a more or less natural death?

These and many other questions present themselves, the answers to which the next telegraph conference (to take place in Madrid in 1932) will be called upon to determine. In the meantime, from October 1, 1929, to 1932, there will be opportunity to observe both the 10-letter and the 5-letter systems in operation side by side and to form an opinion as to the merits of each system. In the end the now complicated rules will have to be simplified by the adoption of a single system.[2]

---

[1] See Friedman, W. F., and Mendelsohm, C. J., *Notes on Code Words*, in *The American Mathematical Monthly*, Vol. XXXIX, No. 7, Aug.-Sept., 1932.

[2] A limited number of copies of the English translation of the documents relating to the Brussels conference' including those of the Cortina committee, are available for distribution for official use. They may be obtained from the Department of State, or from the office of the Chief Signal Officer.

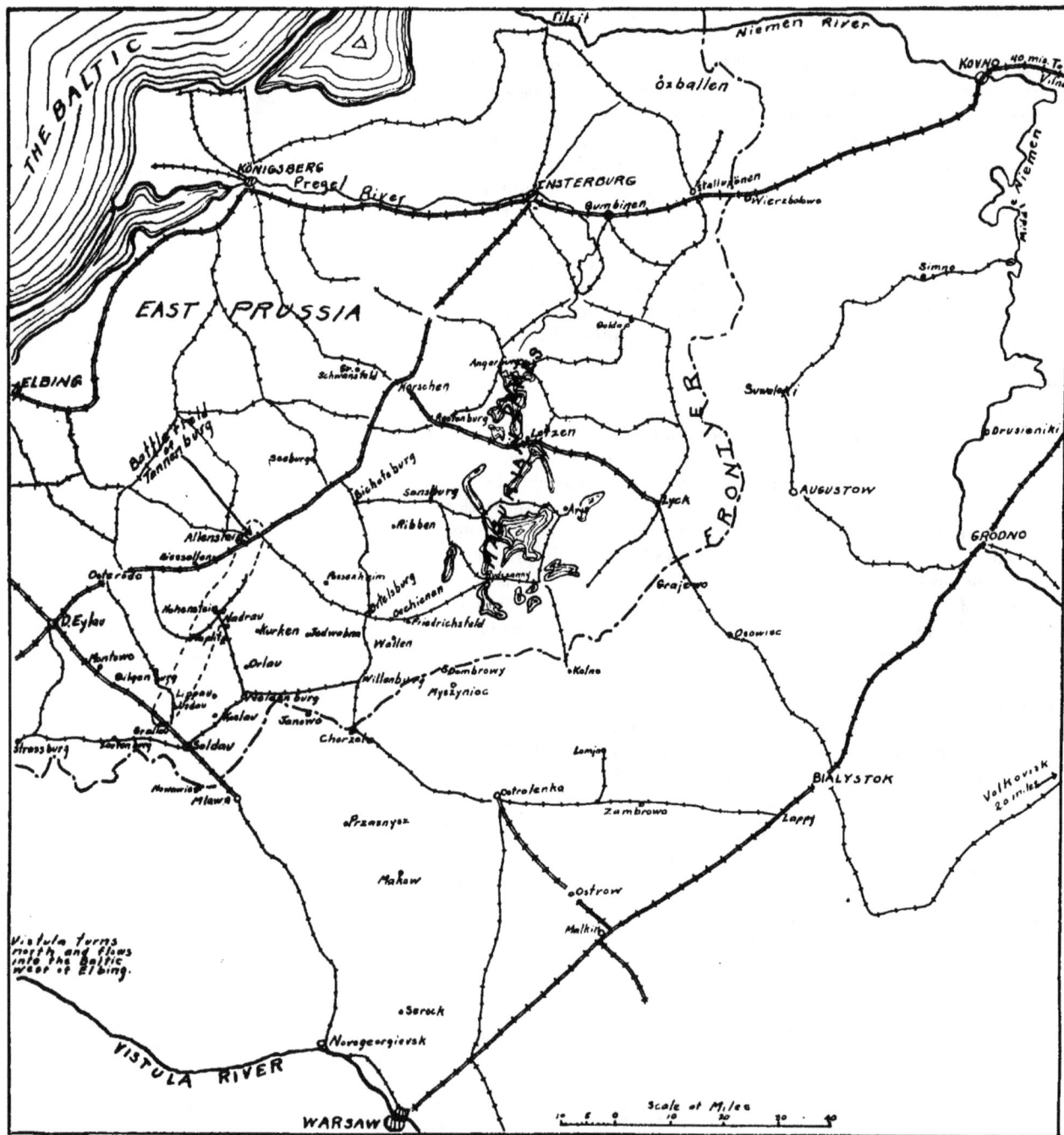

MAP OF EAST PRUSSIAN THEATRE OF OPERATIONS, AUGUST, 1914

GPO O - 478508 (Face p. 41)

TANNENBURG—A STUDY IN FAULTY SIGNAL COMMUNICATION *

By Maj. H. C. INGLES, Signal Corps

The officer who would keep abreast of the military profession can not afford to neglect the study of history. There are many lessons that can be drawn from the success or failure of commanders in the past. This is as true in the study of signal communication as it is with strategy and tactics. Unfortunately, the material available for the historical study of signal communication is extremely limited. However, the campaign of the Russian Second Army in August, 1914, culminating in the Battle of Tannenburg, is an exception in that there is considerable material available to indicate the status of signal communication. Probably no campaign of the World War furnishes such an example of faulty signal communication and the difficulties of command arising therefrom. It is the purpose of this article to briefly review this campaign and, in so far as available source material will permit, to point out the deficiencies in signal communication.

ORGANIZATION

First it is necessary to briefly consider the organization of the Russian Army when war was declared in 1914. The infantry division was the basis of the Russian war organization, as was the case with the other first-class powers. The Russian infantry division consisted normally of two infantry brigades (each consisting of two 4-battalion regiments of infantry), a field-artillery brigade of six 8-gun batteries, and a very small allotment of technical and administrative troops. There was a small signal detachment as a part of the headquarters. In some divisions these signal detachments were apparently quite efficient, but in all cases they had only very scant equipment. They were initially supplied with only a small amount of wire, which was quickly exhausted in the early stages of the campaign and was not replenished. The divisions (with the exception of some of the cavalry divisions) were not supplied with radio.

*(No. 49, July–August, 1929)

41

42

There were small signal detachments in each infantry regiment, but these were indifferently trained and practically without equipment. In all, the Russian infantry division contained about 20,000 men—about the total strength of our present Infantry division—but with a higher proportion of infantry and a less proportion of administrative, technical, and supply troops than our division.

There were also permanent organizations known as rifle brigades. Each of these consisted of four infantry regiments, of two battalions each, and three 8-gun batteries of light artillery. Aside from small detachments of infantrymen partially trained in signal work, these rifle brigades were without signal troops.

The army corps normally consisted of two infantry divisions; one light-howitzer division (two 6-gun batteries) with a howitzer park (repair and ammunition supply) and one battalion of sappers (engineers). It is this battalion of engineers with which we are the most concerned. It consisted of three sapper companies (similar to our combat Engineer companies) and two telegraph companies. In the Russian Army signal communication was a function of the engineers. The telegraph companies were primarily trained and equipped to install and maintain telegraph lines and installations, but they also carried a small amount of telephone equipment.

There was no fixed organization for the army. There were 5,000,000 men in the regular army and its reserve classified for mobilization, about 3,000,000 of which were to be organized into 9 or 10 armies. Each army had a different organization, according to its mission and the theater in which it was to operate.

In addition to the signal organizations mentioned above, there were independent telegraph companies, telegraph columns, telephone establishments, and field radio stations. These were intended to be assigned to the headquarters of the various armies, army groups, and general headquarters.

The independent telegraph companies were organized similarly to the telegraph companies regularly assigned to the army corps but were provided with more wire. These organizations appear to have been fairly efficient as far as line construction was concerned, but very short on operators, and those that they had were poorly trained and inexperienced. We have no signal organizations in our army parallel to these telegraph companies. They seem to have been somewhat similar to the telegraph trains organized by McClellan for the peninsular campaign in 1862.

The telegraph columns were lines of communication troops and were probably somewhat similar to our construction companies. There is little or nothing that has come down to us from which we can determine their organization and equipment.

Telephone establishments were organizations provided with 25 telephone instruments. They had sufficient switchboards, wire, and personnel to establish a telephone installation of not to exceed 25 subscribers' stations.

A field radio station was an organization provided with personnel and equipment to establish and operate one radio station. There is no information available as to the type of set provided for these stations. It was undoubtedly spark equipment and must have had sufficient power to cover a range of at least 100 miles. This is inferred from the fact that messages sent from the headquarters of the Second Russian Army at Ostrolenka were heard and copied at the headquarters of the Eighth German Army at Reisenburg, about 110 miles away. Field radio stations were provided at corps headquarters as well as at army headquarters.

CONCENTRATION AND THE GENERAL SITUATION

With this brief survey of the Russian Army organization, we must next consider the military situation on the East Prussian frontier.[1] Only the Russian Second Army was involved in the Battle of Tannenburg, but in order to clearly understand the situation we must also consider conditions on the entire front of the northwest army group. The army group on the northwest front consisted of the First Army, under General Rennenkampf, and the Second Army, under General Samsonoff. The entire northwest front was under command of General Jilinsky, whose headquarters were at Volkovisk during the first part of August, but about the middle of the month moved up to Bialystok. The First Army consisted of the Third, Fourth, and Twentieth Corps; Fifth Rifle Brigade; First and Second Guard Cavalry Divisions; First, Second, and Third Cavalry Divisions, and First Independent Cavalry Brigade. Its concentration took place generally on the right along the line Kovno–Simno–Drusieniki. During the concentration First Army headquarters was at Vilna (about 40 miles east of Kovno). On August 17 it moved up to Wierzbolowo.

The Second Army, consisting of the Second, Sixth, Thirteenth, Fifteenth, and Twenty-third Corps; First Rifle Brigade, and Fourth, Sixth, and Fifteenth Cavalry Divisions, concentrated along the general line Augustow–Osowiec–Zambromo–Serock, with the Thirteenth Corps concentrating at Bialystok. The headquarters, Second Army, was initially at Bialystok, but on August 18 moved to Ostrolenka.

Opposed to the First and Second Russian Armies the Germans had in East Prussia the First, Seventeenth, and Twentieth Corps and the First Reserve Corps; the First Cavalry Division, and garrisons of all the fortresses. In all, the Germans had available 144 batallions

---

[1] See map.

478603 O - 42 - 4

of infantry and 84 squadrons of cavalry with which to oppose the Russian 250 batallions of infantry and 230 squadron of cavalry. However, the Russian concentration had been ordered before mobilization was complet, and the units were by no means up to strength. The Germans were at least equal in light artillery and had considerable superiority in heavy artillery. The German troops in East Prussia were organized into the Eighth Army under Von Prittwitz with Graf von Waldersee as his chief of staff. The Eighth German Army was later reinforced by two corps from the western front, but these did not reach East Prussia until after the Battle of Tannenburg.

The Russian plan of campaign was for the First Army to advance into East Prussia north of the Masurian Lakes, crossing the frontier two or three days before the advance of the Second Army. It was to draw onto itself the main German forces. The Second Army was to cross the frontier two or three days later and, advancing south and west of the Masurian Lakes, cut off the withdrawal of the Germans to the Vistula River and destroy them. Thus we see that the plan involved a gigantic turning movement or, if this was not entirely successful, an envelopment. The two armies were to effect a junction somewhere west of the Masurian Lakes.

It will be readily appreciated from a glance at the map that by separating the two armies by the difficult lake region this plan greatly increased the difficulties of lateral signal communication. This danger seems to have been appreciated by Russian general headquarters, as the instructions issued Jilinsky contained the following specific order:

The closest liaison must be maintained between the First and Second Armies. a sufficient screen being placed in front of the lake position.

This part of his instructions does not seem to have greatly impressed Jilinsky. His orders to the Second Army directed that the Second Corps advance through the lake region, thereby providing a screen for the lake position, but he did this because he feared a German advance through the Lotzen Gap rather than for the purpose of maintaining liaison between the armies. He did not charge either army commander with the responsibility of maintaining signal communication with the other, nor did he make any provision for maintaining this communication himself. There is nothing to indicate that the principle that lateral communication between subordinate units is the responsibility of the first common superior, now accepted in our Army, was then recognized in the Russian Army.

During the concentration the mainstay of the signal communication system was the network of Government-owned telegraph lines. In general, these lines followed the railroads, but not all railroads had telegraph lines. Since, during the concentration, army and corps headquarters were uniformly placed on the railroads, the existing telegraph system satisfactorily met the situation until the advance started. Instructions sent out telegraphically from army group and army headquarters during the concentration seem to have been uniformly received and acted upon the same day as sent. Since the corps concentration areas were small (in only one case was a corps concentration area more than 10 miles across) the corps commanders had no difficulty in communicating with their divisions.

THE ADVANCE

Pursuant to the general plan outlined above, General Jilinsky ordered the First Army to cross the frontier on August 17, advancing from the line Wierzbolowo–Suwalki to the line Insterburg–Angerburg. The Second Army was ordered to cross the frontier on August 19, advancing from the line Augustow–Grajewo–Myszyniec–Chorzele to the line Rudczanny–Passenheim and thereafter to continue its advance to the line Rastenburg–Seeburg. Instead of issuing one order which contained instructions for each army, General Jilinsky issued a separate order to each army. He informed the commander of the First Army, General Rennenkampf, that the Second Army would advance to the line Lotzen–Rudczanny–Passenheim. General Rennenkampf therefore expected to gain communication with the right flank of the Second Army in the vicinity of Lotzen. However, as we have seen, the orders issued the Second Army directed an advance to the line Rudczanny–Passenheim. Under these orders the right flank of the Second Army would have been at Rudczanny, nearly 30 miles from Lotzen, leaving a gap which could only be partially screened by the Second Corps. However, General Samsonoff did not obey these orders but directed the advance of the Second Army on the line Dombrowy–Mlawa, to be reached August 20, and the line Ribben–Waplitz, to be reached August 24. He thus increased the gap between the two armies by about 30 miles, so that the total gap which actually existed was about 60 miles, with only the Second Corps to cover it. It should be noted that the Second Corps was in this gap and belonged to the Second Army. Samsonoff's only means of signal communication with this corps was by telegraph via the circuitous route Ostrolenka–Ostrow–Bialystok–Lyck. This route also involved several manual relays. The result was Second Army headquarters was almost continuously out of communication with the Second Corps.

The general picture is now complete and we see the First Army north of the Masurian Lakes and moving westward; the Second Army south of the lakes and moving northwest and between the flanks of the armies a gap of 60 miles covered by only one corps, which was out of communication with its own army. The operation of the concentric advance on a concentrated enemy is a classic one in history. There is no operation in the realm of strategy which requires more careful timing and none that requires a more complete and reliable signal-communication system. Here there was no direct signal communication between the First and Second Armies. All communication between the army commanders had to be routed through Bialystok, the headquarters of the northwest front. General Jilinsky had telegraphic communication with each army commander most of the time but failed to inform each commander of the situation in the other army.

The First Army took no part in the battle of Tannenburg, and we will consider only those features of its operations which had a bearing on the fate of the Second Army. In order for the corps to cross the frontier on August 17 as ordered, it was necessary for them to march from the concentration areas not later than August 13. The necessary rear services to supply the troops were not ready to function until August 19. The Second Army started its advance six days before the rear services were ready to function. This had an effect on the signal situation in that when the small initial supply of wire was exhausted it was not replenished. In spite of the exhaustion of the troops and shortage of food and everything else, the First Army crossed the frontier on August 17 on schedule and the Third Corps gained contact with the Germans at Stallupönen. The Germans were successful in this first action but received peremptory orders from Von Prittwitz to withdraw to Gumbinen. The First Army continued a slow advance on August 18 but by night the rear services were in such disorder that they had practically ceased to function. The signal system was blocked with undelivered telegrams. Communication by wire between army headquarters and corps command posts was practically impossible. In desperation the army orders for the 19th, which were to advance to the line Ozballen–Goldap and halt there during August 20, were sent out by radio. These orders were sent out in the clear. They reached the corps on the morning of the 19th, and then only in mutilated form. The corps receiving stations must have been at fault, as the Germans picked up these orders correctly, and were thus informed of the Russian movements for the next two days. Von Francois, the commander of the German First Corps which was opposing Rennenkampf, was quick to take advantage of this information and launched a successful attack. However, the German Seventeenth Corps failed to promptly support him and the action was indecisive. Von Prittwitz now received information that the Russian Second Army had crossed the frontier. He became fearful of the situation and ordered the German forces to withdraw to the west of the Vistula River. When he called the German supreme headquarters at Coblentz and informed them of his action their reply was to promptly relieve both Von Prittwitz and his chief of staff and replace them by the solid Von Hindenburg, with the nimble-minded Ludendorff as his chief of staff.

OPERATIONS OF THE SECOND ARMY

As has been previously pointed out, the Second Army, under General Samsonoff, was to cross the frontier two days after the First Army crossed. Under General Samsonoff's orders they began their advance August 15 and by the 20th had reached the line prescribed by the army commander, Dombrowy–Mlawa. Though the advance started two days later than that of the First Army, the rear services were not yet organized. The country through which the army advanced was a waste land, intentionally left that way by the Russians as a protection against a long-feared invasion of Poland from East Prussia. Roads were few and those that existed were mere sandy tracks. On the 18th the Second Army headquarters moved to Ostrolenka. By August 21 the main body of the army had reached the line Friedrichsfeld–Willenberg–Mlawa. The Second Corps had reached Arys, just east of the Masurian Lakes. Samsonoff was now completely out of communication with the Second Corps and it was acting practically as an independent force. Jilinsky decided that the First Army could better control the Second Corps, and on the 21st transferred it to the command of the First Army. Since Jilinsky was the only one who had any signal communication with this corps, it would have been better to have kept it under his own command. By August 22 the army was so exhausted by continuous marching over abominable roads and from lack of food that only a straggling advance was possible. On August 23 the Sixth Corps advanced to Ortelsburg, the Thirteenth Corps to Jedwabna, the Fifteenth Corps to Neidenburg, the Twenty-third Corps (only one division of this corps was present) to Koslau, and the First Corps (which had been attached to the Second Army on the 20th) to Soldau. It will now be seen that Samsonoff had only one corps, the Sixth, on the line of his original objective. All the remainder were well to the west of it. The dangerous gap between the First and Second Armies was ever widening. Jilinsky saw the danger, and on the 23d directed Samsonoff to march on the line Sensburg–Allenstein. The position of the army now made this practically impossible. As a staff officer at the headquarters of the northwest front expressed it, "Samsonoff was pulling the army to the left, and Jilinsky was pulling it to the right."

On the 24th the Fifteenth Corps encountered the German Twentieth Corps in the vicinity of Orlau and fought an indecisive engagement. The Thirteenth Corps changed its direction of march to strike the German left flank, but during the night, 24th-25th, the Germans withdrew. Samsonoff assumed that they withdrew in the direction of Osterode. Strengthened by this assumption (which was unfounded, as the German Twentieth Corps did not withdraw to Osterode, but to Hohenstein), Samsonoff again requested the commander of the northwest front to permit him to march on the line Allenstein–Osterode. This time Jilinsky yielded to the westward pull of Samsonoff and acquiesced, but directed that at least one corps and one cavalry division remain between Allenstein and the Masurian Lakes.

GERMAN MOVEMENTS

When Ludendorff arrived at German supreme headquarters on August 22 he at once began issuing orders. He and Von Hindenburg arrived at the headquarters of the Eighth German Army on August 23 and assumed control. On August 24 it will be remembered the German Twentieth Corps fought an indecisive engagement with the Russian Fifteen Corps in the vicinity of Orlau and then withdrew to the vicinity of Hohenstein. On the 23d Ludendorff had ordered a withdrawal from in front of Rennenkampf and on the evening of the 24th he decided to make the Twentieth Corps the framework upon which to direct the Germans then withdrawing from Rennenkampf's front. Consequently he placed the Twentieth Corps in position on the line Hohenstein–Gilgenburg and directed the Seventeenth Corps and the First Reserve Corps to concentrate on the left of the Twentieth Corps. He also directed the Third Reserve Division to the left of the Twentieth Corps. The First Corps was directed to the right of the Twentieth Corps. All available garrison troops from the Vistula were also to move to the right of the Twentieth Corps. A landwehr division from Schleswig-Holstein was started to the eastern front and directed to Biessellen.

Ludendorff was able to order these moves without fear of Russian interference because the careless use of radio in the First Army had informed him of Rennenkampf's intention to slow up his advance. On August 24 Samsonoff transmitted, by radio, to his corps commanders his orders for the movements of the 24th and 25th. The Germans picked up these messages, so were fully informed as to the movements of the Second Army.

SITUATION BY EVENING, AUGUST 25

By evening of August 25 the Russian Second Army was disposed as follows: Sixth Corps, Bichofsburg; Fourth Cavalry Division, Sensburg; Thirteenth Corps, Kurken; Fifteenth Corps, Orlau; Twenty-third Corps (with only one regiment now absent), Lippau; First Corps (attached), Usdau–Grallau.

It should be noted that the Sixth Corps and the Fourth Cavalry Division, which had now been attached to the Sixth Corps, were approximately 30 miles from the right flank of the main body of the Second Army—over two days' march.

By the evening of August 25 the German Eighth Army was disposed as follows: First Corps and a detachment aggregating about a brigade, southeast of Montowo; Twentieth Corps on the line Gilgenburg-Hohenstein; Seventeenth Corps, Gross Schwansfeld; First Reserve Corps, east of Seeburg; Sixth Landwehr Brigade, east of Seeburg.

The picture is now complete. Samsonoff had disposed his three cavalry divisions on the flanks of the Second Army instead of in front, where they should have been, so was in complete ignorance of the German concentration and of the blow about to descend upon him. He was about to continue his advance on the line Allenstein-Osterode with the bulk of his army, leaving one corps and one cavalry division isolated on his right at a distance of over two days' march. The troops were tired and unfed. Stragglers were numerous and the army much reduced by sickness. All had been marching over execrable roads since the 15th, and some even before that date.

SIGNAL COMMUNICATION IN THE SECOND ARMY

In addition to the telegraph companies that were integral parts of the corps, Samsonoff had with the army headquarters the following signal troops: One independent telegraph company, one telegraph column, one telephone establishment, two field radio stations.

The existing net of government-owned telegraph lines was depended upon as the mainstay of the signal system. However, this was pitifully inadequate. These lines ran as follows:

(1) Ostrow-Ostrolenka-Myszyniec.
(2) Ostrow-Makow-Przasnysz-Mlawa.
(3) Przasnysz-Chorzele.
(4) Ostrolenka-Lappy-Bialystok.

These towns were the only telegraph offices in the area of the advance. By August 20 all the corps except the Thirteenth Corps had advanced beyond these stations. The Thirteenth Corps was then at Chorzele, but by evening of the 21st it also had advanced beyond the end of the permanent telegraph lines. It then became necessary to extend the permanent lines with temporary construction in order to reach the command posts of the corps.

It is a well-recognized basic principle that the impetus for signal communication must come from the rear and the superior unit must be held responsible for signal communication to the subordinate. This principle was not applied in the Russian Second Army, and the corps were required to extend the telegraph lines from the nearest permanent offices. Each corps had but 50 miles of wire when it entered the campaign, and, due to the disorganization of the rear services, the wire supply was not replenished. The corps soon exhausted their supplies of wire in extending the permanent lines, leaving nothing for the corps signal systems to the divisions. The divisions had only a few miles of wire, insufficient for their own use, and were unable to help out the general shortage.

The Independent Telegraph Company, which should have been employed installing and maintaining wire communication between Second Army headquarters and the command posts of the corps, was employed to build a telegraph line from Ostrolenka to Przasnysz and thence to Mlawa. This line was intended to furnish lateral communication, but it was so slow in building that by the time it was completed it had been decided to move army headquarters to Ortelsburg. Consequently the company was ordered to proceed to Ortelsburg. The army had available only about 80 miles of wire, and about 50 miles had been used in the Ostrolenka–Mlawa line. In order to recover the wire, it was ordered to take down this line, which it had just finished. At Chorzele, on its way to Ortelsburg, the order to proceed to Ortelsburg was revoked and the company was directed to go to Neidenburg. The company eventually arrived at Neidenburg after Samsonoff had left and the fate of the Second Army had been decided.

The wire supply in the Second Army was entirely inadequate. Counting the wire in the First Corps, which was only attached to the army, and counting small amounts of wire in the divisions, the total amount of wire within the army was about 350 miles. If we compare this with the 5,776 miles of wire which would be available in an American Army of only three corps to-day, or if we compare it with the 2,500 miles of wire per day which was being consumed by the American First Army by the fourth day of the Meuse–Argonne offensive, we can readily appreciate how pitifully insufficient the wire supply was. As has been pointed out, the corps used their precious 50 miles of wire in extending the permanent lines in an endeavor to keep in communication with the army, and had nothing left to communicate with the divisions. In the Sixth Corps this did not suffice even to keep in wire communication with the army. This corps used all their wire in extending the line from Myszyniec to Ortelsburg and had to rely upon mounted messengers from Ortelsburg forward. By the evening of August 25, when the Sixth Corps command post was at Bischofsburg, these mounted messengers had to cover a distance of over 25 miles to get to the head of the wire line.

After August 20, the telegraph offices became so jammed with messages and the confusion reached such proportions that army orders sent out in the evening did not reach the corps until late the next morning—sometimes as late as noon. In desperation, army headquarters turned more and more to the use of radio. We have seen the disastrous results of the careless use of radio on August 24. In many cases messages were sent out in the clear. The French mission with the Russian Army reports that the Russians had a cipher for field use but that it was such a simple cipher that even when it was used the Germans probably had no difficulty in breaking it down. General Knox, British Army, who was the British liaison officer with the northwest army group, reports that the general use of the then authorized Russian cipher was impossible, as many of the corps staffs were unable to use the cipher or decipher messages sent in it.

THE BATTLE OF TANNENBURG

The Battle of Tannenburg was really three engagements all starting on August 26. They were all coordinated on the German side but were separate, independent, and widely separated actions as far as the Russians were concerned.

It will be remembered that the Sixth Russian . Corps was at Bischofsburg, nearly 30 miles from the main body of the Second Army. Early on the 26th it was attacked by the German Seventeenth Corps, assisted by the First Reserve Corps and Sixth Landwehr Brigade. The Sixth Corps was disposed with its divisions out of supporting distance of each other. The Fourth Division was very severely punished, while the Sixteenth Division spent the day marching and countermarching. The Russians retreated in disorder for about 21 miles. All communication with army headquarters had been lost and it was not until the morning of the 28th that a mounted messenger reached the army commander and informed him of the disaster to the Sixth Corps. During the 27th the corps withdrew to Oschienen and Wallen, leaving the German Seventeenth Corps and First Reserve Corps free to turn south and assist in the attack against the Russian center.

The Russian First Corps was on the line Usdau-Grallau, on the extreme left of the Second Army. The corps commander had 50 squadrons of cavalry at his disposal and yet the whole German First Corps detrained within one day's march of the Russian position without being detected. The German First Corps was still short some of its artillery and made only a half-hearted attack on August 26. By the morning of the 27th all the artillery was in place and the Germans launched a determined attack at 5 a. m., preceded by an hour's intensive artillery preparation. The half-starved and e hausted Russians were in no condition to withstand it. They beg. to leave the trenches without even waiting for the infantry attac The movement soon became a rout and by 10 a. m. the Russian Fir Corps had ceased to exist as an organized body. By night of tl 27th all that remained of the corps was a rear guard of five regimen from various divisions. The German First Corps pushed on, some c the troops covering 40 miles in 2 days, and by the evening of Augu: 29 was east of Neidenburg, blocking the Russian line of retreat.

The Thirteenth Corps at Kurken, the Fifteenth Corps at Orla and the incomplete Twenty-third Corps at Lippau formed the Rus sian center. On the morning of the 26th these corps continued thei advance on the line Allenstein–Osterode. They soon encountered the German Twentieth Corps all along the line. The Russian: fought well, and, with the exception of the Second Russian Division, which was nearly annihilated, succeeded in pushing the Germans back. Hindenburg wished to gain time for the German First Re serve Corps and the Seventeenth Corps to close in on the north and the German First Corps to close in on the south. To gain this time he ordered the Twentieth Corps, with a landwehr division attached, to attack on the 27th. Because of the total absence of lateral signal communication the Russian corps commanders were in ignorance of what was taking place on their flanks. As we have seen, by evening of the 27th both the right and left flanks of the Second Army had been broken down. The attack of the German Twentieth Corps was successful. The Twenty-third Corps was driven back through Neidenburg and the Russian Thirteenth and Fifteenth Corps left with both flanks exposed.

On the 27th, headquarters of the Second Army moved to Neidenburg. The army was now out of communication with all the corps— in fact, did not even know where the corps command posts were. The breakdown of the signal system had deprived the army commander of any information of the true situation.

Hindenburg ordered the German Seventeenth Corps and First Reserve Corps to attack the Russian center from the north on August 28. while the German First Corps was to close in on the south. The Twentieth Corps was to continue the pressure in the center.

On the 28th the double envelopment struck the flanks of the Thirteenth and Fifteenth Corps. Both corps were shattered, and during the night August 28–29 the remnants started to withdraw. The Germans pursued vigorously and the Russian withdrawal soon became a rout. During the 29th and 30th all organizations broke up and small groups of utterly exhausted men continued to drag themselves to the rear. By evening of August 30 the Second Army had ceased to exist. Of the Thirteenth and Fifteenth Corps there remained of the 50,000 which entered the campaign only 50 officers and 2,000 men. Losses in the other corps were not so heavy, but in all the Second Army lost about 130,000 men.

It is interesting and instructive to trace the movements of army headquarters. When the campaign opened army headquarters was at Ostrolenka. As the advance progressed plans were made to move it to Ortelsburg, and, as has already been described, the Army Independent Telegraph Company was ordered to that place. With the defeat of the Sixth Corps Ortelsburg became an unsafe place for army headquarters, so on the 27th it moved to Neidenburg. However, only the army commander and a few staff officers went to Neidenburg. All the supply and administrative officers remained at Ostrolenka. Messages between these echelons of army headquarters had to be transmitted through five stations—Mlawa–Przasnysz–Makow–Ostrow–Ostrolenka. All signal communication with headquarters of the northwest front at Bialystok was also over this very circuitous route. On the 28th the army commander left Neidenburg and went to Nadrau, where the command post of the Fifteenth Corps was supposed to be, thereby cutting himself off from all signal communication to the rear. On the night August 28–29 he decided to move army headquarters to Janowo. Samsonoff, with a few staff officers, started out to ride from Nadrau to Janowo. They became lost in the forest before they reached Janowo, and Samsonoff in despair committed suicide.

CONCLUSIONS

There are several lessons which commanders, general staff officers, and signal officers may draw from this campaign. It would be an error to say that faulty signal communication was the only cause of the disaster to the Second Army, but it undoubtedly was one of the primary causes. Disorganization of the supply services, which resulted in men and animals being half starved; lack of reconnaissance, which was the result of improper use of the cavalry; and, above all, poor leadership, all contributed their quota to the Russian defeat.

The Russian advance was, with some slight modifications, an execution of the plan of 1910. Though this plan had been in effect four years it contained no provision for signal communication. This indicates to us that no war plan is complete without a signal annex.

The signal supply, particularly wire, was entirely inadequate. There is no doubt that the American soldier is very prodigal of wire, and the large amounts of wire provided for our organization is greater than would be necessary in other armies. Even taking this into consideration, however, we can not but conclude that the Russian supply was pitifully insufficient.

After August 26 there was no time at which army headquarters knew the location of all the corps command posts. In battle we expect frequently to lose communication with battalions. Doubtlessly there will also be times when we do not know the locations of regimental command posts, and there were even times during the World War when division headquarters did not know the location of the brigade command posts. However, losing the command post of a unit as large as an army corps is inexcusable.

Army headquarters greatly multiplied the communication difficulties by its frequent moves. Starting with its movement to Neidenburg on the 27th, army headquarters moved daily for three days. These moves were made without regard to the communication situation, and the commander and staff groups making the moves were not preceded by signal detachments to install signal facilities at the new locations.

It has been possible within the limits of this article to point out only the more glaring defects in signal communication during this campaign. A more detailed study of the Russian operations is recommended for signal officers.

BIBLIOGRAPHY

Tannenburg, the First Thirty Days in East Prussia, by Maj. Gen. Sir Edmund Ironsides.

Russia, 1914–1917, Memories of War and Revolution, by Gen. Basil Gourko.

With the Russian Army 1914–1917, by Maj. Gen. Sir Alfred Knox.

Russland in Weltkriege, 1914–1915 (Russia in the World War, 1914–1915), by Jurij Daniloff. (Translation by Col. Gustavus M. Blech, Medical Corps, United States Army.)

Official Report of the Signal Officer, American First Army, American Expeditionary Forces, for September, 1918.

* **Cryptogram.**—The cryptogram reproduced below was found in the prison yard of an eastern penitentiary and was sent to the office of the Chief Signal Officer for solution. The message was decryptographed in 50 minutes by a group of junior cryptanalysts. Can you solve it? The solution will appear in the next issue of the BULLETIN.

* **Cryptogram.**—How many solved the cryptogram appearing in the last issue of the BULLETIN? The following is the translation:

Dearest Sarah, sweetheart: Just a few lines to let you hear from me. I am well and hoping that these few words will find you enjoying the best health and all the pleasures a happy life affords. Dear, I should have written you long before this had circumstance permitted for, dear, you can not imagine what a torture it has been this being too far away to see you and to hear your voice assuring me that you still care. Back in Newark it was easier to bear because there we could see each other twice a week but here haven't even heard from you in three weeks and it has worried me more than I can say. Well, little sweetheart, I am going to close.

(No signature.)

*(No. 56, September–October, 1930)
*(No. 57, November–December, 1930)

THE INTERNATIONAL TELECOMMUNICATION CONVENTION *

By Maj. WILLIAM F. FRIEDMAN, *Signal Reserve*

FOREWORD

The following article, appearing coincidentally with the effective date of the new International Telecommunication Convention, is deemed timely and of general interest to Signal Corps personnel. The author attended the Conference of Madrid, which drew up the convention. He participated in the work of the conference in a dual capacity—first, as a technical adviser to the American delegation to the International Radiotelegraph Conference, secondly, as a representative of the United States to the International Telegraph Conference.—*The Editor*.

On December 9, 1932, there was signed in Madrid, by specially designated plenipotentiaries from practically all the governments of the world, a document which is at the moment of particular interest to all persons connected with the communication industry, and is in the future likely to become of great historic importance in the art of signaling, namely, the International Telecommunication Con-

*(No. 76, January–February, 1934)

56

vention. This new convention became effective on January 1, 1934, as among the signatory governments which had ratified it on that date.[1] With its accompanying sets of regulations, the convention constitutes a treaty between the signatory governments with regard to the broad, general principles upon which they agree to exchange communications between themselves or to permit them to be exchanged between their respective nationals. In relations between two governments both of which have ratified it, the Telecommunication Convention will supersede and replace all previously existing communication conventions, including the International Telegraph Convention signed at St. Petersburg in 1875, and the International Radiotelegraph Convention signed at Washington in 1927.

In order to appreciate the significance of the new convention, it is necessary to have at least a birdseye view of the historical background of the two older conventions which it replaces. This background, of course, has as its principal features the invention and development of wire telegraphy and wire telephony, the discovery of radioelectric waves, and the consequent development of radiotelegraphy and radiotelephony. In America, in 1835, Joseph Henry, then a professor at Princeton University, demonstrated electric telegraphy, and in the same year Morse constructed his first rude working model. In 1837 Morse was granted the first American patent covering electric telegraphy and gave the first public exhibition of his instruments; and in 1844, with the aid of a governmental grant of $30,000, he established the first public telegraph line in America, between Washington and Baltimore. The development of the new facility was very rapid in the United States, but since it proceeded within the confines of one large country there was no necessity for a considerable time for American participation in any international agreements. Communications with Mexico and Canada were sparse; cable telegraphy was in its infancy. When the time for international agreements did come as a result of the successful establishment of electrical connections with Europe by means of submarine cables (1867), the situation was already quite complicated and such that the United States never became a party to the international agreements drawn up and entered into by most of the other nations of the world. This phase of the subject will be dealt with in detail later in this paper. Suffice it to say at this point that the American companies owning and operating the land wires and ocean cables over which international messages were transmitted retained practically complete freedom to negotiate directly with the foreign governments concerned such

[1] The convention is not yet effective as to the United States. It is understood that it will be submitted to the Senate in January for that body's advice and consent to ratification.

agreements as were necessary to facilitate the handling of this international traffic.

The situation in this respect in other parts of the world, however, was quite different. In Europe, the first patent covering electric telegraphy was granted to two Englishmen, Cooke and Wheatstone, in 1837. Although the earliest practical test of it was made by them in the same year, and the first public line was opened in England in 1843, it was not until 1847 that telegraphy was introduced on the Continent, in Germany. The development of the industry was also rapid, and almost from the very first the new instrumentality of communication was taken over completely by the governments concerned; each state owned and operated its telegraphs, and later, its telephones. But, in contrast with the situation in the United States, European countries, except Russia, were so small in area that the necessity for international agreements soon became pressing. For as the telegraph in each country developed into usage, it was not long before the lines from two countries would reach the boundary between them and would there have to stop. In order to relieve a situation rapidly becoming intolerable, some sort of agreement between the countries concerned was essential. The establishment of agreements in respect to telegraphy was more difficult than that in the case of the mails, on which subject international agreements had long been a common matter, because in the latter only the physical carriage of material objects is involved whereas in the former the transmission of a more or less mysterious force—electric current— is involved, together with such debatable questions as types of apparatus, languages to be used, hours of opening and closing offices, tariffs, and methods of accounting to one another for charges collected, and so on.

The reader may appreciate the situation in Europe if he will imagine that the States of New York and Pennsylvania, for example, were separate, sovereign nations, speaking entirely different languages, and that the telegraph lines and offices were owned by the States themselves. It is apparent that specific agreements would be necessary in order that citizens of one State might exchange messages with citizens of the other.

Let us note now how the first telegraph convention originated. In 1849 Prussia and Austria concluded a convention concerning the establishment and utilization of electromagnetic telegraphs, but only for the exchange of government dispatches. Very soon agreements were made between other portions of what later became Germany and Austria, resulting in the formation of the Austro-German Telegraph Union, which became effective on October 1, 1851. In 1852 France, Belgium, Prussia, Bavaria, Saxony, Hanover, Wurtemberg, Austria, and the Netherlands signed a convention " to assure to international telegraph correspondence the advantages of a uniform tariff and identical regulations." It was not until 1865, however, that a really international union was formed, when, on the invitation of the French Government, plenipotentiaries from 20 European states assembled at Paris for the first International Telegraph Conference and drew up a convention and regulations governing international telegraphy. It was still a regional agreement, however, as there was no participation by countries outside of Europe. Not even Great Britain was a party to it.[2] In 1868, at Vienna, and in 1872, at Rome, delegates from the signatory countries reassembled to revise and add to the rules formulated by the Paris Conference.

In 1875, however, with a view to making the International Telegraph Convention a sound, simple, practical and general agreement, and of such a nature as to facilitate the adherence of governments and large companies, the Conference of St. Petersburg proceeded to establish the convention upon a new foundation by limiting it to provisions of a character considered by all to be basic, as determined by long experience and general consent. The Conference at the same time decided to relegate variable provisions and minor rules to a set of regulations which could, in consequence, be amended, broadened, or made more specific in details as often as became necessary. In 1875 the map of Europe had assumed a form that remained fairly constant until 1914. Because of the absorption of many small states into larger ones, and the consequent reduction in boundary lines, there were only 15 European states represented at the St. Petersburg Conference; but the presence of representatives from Egypt and from the United States made it truly an international conference in which governments from four continents participated. The Telegraph Union was no longer purely a European affair. So well did the St. Petersburg Conference do its work that the convention it formulated in 1875 remained unchanged for over half a century, although the regulations were amended from time to time, at London in 1879, at Berlin in 1885, at Paris in 1890, at Budapest in 1896, at London in 1903, at Lisbon in 1908, at Paris in 1925, and at Brussels in 1928.[8] In the years intervening between 1875 and 1932, practically all governments of the world had signed the St. Petersburg Convention;

---

[2] Great Britain became a signatory to the Rome convention of 1872 after the Postmaster General was empowered to purchase the telegraph lines by an act passed in 1868.

[8] It should be noted that up to and including the St. Petersburg Conference, governmental delegates to the Telegraph Conferences represented their governments as well as their respective telegraph administrations, for they attended these Conferences as diplomatic representatives. But all the Conferences held after the St. Petersburg and until the Madrid Conference were administrative Conferences; that is, the persons who attended them as delegates carried no plenipotentiary credentials and were empowered only to make changes in the regulations, and not in the convention itself. The latter was a treaty, in other words, and as such, a more or less sacred document, to be dealt with only by diplomats with plenipotentiary powers.

the only ones conspicuous by their failure to sign were the United States, Canada, and Mexico.[4]

We come now to the interesting question as to why the United States never became a signatory to the International Telegraph Convention. In the words of the report of one American delegation, to sign the convention and become a member of the Telegraph Union, a government " must be in a position to insure the general acceptance of the principles and rules of the International Telegraph Conference on the part of the private companies within its territory." But electrical communication facilities in the United States, except for a very short time in the early days of development, have always been privately owned and operated. There have been, and still are, instances wherein the Government owns and operates small systems open to public correspondence, but these are sporadic instances only and are of such minor importance that they may be disregarded in this connection. Now the St. Petersburg Convention and its accompanying regulations contain obligatory clauses of a nature such that the signing of these documents by the United States would involve the imposition of restrictions upon the degree of freedom of action deemed essential by private operating companies for the successful conduct of their enterprises. Therefore, when the United States received urgent invitations to join the Telegraph Union as a full member, these were consistently refused " on the ground that telegraphy in this country is a private enterprise not subject to control of government." However, the invitation to join did not preclude the possibility of participation by sending representatives who acted in the capacity of nonvoting delegates or " observers " and this is what has happened at practically every Telegraph Conference since 1865, when President Grant, on repeated, earnest solicitation by Russia, directed our minister at St. Petersburg to " attend the Telegraph Convention and report results without committing this Government."

Private ownership and operation of electrical communication facilities in the United States has for a long time been such an obvious and satisfactory arrangement that one is apt to take it for granted and overlook the fact that in the early days this Government was not at all certain whether to take over telegraphy as a matter of public interest or to permit its development as a private enterprise.[5]

---

[4] According to the 1932 Annual Report of the International Bureau of the Telegraph Union the following governments are not signatories to the St. Petersburg Convention: Canada, Costa Rica, Cuba, Dominican Republic, El Salvador, United States of America, Guatemala, Haiti, Honduras, Liberia, Mexico, Nicaragua, Panama, Paraguay, and Peru.

[5] There is, indeed, on the statute books even now a fundamental permissive law which arose as a result of early experiments in public ownership. On July 24, 1866, Congress passed an act (37 Stat.L. 560; R.S. 5263) in which the following is stated:

"The United States may at any time after the expiration of 5 years from the date of the passage of this act purchase all the telegraph lines, properties, and effects of

In the majority of the countries of the world the communication facilities, as already noted, are owned and operated by the respective governments. But there are cases in which even though these facilities are private enterprises, the governments concerned are nevertheless signatories to the telegraph convention and the regulations, which provide that in these cases and solely in connection with their participation in the international service, the privately owned systems shall be regarded as forming integral parts of the telegraph systems of the States concerned. A private company conducting an international service in a country not signatory to the convention can "adhere" to it and to the regulations on notification through diplomatic channels from its own government that it is ready to abide by the obligatory clauses contained therein. Thus, privately owned cable companies, by formally adhering to the convention and to the regulations, can, if they wish, have the opportunity to enjoy all the advantages of full signature except the right to vote at conferences. But the American cable companies apparently have not found it to their interest to "adhere" officially to all the obligatory clauses of the convention and of the regulations; they do, however, conform in a general manner to those clauses and correspond regularly with the International Telegraph Bureau. Indeed, conformity with the convention and the regulations is more or less compulsory if they expect to do business in foreign countries that are members of the Telegraph Union, for otherwise their messages would not be accepted or delivered over the lines of those foreign countries. Nor, of course, would those countries accept messages for transmission over the lines of the companies unless the latter conform to their rules. The reason why the American cable companies impose the international regulations upon all messages destined abroad should now be clear; and it also becomes clear why it is that even though their own government is not a signatory, American business men desiring to exchange messages with their agents or with other business men in foreign countries (except Mexico and Canada) find that their messages have to conform to international rules and regulations which are quite different from domestic rules and regulations. For example, in domestic practice no charge is made for words in the address or signature; in cablegrams, on the other hand, every word in these important parts of a message is charged for. Again, under domestic rules the method of counting and charging for code or cipher groups is far different from that under international rules.

To go back now to the International Telegraph Convention itself, that a treaty drawn up as early as 1875 should have remained even

---

any or all of said companies, at an appraised value, to be ascertained by 5 competent disinterested persons, 2 of whom shall be selected by the Postmaster General of the United States, 2 by the companies interested, and 1 by the 4 so previously selected."

reasonably satisfactory for almost 60 years, during which the technology to which it applied grew by leaps and bounds until it had come to occupy one of the foremost positions in those industries which make civilization possible, is a tribute to the perspicacity of the framers of the St. Petersburg Convention. But the time had come when that convention had to be broadened in its scope. In 1875 wire telegraphy alone occupied the field of electrical communications; but by 1932 many other agencies of signal communication—wire telephony, radiotelephony, radiotelegraphy, broadcasting, television, radiobeacon, radio compass, telephotography—had to be considered, especially if an efficient, world-wide system of communication was to be established. Thus, it seemed time to revise the now hoary St. Petersburg Convention and replace it with a more up-to-date treaty.

The Telegraph Convention was, however, not the only convention dealing with electrical communication matters. There was, of course, the Radiotelegraph Convention, born long after the Telegraph Convention had reached manhood and now threatening to supersede it in importance. Let us see how the Radiotelegraph Convention came into existence and grew up to occupy such a prominent place in the field of electrical communication.

Although the history of radio communication may be traced back to 1827, when Savary found that a steel needle could be magnetized by the discharge from a Leyden jar, or to 1840, when Henry first produced high-frequency electric oscillations, or to 1873, when Clerk-Maxwell noted that electric waves were set up in the space surrounding a circuit through which high-frequency currents were passed, it was not until 1887 that the fundamental theory upon which all modern radio devices are based was established by Hertz, who in that year showed that electromagnetic waves act in accordance with the laws underlying light and heat waves. In 1896 Marconi entered his application for the first British patent for wireless telegraphy, and the entrance of radio in the field of public correspondence may accurately be dated as having taken place on June 3, 1898, when the first paid radiogram was transmitted from a station on the Isle of Wight. In 1901 the letter " S " was transmitted across the Atlantic by Marconi between two stations 1,800 miles apart. From then on the use of radiotelegraphy grew by leaps and bounds, improvements as a result of new inventions acting as a stimulus to increased public use of radio, and the latter resulting in turn in a further stimulus to inventors to improve methods and apparatus. It is one of the characteristics of electrical communication that it rapidly breaks down or through national boundaries, and this is especially true of radio communication. In order to permit of orderly progress and, in the case of radio, to prevent actual chaos, international agreements are, of course, absolutely essential.

It was noted in the case of wire telegraphy that the establishment of the first agreement between two nations in regard to the exchange of telegrams practically coincided with the introduction of this means of communication within each of the nations concerned. Since radio waves are no respecters of national boundaries, one might naturally expect that the first international agreement concerning their use would be established almost simultaneously with the introduction of radiotelegraphy because of this obvious characteristic. Strange to relate, however, when finally the first radio convention was established it did not come about primarily because of this fundamental property of radio, but because of the refusal of certain radio companies to permit stations employing their apparatus to receive messages from stations employing competing apparatus. The object behind this refusal was obvious enough: The building up of a monopoly by the Marconi Co., which had the support of not only Italy but also Great Britain. This state of affairs could, of course, not be tolerated for long. In 1903 a preliminary conference met in Berlin, with a view to drafting an international agreement in regard to the general principles upon which a radio convention and a set of regulations might later be established. Although the German Government invited 18 nations to participate, only 8 attended and 7 of these were European. The only non-European country represented there was the United States, showing that it recognized the importance of the pending negotiations upon the future development of radio. It is interesting to note that the then Chief Signal Officer, Maj. Gen. A. W. Greely, was head of the American delegation. This preliminary conference drew up no treaty but only resolutions,[6] and in 1906, in the same city as before, a conference was held to adopt the first radio convention and regulations. Whereas in 1903 only 8 nations participated in the discussions, in 1906 30 governments from 4 continents were represented, showing that in a brief space of 3 years radio had become world-wide in its importance. The convention comprised 23 articles, fundamentally legal in character, and the regulations, 42 articles of technical details. There was also a supplementary agreement to cover a point on which unanimous approval could not be obtained, and a final protocol. This treaty

---

[6] According to Clark in International Communications, the reason why no convention was drawn up at this time can be found in General Greeley's address at the opening of the second session, during the course of which he said:

"Recognizing the inchoate state of the science of wireless telegraphy, it is our firm conviction that detailed regulations are impracticable . . . that general resolutions . . . ensure the greatest advantage to the trade and commerce of the world. (Since interchange of ship signals was not internationally obligatory, he believed it) inadvisable to insist, for the present at least, on interchange between ships on the high seas, especially in view of the impracticability of efficaciously enforcing any such regulations."

contained basically good material, for it served as the framework for the subsequent conventions of 1912 and 1927. In 1912 a second convention was adopted at London; it merely widened the scope of the Berlin Convention, but made many changes in the regulations to keep pace with the development of the art. The third radio conference was scheduled to take place at Washington in 1917, but the World War forced its postponement. During the World War radio-communication control among the Allies was exercised by the Inter-allied Wireless Commission, and at the Paris Conference the Principal Allied and Associated Powers issued a draft of revised International Regulations known as the "Radio Protocol." In 1920 a preliminary conference of the 5 great powers was held at Washington to discuss the whole field of communication control. It was there that the idea of a single convention was first officially discussed. The conference drew up a draft convention and regulations of a "Universal Electrical Communication Union." A technical committee revised the draft at Paris in 1921, but the conference which was to adopt the treaty was never called. The decade 1917-27 witnessed most remarkable advances in the radio art. Broadcasting as an educational, recreational, industrial, and political medium began in 1920 and by 1927 almost overshadowed its much older progenitor, radiotelegraphy. Governments were quick to recognize the great importance of the new medium and of the necessity for safeguarding their individual, national interests. In 1927 the Conference of Washington, originally scheduled for 1917, took place and was attended by delegates from 80 countries. The successful labors of this conference extended the scope of the convention and brought about a degree of order and coordination so necessary for the most efficient use of radio, at the same time not setting up restrictions that would hamper future development. The most important problem that confronted the Washington Conference was, of course, that of allocation of radio frequencies, and this was accomplished on the basis of "services", designated by various names such as "fixed", "mobile", "broadcasting", and so on. It was recognized as being entirely impossible, impracticable, and impolitic to allocate specific frequencies to specific countries. Authority was permitted to each country to assign any frequency and any type of wave to any radio station within its jurisdiction, provided no interference with any service of another country resulted from such assignment.

The International Radiotelegraph Conference of Washington drew up a Convention, a set of General Regulations, and a set of supplementary Regulations. The last-named regulations embodied certain provisions such as those concerning rates, priority of transmission, accounting, etc., which are established in this country by private companies rather than by the Government. This separation of regulations into two sets was, of course, done for the benefit of the countries in which the radio facilities are not government owned, among them the United States and Canada. Since the Convention and the General Regulations were so drafted as to cover matters which were essentially governmental in character and were of the type with which governments usually concern themselves, the United States was able to sign these documents and thus enter into full membership in the radiotelegraph section of the International Telegraph Union. The Convention and the General Regulations were signed by 78 of the 80 governments represented at Washington, and thus these documents became one of the most generally accepted treaties in the world.

It has been noted that although the United States never became a signatory to the International Telegraph Convention, it did become one of the first signatories to the International Radiotelegraph Convention. There is undoubtedly a perfectly valid basis for this difference in attitude, lying in the different media through which the electric waves are propagated in the two cases. In that of land wire and cable telegraphy, the electric currents are confined to physical conductors and nature imposes no limitations with respect to the number of such conductors that may be established; practical considerations of finance, politics, industry, and so on are the determining factors. Moreover, these conductors can be established wholly on or within territory belonging to each government, and signals traversing these channels, no matter how contiguous, within reasonable degrees, do not interfere with one another. But in the case of radio, nature imposes rather severe limitations. First, the electric waves are practically free to move in all directions; no physical conductors are required for their propagation in space. Hence, once they have been started their control passes out of human hands and signals which are national in origin may become international in their effects. Secondly, the available channels for the propagation of these waves are quite limited in number and they must be shared in a more or less equitable manner among all the governments of the world. Thirdly, radio waves readily interfere with one another if the channels are close together, thus impairing the efficiency of the signals or nullifying them altogether so far as their usefulness is concerned. Fourthly, radioelectric waves are the sole means by which communication can be established over long distances between moving objects and the latter may be moving in different national territories or on the high seas. There are other differences, too, which necessitate a much greater degree of international cooperation in the case of radio than in that of wire telegraphy. But it is to be admitted that there are persons who see in these arguments no valid reason why the United States should so willingly have become a signatory to the Radio Convention and should have refused all invitations to become a signatory to the Telegraph Convention. For example, American business men are vitally affected by the rules for determining word count and by the rates and methods of charging for cablegrams; however, at present they have no recourse such as is available in the case of these same factors in domestic messages. Hence, they feel that their Government should be a party to the agreement whereby these regulations are established, so that American business men may be safeguarded against what they believe to be inequitable provisions when changes in these regulations are under consideration by other countries. However, this view has not gained sufficient support to influence or modify the position taken by the United States in the matter. When, therefore, the time came for the Telegraph and Radio Conferences at Madrid, the United States appointed no delegates to the International Telegraph Conference, but only to the International Radiotelegraph Conference. However, as noted above, since this Government has usually been invited to participate in the deliberations of the Telegraph Conference, without right to vote, the matter of participation was easily settled by designating certain members of the American delegation to the International Radiotelegraph Conference to serve also as representatives of the United States to the International Telegraph Conference. It is of interest to relate that when the question arose of whether the representatives of the United States had the right to vote in the meetings of the Telegraph Conference at Madrid, it was decided that full voting participation was within their right—but, under instructions from the Government, this right was not exercised.[7]

We hasten now to that part of the story which deals with the fusion of the Telegraph and Radiotelegraph Conventions.

It was noted that the idea of a single Communications Convention was the basis of the draft convention drawn up in Washington in 1920. That convention never was adopted. The Telegraph Conference of Paris in 1925 expressed a desire to combine the Telegraph

---

[7] The basis for this unprecedented grant of voting privileges to the American representatives lay, of course, in the facts that the telegraph and the radio conventions were to be fused into a single convention and that the United States had indicated its intention to sign the convention, if satisfactory. The decision to waive their right to vote in the discussions relative to telegraph matters, both in committees and plenary sessions of the Telegraph Conference was based upon their indicated intention not to sign the telegraph regulations. To participate in the voting and then refrain from signing would, of course, have been most inconsistent. At the same time it must be admitted that it was only logical that the previously announced intention not to sign the telegraph regulations should have had the important consequence of greatly weakening the position taken by the American representatives in regard to such controversial matters as changes in code language rules, rate coefficients, and minimum word counts, matters which vitally affect the international messages transmitted by American business firms.

and the Radio Conventions into a single convention to apply to all electrical communications.[s] The Radio Conference of Washington in 1927 was in accord with this wish and adopted the following recommendation:

" The International Radio Conference at Washington expresses the desire that the contracting Governments shall examine the possibility of combining the International Radio Convention with the International Telegraph Convention, and that, where necessary, they shall take the necessary steps for this purpose."

To fulfill this wish was one of the principal aims of the Madrid Conference of 1932. It may be stated that the fusion of the two Conventions was not brought about without many difficulties, acrimonious discussions, and what seemed interminable delays, but it was finally accomplished. It took years of preliminary work and four solid months of constant discussion in conference.

One may visualize the document and its accompanying regulations more easily by a study of the following diagram, which shows the relationship between the various acts of the conferences. According to article 2 of the convention, in order to become a signatory or an adherent to the Convention, it is necessary to sign or adhere to at least one of the regulations.

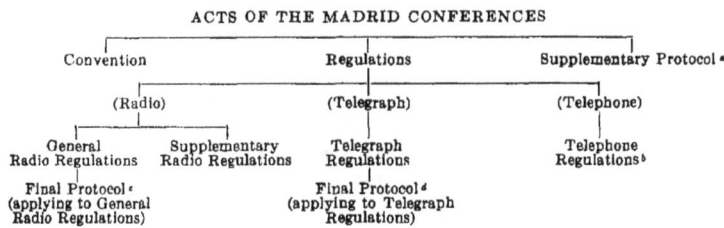

ACTS OF THE MADRID CONFERENCES

```
        Convention              Regulations            Supplementary Protocol a

          (Radio)               (Telegraph)                 (Telephone)

   General        Supplementary      Telegraph              Telephone
Radio Regulations Radio Regulations  Regulations            Regulations b

Final Protocol c                 Final Protocol d
(applying to General             (applying to Telegraph
Radio Regulations)               Regulations)
```

[s] The Telegraph Conference of Lisbon, 1908, was the last held before the World War. The Conference scheduled for 1915 had, of course, to be postponed.

[a] This document, entitled " The Supplementary Protocol of the Acts of the International Radiotelegraph Conference of Madrid Signed by Governments of the European Region ", deals with a subsidiary conference to be held in Switzerland for the purpose of concluding an agreement concerning the allocation of frequencies to various broadcasting stations of the European region and the fixing of methods of employing these frequencies. The Conference met at Lucerne in May 1933, and reached satisfactory agreements on the subjects indicated. These, of course, are of no direct interest to the United States. See, in this connection the remarks made below, under article 13 of the convention.

[b] The telephone regulations deal almost entirely with matters concerning telephony in Europe.

[c] The final protocol applying to the general radio regulations sets forth certain reservations made by several governments to specific articles of the regulations. Among them, the Union of Soviet Socialist Republics reserves the right to use certain frequencies for services otherwise than as indicated in the regulations. This reservation brought in its wake reservations by other countries with regard to their retention of full liberty of action to protect themselves against radio interference resulting from such special usage of the frequencies indicated.

[d] The final protocol to the telegraph regulations contains two parts. The first merely stipulates that the signatories agree to place certain of the regulations into effect on April 1, 1933. The second part contains reservations by practically all the signatories

68

The documents to which the United States delegates appended their signatures at Madrid are:

(1) The International Telecommunication Convention.

(2) The General Radio Regulations.

(3) The Final Protocol Applying to the General Radio Regulations.

They did not sign:

(4) The Supplementary Radio Regulations.

(5) The Telegraph Regulations.

(6) The Final Protocol Applying to the Telegraph Regulations.

(7) The Telephone Regulations.

(8) The Supplementary Protocol to the Acts of the International Radiotelegraph Conference of Madrid (European Radio Protocol, see footnote a, p. 12).

The new convention and its accompanying sets of regulations are certainly not perfect and some time must pass before their real value can be measured. It is true that they contain many basic articles concerning which there was from the first practically unanimity; but they also contain many more articles concerning which there was up to the bitter end much haranguing and wordy combat so that the final results must obviously represent compromises between widely divergent original views.

Since the single convention is applicable not only to radio but also to telegraphy and telephony, one may wonder whether its acceptance by the American delegation represents a departure from the policy discussed above in setting forth the reasons for the refusal of the United States to sign the International Telegraph Convention. But it must be emphasized that the statements contained in the Telecommunication Convention are, as already indicated, only of the character of general principles. The efforts of the American delegation were entirely successful in eliminating all those features relating to, telegraphy and telephony which had made it undesirable or impractical for the United States to accept the Telegraph Convention. These objectionable clauses, and the detailed provisions applicable to telegraphy and telephony are, as noted above, contained in separate documents, neither of which was signed by the American delegation. At the same time that objectionable clauses relating to telegraphy and telephony were eliminated from the Telecommunication Convention to meet the wishes of the American delegates, the latter were

---

to the effect that they accept no obligation whatsoever with regard to paragraph 3 of article 26 (composition of rates) or to article 31 (fixing of monetary equivalents). Space forbids a discussion of the reasons for the latter reservations; they are, of course, intimately associated with the present-day difficulties connected with the maintenance of the gold standard. The arguments that centered about these reservations very nearly broke up the conference.

nevertheless able to keep in the convention certain important, rather specific articles relating directly to radio.

Only a few explanatory details with respect to the convention itself can here be given. It consists of 5 chapters containing 40 articles. Practically every word of each article was carefully selected as to its exact meaning (in French), its connotations and implications. The present verbiage represents the result of collective efforts in the dissection and synthesis of literally dozens of preliminary drafts. For the benefit of readers who may not have opportunity to learn by direct examination what subjects are treated in a convention of this type, a brief outline of its contents will be given. The titles of each article will be indicated, together with a very brief résumé of its subject matter.

THE INTERNATIONAL TELECOMMUNICATION CONVENTION

CHAPTER I. ORGANIZATION AND FUNCTIONING OF THE UNION

ARTICLE 1. *Constitution of the union.*—Merely states that the countries which are signatory to the convention form the International Telecommunication Union. (Many hours were spent in unsuccessful attempts by certain European countries to include a statement as to the purpose of the union.)

ART. 2. *Regulations.*—States that the provisions of the convention are completed by telegraph, telephone, and radio regulations, which bind only the contracting governments that have signed them and apply only as between governments that have undertaken the same obligations. Only signatories to the convention or adherents can sign or adhere to these regulations. Each signatory to the convention must adhere to at least 1 of the 3 sets of regulations. The supplementary radio regulations can be accepted only in conjunction with the general radio regulations, although acceptance of the latter does not involve acceptance of the former. The last paragraph of this article is very important to note. It states that the provisions of the present convention bind only the contracting governments with respect to the services governed by those regulations which these governments have signed. Thus, since the United States signed only the radio regulations, this government will have obligations only with respect to radio and not with respect to telegraphy or telephony.

ART. 3. *Adherence of governments to the convention.*—Sets forth the procedure by which a country that is not a signatory to the convention may become an adherent to same. (Adherence carries with it the same advantages and obligations as signature.)

ART. 4. *Adherence of governments to the regulations.*—Same subject matter as under Article 3, but applicable to the regulations only, for the benefit of countries which are already parties to the convention and 1 or 2 of the 3 sets of regulations.

ART. 5. *Adherence of colonies, protectorates, etc., to the convention and the regulations.*—States that each contracting government may indicate either at the time of signature, ratification, adherence, or afterward, whether acceptance of the convention is also valid for the totality, or a group, or a single one of its colonies, protectorates, etc. But the latter may at any time separately adhere.

ART. 6. *Ratification of the convention.*—Details of ratifying and depositing the ratifications by diplomatic channels. (Ratification by the United States is effected by the President, " with the consent and advice of the Senate." By withholding its consent, the latter can, of course, prevent ratification. See footnote 1, p. 2.)

ART. 7. *Acceptance of the regulations.*—Governments must indicate, as promptly as possible, their intentions with regard to their acceptance of the regulations drawn up in conference. If one or more governments fail to accept the new regulations, the latter are nevertheless valid as between those governments which have accepted them.

ART. 8. *Abrogation of previous conventions and regulations.*—It was deemed necessary to include a statement expressly abrogating all prior documents of this nature so far as they concern the relations between countries which have ratified or adhered to the later convention and regulations.

ART. 9. *Execution of the convention and the regulations.*—This article is of such importance as to warrant quoting in full:

SECTION 1. The contracting governments undertake to apply the provisions of the present convention and of the regulations accepted by them in all the offices and in all the telecommunication stations established or operated by them, and which are open to the international service of public correspondence, to the broadcasting service, or to the special services governed by the regulations.

SEC. 2. Moreover, they agree to take the steps necessary to enforce the provisions of the present convention and of the regulations which they accept upon the private operating agencies recognized by them, and upon the other operating agencies duly authorized to establish and operate telecommunications of the international service, whether or not open to public correspondence.

ART. 10. *Denunciation of the convention by governments.*—Details of procedure to be followed by a signatory that wishes to withdraw from the convention.

ART. 11. *Denunciation of the regulations by governments.*—Same as regards the regulations.

ART. 12. *Denunciation of the convention and the regulations by colonies, protectorates, etc.*—Same as regards colonies, protectorates, etc.

ART. 13. *Special agreements.*—A very important article under which the contracting governments reserve for themselves and for their private operating companies all rights to make special agreements with regard to service matters not of interest to all governments. But such special agreements must remain within the limits of the convention and the regulations as regards interference with the services of other countries.[9]

ART. 14. *Relations with noncontracting States.*—Governments reserve rights on their own behalf and on behalf of their private operating companies to establish the conditions under which they will exchange telecommunications with a country that does not adhere to the convention or to the regulations. (This article is designed primarily for the relations of governments which accept the telegraph regulations, but its phraseology is not objectionable to governments that do not accept the latter.)

ART. 15. *Arbitration.*—This is a long and complicated article dealing with the mechanics of settling, by arbitration, disputes relative to the execution of the convention and the regulations.

ART. 16. *International consulting committees.*—A short article dealing with advisory committees appointed to study questions relative to the telecommunication services; details are given in the regulations. (A great deal of argument centered around this matter. The efforts of the United States were directed toward reducing the functions of these committees to a minimum.)

ART. 17. *Bureau of the Union.*—The official name of the " Berne Bureau ", formerly designated as " The International Bureau of the Telegraph Union ", becomes " The Bureau of the International Telecommunication Union."

This article sets forth the functions and responsibilities of the Bureau, together with specific indications as to how its expenses are to be shared by members of the union. Two separate accounts must be maintained, one relating to the telegraph and telephone services, the other, to the radio services. (The reason for this is that certain countries are signatories or adherents to the documents applying to only one type of service and therefore should not be expected to share the costs of the Bureau incurred in connection with other types of service. For example, the United States contributes only to the support of the Bureau as regards the expense occasioned by the services rendered by the Bureau in connection with radio matters.)

CHAPTER II. CONFERENCES

ART. 18. *Conferences of Plenipotentiaries and Administrative Conferences.*—Delegates for the purpose of revising the convention

---

[9] The radio conference held at Mexico City in 1933, attended by representatives from governments of North and Central America, is a good example of how special or regional agreements can be reached under this article. This conference adopted recommendations for the further allocation of frequencies between 1,500 and 4,000 kilocycles.

must have plenipotentiary powers, and revision can be made only when it has been decided upon by a previous conference of plenipotentiaries or when at least 20 contracting governments have indicated a desire for revision. Revision of the regulations, however, can be made by administrative Conferences, each conference setting the time and place of the next Conference.[10]

ART. 19. *Changing the date of a Conference.*—Conferences may be advanced or retarded in date when at least 10 contracting governments wish to do so. The place of meeting remains as fixed by the last Conference, or if this is impossible, a consultation on the matter is held among the contracting governments.

ART. 20. *Internal regulations of Conferences.*—This refers briefly to the rules of procedure to be followed in the deliberations. The rules of the preceding Conference are to be taken as a basis for the establishment of the rules for a new Conference.

ART. 21. *Language.*—French is the official language for the acts of the Conferences and for all the documents of the union, but French and English may be used in the debates; each language must be immediately followed by a translation into the other language by official interpreters furnished by the Bureau of the Union. Other languages may also be used provided interpreters are furnished by the delegates to translate into French or English.[11]

CHAPTER III. GENERAL PROVISIONS

ART. 22. *The public telecommunication service.*—In a single paragraph the right of the public to avail themselves of the telecommunication facilities for the purpose of correspondence is recognized, without granting anybody special prerogatives not provided for in the convention or the regulations.

ART. 23. *Responsibility.*—The contracting governments declare that they accept no responsibility with regard to the users of the international telecommunication service. (In the domestic service in this country the telegraph companies are liable, but only to a limited degree, for mistakes or delays in transmission or delivery or for non-delivery of messages. On the contrary, in other countries where the

---

[10] The next Conferences are scheduled to be held in Cairo, in 1937. They will be administrative Conferences. Curiously enough, when the question came up as to whether a single telecommunication Conference or two separate Conferences, telegraph and radio, would be called, the Madrid Conference decided in favor of the latter.

[11] To give the background of this article and to tell in detail how it came finally to be adopted as it stands would require a separate paper. Suffice it to say here that the question of language, instead of being definitely settled at the very first session, was left open practically throughout the duration of the Conferences; but in the meantime, both English and French were used, the delegation of the United States furnishing the interpreters. By common consent, the irregularity in parliamentary procedure and the anomalous situation presented by the way in which the matter was being handled was blinked at with considerable humor.

communication facilities are owned and operated by the government, no such liability whatever is recognized.)

ART. 24. *Secrecy of telecommunication.*—This is an important article under which the secrecy of international correspondence is assured. However, the contracting governments reserve the right to communicate international messages to competent authorities in order to insure the application of the internal laws or the execution of the international conventions to which these governments are parties. (The latter makes it possible for one government to turn over to another messages dealing with violations of laws based upon international treaties, for example, laws against narcotics smuggling.)

ART. 25. *Constitution, operation, and safeguarding of installations and telecommunication channels.*—This article is of a general nature in regard to insuring the use of up-to-date equipment, its operation according to the best methods, and its protection against willful damage within the limits of the jurisdiction of each country.

ART. 26. *Stoppage of telecommunications.*—This article allows each government to stop the transmission of private communications (including telephone conversations) which appear to be dangerous to the safety of the state, or contrary to the laws of the country, public order or decency. But the office of origin must immediately be notified of such stoppage, except in case such notice can appear dangerous to the safety of the state. This article is the basis upon which censorship of communications, especially of press messages, is exercised. Attempts by some countries to make its provisions more rigid terminated in liberalization of the article, so that certain censorship practices will, in future, be more difficult.

ART. 27. *Suspension of service.*—Each government reserves the right to suspend the international telecommunication service for an indefinite period, in whole or in part, provided it notifies each of the other governments immediately through the bureau of the Union.

ART. 28. *Information concerning infractions.*—The governments agree to inform one another as to violations of the provisions of the convention and of the regulations approved by them, in order to facilitate action with a view to their elimination.

ART. 29. *Rates and franking privileges.*—This article simply makes a reference to the fact that this subject is set forth in detail in the regulations.

ART. 30. *Priority of transmission of government telegrams and radiotelegrams.*—Priority in transmission is accorded such messages except when the sender specifically renounces this right.

ART. 31. *Secret language.*—All government messages may be in secret language; private messages may be admitted in secret language between all countries except those which have previously indicated that they do not admit them. However, a country which does not admit such messages must allow them to pass in transit.

ART. 32. *Monetary unit.*—This sets up the gold franc of 100 centimes, 10/31 grammes in weight and 0.900 in fineness as the monetary unit employed in the composition of rates, and in the settlement of accounts.[12]

ART. 33. *Rendering of accounts.*—The governments undertake to account to one another for the charges collected by the respective services.

CHAPTER IV. SPECIAL PROVISIONS APPLICABLE TO RADIO

This chapter, comprising six articles, contains provisions relating particularly to radio. Their contents are practically identical with the corresponding articles of the 1927 Radio Convention, but for the sake of completeness they will be outlined below.

ART. 34. *Intercommunication.*—Under this article the reciprocal exchange of radiocommunications of the same character in the mobile service is guaranteed, without distinction as to the radio system employed by the various stations. This, of course, does not prevent the use of a system incapable of communicating with other systems, provided this incapacity is of a nature inherent in the system and is not the result of devices solely employed to prevent intercommiunication.

ART. 35. *Interference.*—So far as radio is concerned, this is probably the most important article in the convention. It reads as follows:

SECTION 1. All stations, whatever their purpose, must, so far as possible, be established and operated in such a manner as not to disturb the radio communications or services either of the other contracting governments or of the private operating companies recognized by these contracting governments and other duly authorized agencies which conduct a radio service.

SEC. 2. Each of the contracting governments not itself operating the radio facilities undertakes to require of the private operating companies recognized by it, and of other duly authorized operating agencies, the observance of the provision of section 1 above.

ART. 36. *Distress calls and messages.*—Stations participating in the mobile service are obliged to accept with absolute priority distress calls and messages, whatever be their origin, to answer these

---

[12] In this connection, see footnote *d* on p. 48. No reservations were made by any government to this article as were made to article 31 of the telegraph regulations. What might on first glance appear to be an inconsistency in attitude in respect to reservations on this matter can be explained by noting that while it is agreed that rates and accounting are to be expressed in terms of the gold franc, the number of units of a specific currency that are considered to be equal in value to that of a gold franc is another matter and one that is subject to change as determined from time to time by the country issuing that currency.

messages themselves, and to take whatever action they require immediately.

ART. 37. *False distress signals—Illegimate use of call signs.*—The contracting governments agree to take necessary measures to suppress the transmission or the circulation of false or erroneous distress signals or distress calls, and the use by a station of call signs which have not been legitimately assigned to it.

ART. 38. *Limited service.*—This permits a station to establish a restricted international service determined by the object of the telecommunication or by other circumstances independent of the system employed. (The purpose of this is to except certain stations from the obligation to exchange communications as required under section 1 of article 34. For example, stations carrying on a news service to ships at sea are not required to accept private messages for transmission or relay.)

ART. 39. *Installations of national-defense services.*—This article is, of course, of particular interest to the military service, and is therefore worth quoting in full:

SECTION 1. The contracting governments retain their entire liberty with respect to radioelectric installations not covered by article 9 and, in particular, to military stations of land, maritime, or aerial forces.

SEC. 2. (1) However, these installations and stations must, so far as possible, comply with the regulatory provisions relative to aids to be furnished in cases of distress and to measures to be taken to prevent interference. They must also, so far as possible, observe the regulatory provisions concerning the types of waves and the frequencies to be used, according to the kind of service which the said stations conduct.

(2) In addition, when these installations and stations make an exchange of public correspondence or participate in special services governed by the regulations annexed to the present convention, they must comply, in general, with the regulatory provisions for the conduct of these services.

CHAPTER V. FINAL PROVISION

ART. 40. *Effective date of the convention.*—The new convention becomes effective on January 1, 1934.

*   *   *   *   *   *   *

There then follow the signatures of the various plenipotentiaries empowered by their governments to sign the convention. The original is deposited in the archives of the Spanish Government and one copy is sent to each government.

The convention proper is followed by a single annex defining certain of the terms employed in it, such as " telecommunication ", " radiocommunication ", " radiotelegram ", " administration ", " public service ", etc., each of which has a specific meaning that was agreed upon only after much discussion. In case of future disputes, undoubtedly much will depend upon the interpretation to be given certain of these definitions.

It is interesting to note that the guiding minds at the Madrid Conferences were extremely careful to observe all juridical formalities deemed essential for the validity of the new single convention. For instance, the fact that two separate and distinct Conferences, Telegraph and Radio, were in session was constantly emphasized. Indeed, from a legal standpoint previous conventions still exist and will continue to be in force as between specific governments until the new convention is ratified by the governments concerned. For example, although the French delegates signed the Washington convention of 1927, the French Government never ratified this treaty.[13] Consequently, as between France and other countries, the London Radio Convention of 1912 has been in effect since the date of ratification of that treaty and will continue in effect until France ratifies the Madrid convention. Suppose she fails to ratify the latter, and suppose the United States and Great Britain do ratify it, and further, suppose Canada, which did ratify the Washington convention, does not ratify the Madrid convention; then the situation between the United States and these three countries as regards the convention in effect may be depicted as follows:

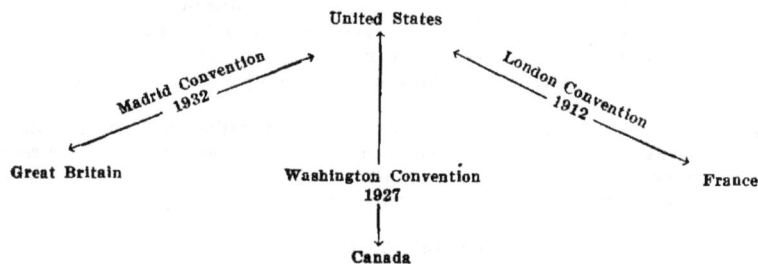

Would such a complicated situation cause much difficulty? Not necessarily, for much depends upon the proximity of the countries and the extent of their radio relations. The fact that France failed to ratify the Washington convention meant very little so far as this country is concerned; but so far as France's neighbors are concerned, the situation is different.

It can almost be taken for granted that not all the governments will ratify the Madrid convention at first. It may take several years and perhaps many will have failed to ratify it by the time the next Conference takes place, which is scheduled to open at Cairo.

[13] Recent information indicates that France may yet ratify the 1927 radio convention.

There is no question but that the fusion of the telegraph and the radiotelegraph conventions into a single telecommunication convention marks a distinct and very important step forward, not only in the art of signaling, but in the advance of civilization itself. While some countries objected strenuously at the outset to a fusion of the two conventions, foreseeing some loss perhaps in advantages to them, in the end the weight of the majority opinion prevailed. The phrase " weight of the majority opinion " is used advisedly, for in matters such as these there can be no coercion, pressure, or force applied as between sovereign States. A single document, signed by practically the whole world, and covering the transmission of intelligence by every agency of electrical communication cannot fail to lead to unification, coordination, and better employment of these agencies, to the material advantage of all concerned. But in a larger sense, the unification is much more important. In these difficult days, when the labors of international conferences are beset with apparently insurmountable obstacles, when human efforts to iron out honest differences of opinion between nations in a spirit of cordial cooperation, justice, and conciliation seem baffled on all sides, the fact that an accord was reached at Madrid between 81 governments and on matters vitally affecting each of them, stands out as a bright light in the otherwise dark heavens. For, before nations can reach any agreement on matters of mutual concern, they must be able to communicate with one another and exchange ideas; and anything that will facilitate such communication and exchange materially assists in clearing a way to the reaching of those accords without which civilization stagnates. Thus, if the birth of the telecommunication convention is noteworthy from a materialistic or economic point of view, and is therefore of particular interest to those concerned with signal-communication matters, it also presents a spiritual significance that merits the attention of everybody the world over.

SECRET CAUSES OF GERMAN SUCCESSES ON THE EASTERN FRONT [7]

By A. M. NIKOLAIEFF [8][*]

(Reprinted from the September–October 1935 issue of the Coast Artillery Journal with the courteous permission of its editor)

It was commonly believed during the World War, and even now the opinion prevails, that the main causes of the military successes of the Germans on the Eastern front lay as much in the superiority of their artillery and aircraft, and in the well developed system of their strategic railways, as in the clever stategy of the German military leaders. However, in the opinion of some Russian students

[7] EDITOR'S NOTE.—The author of this article was a colonel in the Imperial Russian Army and served on the Russian General Staff during the World War. He was formerly a military attaché at both Washington and Tokyo.

[8] EDITOR'S NOTE.—For a more recent example of military defeats caused in part by improper use of radio, see, under The Editor's OP of this issue, the item "Radio, a Contributing Cause of Military Disasters." See also the articles, "Tannenberg—A study in Faulty Signal Communication", by Lt. Col. H. C. Ingles, Signal Corps, in the July–August 1929 issue of the Bulletin.

*(No. 91, July–August, 1936)

of the War, these causes taken alone did not offer an adequate explanation of those episodes of the struggle in the East in which the relative strength of the opposing forces was approximately equal and the strategic skill of the Teutonic leaders was not particularly brilliant though the results obtained by the Germans were so. Some of the episodes were: The extraordinary German victory at Tannenberg, the forestalling by the Germans of the Russian offensive after the defeat of the Austro-Hungarian army in the battle of Galicia, and the escape of the German Army Corps surrounded by the Russians at Lodz. The fortunes of war, usually so changeable, here constantly favored one side, and this suggested that there must have been another cause to explain in a more satisfactory way the remarkable successes of the Germans, and the reverses and half-successes of the Russians. What was that cause? For some time it remained a secret, and then the curtain began to rise.

Light was thrown on the secret for the first time when the German military leaders published their memoirs and accounts of the war events on the Russian front. In 1919 General Ludendorff, describing in his Own Story the situation before the Battle of Tannenberg, made the following significant statement: "On the journey from Marienburg (the Headquarters of the German Army in East Prussia) to Tannenberg an intercepted enemy wireless message was sent us (that is, to Hindenburg and Ludendorff) which gave a clear idea of the opponents' dispositions for the next few days."

Next came the admission of Field Marshal Hindenburg. In his reminiscences (Out of My Life) published in 1920, he said, speaking of the campaign in Poland: "By tapping the enemy's wireless we were not only able to learn what the situation was, but also the intentions of the enemy." Finally General Hoffmann, with whose work "all the important military events on the German Eastern front are closely bound", supplied detailed information on the question of the Russian wireless messages before the Battle of Tannenberg. In his account of that battle (Tannenberg wie es wirklich war), published in 1926, he disclosed what those messages were. One, sent from the army of Rennenkampf, made it clear that the army was not marching in a southwesterly direction toward the army of Samsonoff, as the Germans had feared, but was continuing its advance westward, toward Königsberg; it could not, therefore, arrive in time to the assistance of Samsonoff's army, against which the Germans were planning an attack. The second message was sent from the army of Samsonoff. This message showed that Samsonoff, having mistaken the retreat of one German Army corps (the 20th) for the withdrawal of all the German forces facing his army, had given orders to his own army corps to pursue the retreating Germans in a northerly direction (from the line Ortelsburg-Soldau toward the line Allenstein-Osterode), and by that pursuit had exposed his left flank to a German attack. According to Hoffmann, neither of these Russian messages was sent in cipher. Their importance to the Germans cannot be overemphasized. The situation was similar to that of a bridge game in which one team is not only holding its cards face up, but is even informing its opponents in advance of what cards it is going to play.

How could it happen that wireless messages of vital importance were sent unciphered? In his study of the first battles in East Prussia in 1914, General Golovine, one of the Russian Army leaders in the War and a writer of note, sees the cause of that fact in the want of organization and the disorder which characterized the work of the headquarters of the Russian armies in the beginning of the campaign.[9] According to another Russian author, General Daniloff, who was Director of Military Operations at the Russian General Headquarters in the first year of the War, the sending of unciphered radio messages by various Russian headquarters was a result of their lack of familiarity with the new means of liaison. He writes: "To the various headquarters of our army, the use of the wireless in the field was something completely new."[10] Whatever may have been the real cause of the Russian blunder, whether a lack of organization or of familiarity with the wireless, it was more because of their error than because of the strategic skill of the Germans that the battle of Tannenberg turned out to be such a disaster for the Russians.

Following the Russian reverses in East Prussia, measures were taken by the Russian High Command to keep secret the dispositions and movements of troops. In the beginning of the War wireless messages were often sent with a part of the text in cipher and a part unciphered. Soon it was realized that the deciphering of such messages was comparatively easy for the enemy, and the practice of sending messages in this form was therefore discontinued. Besides this, the cipher used by the army in the field was changed from time to time. The Russian military leaders believed in the efficiency of these measures and were under the impression throughout the War that the contents of their wireless messages remained unknown to the opposite side. In the period which followed the war, some suspicion as to the secrecy of the Russian radio messages was expressed in the Russian military press abroad, but for a long time there was nothing to prove that those suspicions were justified. Now, however, after all these years, a new light has been thrown on this puzzling question,

---

[9] N. Golovine. Iz istorii kampanii 1914 g. na russkom fronte. Nachalo voiny i operatzii v Vostochnoi Prussii (The history of the campaign of 1914 on the Russian front. The beginning of the War and the operations in East Prussia.) Prague, 1926, p. 220.

[10] Y. Daniloff Rossiya v Mirovoi voine (Russia in the World War). Berlin, 1924, p. 153.

and the secret cause of the military successes of the Teutonic armies on the Eastern front has been revealed.

These striking revelations are made by General Max Ronge, Chief of the Intelligence Service at the Austro-Hungarian General Headquarters during the World War, in his imposing book, Kriege and Industrie Spionage (Military and Industrial Espionage). Here we learn that on September 19, 1914, an intercepted Russian wireless message was deciphered by the Austrian intelligence service for the first time; and we are told that from this time until the end of the War the messages sent in cipher by the Russian radio stations in the field were regularly intercepted by the Austrian stations, and successfully deciphered by the experts of the Austrian intelligence service. The contents of these messages were known to the Austrian and German High Commands within a few hours after their original dispatch. Thus the dispositions and movements of the Russian troops, and therefore the Russian strategic plans, were not a secret for those Commands. It is quite obvious that this detailed and reliable information made it easy for the German and Austrian strategists not only to take counter measures to prevent the execution of the Russian plans, but to launch attacks on the weakest parts of the Russian front as well.

The combatant who knows his enemy's plans has, of course, an extraordinary advantage, and in the whole of military history there is perhaps no better illustration of this advantage than that offered by the checking of the Russian offensive in the initial period of the War, after the defeat by the Russians of the Austro-Hungarian army in the battle of Galicia.

The strategic situation after the battle of Galicia, fought from August 24 to September 12, 1914, was as follows: The remnants of the defeated Austro-Hungarian army had retreated from Russian Poland and East Galicia toward Cracow, and had gathered in the western corner of Galicia behind the Visloka River. The Austrian losses were so heavy [11] that for some time the Austrian armies were not even able to protect their own and the adjacent German territory from a possible further invasion; the Germans, therefore, had to move four of their army corps from East Prussia to Silesia in order to bar the roads, should the Russians attempt to invade this province and to dominate its rich resources of coal and iron.

A difficult task now confronted the Austro-Hungarian commander in chief. He had to solve a problem of vital importance—what

---

[11] From a remark in General Ludendorff's memoirs one may judge the extent to which the strength of the Austrian armies had been reduced by their heavy losses. He expresses great surprise at the fact that four Austrian armies were crowded into an area so narrow as the corner of Galicia behind the Visloka River, between the Vistula and the Carpathians.

would the victorious Russian Army undertake next? The further advance of that army might be undertaken in any one of three directions: First, the Russians might invade the plain of Hungary; second, they might continue their drive toward Cracow, and, finally the Russian armies might concentrate on a new line, for instance, behind the middle Vistula (as they actually did), with the object of starting an offensive in the direction of Silesia (toward Breslau). However, the problem of finding out the further movements of the Russians proved to be an easy one for the Austrian High Command. The solution of that problem was obtained by deciphering the intercepted wireless messages sent by the Russian army leaders.

The first information was received by the Austrian High Command from three messages, of which two had been sent by the Ninth Russian Army on September 25 and 28 and one by the commander of the Russian cavalry corps on September 25. The Ninth army formed the right flank of the Russian front; it had been pressing upon the heels of the retreating Austrians in Galicia, and by September 25 had crossed the Visloka River. Now, according to the first radio message, all its army corps, "in view of the new maneuver decided upon" by the Russian High Command, were to fall back on the next day (September 26), leaving on the Visloka River only vanguards. The second message disclosed that the Ninth army was to assemble in a new area, behind the Vistula to the north of the mouth of the San River. Finally, the message of the commander of the Russian cavalry corps presented a clear picture of the whole situation (as the Russians saw it) in the wide region to the west of the Vistula; and besides this, it contained information with regard to the movements planned by the Russian cavalry with a view to preventing the enemy cavalry from reconnoitering the Russian front. The subsequent Russian radio messages, intercepted and deciphered up to the 5th of October, disclosed that not only one (the Ninth) but two more Russian armies (the Fourth and the Fifth) were being withdrawn from Galicia to take up a new front, behind the middle Vistula, the latter two armies to occupy a line to the north of the Ninth Army. Furthermore, it was learned that two Russian Armies of the Northern front were being moved southward toward the Novogeorgievsk and Warsaw to form the right flank of the new Russian front.

No information about the enemy, more complete and accurate than that contained in these intercepted messages, was ever received by an army engaged in military operations. The Austrian and German High Commands now knew in detail just what forces and what movements they had to deal with, and of even greater importance was the fact that the information about the enemy's movements and intentions had reached these High Commands at a time when the Rus-

sians were just starting to carry out their new plan. This plan called
for a huge shifting and a complicated regrouping of five Russian
armies, and at least 3 weeks would be required for these operations. That is, the Russian armies would not be ready to take the

Eastern Theater of War

offensive from the new front until about October 20; in the meantime the advance units of the Austrian and German forces were only
1 day's march away from the midde Vistula (at Opatov and opposite Sandomir). With the obvious purpose of taking advantage of
the precarious situation in which the Russian armies stood during the

slow process of their regrouping, the Germans and Austrians pushed on toward the Vistula; on October 9–12 they attacked the Russian Army corps (of the Fourth and Second armies) which had crossed the river in order to enable the Fifth Russian army to take up its position to the south of Warsaw.[12] Although those army corps were pushed back by the Germans and had to withdraw to the right bank of the Vistula, they put up a stubborn resistance on the line of that river (at the fortresses of Ivangorod and near Warsaw), and were able to hold their own until all the Russian armies had reached the positions assigned to them, and were ready to advance. The Russian offensive was scheduled to begin on October 21, and the main attack was to be launched from the region of Novogeorgievsk and Warsaw by the combined force of two Russian armies (the Second and Fifth); the attack was aimed at the left flank and rear of the German front. But quite unexpectedly in the night of October 19 the German left facing the Vistula to the south of Warsaw began to fall back, and soon the whole German-Austrian front was in full retreat. Thus the attack planned by the Russians did not materialize; the enemy had escaped. Had the Germans remained on their front 2 days longer, their position might have become critical. At the time of that retreat the "clairvoyance" of the German High Command could be little understood, but now the mystery has been explained. The author of Kriegs and Industrie Spionage tells us that the retreat from the Vistula toward Silesia was ordered by General Hindenburg because it had become clear, after the deciphering of the Russian radio messages, that the German and Austrian forces were greatly outnumbered by the Russians. To prove the accuracy of his statement General Ronge cites figures which show the distribution of the Russian divisions among the various parts of the front at that time; from these figures the numerical superiority of the Russian forces facing the German left may be clearly seen.

The blow aimed at the German left and rear had been averted, but the danger of a Russian offensive was still present—the round was not over. The retreating Teutonic armies might be pursued and overtaken. In point of fact the Russian High Command, upon learning of the escape of the Germans, changed its plan and immediately gave orders to pursue the enemy and force them to accept a battle. The situation of the Teutonic armies remained serious, but one important circumstance was still favorable to them. General Ronge writes: "Our radio service was able to discover at once the intentions of the enemy leaders, and already by the end of October our information about the enemy forces was subjected to such a thorough

---

[12] On October 9 that army only started to assemble at the city of Lublin to entrain there in order to be transported to Warsaw, about 100 miles away from the former place.

checking that our data about the daily disposition of the Russian troops, from a division up, could not have differed very much from those of the Russian General Headquarters." In this struggle in which one side knew every move of its opponent, while the other side had to grope in the dark, the outcome might have been told in advance. What actually happened is as clear now as it was mysterious and unexpected to the Russians at the time when their offensive was in progress. The facts were as follows: The German and Austrian armies retreated from the line Warsaw-Ivangorod-Sandomit in a southwesterly direction, toward Breslau and Cracow; as they fell back they destroyed the railways and bridges and offered a strong resistance to the pursuing Russians. By November 8 the main German force reached the line Kalish-Chenstokhov, running along the westernmost frontier of Russian Poland (the western face of the "Polish salient"), and, according to the Russian information, started to fortify that line. On November 13 an order was given to the Russian armies, which were less than 2 days' march away from the enemy front, to take the offensive against the line Kalish-Chenstokhov where the main German force was supposed to have taken up a position. But in the afternoon of the same day (General Ronge writes) the wireless message in which this order had been sent to the Russian armies "lay deciphered on the desk in our (the Austrian) office of military operations and on the desk of the office of the German Headquarters in Posen as well." The information contained in this message "immediately put an end to the divergence of opinion of the (Teutonic) Allies" as to the best plan for further action. Knowing that the Russian forces were concentrated in front of the line Kalish-Chenstokhov, with their right flank exposed to an attack from the northwest, the German High Command gathered a strong force to the north of Kalish, between the rivers Varta and Vistula,[13] and launched that force from the line Wreschen-Thorn along the left bank of the Vistula with the object of turning the right flank of the advancing Russian front. The Russian offensive was stopped for the second time. Evidently proud of the invaluable achievements of the Austrian radio intelligence service, of which he was in charge, General Ronge makes an ironical remark with regard to the inability of the Russians to find out how such complete information reached their opponents. He writes: "For a long time the Russians had wondered about our excellent orientation, but finally they came to the conclusion, which the Novoye Vremya (a Russian daily) ex-

[13] The German Ninth army under Mackensen, reinforced by two corps of the German Eighth army in East Prussia; in the latter part of November this force was increased by four corps from the Western front and by the garrisons of the fortresses Thorn, Posen, and Breslau.

pressed in an article of November 11, that the German air reconnaissance was responsible for it."

The German counter-offensive between the rivers Varta and Vistula progressed quickly and eventually led to the extremely complicated battle of Lodz (November 18–24). The whole operation which ended with the battle of Lodz is of special interest because in that operation more than in any other episode of the War it was made clear to what extent the successful action of the Germans depended on the good services of the Austrian radio intelligence. Having succeeded in cutting off two Russian armies (the Second and the Fifth) from the remaining Russian force, the Germans were doing their utmost to surround these armies. But at the time of these important engagements an unexpected thing happened: the Russians changed their cipher. General Ronge thus describes the effect which that change had on the Austro-German leaders: "We were living through a crisis. At the very time when our encircling movement seemed to have reached its highest point, and the surrender of the two Russian armies, surrounded by the Germans near Lodz, seemed certain, our best means of securing information became useless. The radio stations, both ours and the Germans', set to work together on the newly received ciphered messages * * * and as a result of the joint effort the new code was deciphered on November 22." Thus during the few days preceding the above date, the Germans were in the same position with regard to the knowledge of the situation of the opposing side as were the Russians, and it is highly significant that during those decisive days the German plan of surrounding the Russian armies failed, and a part of the German turning force (the Twenty-fifth Reserve corps and the Third Division of the Guard) was surrounded by the Russians and escaped from the Russian ring only with the greatest difficulty, leaving behind many prisoners. The first Russian message deciphered by the Austrians after they succeeded in working out the new Russian cipher, contained information (General Ronge writes) "about the breaking of the German encirclement" by the Russians and also information about the directions in which the retreating Germans were being pursued. Thus the hopes of the Germans for a great victory were wrecked, but the information enabled them to carry out their retreat safely.

How is one to explain the remarkable results obtained during the War by the Austrians in the deciphering of intercepted messages? One factor to be taken into account in attempting an explanation is the experience in work of this kind gained by the experts of the Austrian cipher service ("Chiffredienst") during the years preceding the War. Another factor to be considered is that the Russians made mistakes in the employment of their ciphers. From General Ronge's book it may be learned that as early as 1908—that is, at the time when the relations between Austria-Hungary and Serbia became strained on account of the annexation of Bosnia and Herzegovina, the Austrian intelligence service was busy deciphering Serbian messages. Later in 1911–12, during the Turko-Italian war in Tripoli, a special section was formed in the Intelligence Bureau of the Austrian General Staff for the purpose of deciphering the radio messages intercepted by the Austrian naval wireless station. Still later, during the Balkan wars of 1912–13, the Austrian cipher experts acquired an important fund of material, namely, a large number of intercepted Serbian messages. Working on that material, the experts succeeded in obtaining excellent results, thanks to which "the deciphering of Serbian messages (before the War) presented no difficulties." As regards the deciphering of Russian messages before the War, the Austrian General Staff was less fortunate. The secret of the Russian cipher was not disclosed until 50 days after the World War began—that is, on September 19, 1914, as it has been already said. From that time on, General Ronge says, the deciphering of Russian messages was, "with the exception of some unavoidable mutilations, no longer difficult." This statement is supported by the following figures: Up to the beginning of 1915, 16 Russian ciphers were unraveled, and during the War there were days when the number of deciphered messages reached as many as 70; for instance, this was the number of messages deciphered on June 4, 1916, the day when the Brusiloff offensive began.

What were the Russian mistakes in using the cipher? One mistake made in the beginning of the War, and righted after 6 weeks, has been already pointed out. It consisted in sending messages of which only certain parts were in cipher. Another mistake—we learn from General Ronge's revelations—consisted in using two ciphers, the old and the new, for identical dispatches. This violation of the fundamental rules of ciphering was made on the occasions when a change of cipher was taking place. Stations that had not received the new cipher in time, would report their difficulty, and the message that had been communicated to them in the new cipher would be put into the old cipher and dispatched again. "Nothing more was required by our cipher experts", Ronge remarks with regard to this careless way of overcoming a difficulty. Still another mistake, according to the Austrian general, was that "the systematic Russians stuck pretty near to the method of ciphering to which they had become accustomed." This, of course, facilitated the process of deciphering their messages.

Thus the wireless telegraph proved to be a great disadvantage for the Russians. Their army orders and reports sent by radio were known to the opposing side as well and as soon as they were known to those to whom they had been addressed. Speaking of this fact in his review [14] of General Ronge's book, General Batyushin, of the former Russian General Staff, maintains that the military action of the Russians in the World War would have been much more successful if they had not used wireless telegraphy at all. The correctness of this statement he proves by citing two examples: First, the defeat of the Austro-Hungarian armies in the battle of Galicia in August and the earlier part of September 1914; and, second, the initial success of the Russian Army of General Rennenkampf in East Prussia in August 1914; both Russian successes were won at a time when the Austrians and the Germans had not yet succeeded in discovering the secret of the Russian cipher. These two examples constituted exceptions from the general order of things during the World War in which as a rule the Russians had to fight in the dark, while for the Germans and the Austrians the military situation of their opponent was as clear as daylight.

It now remains to be seen what lessons may be derived from all that was said above. It seems that the sad experience of the Russians fully reveals the extreme disadvantage at which an army in the field may be placed if it freely uses the wireless telegraph. Hence it follows that, except in circumstances when no other means of liaison can be resorted to, the wireless must not be used by an army for strategic communications or for any other dispatches that contain information useful for the enemy. Furthermore, the cipher in which radio messages are sent must be as difficult as possible to decode.

However, the elimination of the wireless as a means of sending strategic directives, long orders, and detailed information does not mean that this invention may not be of the greatest service in time of war. But to be of such service, the radio, when used for strategic purposes, must be limited to the sending of brief messages and commands which are rather signals for initiating, changing, or stopping movements previously decided upon. Next, the radio should be used for purposes other than strategical. In this respect the tactical use of the radio should be placed first. Tactically the radio may be used for giving orders which call for immediate execution and which the enemy would not be able to prevent from being carried out should the messages be intercepted. For instance, an order to a firing battery to open fire against a new target may be sent over the radio because the fire of the battery will be carried over to the

---

[14] Vestnik Voennykh Znanii, Sarajevo, 1931, nos. 9, 10.

new target whether the enemy intercepts the order or not. Furthermore, the wireless should be used for the interception of radio messages of the enemy, not only to find out what is going on on his front (provided the enemy messages relate to the conduct of military operations), but also to get information of the situation in the rear, that is, in the interior of the enemy country. Another important service of the radiotelegraph may consist in broadcasting messages with a view to disseminating news and communications which may lower the morale of the enemy, contribute to the breaking of his resistance, and induce him to ask for peace.

POWERS AND LIMITATIONS OF RADIO COMMUNICATION WITHIN A MODERN FIELD ARMY *

By Maj. R. B. MORAN, *Signal Corps*

INTRODUCTION

This paper was undertaken with the primary purpose of determining as far as practicable from a theoretical study, whether in the field in time of war the various units which go to make up a field

*(No. 91, July–August, 1936)

army can expect to operate satisfactorily the radio sets which have been allotted for their use. If the answer should be negative, it was then desired to formulate some basis of priority for the use of radio.

The study has been revised for publication as an article in the Signal Corps Bulletin by modifying the form slightly, by the addition of some information which has come to the attention of the author since the original paper was completed, and by the elimination of the detailed application of conclusions to a particular tactical situation, although a statement of the tactical situation in general terms is included, together with the method followed in providing radio communication therefor.

THE PROBLEM PRESENTED

The problem presented in this study is a determination of the powers and limitations of radio communication within a modern field army. In studying the problem we should assume that both Red and Blue have radio equipment, and that each has a mechanized force and combat aviation attached.

BASIS OF CONSIDERATION

The problem presented is considered in this study on the basis of operating practicability with the technical equipment available, after a careful consideration of the needs of the various arms and services involved. Some consideration will also be given to the trend of future development.

Many items which actually affect the powers and limitations of radio, such as the availability of competent operators, availability of transportation, availability (production) of radio equipment, and suitable power supply therefor, are not considered to be within the scope of this study. Each one is a suitable subject for study and investigation. It is assumed in this paper that these requirements can be met.

An analysis of the problem dictates its division into two main phases: First, what are the needs for military radio? This question will be answered insofar as possible by a study of historical examples and the results of tests and experiments. The result of this study should lead to certain conclusions concerning the relative needs for radio communication by different elements in a field army. Second, it is possible, based on the conclusions drawn as a result of the preliminary study, to provide radio communication of the type desired and in the amount desired by the various elements of the field army? The answer to this question should be determined by an actual radio set-up for a tactical problem taken from the course of instruction at the Command and General Staff School.

91

THE RADIO SPECTRUM

The transmission of radio waves and their manipulation to produce signals, and hence convey intelligence, are natural physical phenomena and are therefore governed by fixed natural laws. Those ether vibrations which occur approximately between a low-frequency limit of 7,500 to 10,000 cycles per second and a high-frequency limit which has not yet been determined are known as radio waves. For convenience frequencies of the order of thousands per second are expressed in kilocycles per second, as 7,500 cycles per second equals 7.5 kilocycles per second. Frequencies of the order of millions per second are expressed as megacycles per second. That is, 62,000,000 cycles per second would be expressed as 62 megacycles per second.

The low-frequency limit is rather well established in present-day development since installations employing low-frequency transmissions are costly to build and operate, and at the same time can transmit only short distances per unit of energy expended as compared to so-called high-frequency transmissions. Due to the great saving in weight, size, original cost, cost of operation, and due to the decreased problem of supply, all development of field radio sets for the United States Army is taking place in the high-frequency ranges. Low frequencies are adaptable only to fixed installations. The practical limits so far determined for field sets are about 150 kilocycles per second and 62 megacycles per second.

The ultrahigh frequencies have certain peculiarities which lend themselves well to use in front-line situations. Waves of extremely high frequency do not travel very far regardless of the amount of power used at the transmitter. They may be reflected to some extent in a manner similar to that in which light is reflected. Usually no fading (alternate rise and fall in the volume of the received signal) is experienced. However, the waves in transmission are subject to deflection and absorption in some degree.[1]

TYPES OF TRANSMISSIONS

There are two general types of radio transmissions, or, putting it another way, there are two general forms of radio waves, each produced in a characteristic manner, each having definite qualities, and each producing quite different effects in the receiver.

The first of these types is the damped wave such as is emitted by a spark transmitter. Its chief characteristic is that, when transmitted on a given frequency, it really contains several frequencies differing more or less from the principal frequency and containing

---

[1] Saxl; Chandler, pp. 455 and 458; BC, pp. 44 and 45; Borden, pp. 52 and 53.

less energy than the principal frequency (when the transmitter is properly tuned). This results in what is known as a broad wave; that is, it takes up considerable space in the radio spectrum.[2]

The second type is known as a continuous wave and is emitted on one fixed frequency. This is the type used in all modern transmitters, military or otherwise. It can be seen that the latter type of wave is much more economical of frequency space in the radio spectrum. It has many other advantages, but they are not important to this paper.

Characteristics which are important in the consideration of military radio are: Damped waves may be received by any type of receiving equipment and the signals have a fixed tone or pitch determined entirely by the transmitting set.[3] They cannot be used as a practical means of voice transmission.[4] Continuous waves, as such, cannot be heard by means of an ordinary receiver unless modulated or shaped by audio-frequency tones or sounds such as the voice or music.[5] They may, however, be detected by the operation of a small transmitter in connection with the receiver which produces a beat note equal to an audio-frequency difference between the incoming radio wave and the wave set up by the local oscillator.[6] This effect makes it possible for an operator receiving telegraph signals to vary the tone or pitch to best suit his ear and thereby enable him to receive through otherwise serious interference.[7] The continuous wave may be modulated at the transmitter by any type of sound which may then be heard in a receiver without the aid of a local transmitter or oscillator.[8]

It will be obvious from this discussion that each type of wave occupies a certain amount of space in the radio spectrum; the lesser amount being required for the continuous wave. If the continuous wave be modulated, somewhat more frequency space will be required.

ASSIGNMENT OF FREQUENCIES

The total frequency space occupied by a transmission and an adjacent clear space forms a channel. There are certain basic principles which govern the allotment and assignment of the frequencies from the available frequency bands. These must be observed if a minimum of interference is to result.

The ideal assignment of frequencies is one in which, if each net operates on its assigned frequency, it will not cause interference

[2] Morecroft, p. 398.
[3] Morecroft, pp. 405-411 and 676.
[4] Morecroft, p. 742.
[5] Morecroft, p. 722.
[6] Morecroft, p. 724.
[7] Morecroft, p. 676.
[8] Morecroft, p. 746.

with any other net operating on the assigned frequency of the latter. In making frequency assignments, it is difficult to formulate a general rule designating the minimum width of the frequency band in which a given type of set is to be operated, unless all the conditions under which the sets are to be operated, and their physical relationships to other sets with which they might interfere, are definitely known. The band of frequencies over which a given transmitter may cause interference to receivers operating on another frequency, depends upon numerous factors such as:

(1) The distance between transmitter and receiver. As an example, the 75-watt radio set SCR-193 is likely to cause interference to any set having a receiver such as the receiver BC-189, over a frequency band of approximately 125 kilocycles at distances from the transmitter up to 2 miles. With such a receiver located 40 miles away from the transmitter of a set SCR-193, the interference band of the transmitter is reduced to approximately 10 to 15 kilocycles. Similarly if each of two sets SCR-177 at a corps command post were to operate on frequencies having a minimum of separation in kilocycles, interference between the two sets would be almost a certainty whereas if the nearest two sets SCR-177 operating on these same two frequencies were 75 miles apart, probability of interference between them would be negligible.

(2) Power of the transmitter, which in turn is dependent in part upon the efficiency of the antenna system and the watts rating of the transmitter. Under the same conditions as those given in (1) above for the radio set SCR-193, the interference band of a 10-watt transmitter has been shown to be approximately half of the above figures.

(3) The type of transmission used; i. e., c. w., voice, or tone. A given transmitter usually has the narrowest interference band when operated on c. w. telegraph, and the widest on tone telegraph. This latter is particularly true between nearby stations due to key thumps and constant high-percentage modulation. However, voice operation in some sets covers the widest band.

(4) The frequency used. Generally speaking the greater the frequency used by a transmitter the greater must be the frequency separation for sets operating within their rated transmitting distance of each other.

(5) The frequency stability of the transmitter. To be considered with this factor are the initial accuracy of the transmitter frequency setting, and the frequency drift after the transmitter is once set on a particular frequency.

(6) Characteristics of the receiver with which the transmitter is apt to interfere, including particularly its sensitivity and selectivity.

(7) The dimensions of the receiver antenna system.

(8) Propagation characteristics in the part of the country where the sets are operating. For example, attenuation of the ground wave is much greater along the eastern seaboard than in the Middle West. With radio sets separated by the same distance, interference over a wider band can be expected in the Middle West than on the eastern seaboard.

However, in making preparation for field operations of a large unit, a corps, Army, or GHQ signal officer must arrange for distribution and assignment of frequencies and blocks of frequencies before tactical dispositions and the resulting locations of radio stations are decided upon. Consequently he must make an as nearly equitable distribution of suitable frequency assignments as he can from information at his disposal concerning the characteristics and locations of the radio sets which are to employ those frequency assignments. He later can expect to have to make an adjustment of his initial assignment of frequencies as need therefor becomes apparent. As a very rough guide in making such initial assignments of frequencies to radio nets the sets of which are to operate within their rated transmitting distance of each other, it is recommended:

First. That the adjacent frequency assignments of radio frequencies for nets in which only radio sets SCR–131, 161, 163–A, or 171 are to operate, be separated by at least 20 kilocycles.

Second. That adjacent frequency assignments to nets in which the radio set SCR–194 is to operate, be separated by at least 500 kilocycles.

Third. That for nets in which any other than the above-mentioned military radio sets are to operate, the separation between any two net frequency assignments be made at least 1 percent of the higher frequency assigned, and never less than 20 kilocycles.

Fourth. That adjacent frequencies be not assigned to nets each having a set operating at the same location; e. g., to the corps and Army (command) nets each of which has a station at the corps command post.

It must be emphasized that this is only a very rough guide, that later a more detailed and accurate guide may become available to the service, and that whatever the guide used, adjustments will very probably have to be made to correct individual cases of interference. Also, it must not be forgotten that frequencies used by the enemy and by other governmental or commercial agencies may also make necessary a readjustment of assignments of frequencies to military radio nets.

TRANSMITTING DISTANCE

The distance over which a radio set will transmit is the greatest variable with which one has to deal. The distance depends upon a large number of factors, many of which are themselves variable. The most important of these factors are:

a. Power of the set.

b. Time of day.

c. Season of the year.

d. General frequency band of the set.

e. Terrain over which the transmission is made.

f. State of training of operators.

g. Interference.

It is necessarily the policy of the Chief Signal Officer to develop sets which will operate over the minimum distance required under unfavorable conditions. This indicates at once that under favorable conditions greater distances will be covered except in the case of ultrahigh frequency sets which have the peculiar characteristic of limited range more or less irrespective of added power, as previously mentioned.

NONDIRECTIONAL CHARACTERISTIC OF RADIO

One of the outstanding characteristics of radio transmission is that waves radiated at the transmitter travel in all directions. The extent of travel in all directions is not the same but, except in the case of ultrahigh frequencies, this fact may be neglected in military sets since they are designed to transmit over a minimum distance in any direction.

This characteristic is both advantageous and disadvantageous. The advantage is that communication can be established quickly between stations without orientation and usually regardless of intervening terrain. It has the important disadvantage that enemy receivers located within range of friendly transmitters may pick up any transmission and make use of information thus obtained. This matter is more fully discussed in a later portion of this paper on goniometric and intercept activities. Since the enemy may and will intercept radio messages, they must be sent and received, and the information they contain utilized before the enemy can make use of it. The use of codes and ciphers increases the delay to the enemy although their use consumes time in the transmission of messages.

It has, therefore, become the policy of all nations to encode or encipher all radio messages containing information of value to the enemy, and to send in clear only messages which, if intercepted by an enemy, will be of no value to him. The idea must not be gained that encoded or enciphered messages cannot be read by the enemy. They can. The advantage of cryptographed messages is that they force the enemy to consume time in securing the information he seeks.[9]

---

[9] Gylden–75, pp. 25 and 26.

96

GENERAL MILITARY VALUE OF RADIO

Radio was not put to any practical military use in the field prior to the World War, although some experiments were made involving the use of radio by the British in the Boer War in South Africa in 1899.[10] Since 1906 the principal armies of the world have had some radio equipment. The first field radio equipment made its appearance in our army in 1903 and was used in maneuvers held in Kentucky under General Bates.[11]

Radio was early recognized as a valuable means of signal communication for forces whose movements were rapid. The British entered the World War with radio provided in a meager manner for independent cavalry.[11a] The increase in the use of radio during the World War as a means of signal communication continued throughout its length, as is ably demonstrated by Priestly's account of the British Signal Service, Carlsward's description of the German Signal Service, and the report of the Chief Signal Officer, United States Army, 1919. Its value is shown not only to cavalry but to aviation, artillery, tanks, and forward infantry units.

RADIO COMMUNICATION IN THE OPERATIONS OF INFANTRY (LESS TANKS) AND FIELD ARTILLERY

One of the first uses to which radio was put was that of providing communication between airplanes in flight and ground stations. While radio was early employed for this purpose, other means such as dropped messages and visual seemed to be preferred both in the British and American services.[12] There was one type of operation, however, which required the use of radio, that was "spotting" for artillery. Prior to the Aisne offensive in the fall of 1914 spotting for artillery by observation aviation was unknown in the British service. On October 1, 1914, the first experiment in spotting was conducted, using radio for communication, with conspicuous success. Priestly says:

> The new invention quickly showed that it had come to stay, and from this date a great organization was built up for this purpose alone, with ramifications which embraced the Signal Service, the R. F. C. (Royal Flying Corps), and the Intelligence Branch of the General Staff.[13]

That the Germans considered this use of radio important is shown by the following quotations contained in translations of German documents:

---

[10] Priestly, p. 9 ; Wade, p. 186.
[11] Harbord, p. 31 ; Carlsward, pp. 5–10.
[11a] Priestly, p. 28.
[12] Priestly, pp. 145 and 330 ; CSO–3, p. 484.
[13] Priestly, p. 38.

It (wireless telegraphy) is the only rapid and reliable means of communi- cation between aircraft and the ground.[14]

Artillery airplanes employ wireless telegraphy as the only means which enables them to transmit the results of their observations to the batteries fir- ing promptly and safely, without interrupting their flight.[15]

The British and American forces used wire communication when- ever it was possible to do so. The Germans also made extensive use of it. In stabilized situations wire buried deep in the ground was seldom interrupted. Both Priestly's account of the British Signal Service in France and the report of the Chief Signal Officer, 1919, show the preponderance of importance given to wire telephone when it was possible to use it. It was when this means failed that radio was in demand.

To show the natural inclination of an American to use the tele- phone, the following example is mentioned. It occurred in the course of the Allied offensive which began on July 18, 1918. On August 7 the Sixth Brigade of the Third Division was temporarily out of wire communication. (It was operating independently.) Radio was available but the brigade commander preferred to wait until the lines were in again rather than use it.[16] Also previous to this time in the St. Mihiel offensive it was not uncommon to receive the following message from a brigade commander by radio: "I am absolutely out of all communication."[17] This condition improved, however, as the value of radio became more apparent.

The British found that during their 1915 fighting in nearly every operation, whether offensive or defensive, the hostile artillery early destroyed forward wire lines. Visual signaling did not fill the need. The obvious answer was radio, but at that time no suitable set had been produced.[18] After a trial at the battle of Ypres in June 1915,[19] the tactical importance of short-range sets was demonstrated to the British in the battle of Loos in September 1915. Only eight sets were available to the First Army but they functioned well and on three critical occasions radio messages got through when all other means of communication failed.[20] Radio communication with front- line units always jumped in importance when movements were rapid or distances to be covered were great. During stabilized periods extensive wire installations reduced the necessity for radio. The British found radio of particular value in their Somme offensive when units passed beyond the limits of the extensive wire system.

---

[14] Signal Service, July, p. 6.
[15] Signal Service, December, p. 18.
[16] CSO–3, p. 412.
[17] CSO–3, p. 448 ; Harbord, p. 28.
[18] Priestly, pp. 81 to 84.
[19] Priestly, p. 86.
[20] Priestly, p. 88.

At times radio was the only means of communication available.[21] Again during the battle of Cambrai radio became extremely valuable both to the infantry and cavalry due to the comparatively great depth of the advance and also to the fact that tanks wrought havoc to wire lines.[22] In spite of excellent radio communication, however, this means was not used to its full advantage, largely due to its newness and to the difficulty involved in the use of codes or ciphers.[23]

All available radio was concentrated on service between divisions and brigades.[24] Later in the battle when the Germans counterattacked the southern part of the salient, radio was the most used of all alternate methods of signaling. That it did not play even a more important role was due to the fact that one alternate wire line remained intact throughout two critical days.[25] The British learned the full value of radio in their retreat from the Oise-Arras front to Amiens in March 1918 over the completely devastated area in their rear. The figures of wireless traffic during these few days had never been approached before.[26] Radio proved its great usefulness in maintaining contact with flank units. So long as flank radio stations were in operation there was little fear of a breakthrough taking place to the right or left without information reaching the divisional commander in time to permit him to organize a defensive flank or hasten his retreat.[27] Later radio again proved its value in the advance during the German retreat from the Marne. In one instance a British division had only radio communication for 2 or 3 days.[28]

All accounts show the need for radio communication when wire failed, and the lack of its use for command purposes when wire was available. During the bombardment of the Third American Division by the Germans on July 14 and 15, 1918, every line of the Fourth Infantry was severed. Eight pairs of linemen went out in an endeavor to repair the breaks but every man was either killed or wounded. Radio was then resorted to and operated successfully.[29] Heavy shelling of the command post of the Sixth Brigade at Courboin spared nothing. Wire was cut into pieces 15 to 20 feet long, and radio and visual stations were destroyed. The same thing happened to the Seventh Infantry. However, repairs were made the next day.[30] Radio could be put into operation as soon as sets could

[21] Priestly, pp. 150 and 151.
[22] Priestly, p. 237.
[23] Priestly, pp. 239 and 240.
[24] Priestly, p. 241.
[25] Priestly, p. 243.
[26] Priestly, p. 273.
[27] Priestly, p. 274.
[28] Priestly, p. 290.
[29] CSO-3, pp. 398 and 399.
[30] CSO-3, p. 399.

be brought up. It is interesting to note that most of the radio messages sent at this time within the Third Division were of an emergency nature calling for reinforcements, water, and action against new moves of the enemy. These were sent *in clear*.[30] On the contrary when the Third Division took up the pursuit of the Germans on July 21, good wire communication had been established well forward and radio was seldom used.[31] In the advance of the Thirty-second Division from August 27 to September 3 wire was used exclusively for command purposes. Radio was not used except for communication with airplanes in which it was very successful. There were no other means of signal communication available.[32] The Thirtieth American Division demonstrated the value of radio in the British attack on the Hindenburg line which began September 29 in which tanks tore up wire lines.[33] The One hundred and eighteenth Infantry of the Thirtieth Division had particularly hard fighting in the latter stages of this offensive and while they were able to maintain some wire communication, they used radio every hour in the day. Long messages were often sent. Cipher was used.[34] In the beginning of the St. Mihiel attack the wire lines of the Fifth Division were broken time and again by shell fire. During such times service was rendered by radio.[35] In the attack of the Twenty-sixth Division on October 23 in the Meuse-Argonne offensive against the woods to the north and east of the Ravine de Molleville, telephone lines and one radio set accompanied infantry battalions in the attack against Molleville farm and Ravine de la Reine. When all telephone lines in the area went out at 6 A. M., the first message back to division headquarters came from the continuous-wave radio station at the advance brigade command post.[36] At the end of October, during the rapid advance of the V Corps, considerable difficulty attended the maintenance of signal communication. In one instance radio had to be relied upon during a forced march of 2 days and nights.[37] During the advance of the Ninetieth Division to Montigny in the same offensive, lines were broken continuously and radio was called upon to maintain communication.[38] The Seventy-eighth Division, after taking Grandpre and after a few days of rest, again entered the offensive. Its advance was so rapid that after the first few hours no attempt was made to maintain telephone communication with the regiments. Radio had to be resorted to as

---

[31] CSO–3, p. 410.
[30] CSO–3, p. 414.
[32] CSO–3, p. 437.
[34] CSO–3, p. 439.
[35] CSO–3, p. 447.
[36] CSO–3, p. 480.
[37] CSO–3, p. 491.
[38] CSO–3, p. 493.

the troops advanced through Germont and Auths to Brieulles-sur-Bar. For a time the radio station at Brieulles-sur-Bar was the only point of contact which the division had with the rear, after it had moved its command post to that place on November 5.[39] The First Division went into the line near Chehery, just south of Sedan, after a forced march of 40 kilometers on the night of November 6, and went into the attack at 9 A. M. the following day. The division command post was established at Chehery from which point radio was the only means of communication to the rear.[40]

In the Champagne offensive the Second Division had an extensive wire system and used it as its primary means of signal communication. However, while radio was not used along the main-wire axis, sets moved with regimental and brigade command posts and furnished direct and practically continuous communication.[41] In the rapid advance of the Thirty-sixth Division in this operation neither wire nor radio gave entire satisfaction. Command posts were moved so frequently and on such short notice that wire lines often could not keep up. On one occasion during the move of the division command post from Machault to Dricourt there was a period of 7 hours during which telephone connection to corps was lost. The radio section was virtually the first command post personnel to enter Dricourt. Three stations were immediately set up.[42]

The great difficulty of maintaining wire communication in a rapid advance is well illustrated by the experiences of the Thirty-seventh and Ninety-first Divisions with the Belgians in the Lys-Scheldt drive.[43] Under such conditions the need for emergency means of signal communication becomes acute.

Artillery fire is a considerable menace to radio antennas when they are of appreciable size. It was a common occurrence during the World War for them to be shot out. However, they are quite easily replaced. The Fourth Division experienced this difficulty in the Meuse-Argonne offensive, although it did not seriously interfere with radio communication which was maintained.[44] In one day during this operation the radio station at division command post sent 80 messages, one containing more than 400 words. This service was maintained in spite of the fact that good wire communication existed at the time.[45] This appears to be unusual. An incident related by the Chief Signal Officer in his report of 1919 indicated both the value of radio in an emergency and the effect of artillery fire. It

[39] CSO-3, p. 497.
[40] CSO-3, p. 498.
[41] CSO-3, p. 456.
[42] CSO-3, p. 458.
[43] CSO-3, p. 463.
[44] CSO-3, p. 477.
[45] CSO-3, p. 476.

occurred at the headquarters of the One Hundred and Forty-fifth Infantry, Thirty-seventh Division, in the early stages of the Meuse-Argonne offensive.

A runner had just brought in information to the One Hundred and Forty-fifth Infantry commander that the enemy had begun a bracketing fire on the front line. The regimental position would unquestionably come under fire in a matter of minutes, and as the colonel dashed off a message to the artillery to begin counterbattery action, all personnel prepared to leave the regimental post. Sergeant Mulzer ordered his men to seek shelter with the colonel and his staff as the enemy was beginning to concentrate on the wireless antenna at the command post. The sergeant alone remained and began to flash his message just as a shell concussion blew down the antenna. Mulzer put the antenna up again and started on the message while lying flat on the ground. This time he succeeded, and a few minutes later the American batteries opened fire.[46]

In the march of the Third Army into Germany radio demonstrated its importance. Limitations placed upon the use of the telephone brought radio into prominence, and the efficiency of that type of signal communication was soon appreciated more fully than it had been during combat. Contact between brigades and divisions often depended entirely upon radio, and within brigades radio frequently became the only means of transmitting information.[47] The Thirty-second Division used no other means of signal communication within its brigades during the march. For the larger units civil and military telephone lines were used whenever possible.[48] The British also used radio extensively on their march into Germany.[49]

The dependence of the First, Second, Third, and Fourth German Armies on radio communication during their early advance into France is well known.

The failure of German wire communication was due to a number of causes, among which were: The presence of the largest military communication problem the world has ever known.[50] Reorganization of telephone units was taking place when the war opened. This caused a mixing of personnel and equipment.[51] The responsibility placed on lower units to connect with higher units was often impossible of accomplishment, and usually resulted in delays and wrong connections due to the ignorance of forward troops concerning rear wire systems.[52] Shortage of wire. The telephone detachment with the First Army had initially only 115 miles of wire, none of which was suitable for the construction of permanent lines.[53] Dis-

[46] CSO–3, pp. 478 and 479.
[47] CSO–3, p. 509.
[48] CSO–3, p. 511.
[49] Priestly, pp. 325, 326.
[50] Carlsward, p. 258.
[51] Carlsward, pp. 22–39.
[52] Carlsward, p. 28.
[53] Carlsward, p. 22.

tances as great as 510 kilometers separated GHQ from army head-quarters (First Army) of which 325 kilometers extended through hostile territory.[54] Lines were frequently cut by hostile inhabitants and destroyed by fire and friendly transportation.[55] The first wire communication established between GHQ and the right wing was to the Fourth Army on September 8, the day before the momentous decision was made to retire to the Marne.[56] A wire line between the First and Second Armies was completed on September 9, just after the retreat order was issued.[57]

The pre-war German signal organization provided only for tele-phone and radio communication.[58] Radio was provided only for army headquarters and for cavalry divisions.[59] Frequently there was no signal communication between army headquarters and lower units.[60]

Each Army headquarters was provided with two radio sets, each of a different type and range. One worked with GHQ and the other with adjacent armies. GHQ had only one radio set with which to communicate with all seven armies on the western front in addition to several fortress stations. This resulted in hours of delay in clear-ing radio traffic. The total inadequacy of this station forced the designation of the fortress station at Cologne and later the one at Metz as stations to operate with the armies.[61]

Some of the field radio units started the march without having received orders or instructions as to radio traffic, station-call signs, wavelengths (frequencies), or the use of cipher. It was therefore necessary for station chiefs to get together during the first few days of the campaign in order to regulate the traffic.[62]

In all of Carlsward's extremely detailed description of German signal communication up to the battle of the Marne, he mentions only one delay due to the failure of radio. In that case, a message from the First Army to GHQ which was to be sent at 10 p. m. on August 31 could not be transmitted until 4 a. m. September 1.[63] Contrary to some opinion, radio was functioning satisfactorily on September 8 and 9 during the critical period of decision at the Marne but for some unknown reason was not used to get information of the situ-ation on the fronts of the First, Second, and Third Armies.[64]

---

[54] Carlsward, p. 130.
[55] Carlsward, p. 101.
[56] Carlsward, p. 227.
[57] Carlsward, p. 221.
[58] Carlsward, p. 11.
[59] Carlsward, p. 31 ; Schndt., p. 3.
[60] Carlsward, pp. 143, 146, 149 ; Schndt., p. 9.
[61] Carlsward, pp. 224 to 226 ; Schndt., pp. 3 and 4.
[62] Carlsward, p. 36.
[63] Carlsward, p. 135.
[64] Carlsward, pp. 206 to 209.

Von Kluck well describes the signal communication situation in general and that of radio in particular during the days immediately preceding the battle of the Marne, in the following words:

Army headquarters had up until then been under the assumption that the German plan of operations had been so far carried out as arranged, that all the armies were advancing from victory to victory, and that the enemy was being beaten along the entire front. That such was not the case—particularly that the German left wing to the southwest had withdrawn from the front of the French line of fortresses—was not realized at First Army headquarters, owing to the scanty information which was given to it concerning the general situation of all the armies. The rapidity of the advance frequently made it difficult to maintain the telephone lines leading to the rear, which were often destroyed by the inhabitants or by fire, sometimes accidently by our own troops, and in other ways. Communication with the Supreme Command had therefore to be carried on mainly by radio stations, which again were overworked in communicating with the Cavalry Corps and the neighboring armies, a fact which the army commander was frequently made aware of by personal experience. There was consequently no means for the personal exchange of views so urgently needed between army headquarters and the General Staff of the Supreme Command.[65]

It is remarkable that radio rendered such splendid service in the first month of the German operations in view of the fact that there seemed to be no plan for any kind of signal communication, and that radio carried the whole load except that which was handled by messenger and by the personal visits of staff officers. There were no message centers, no liaison officers attached to units, no airplane messengers, and no wire.[66] Much better radio service could have been rendered had plans been made and had supervision led to the early correction of errors.[67] Carlsward places the blame for the lack of planning directly at the door of the chief signal officer (chief of field telegraphy) although Schniewindt indicated that he was not free to make the necessary decisions.[68]

Lieutenant General Schniewindt in his report submitted to the Reichswehr Ministry following a study of the signal communication of the German armies of 1914 on both the western and eastern fronts, concludes that:

Radio communication, according to the state of technique at that time, did well and often replaced the lacking wire connections. For a complete replacement it was not suitable, which is also the case today. First of all, radio communication is correctly considered as the most exposed means of signal communication, since radio messages are accessible to the enemy. * * * Rightly used, radio communication can always be an important means of exercising high command, as is shown by its employment on the right wing of the command on the western front.[69]

---

[65] von Kluck, p. 89.
[66] Carlsward, pp. 225 and 226.
[67] Carlsward, pp. 227 to 235.
[68] Carlsward, pp. 116, 138, 183, and 184; Schndt., pp. 6, 10, and 11.
[69] Schndt., p. 25.

104

To show the German appreciation in 1917 of the value of radio in forward units (which had none when the war began) the following is quoted from the translation of a German document dated December 15, 1917:

> The artillery, in particular, must bear in mind that it is absolutely impossible to rely on the transmission of orders and reports by telephone in the forward area during a battle. Wireless means of communication must therefore form the basis of the entire system of communications within the zone of effective hostile fire.[70]

Since the World War considerable research has been devoted to the development of ultra-high frequency radio telephone for artillery communication. Radio set SCR-194 is the result of this effort. It operates in the frequency band of 28 to 52 megacycles, which removes it far from other bands employed in the infantry division. Results of tests on this set are not available. However, in the course of a test of a similar set operating in the frequency band of 45 to 75 megacycles, First Lt. Rex E. Chandler, Field Artillery, found it to be suitable for artillery communication due to the facts that the range is limited—5,000 yards in this particular case; there is no fading; telephone is employed; and sufficient channels can be obtained.[71] He says:

> Radio, not wire, will be the only means of communication capable of keeping up with the situation.[72]

Captain D. A. L. Wade, writing in the June 1933 issue of Fighting Forces, says:

> No matter what decision regarding the use of wireless strategy may demand in the opening stages of battle, the fact remains that once the forces are engaged it must become the backbone of the system of communications; for it alone can compete with the mobility of modern weapons.[73]

RADIO COMMUNICATION IN THE OPERATIONS OF CAVALRY (HORSE)

The need for radio communication for cavalry was recognized early by the British as has already been mentioned, and that the Germans forsaw its need is indicated by their assignment of at least three, and in some cases four, radio sets to each cavalry division, while each field army had but two.[74] Since cavalry was little used on the western front after the initial stages of the World War, other theaters must be searched for historical examples. It may be stated in passing, however, that radio formed the only connecting link between German GHQ, the cavalry, and the field armies

---

[70] Signal Service, December, p. 22.
[71] Chandler, p. 458.
[72] Chandler, p. 456.
[73] Wade, pp. 190 and 191.
[74] Carlsward, p. 31.

on the western front in the early days of the conflict. Marwitz's misuse of radio is discussed later in this paper under intercept and goniometric activities.

Probably the best-known use of cavalry made during the World War was that by Allenby in Palestine in September and October 1918. While this operation was conducted by a force of all arms,[75] cavalry operations played a very important part in it. Its success was largely dependent upon surprise, rapidity of action, and careful preparation.[76]

The British relied instinctively on good wire communication, as has already been brought out, and never felt quite secure without it. For this reason, while it was recognized that the advance of the Desert Mounted Corps comprising the Fourth and Fifth Cavalry Divisions, and the Australian Mounted Division would be rapid, and that it would be impossible to build wire lines fast enough to keep up with it, they were unwilling to rely on radio alone but planned on using the captured Turkish telegraph lines which would fall into their hands. They had done it before.[77] In this case, however, this ability to utilize the Turkish telegraph system was in no small measure due to a stroke of luck. When the Thirteenth Cavalry Brigade captured the headquarters of the Yilderim Army Group at Nazareth on September 20th, among the papers that fell into their hands was an up-to-date map showing routes, number of circuits, etc., of the entire Turkish telegraph system in Palestine. This information was promptly made available to all concerned.

Notwithstanding the extensive use of Turkish wire lines, it was often impossible to provide wire communication between the command post of the Desert Mounted Corps and its divisions. In such cases radio was extensively used. During the 120-mile march of the Fourth Cavalry Division from Beisan to Damascus, September 26th to 30th, radio furnished the only means of signal communication. During the entire period this division was in communication with the Desert mounted Corps at least twice daily.[78]

Chaytor's Force which consisted of the Australian and New Zealand Mounted Division, the Twentieth Infantry Brigade, four additional battalions of infantry, a mixed artillery contingent, and a detachment of engineers, operated east of the Jordan River in a country devoid of wire lines, and until Es Salt was captured (a period of 3 days from September 21st to 23d), had to rely on radio. At one time, due to the loss of its radio set over a cliff and to the fact that it was not provided with a signal unit, General Chaytor's

[75] Ingles–1, pp. 13 and 14.
[76] Ingles–1, p. 14.
[77] Ingles–1, pp. 19 and 20.
[78] Ingles–1, pp. 17 and 20.

headquarters was out of touch with general headquarters for more than a day.[79]

The cavalry divisions were equipped with both pack and wagon radio sets. In several cases radio and messengers of the Desert Mounted Corps were the only means of communication with some of the divisions for 2 or 3 days at a time.[80]

Considerable difficulty was encountered at times in keeping wire lines up behind the rapid advance of the infantry. The greatest difficulty was experienced in the zone of action of the XX Corps through the rough, hilly country north of Jerusalem. Due to the character of the country, the clear atmosphere and sunshine at this period of the year, heliograph solved the problem.[81] This incident is mentioned here merely to note the use of a means of signaling little used today. It emphasizes the point that no available means of signal communication should be neglected.

Prior to the final offensive in Palestine, radio played important roles in raids and other operations despite the fact that a most excellent wire system was maintained. In one instance a raid was directed on Amman from Jerico, a distance of 30 miles. Signal communication with the raiding force was entirely by radio and was successfully maintained during the 12 days which the raid lasted.[82]

In the 1932 maneuvers of the First Cavalry Division (US) radio was used extensively although one wire circuit was maintained to the rear, and in the defensive phase of the maneuver one wire line was laid as far forward as regiments. The single circuit to the rear over field wire was too long to permit telephone communication although telegraph was practicable.[83] The training policy for signal communication stressed radio telegraphy and emphasized the need for the maintenance of communication during rapid movements over long distances.[84] Contact was maintained between a moving counter-reconnaissance screen and division headquarters by means of radio at hourly intervals while the division was on the march.[85] Constant radio communication was maintained between the division command post, observation aviation, brigade command posts, the field artillery battalion, and the division rear echelon.[86] It is not difficult to imagine the importance of radio had the one-wire circuit between the various command posts and the rear been interrupted.

---

[79] Ingles–1, pp. 1, 17, 20, and 21.
[80] Ingles–1, p. 23.
[81] Ingles–1, p. 21.
[82] Ingles–1, p. 10.
[83] Rumbough, pp. 8 and 9.
[84] Rumbough, p. 1.
[85] Rumbough, p. 7.
[86] Rumbough, p. 9.

RADIO COMMUNICATION IN THE OPERATIONS OF TANKS AND MECHANIZED CAVALRY

Since tanks were used comparatively little in the World War and mechanized cavalry not at all, an estimate of the radio requirements for these forces must be made largely on a theoretical basis supplemented by conclusions drawn from such peace-time tests as may be found.

The most extensive use of tanks made in a World War operation occurred at the second battle of Cambrai. This operation came at a time early in the development of radio as a whole, and little attention had been given to tank radio. Visual methods were used prior to the battle with indifferent success. Pigeons proved to be of more value.[87] Radio sets were carried by fighting tanks in the battle, and were used with good effect. They were not especially designed for the purpose but were originally intended for use by the artillery. Radio in the battle encountered some failures the principal one of which was the nonuse made of such radio facilities as existed. The success attained, however, demonstrated the need for tank radio, and development continued to finally include the use of radio telephone.[88]

The experiences of the First Cavalry (mechanized) throw some light on the need for radio communication from and to fast moving vehicles. In the march of this unit from Marfa, Tex., to Fort Knox, Ky., a distance of 1,600 miles, in the winter of 1932–33, the lack of radio in the column was a serious handicap to its control.[89] This was in the early period of the organization of this regiment. Radio has now been provided. The columns of mechanized cavalry move at 25 miles per hour on the march, and a day's march usually averages 150 miles. Indications point to an increase in the rate of speed and in the daily distance covered in the future. Under such conditions situations change rapidly. It is important that information of such changes reach the command headquarters quickly and that orders be issued to distant units with no loss of time, even though these units and their headquarters are on the move. These considerations indicate, in the opinion of the communication officer of the regiment, certain definite conclusions as follows: Wire communication cannot be used. Visual signaling can only be employed when the units or vehicles are within view of each other. Motorcycle messengers can be used profitably between points that are fixed and are not too far apart. This exhausts about all the means of signaling except radio. It is difficult to operate radio telegraph from vehicles that are moving rapidly over rough ground. Also, radio operators

[87] Priestly, p. 247.
[88] Priestly, p. 248.
[89] Withers, p. 15.

108

must be provided. Thus, only radio telephone remains as the solution to the problem. This means works very well and development is increasing its reliability.[90] The principal difficulties encountered in the use of radio telephone were technical breakdowns due largely to dust and moisture [91] and to the lack of proper training on the part of using personnel.[92]

No descriptions of post-war tests to determine the need for radio communication with tanks, are available. However, it is known that much thought and effort have been devoted to this subject and sets have been designated for tank use. It would seem reasonable that fast-moving tanks which operate at a considerable distance from their headquarters and from troops which they support, will require radio to at least as great an extent as does mechanized cavalry.

RADIO COMMUNICATION IN THE OPERATIONS OF AVIATION

Some references have been made to the use of radio for communication between airplanes and the ground for the purpose of reporting the results of reconnaissance and to the necessity for its use in the control of artillery fire. This use was confined to telegraph during the World War because suitable radio telephone equipment had not been developed at that time. The operations of aircraft were not as great nor as varied as they may be expected to be in a future major conflict. It appears self-evident that if technically satisfactory equipment can be produced, radio offers an excellent means of communication between aircraft and the ground and more important, between aircraft in flight. While visual and sound signals, and dropped and pick-up messages can be used over short distances between airplane and ground quite successfully, there is no method, other than radio, which will provide communication between individual planes in the air and between planes in the air and ground stations when the latter are separated by great distances.

In order to make some estimate of the radio requirements for aviation it is necessary to observe the results of peace-time tests. The latest and probably the most extensive test of radio communication for an air force was that made in connection with the air force maneuvers of 1933 on the west coast. These maneuvers consisted of five phases; viz., a rapid mobilization and concentration at March Field, Calif., involving a convergence of units from as far as the east coast; a series of exercises at March Field; a move of the air force and subordinate staffs to Seattle; and the return of the skeletonized air force units to their respective home stations.[93]

[90] Withers, pp. 16 and 17.
[91] Withers, p. 24.
[92] Withers, p. 25.
[93] Murphy, p. 3.

The air force was composed of two bombardment wings and an additional bombardment group, one attack wing, two observation groups, and a provisional transport squadron, in all of which a total of 136 planes were equipped with radio.[94]

While full advantage was taken of all ground wire communication facilities, a considerable amount of radio communication, both interplane and air-ground, was essential. Radio was the vital link on which the success of the exercises depended.[95] Four groups of frequencies were established as follows: One for command, one for secondary communication such as position reports, one for observation, and one kept clear for emergency use or for night missions over water. The latter was never required.[96] Frequency assignments had to be made to avoid mutual interference and interference from harmonics* of broadcasting stations.[97] In time of war a strict control of our own nonmilitary radio would reduce the interference from this source but it would be more than equaled by hostile radio interference. It was found entirely practicable to control airplanes in flight in this maneuver, to receive orders from the ground, and to report the results of observation by radio.

The author of this paper has talked to Maj. Hugh Mitchell, Signal Corps, who was signal officer for the 1931 air division maneuvers held in the eastern part of the country. His experience bears out the facts that it is entirely practicable to control air units in the air by means of radio and that radio is absolutely essential as a means of communication for such a force.

Radio was used successfully to control the pursuit group (Red) defending the Fort Knox, Ky., area in the 1933 antiaircraft Air Corps exercises, both from the ground and from the air. Second Lt. D. C. Doubleday, Air Corps, in commenting upon the operation of this group said:

> The exceptional performance of the radio equipment of the First Pursuit Group was what spelled success for it in the exercises. Without dependable radio communication it would have been impossible to make the numerous interceptions with such a small defending force.[98]

RADIO COMMUNICATION FOR THE TRANSMISSION OF INFORMATION CONCERNING THE APPROACH OF HOSTILE AIRCRAFT

It is obvious that if protection against hostile combat aviation is to be secured, early information of the approach of hostile air-

---

[94] Murphy, pp. 3 and 4.
[95] Murphy, p. 7.
[96] Murphy, pp. 8 and 9.
* AUTHOR'S NOTE.—Harmonics are waves emitted on multiples of the basic frequency but at greatly reduced strengths. They are practically eliminated in the better types of permanent installations.
[97] Murphy, p. 10.
[98] Doubleday, p. 13.

planes must be available to the protective arms; that is, friendly aviation and antiaircraft artillery. Due to the speed of its approach, the time elapsing between the time of sighting the hostile aircraft and the time antiaircraft artillery goes into action or the time of take-off of friendly aviation, must be as short as possible.

In order to secure early information of the approach of hostile aircraft, antiaircraft artillery establishes observation posts well to the front and flanks of the army.[99] Insofar as practicable direct telephone communication is provided for the transmission of alarms and the collection of information by the antiaircraft intelligence service,[1] although radio supplements the telephone.[2] Great reliance is placed on information received from supporting troops.[1] Since observation posts are located well to the front, signal communication for antiaircraft intelligence purposes is subject to the same conditions of combat as is signal communication for infantry and field artillery already discussed in paragraph 9.

Warning to friendly aviation of the approach of hostile aviation must first be given at least 100 miles forward of the location of the friendly airdrome in order to give pursuit aviation sufficient time to receive the warning and be in the air. This is simply a matter of arithmetic. This distance becomes greater with the increase in the speed of aircraft. In the joint antiaircraft—Air Corps exercises held in the vicinity of Fort Knox, Ky., in May 1933, it was estimated that not more than 4 minutes could be allowed to elapse between the sighting of a hostile bomber at 100 miles from the friendly pursuit airdrome, in order to permit the pursuit aviation to take-off, gain the necessary altitude, and maneuver for interception.[3]

A most carefully prepared and coordinated wire system was used to transmit the alarms. This system consisted of commercial circuits the coordination of which received the close attention of the civil telephone and telegraph officials. The average time required for the transmission of a telephone message over this system from the most distant point was 2.65 minutes.[4]

A radio net was also provided comprising sets operated by military personnel.[5] The average elapsed time for the transmission of a radio message was 2.82 minutes.[4]

The antiaircraft net of the First Army (U. S.) in the Meuse-Argonne offensive numbered 14 stations. These stations transmitted reports from forward observation posts to pursuit airdromes.[6]

[99] CACFM, Vol. II, p. 91.
[1] CACFM, Vol. II, p. 84.
[2] CACFM, Vol. II, p. 92.
[3] Bender, p. 2.
[4] Bender, p. 8.
[5] Bender, p. 3; Green, p. 249.
[6] CSO-3, p. 467.

111

BIBLIOGRAPHY *

Beamcasting, published in Signal Corps Bulletin, November–December, 1933. M–411–C73–B6. Key: BC.

Bender, L. B., Major, Signal Corps, *Signal Operations in the Defense Forces (Red) During the Joint Antiaircraft-Air Corps Exercises, Fifth Corps Area, 1933*, published in Signal Corps Bulletin, November–December, 1933. M–411–C73–B6. Key: Bender.

Borden, F. G., Captain, Signal Corps, *Some Peculiarities of High Frequency Radio Communication*, published in Signal Corps Bulletin, July–August, 1933. M–411–C73–B6. Key: Borden.

Carlsward, Tage, *Den Strategiska Signaltjansen Vid Tyska Vastharens Hogra Flygel (The Strategical Signal Communication With the German Right Wing)*. A translation from the Swedish. The Signal School, Fort Monmouth, N. J. Key: Carlsward.

Chandler, Rex E., 1st Lieut., Field Artillery, *The Adaptability of Ultra-Short Wave Radio to Field Artillery Communication*, pubblished in Field Artillery Journal, September–October, 1933. M–407–C73–B6. Key: Chandler.

Chief Signal Officer, *Report of the Chief Signal Officer*, 1919. M–411–C73–1. Key: CSO–3.

Doubleday, D. C., 2d Lieut., Air Corps, *Signal Communication in the First Pursuit Group During the Joint Antiaircraft-Air Corps Exercises, Fifth Corps Area, May 1933*, published in Signal Corps Bulletin, November–December 1933. M–411–C73–B6. Key: Doubleday.

German Document, *The Signal Service*, a translation, July 15th, 1917. M–9403–G11–J.43. Key: Sig. Serv.—July.

German Document, *The Signal Service and its Employment*, a translation, December 15th, 1917. M–9403–G11–J1–A.43. Key: Sig. Serv.—Dec.

Green, J. A., Lieut. Colonel, Coast Artillery Corps, *The Fort Knox Distant Intelligence Net*, published in the Coast Artillery Journal, July–August 1933. M–408–C73–B6. Key: Green.

Gylden, Yves, *Chifferbyraernas Insatser I Vardskriget Till Lands (The Contribution of the Cryptographic Bureaus in the World War)*. A translation from the Swedish, Stockholm, 1931, published serially in the Signal Corps Bulletin from November–December 1933 (No. 75) to November-December 1934 (No. 81). M–411–073–B6. Key: Gylden, followed by a number indicating the issue of the Signal Corps Bulletin involved, i. e., Gylden–81.

---

* EDITOR'S NOTE.—The Bibliography is inserted here instead of at the end of the last installment, where it normally belongs, to facilitate reference to it by readers of this first section of this article, before the later sections appear.

Harbord, J. G., Major General, U. S. A., *Radio in War*, an address made to the New York Society of Military and Naval Officers of the World War, December 5th, 1933, published in Signal Corps Bulletin, March–April 1934. M–411–C73–B6. Key: Harbord.

Ingles, H. C., Major, Signal Corps, *Allenby's Final Campaign in Palestine*, published in Signal Corps Bulletin, November–December 1929. M–411–C73–B6. Key: Ingles–1.

Ingles, H. C., Major, Signal Corps, *Tannenburg, a Study in Faulty Signal Communication*, published in Signal Corps Bulletin, July–August 1929. M–411–C73–B6. Key: Ingles–2.

Morecroft, John H., *Principles of Radio Communication*, John Wiley and Sons, Inc., New York. M–605–F1–73. Key: Morecroft.

Murphy, Wm. H., Captain, Signal Corps, *Signal Communication in the 1933 Air Force Maneuvers*, published in Signal Corps Bulletin, July–August, 1934. M–411–C73–B6. Key: Murphy.

Neame, Philip, Lieut. Colonel, Royal Engineers, *German Strategy in the Great War*. Edward Arnold & Co., London, 1923. M–9403–H1–D.42. Key: Neame.

Priestly, R. E., *The Signal Service in the European War of 1914 to 1918 (France)*. W. & J. Mackay & Co., Limited, Chatham, 1921. M–9403–G10–C.42–A3. Key: Priestly.

Randeweg, *German Radio Interception in the Battle of Tannenburg*. Reviewed from Wissen and Wehr, March 1932 in Review of Current Military Literature, C. & G. S. S., No. 45. M–209–C.73–D4E–2D. Key: Randeweg.

Review of Current Military Literature, C. & G. S. S., No. 34, *The Battle of Radio Intercepts*, reviewed from Militar-Wochenblatt, April 25th, 1929. M–209–C.73–D4E–2D. Key: RCML No. 34.

Rumbough, Wm. S., Major, Signal Corps, *First Signal Troop in the First Cavalry Division Maneuvers of 1932*, published in Signal Corps Bulletin, March–April 1933. M–411–C73–B6. Key: Rumbough.

Saxl, Dr. Irving J., *Micro Waves and Their Application for Military Purposes*, published in the Coast Artillery Journal, January–February 1934. M–408–C73–B6. Key: Saxl.

Schniewindt, Lieut. General, *Signal Communication Between the Headquarters Staffs During the Warfare of Movement in 1914*, translated from Wissen and Wehr, published in Signal Corps Bulletin, September–October 1933. M–411–C73–B6. Key: Schndt.

von Kluck, *The March on Paris and the Battle of the Marne, 1914*. Alexander von Kluck, Longmans, Green & Co., N. Y., 1920. M–9403–J.44:4–N5.43. Key: von Kluck.

Wade, D. A. L., *Wireless Developments*, published in Fighting Forces, June 1933. (Aldershot, England) M–104–C.42–B6. Key: Wade.

War Department, *Coast Artillery Field Manual, Vol. II. Antiaircraft Artillery, Part One. Tactics. 1933.* M–408–G.73. Key: CACFM.

War Department, *Basic Field Manual, Vol. IV. Signal Communication. 1931.* M–506–A4. Key: BFM, Vol. IV.

War Department, *Signal Corps Field Manual. Vol. I, Signal Corps Troops*, 1931. M–411–G.73. Key: SCFM, Vol. I.

War Department, *Signal Corps Field Manual, Vol. II, Signal Corps Operations*, 1931. M–411–G.73. Key: SCFM, Vol. II.

Withers, W. P., 1st Lieut. Cavalry, *Mobile Communication for Mechanized Cavalry*, published in Signal Corps Bulletin, March–April 1934. M–411–C73–B6. Key: Withers.

EDITOR'S NOTE: This paper will be continued in the next issue of the Signal Corps Bulletin.

---

* *Radio, a contributing cause of military disasters.*—Recent advices show the influence that Ethiopian radio messages in clear had on their disastrous defeats in the northern and southeastern sectors. During the battle in the Tembien, Italian headquarters were fully aware of the enemy's advance through the interception of Ethiopian radio messages in clear, and knew that it was directed on Hauzien. The Italians attacked and successfully drove back the advancing enemy. Again in the Dolo-Neghelli operations Ras Desta had been advancing for some time toward Dolo and, as he reported his movements daily to Dessie by radio in clear, his progress was accurately known to General Graziani. The latter waited until Ras Desta had reached Filta and then advanced. General Graziani's offensive was completely successful and Ras Desta's army to all intents and purposes, was destroyed. These recent results of the use in actual warface of radio messages in clear, duplicate those described in the preceding article in this bulletin on Secret Causes of German Successes on the Eastern Front, which article was introduced in the Coast Artillery Journal by the remark, "The sad experience of the Russians fully reveals the extreme disadvantage at which an army in the field may be placed if it freely uses the wireless telegraph."

*(No. 91, July–August, 1936)

POWERS AND LIMITATIONS OF RADIO COMMUNICATION WITHIN A MODERN FIELD ARMY *

By Maj. R. B. MORAN, *Signal Corps*

EDITOR'S NOTE.—This is the second and concluding installment of Major Moran's study. The first installment and the bibliography appeared in the preceding issue of the Signal Corps Bulletin (No. 91, July–August 1936).

RADIO INTERCEPT

Since radio waves travel to a greater or lesser extent in all directions from the transmitter, a belligerent may receive messages sent from one enemy headquarters to another, and if he can determine their contents quickly, he may be able to make use of the information thus secured. For this reason all field forces establish radio-intercept stations. Such stations also function to supervise friendly transmissions to see that radio regulations are obeyed in order that the securing of valuable information by the enemy will be reduced to the minimum.

Perhaps the best example of information obtained from intercepted radio messages is the German interception of Russian radio traffic at the opening of the World War during the advance of the Russian First and Second Armies which culminated in the Battle of Tannenberg.

Telegraph lines paralleled some of the Russian railroad lines, and it was on these that the Russians relied for their principal means of signal communication. However, both armies advanced before their supply services were ready to function, and they were thus deprived of sufficient wire to make the necessary extensions as they advanced. General Jilinsky at Bialystok had communication to the First and Second Armies most of the time but there was no direct communication between the armies.

The First Army crossed the frontier on August 17 and gained contact with the Germans at Stallupönen. It followed the Germans in their withdrawal to Gumbinnen on the 18th. By nightfall the signal system was blocked with undelivered telegrams. Communication by wire between army headquarters and corps command posts was practically impossible. In desperation the army orders for the 19th, which were to advance to the line Oszballen-Goldap and halt there during August 20, were sent out by radio *in the clear*. They reached the corps on the morning of the 19th but in mutilated form. The

*(No. 92, September–October. 1936)

115

Germans, however, picked up the messages correctly and were thus informed of the contemplated Russian movements for the next 2 days. General von Francois, commanding the German I Corps which was opposing the Russian First Army under Rennenkampf, was quick to take advantage of this information and launched a successful attack.[1] von Prittwitz, the German supreme commander, received information that the Russian Second Army had crossed the frontier, and becoming fearful of the situation, ordered the German forces to the west of the Vistula River. This action resulted in the relief of von Prittwitz and his replacement by von Hindenburg with Ludendorff as his chief of staff. Ludendorff arrived at German supreme headquarters on August 22 and at once began issuing orders for new dispositions. He was able to do this because of information secured by the careless use of radio by the Russian First Army indicating a slowing up of its advance. On August 24 Samsonoff transmitted by radio to his corps commanders his orders for the movements of the Russian Second Army on the 24th and 25th. The Germans picked up these messages and so were fully informed of the movements of the Second Army. Many messages were sent in clear and others in a very simple cipher which the Germans had no trouble in reading.[2]

The danger of the enemy securing information from radio messages was deeply impressed on Field Marshal von Hindenburg, and as late as the spring of 1917 he was strongly against the use of radio of any description. He attributed his victory at Tannenberg entirely to the fact that during the whole of the action he was able to overhear and follow the plans of the Russian higher command as transmitted by radio to the fighting formations. He was greatly in fear of similar indiscretions and considered the function of radio should be the interception of information which might be obtained from a less careful enemy radio service. His objections were overruled and the Germans soon developed field radio to a considerable extent.[3]

The Russians continued to keep the enemy well informed by means of radio.[4] General Ronge of the Austrian Army sites innumerable instances in his book Krieges- und Industrie- Spionage in which valuable information was secured in this manner. The following examples will serve to illustrate the point:

An effective unsurpassed source of information was, however, opened to us by the Russian radio messages which were transmitted with a carelessness

[1] Ingles–2, p. 6 ; Gylden–80, pp. 51 and 52.
[2] Ingles–2, pp. 8 and 1b ; Gylden–80, pp. 52 and 53 ; Randeweg, p. 60 ; Neame, p. 52.
[3] Priestly, p. 151.
[4] Neame, p. 52.

similar to that of which the Germans were guilty when opposite the French troops at the beginning of the war.

and

> The Russians acted just as if we were not in possession of similar devices and were not able to tune to their wavelengths. We used our radio stations much more sparingly and more carefully in transmitting orders, but on the contrary, we used them very extensively for intercepting purposes.[5]

Again Ronge says:

> It was reassuring to our command that the radio-intercepting service, played on the Russian grouping as on a piano, instantly was able to report the intent and purposes of the enemy's command, and so well helped in the determination of the enemy's forces that as early as the end of October the diagram of the daily dispositions of the Russian forces even down to the divisions, could not have been much unlike the diagram which was found at Stavka or at the headquarters of the command on the southwestern front at Cholm. Consequently we may be certain that a troop unit which disappeared from the front without any explanation as to what had become of it could be located within a short time in its new position.[6]

The preparations made by the Germans for the battle of Kutno were aided to a great degree by information obtained from intercepted Russian radiograms. Of special importance was one sent by the chief of staff of the Second Army, General Chagin, on the morning of November 13 in a rather simple cipher which was solved on the afternoon of the same day. It gave the clearest possible picture of the Russian idea of the grouping of the German forces, of their own intentions and the consequently necessary grouping of their own forces, of the measures taken to provide flank protection, etc. This permitted the German command to plan its operations most accurately. During the course of the battle more Russian radiograms were intercepted which gave the locations and movements of corps.[7]

The story later in the war was much the same. For instance, in April 1915 a great many Russian radiograms were intercepted. These informed the Austro-German commands concerning the condition and situation of the Russian troops and their grouping. In particular it was learned that the Third Russian Army was in serious need of men and ammunition, and had suffered great losses in the battle of the Carpathians from which they had been able to recover only very slowly. Here was an opportunity for the Central Powers to obtain great results by combining their forces. On May 2 General von Mackensen's attack via Gorlice against the Third Russian Army was made.[8]

---

[5] Gylden–80, p. 54.
[6] Gylden–80, p. 65.
[7] Gylden–80, pp. 65 and 66.
[8] Gylden–81, p. 51.

Russia finally discontinued the use of radio for strategical purposes on October 24, 1916. Even this order was sent by radio and was intercepted by the Austrians.[9]

The following statement is attributed to von Glaise-Horstennau, chief of the war archives at Vienna, privy councilor, and former officer of the Austrian General Staff in an interview in Stockholm:

If we had not intercepted the Russian radiograms we should most probably have lost the war as early as the winter of 1914–15.[10]

The Russians were by no means the only warring nation to be guilty of such carelessness. The Germans on the western front generally used cipher in the early period of the war but frequently names appeared in clear text, as well as words and even whole sentences which had not been understood by the person for whom the messages were intended. There were even entire radiograms with the signature of the sender sent in clear text. In this way, in only a few days, it was learned that von Marwitz was in command of the cavalry corps which used the call sign beginning with the letter S and that von Richthofen was in command of the corps with the call sign beginning with the letter G. In the same way other radiograms sent in clear text informed the French that two German cavalry divisions had entered the valley of the Woevre, probably via Audun-le-Roman, and were advancing toward Verdun via Malavillers and Xivry-Circourt, where one of the divisions had established headquarters. This advance had been entirely unknown to the French high command up to that time.[11] Frequently messages contained part clear text and part cryptographed text, and at times explanations of cryptographed messages were made in clear text. This practice was particularly bad on the part of Marwitz's cavalry corps and it permitted a direct attack on the German cryptographic system.[12]

The French made the same mistakes, although not to such an extent as some of the other forces. This was due largely to the fact that in the early stages of the war they were able to use wire communication to a much greater extent than the Germans, thus enabling them to utilize radio stations more for interception purposes. As a result they learned much from the German misuse of radio and avoided to some extent the German mistakes. In addition to this they believed in the use of radio as an emergency means of communication to be used only when regular telephone and telegraph connections could no longer be maintained.[13] Added

[9] Gylden–81, p. 55.
[10] Gylden–80, p. 70.
[11] Gylden–77, p. 50.
[12] Gylden–77, pp. 51 and 52
[13] Gylden–78, p. 50.

to this, the Germans did not at first appreciate the value of intercept and the value of information to be derived from intercepted messages. It is probable, because of the importance attributed before the war to interfering with enemy radio traffic, that the German radio operators devoted themselves more at first to that sport than to any careful interception of French radiograms. German cryptanalysts after the war expressed the belief that much valuable information was lost due to the neglect to intercept it.[14]

During the period from 1914 to 1916 the Germans did practically no cryptanalytic work on the western front. The French reports to the effect that the Germans did not succeed in breaking down the French cipher until the winter of 1917–18 seem, to judge from all circumstances, to be correct.[15] That this should be so seems difficult to understand in view of the German success on the eastern front until we realize that the Germans before the war gave little consideration to the solution of anything but simple ciphers.[16]

Italy furnished the Austrians with much valuable information especially before the arrival of French and British troops on the Italian front.[17] During the great offensive on the plateau at Lavarone and Folgaria in the late spring of 1916, the Italian counteroffensive was betrayed by decrypted radiograms. During the night of May 20 an Italian radiogram was intercepted containing descriptions of the arrangements made for a large-scale counterattack with the reserves. By 3 a. m. the radiogram had been decrypted and 1 hour later countermeasures ordered which successfully checked the counterattack.[18] On November 22, 1917, the chief of the Italian radio service, because of confusion arising during a retreat, committed the blunder of asking all stations under his command to report their locations and relation to other troops. This gave the Austrians information about the whole grouping of the Italian forces, including the reserves, and the distribution of the medium and heavy artillery.[19]

During the latter part of the war much less information of value was obtained due to improved radio discipline and improved methods of cryptography.

The French divided the western front into three intercepting zones with centers at Paris, Lyons, and Bordeaux. At first, messages sent from the German rear stations received the greatest attention, but later they concentrated upon intercepting messages sent over the enemy's field radio sets. General Cartier, who was chief

[14] Gylden–80, p. 52.
[15] Gylden–78, p. 63.
[16] Gylden–75, pp. 30 to 32.
[17] Gylden–81, p. 64.
[18] Gylden–81, p. 62.
[19] Gylden–81, p. 63.

of the French signal service, states that more than 100 million words were intercepted during the World War by French stations.[20]

The British started with one intercepting station in 1914 and by 1917 this activity had become firmly organized in the wireless observation group of the Army wireless company. The intercept and goniometric service had become so important by this time that a special section of the intelligence staff at G. H. Q. was organized to direct its activities and coordinate the results obtained.[21] It was known that certain radio stations were associated in the German Army with certain definite formations. The work of the British goniometric and intercept stations contributed in no small degree to the efficiency of the intelligence service.[22]

In the A. E. F., radio intercept stations were operated in the First and Second Armies. On November 11, 1918, there were 8 officers and 214 enlisted men engaged in operating intercept and goniometric stations. There were six intercept stations which, during the period December 1917 to November 1918 intercepted 17,688 messages and 237,977 calls.[23] Numerous instances show the value of information obtained by intercept.[24]

A valuable service rendered by intercept stations was the policing of friendly radio stations. Watch was maintained on frequencies in use, and reports of infractions of radio discipline were promptly reported. In a test conducted in the late summer of 1918 by General Nolan, who was then G-2, A. E. F., an American radio operator was sent out to see what he could pick up from our own stations. He was to consider himself an enemy, and had no data given him that was not available to the Germans. Before the St. Mihiel attack this operator reported the American order of battle, locations of certain divisions in reserve, names of commanders, and the nature of instructions given them.[25]

Priestly says, in speaking of this phase of radio:

The second duty of the Army wireless station was of yet more general importance. It was its duty to watch for errors in wireless discipline from the signal point of view. * * * A careful watch for indiscretions must be kept by the Signal Service itself. * * * Innovations in procedure, little mannerisms in the key, irrelevant remarks between operators, indiscreet messages; all of these things needed to be controlled and eliminated so far as was possible, since they might give so much away to a presumably watchful enemy. It was in preventing such occurrences and in tightening up discipline, that the greatest utility of the Army wireless section lay, though its other functions were also of importance.[26]

[20] Gylden—79, p. 49.
[21] Priestly, p. 165.
[22] Priestly, p. 55 ; Carlsward, p. 31.
[23] C. S. O.—3, pp. 326 and 327.
[24] C. S. O.—3, p. 332.
[25] Harbord, p. 33.
[26] Priestly, pp. 191 and 192.

Cryptanalysis of secret messages often depends upon apparently inconsequential errors, the most common of which are: Telegraphing from one station to another in clear text; making and filing together of clear-text copies of secret messages; telegraphing in mixed text (part clear text and part code or cipher); and using one code or cipher to repeat text which has already been sent in another. The early success of the French over the Germans was largely due to such blunders.[27] A good example of the danger of such practices is shown by the routine transmission of weather reports. In 1914 the German station at Norddeich sent out by radio telegraph regular weather reports in mixed text. In these messages the cipher clerks had not taken the trouble to encipher the letters and numbers ordinarily used to indicate the strength and direction of the wind, etc. The station at Brugge, on the contrary, transmitted the same radiograms after enciphering the figures and letters. A comparison of the messages gave an exceedingly valuable clue to the code used and thus permitted its early solution.[28] We now use in our Army a nonsecret code for the transmission of meteorological data. Another item which greatly assists in the solution of codes and ciphers is the use of stereotyped military forms. This characteristic of German messages formed one of the most useful sources for the French experts in their work of cryptanalysis.[29]

The number of German radiograms intercepted by the French varied with war conditions. During periods of calm the messages were mostly of local importance and were comparatively carefully enciphered. On the other hand, such periods were always characterized by stereotyped messages, and as a rule only a few days were necessary to recognize the habits of the crytographers concerned. Despite numerous and quick changes of call signs, even the telegraph operators of the various stations were identified by their individual peculiarities in operating, a circumstance which is well known to every experienced operator. During periods of great activity, on the contrary, for instance during the great spring and summer offensive of 1918, numerous larger units and staff radio stations added to the traffic, and it frequently occurred that about 60 radiograms concerning the operations of the larger units were intercepted during one 24-hour period, not including the innumerable radiograms from smaller units. It was during such periods that the most ordinary errors and blunders were made and the regulations most disregarded.[30]

[27] Gylden–78, p. 60.
[28] Gylden–78, p. 62.
[29] Gylden–77, p. 52.
[30] Gylden–79, p. 58.

The number of messages sent in clear, or which in other respects violated the radio regulations, transmitted by American field stations and intercepted by the intelligence intercept stations, demonstrated the need for stations which specialized in copying messages from American operators. Such a station was established at Toul on July 11, 1918, for the interception of damped-wave transmissions, and soon thereafter another control station was installed to copy messages from continuous-wave stations. Two additional stations were later established at Souilly. The stations supervised the work of American operators and by promptly reporting violations on several occasions succeeded in nullifying slips which might otherwise have been disastrous.[31]

The matter of supervision of friendly radio is of such importance that specific provision is made for it in the radio-intelligence company of an army.[32]

The following brief reports concerning the Italian-Abyssinian campaign are quoted as further examples of information to be obtained from the misuse of radio:

From a report of operations on the Tacazze River and in the Tembian:

As regards the recent battle in Tembian, Italian headquarters were fully aware of the enemy's advance through the interception of Abyssinian wireless messages sent in clear.

From a report on the Dolo-Neghelli operations:

For some time Ras Desta had been advancing towards Dolo and, as he reported his movements daily to Dessie by wireless "in clear" his progress was accurately known by General Braziani.

RADIO GONIOMETRY

After the value of intercepted messages became evident, it was immediately desirable to secure additional information concerning the location and size of the station transmitting. This led to the formation of the radio goniometric service in all armies in the World War. By listening to an enemy station from two or more definitely located points, radio-compass stations were able to obtain bearings on the transmitter, and by means of intersection could locate it.[33] Estimates of its power could also be made, and in this manner, together with the contents of intercepted messages, the identification of the unit to which the station belonged and its location could be determined.

The French entered the war without goniometric equipment, although its need had been pointed out by General Cartier before the

[31] C. S. O.-3, p. 323.
[32] S. C. F. M., vol. I, p. 63; S. C. F. M., vol. II, p. 126.
[33] C. S. O.-3, p. 322.

war. Even without this equipment much was done in the way of identification by intercept alone. The strength of signal, frequency of transmission, and analysis of call signs led to quite accurate identification as has already been mentioned in the case of Marwitz's cavalry.[34] At the close of the war a French goniometric network extended from Le Havre to Saline.[35]

The Austrians were able most of the time to keep well informed of the locations of Italian units by the use of radio goniometers in spite of frequent changes in call signs of Italian radio stations.[36]

The success of radio intercept against the Russians has been mentioned earlier in this paper. This, together with radio goniometry, left little that was not known to the Germans and Austrians concerning the locations and strength of Russian units.

Radio goniometry formed a very important work of the Army signal service in both the First and Second American Armies. In one instance the American goniometric station at Menil la Tour, operating continuously for 24 hours on May 27, 1918, took 670 bearings.[37] Goniometric stations were mounted in trucks in order that they might keep up with the troops in fast-moving situations.[38] In his report to the officer in charge of radio, the radio intelligence officer of the First Army said on September 20, 1918:

The location of all enemy radio stations in their proper places by means of gonio bearings on the night before the attack was the determining factor in the decision of the chief of intelligence that the enemy had not already withdrawn from the St. Mihiel salient.[39]

That the German goniometric stations were not idle is indicated by the experience of the Forty-seventh Infantry on July 6, 1918, in the big German offensive. As soon as the radio set at the regimental command post began calling brigade, hostile shell fire was centered on the command post.[40]

At the time of the armistice there were 28 goniometric stations in operation of which 8 were aero stations. The 20 ground stations had taken 176,913 bearings and the aero stations 5,342 registrations and 102 alerts.[41]

A variation of the goniometric service was the location of hostile airplanes by aero goniometric stations. Ordinarily the ground goniometric stations were engaged in locating enemy ground stations, but when an enemy airplane was heard by the special intercept

[34] Gylden—77, p. 49.
[35] Gylden—79, p. 49.
[36] Gylden—81, p. 63.
[37] C. S. O.—3, p. 324.
[38] C. S. O.—3, p. 323.
[39] C. S. O.—3, p. 323.
[40] C. S. O.—3, p. 402.
[41] C. S. O.—3, pp. 327 and 328.

station, all goniometric stations were notified and bearings taken, so that its position could be found. Alerts were sent to the air service by wire, giving the location of the plane or planes so that pursuit aviation could be sent out. Fine work was done in locating hostile planes directing artillery fire. In the Verdun sector it was impossible to maintain wire communication between the goniometric stations on account of the continual movement and the intense shell fire. Yet one goniometric and aero intercept located at Verdun was able to locate many hostile airplanes operating along the front. By means of a special telegraph wire to the intelligence bureau, General Staff, notification was given as soon as an enemy spotting plane started calling its battery. The General Staff warned the corps commander in whose area the plane was operating many times being able to identify the battery about to open fire. The counter-battery officer at corps headquarters was able to counteract the fire from the enemy battery, sometimes even before it started, and notify the sound and flash stations so that they could take observations.[42]

The Chief Signal Officer, in his report for 1919, says:

This service, however, primarily belonged to war of position, since a complete system of telephone lines between goniometric stations and a control station from which warnings of these flights could be sent to air pursuit groups was necessary. During movement of the front it was necessary frequently to move goniometric stations forward so that it was practically impossible to maintain the proper telephone lines. Hence, with the exception of the brief time when the First Army was engaging in position warfare, this branch of the service received no opportunity to function at its full value.[43]

RADIO CAMOUFLAGE

As soon as the value of radio intercept and goniometric services became evident it was a natural result that defense against them should be sought in deception. This was done to a very great extent and in many cases with considerable success.

This scheme, together with other means of deception, was used by Allenby in his preparations for his attack on the Beersheba–Geza line. He decided to attack Beersheba first while making every effort to convince the Turks that Geza would be the first objective. Many doctored messages, in a cipher which it was known the Germans with the Turkish army could break, were sent between the larger headquarters. The radio traffic meant for Turkish consumption was carefully handled so as to give the impression merely of an indiscreet use of radio. The attack was launched against Beersheba on October 31, 1917. It came as a complete surprise to the Turks and by evening Beersheba was in British hands.[44]

[42] C. S. O.–3, p. 324.
[43] C. S. O.–3, p. 331.
[44] Ingles–1, pp. 8 and 9.

124

Again when Allenby decided to attack the Turkish line along the coastal plain west and northwest of Ludd instead of north of Jerusalem or in the Jordan Valley as the Turks expected, he made extensive use of measures to deceive the enemy, one of which was radio camouflage. He desired to concentrate the Desert Mounted Corps (less the Australian and New Zealand Mounted Division) in rear of the main attack. To move them from their bivouac area in the Jordan Valley would immediately attract the notice of the Turks. The picket lines of the Fourth and Fifth Cavalry Divisions were left standing with dummy horses on them. The headquarters of the corps at Talaat ed Dumm, in view from the hills in the Turkish lines, remained standing for a fortnight after the staff had departed for the coast. It was lit up every night and radio traffic to and from it continued with normal regularity.[45]

On the eastern front, while the Germans were receiving much valuable information from Russian radio, they resorted to the ruse of transmitting fake orders in clear text in the hope that the Russians would read them.[46] The Russians themselves sent faked messages in the spring of 1916 for the purpose of deceiving the Austrians. The attempt failed, however, because the ruse was discussed in earlier radiograms one of which was intercepted and decrypted by the Austrians, and also because at the end of the spurious radiogram, in a cipher which had already been analyzed by the Austrians, was the statement: "Do not be disturbed; this is merely intended to mislead the enemy." [47]

In the spring of 1916 the Austrians started an offensive against Italy. With a view to misleading the enemy concerning the sector of front on which the attack was to be made, faked radio traffic was started on the eastern Carinthian front. A very simple cipher system was used for this purpose; one which it was assumed the Italians would be able to break without difficulty. The results cannot be determined accurately but the scheme is reported to have been successful.[48] Similar faked traffic was established in connection with the battle of the Piave in 1917 and it cost the Italians 60,000 prisoners.[49]

By changing his call sign just before the battle of Jutland, Admiral von Scheer tricked Admiral Beatty into believing he was confronted only by the German cruiser squadron instead of the entire German fleet.[50]

---

[45] Ingles–1, pp. 14 and 15.
[46] Gylden–80, p. 55.
[47] Gylden–81, p. 53.
[48] Gylden–81, p. 61.
[49] Gylden–81, p. 61; R. C. M. L. No. 34, p. 111.
[50] R. C. M. L. No. 34, p. 111.

As has already been pointed out, the primary function of the goniometric service was to locate daily all enemy stations heard, and by connecting these stations by lines indicating an exchange of messages, to determine the groups of stations belonging to divisions, corps, and armies. The radio traffic of a division would normally be contained almost entirely within its own limits, and similarly with corps and armies, so that theoretically the intercommunication of stations would disclose clearly the boundaries of units. But actually the enemy, with the intent of destroying this source of information, indulged in a carefully regulated camouflage activity whenever possible, having stations communicate regularly across divisional, corps, and army boundaries, so that the grouping of stations into actual nets was very difficult. However, under very active conditions, the necessary traffic of stations was so great that camouflage was impossible and the various nets showed up clearly.[51]

In preparation for the second phase of the Meuse-Argonne operation radio deception achieved considerable success. Prisoners taken east of the Meuse between Beaumont and Fresnes, about October 30, declared that the Germans were fearful of an attack in the direction of Briey and Metz. Accordingly a plan was evolved to increase these fears and thereby divert the enemy's attention and his forces from the west of the Meuse. This plan, among other features, included the establishment of a dummy Army radio net opposite the Beaumont-Fresnes front and sending messages between stations of the net in a cipher which the enemy could solve through apparent carelessness in its use. The messages were of a nature which would make the Germans think that an attack by this new "army" was imminent. The plan was put into effect on October 23 and was carried on until after the operations west of the Meuse started on November 1. This camouflage apparently met with considerable success. It later developed that two enemy divisions were held in reserve in Metz, even after the attack west of the Meuse began, because of the fear of an attack east of the river.[52]

RADIO INTERFERENCE

One of the most valuable characteristics of a radio receiver is that it is capable of picking up radio impulses from any direction. From some directions, however, signals may be stronger than from others. Due to the nondirectional characteristics of a receiver, it will record all radio impulses received at the frequency to which it is tuned. As a result many sounds other than those desired will be heard. Such

[51] C. S. O.-3, pp. 329 and 330.
[52] C. S. O.-3, pp. 336 and 337.

sounds are known as interference. The principal sources of interference are:

(a) Undesired signals on the frequency being used.

(b) Atmospheric disturbances (static).

(c) Sounds similar to static produced by various electrical devices such as X-ray machines, motors, etc.

As mentioned earlier in this paper, an operator receiving continuous-wave signals can overcome interference to some degree by changing the pitch of the received signal. Modulated (voice) transmissions cannot be so controlled.

Interference from friendly transmitters can be eliminated by a system of frequency assignments and by careful supervision. Atmospheric interference can be overcome by using sufficient power to drown it out. Interference from electrical machines can be eliminated or reduced by shielding the offending device or by changing the location of the receiver.

Deliberate, hostile, powerful interference cannot be controlled. This would then seem to present a very serious limitation to the use of radio. Let us discover, if possible, the extent to which deliberate interference or "jamming" is practicable.

Hostile interference may be produced effectively in two different ways. A radio transmitter must be used in either case. Let us consider first that the enemy uses a powerful transmitter of the damped-wave type, so tuned that there is little or no predominating frequency and there is a large number of frequencies present, thus occupying a very large portion of the radio spectrum. It is not possible to direct this type of transmission in a given direction (as is possible to a limited extent with continuous-wave radio) so that if the power used is sufficient to prevent our radio receivers from functioning it also prevents the enemy's from operating. Such a scheme would be costly to operate and the moment it stopped our sets could continue their operation. Another method which might be used would be to transmit a continuous wave on the frequency used by a particular set which the enemy wishes to silence. A slight change in frequency of our net would nullify his efforts. Such a scheme would be an impossibility as a practical matter.

Considerable interference must be expected, however, from the congested traffic of both friendly and hostile sets operating close together within a comparatively narrow frequency band. This is true at the present time in the amateur bands but communication is not prevented.

From the discussion already given under intercept and goniometric activities it is unnecessary to stress further the value to be obtained from careless radio transmission. Even the smallest errors are often a source of valuable information. This source of information is lost to the enemy if he succeeds in jamming friendly radio traffic.

Prior to the World War, Germany leaned to the viewpoint that the operation of enemy radio sets should be interfered with. As early as the first mobilization day (Aug. 2, 1914) the German chief of field telegraph (chief signal officer) issued orders to all permanent radio stations on the western border to interfere with radio traffic between France and Russia, and at the same time he ordered stations on the eastern front to intercept this traffic.[53] It is probable that some organized effort was made by Germany to interfere with the field radio transmissions of her enemies, for Priestly mentions the appearance early in the war of special German jamming stations.[54] Again he mentions such stations during the period immediately following the Somme offensive. It is interesting to note, however, that German jamming stations immediately ceased operations when they realized that a British ground station was endeavoring to send a message of tactical importance.[55] Reference has heretofore been made to the slow development of German intercept service and to the probability that the Germans were more concerned on the western front in attempting to prevent enemy radio operation than in securing valuable information therefrom.

A careful search has been made by the author of this paper for reference to instructional or training literature, lists of special equipment for the purpose, organization for the purpose or any other evidence indicating an organized effort to conduct jamming operations. No such evidence has been found in publications pertaining to the French, British, German, or United States Armies. It seems reasonable to suppose that some mention would be made of such a practice had it been considered valuable, especially since most training documents contain warnings against the danger of hostile interference, whether intentional or not.

Some interesting facts were brought out with respect to jamming in connection with the joint antiaircraft Air Corps exercises held at Fort Knox, Ky., in May 1933. The Blue force seeking to attack Fort Knox from the air discovered a Red observation plane was transmitting data on Blue operations. They immediately tried to block the frequency of the Red plane. There ensued several days of effort to interfere with the observer's transmissions, but without success. The longest delay was of about 1 minute's duration, which was required to retune the transmitter. The man doing the transmitting has a decided advantage because he can change his frequency quickly and the would-be blocker must find him. It was

---

[53] Carlsward, p. 38.
[54] Priestly, p. 88.
[55] Priestly, p. 151.

found that if the two stations working with each other could change their frequency on a prearranged code signal, it was impossible to jam them even though several transmitters were used for the purpose. All attempts at deliberate interference during these exercises failed.[56]

The matter of interference between friendly stations or between friendly and enemy stations operating in close proximity to each other is quite another matter. The records available to the author of this paper all indicate the seriousness of this problem. It was, however, much more serious when damped-wave sets were involved, due to the width of the band required by each transmitter. The almost universal use of continuous-wave sets has greatly reduced the problem.

A 2-kilowatt Marconi tractor set (damped wave) used by the Americans for rear-area communication during the march into Germany after the armistice so interfered with other radio traffic that its use had to be discontinued until it could be converted for continuous-wave transmission and its frequency changed.[57]

During the period of heavy radio traffic on the western front in the early stages of the war considerable interference as well as jamming was experienced. The messages became so garbled that many had to be repeated three or four times. Also the time required for cryptographing was so great that at times the transmission of an important radio message required 24 hours.[58]

In order to prevent interference between friendly stations a careful allotment of frequencies must be made and radio discipline must be exercised in nets.[59] Interference from hostile stations is avoided by shifting frequencies.

There is one situation in which it is probable that jamming could be used effectively. That is the case in which one side was so well provided with wire communication that it could forego entirely the use of radio. For example, in the defense of a limited coast line where the defender had an extensive system of underground cables so well protected that artillery fire and air bombs could not blast it out. In such a case damped-wave radio transmitters might be employed to silence the much-needed radio of a landing force. Even in this case, however, there is certainly a question as to whether the information to be gained from intercepted hostile radio might not be worth more than depriving the enemy of its use.

Upon reaching this point in this discussion one may wonder whether the danger in the use of radio is not sufficiently great to

[56] Doubleday, p. 13.
[57] C. S. O.–3, p. 514.
[58] Gylden–77, p. 46; Carlsward, p. 234.
[59] R. F. M., Vol. IV, p. 112; Wade, p. 188.

warrant its prohibition for tactical purposes, and to conclude with von Hindenburg that it should only be used to secure information from the enemy. It is therefore reassuring to see what Glyden has to say after a most exhaustive survey of the intercept and cryptographic services of the nations involved in the World War. His words are as follows:

The said dangers are very great; that fact cannot be denied. But it would be like throwing out the child with the bath water to give up such a valuable, rapid, and simple means of communication as radio for this reason alone. Its value as a means of communication is undeniable, and, strikingly enough, it has been assigned a much greater importance in the armies of the great powers on the Continent since the war. Nor was it radio as a means of communication which so often failed, but the cryptographic service, a fact which can never be too greatly emphasized. But if used with a well-organized cryptographic service, fully experienced in cryptanalysis, radio becomes an invaluable means of communication. When used by a personnel ignorant of the principles of cryptanalysis and poorly prepared, it, on the other hand, becomes to the highest degree dangerous for the activities of the armies using it. Common sense alone tells us that the use of a means of communication which goes both to friend and foe must necessarily presuppose exceptionally great knowledge of cryptography and cryptanalysis on the part of the personnel responsible for the operation of that means. Such knowledge must be made compulsory.[60]

CONCLUSIONS

Radio communication is based on a physical phenomenon governed by natural laws which must be considered in its use for military purposes. The most important of these facts are:

(1) Radio sets capable of utilizing both telegraph and telephone transmission are practicable for military use.

(2) Radio waves travel in all directions, hence radio messages will be received by enemy stations within range as well as by our own.

(3) The number of sets which can operate within a given band of frequencies is limited.

(4) The total number of frequency bands within which radio transmission is practicable is limited.

Wire communication (telephone and telegraph) is the primary means of communication for infantry (less tanks) and artillery, including antiaircraft artillery.

Radio is the most important alternate means of communication for infantry and artillery and may become their primary means when wire lines fail; for example, in forward areas when lines have been shot out, in rapid advances or retreats when time does not permit the establishment of maintenance of wire lines.

Radio, as a secondary means of communication, is necessary for intercommunication between infantry and artillery.

---

[60] Gylden-81, pp. 56 and 57.

Radio communication is essential to the operations of cavalry (horse), as a secondary means of communication between the larger headquarters and to the rear when the rate of movement is not so great as to preclude the establishment of wire lines, or when the distance over which communication is to be carried on is not in excess of the transmission ranges of telephone or telegraph. If either of the two conditions mentioned exist, radio becomes the primary means of communication. Radio is the primary means of communication for small cavalry units over distances too great to be covered by mounted messengers.

Radio must be relied upon as the primary means of signal communication for fast-moving tanks and mechanized cavalry. Slow-moving tanks operating close to supporting infantry may be able to use visual and messengers, but radio is at least as important and probably should be considered a primary means of communication even for slow tanks. Wire can of course be used at the headquarters of tank units for communication to the rear and to adjacent units.

Radio is the primary means of communication for all classes of aviation. It must be relied upon exclusively for contact between planes in the air and between planes in the air and ground stations when the latter are separated beyond visual distance. It is the only means of communication between "spotting" planes and artillery.

Radio is desirable as an alternate means of communication for reporting the approach of hostile aviation to antiaircraft artillery and friendly aviation.

Radio messages can be read by the enemy after interception and therefore should always be cryptographed except when the information which they contain can not be made use of by the enemy. Using personnel must be well trained and radio discipline must be enforced.

Radio transmitting stations give away information of the unit to which they belong. Therefore silence must be observed frequently, and at times radio camouflage must be resorted to.

Radio goniometric and intercept stations must be maintained in order to secure information from the enemy and to supervise the operation of our own radio.

Radio stations are vulnerable to artillery fire, and therefore should have as must cover as possible. A reserve supply of sets should be maintained.

While it is technically possible to "jam" the operation of enemy radio stations, it is unwise to do so because it is a costly operation of limited value, it denies the use of our own radio, and closes the door to valuable information to be obtained from enemy radio stations.

The development of ultra-high-frequency radio sets promises to fill a need in front-line units because of their short range and light weight. Hostile intercept stations would have to be located well forward in order to intercept their traffic.

The radio activities on a particular front must be controlled by a central authority in order to eliminate interference and insure smooth operation.

Priorities for the use of radio by units of a command must be established in each situation.

APPLICATION OF CONCLUSIONS TO A CONCRETE PROBLEM

A highly important phase of this study consisted of making the actual assignment of frequencies for the nets of a field army in a particular tactical situation. Although essential to this study, the details of the tactical situation and detailed assignments of frequencies would be of little interest to the readers of this article. Therefore only a brief summary of the problem will be given together with the methods used in its solution and the final conclusions reached.

The problem selected was that of a field army in attack. The field army comprised the following units: Army headquarters and army troops, three army corps of two divisions each, one army corps of three divisions, one division in army reserve, and two cavalry divisions. The following troops were attached to the army: Ten regiments of field artillery; one regiment of mechanized cavalry; one brigade (3 regiments) of antiaircraft artillery; two observation squadrons (separate); six balloon squadrons; an air force wing consisting of a wing headquarters, one fighter group, one attack group, one bombardment group, one pursuit group, and one observation squadron (separate); three chemical regiments; two regiments of medium fast tanks; one regiment of light slow tanks; and one regiment of light fast tanks.

One cavalry division was on each flank. The mechanized cavalry regiment and the majority of the tanks operated on the left flank in support of the main attack.

The first step in the assignment of frequencies in the situation was a determination of the number of channels required for the operation of all radio nets provided for the units of this force. It was determined that 378 CW channels and 307 telephone channels, or a total of 685, were necessary.

The area over which the action was to take place was studied with the view of determining maximum distances over which particular sets would have to operate in order to ascertain the channels which could be repeated within the army area without causing mutual interference. As a result of this study it was evident that the only channels which could be repeated were those used by the small infantry and artillery sets having maximum operating ranges of five miles or less.

The duplication of channels thus obtained reduced the number of separate CW channels to 296 and the number of separate voice channels to 275.

In order to obtain a uniform unit with which to work, it was arbitrarily assumed that voice channels would have to be twice the width of CW channels. This then made a total of 846 CW channels, or equivalent, necessary. The width of any channel depends on the location of that channel in the radio spectrum as brought out earlier in this article.

A casual inspection was all that was required to clearly indicate that not all nets could be assigned noninterfering channels. It then became a matter of determining the priority of different units in this situation for the assignment of such channels as could be made available. This priority was determined to be as follows:

1. (a) Air nets for the air force wing.
   (b) Mechanized cavalry.
   (c) Tank units on leading and exploiting missions.
   (d) Air-ground communication between artillery and observation aviation.
   (e) Air-ground communication between the headquarters of army, corps and cavalry divisions; and their observation aviation.
2. (a) Infantry units.
   (b) Divisional artillery.
   (c) Air-ground communication between the headquarters of infantry divisions and their observation aviation.
3. (a) Ground nets for air force units.
   (b) Army antiaircraft intelligence net.
   (c) Communication between corps artillery battalions and their observation posts.
4. All other nets.

Based on the priorities listed above, considering the radio equipment available, and substituting CW channels for voice channels wherever possible, there were assigned 280 CW and 123 voice, noninterfering channels.

In the assignment of channels in any priority, preference was given to those channels required by units making the main attack. Assignments of channels which had to be duplicated were made in order from left to right so that units employing the same operating frequency would be as widely separated in distance as possible. The division in Army reserve had to be considered in this allotment. The channels assigned to it had to be based on its probable employment on the left where the main attack was to be made.

The final assignment of frequencies provided for all the requirements in priorities one and two and some in third priority; no assignments of channels were made in fourth priority, except in a few cases where frequencies which could not be used elsewhere were available. No alternate frequencies were available.

Under field conditions assignment of frequencies would be made in blocks by unit signal officers to subordinate units. However, the unit signal officer must go through some such process as the one here indicated in order to insure the adequacy of channels for essential needs.

FINAL CONCLUSIONS

In addition to the conclusions stated earlier in this article the following have been reached as a result of this study:

(a) The problem of finding a sufficient number of noninterfering channels for use in a field army, employing the radio equipment available, is difficult.

(b) Only those types of services requiring radio communication on high priority can be accommodated.

(c) Priorities must be set up for a given tactical situation by the highest authority in a theater of operations, and close central supervision must be maintained.

(d) The minimum assignment of channels should be made for those classes of service in which radio is a secondary means of communication, and the use of radio for such services should be limited to times when primary means fail. This will provide the essential channels for those services having primary need for radio.

(e) Channel assignments should be kept flexible by all signal officers so that frequencies may be "borrowed" during certain periods from units which are out of action at the time.

(f) In the course of this study one is impressed with the large number of radio nets authorized for a field army. When it is remembered that each net contains from 3 to 18 sets, the large number of sets becomes evident. These sets are comparatively delicate instruments and one may fail or be put out of action just when it is most needed. For this reason spare sets should be carried by all units having a high priority need for radio. Also it is frequently necessary to organize special detachments in the division and higher units which should be provided with sets from this reserve.

(g) The efficient operation of a radio goneometric and intercept service is essential for the purposes of securing enemy information and of insuring the satisfactory operation of our own radio communication service.

RECOMMENDATIONS

(a) That all effort be directed toward the provision of adequate radio communication: First, to units or services dependent upon it as a primary means of signal communication, and second, to those units and services which must rely upon it as a primary means in case their normal primary means should fail. This effort should be coordinated from the viewpoints of design and development, supply, operation, and training.

(b) That radio communication be used only when other means are nonexistent or inadequate.

(c) That a definite policy be maintained which will provide for the control of all frequencies in use in a theater of operations by highest unit operating in that theater.

(d) That this study be continued to develop the condition presented by the simultaneous operation of at least four field armies in a given theater of operations. Also to determine the classes of commercial radio which operate during peacetime in the bands designated for army use, and formulate a plan of coordination to be put into effect in time of war. The requirements of naval radio should also be considered.

SOLUTION OF A PLAYFAIR CIPHER [1] *

By Private ALF MONGE, *Ninth Signal Service Company*

The Playfair cipher, for many years used by the British Army, and by the United States Army to a limited extent during the World War, was long thought to be proof against analysis, but does now no longer present such a difficult problem.

All publications on the solution of Playfair ciphers, that have come to the attention of the writer, have been confined to an analysis based on the frequency method; a method which cannot be applied if the message under consideration is too short to show any amount or repetitions.

Inasmuch as the following cryptogram—given as a challenge message by Sir George Aston, Major General, British Naval Intelligence, in his book "Secret Service", consists of only 30 letters and shows no repeated digraphs, the writer fancied that, perhaps, an analysis of this short message may be of interest to the readers of the Bulletin.

The cryptogram:

BUFDA   GNPOX   IHOQY   TKVQM   PMBYD   AAEQZ

Since it is known that this cryptogram is a Playfair, we may proceed immediately to break up the message into digraphs, as follows:

BU	FD	AG	NP	OX	IH	OQ	YT	KV	QM	PM	BY	DA	AE	QZ
1	2	3	4	5	6	7	8	9	10	11	12	13	14	15

---

[1] For the readers, who are not familiar with the structure of a Playfair cipher, a short explanation has been added to the end of this article.

*(No. 93, November December, 1936)

As there are no repeated digraphs in this extremely short message, the usual method of solution based on frequency, is, as mentioned above, obviously out of the question, and our only hope lies in an attempt to reconstruct the keyword, from a study of digraphic combinations in the message.

A short study of the cipher text will bring the digraphs OQ (7) and QM (10) to notice, because of the proximity of these letters in a normal standard alphabet. The high-frequency digraphs NO, ON, and OU show a similar proximity in a normal standard alphabet, and if we could assume the cipher groups OQ and QM to represent the plaintext digraphs ON and OU, respectively, a definite beginning would have been made. This assumption, if true, would place the letters P, R, S, and T in the keyword, which is quite probable.

Our partially reconstructed cipher square would then appear as follows:

1	2	3	4	5
6	7	8	9	10
11	12	13	14	15
M	N	O	Q	U
V	W	X	Y	Z

Substituting possible plain-text equivalents in the cipher, we have:

Group....	1	2	3	4	5	6	7	8	9	10	11	12	13	14	15
Text......	BU	FD	AG	NP	OX	IH	OQ	YT	KV	QM	PM	BY	DA	AE	QZ
Plain......					-O		NO			OU					UY

If we further list under each cipher letter all the plain-text equivalents possible, we have the following:

Group....	1	2	3	4	5	6	7	8	9	10	11	12	13	14	15
Text......	BU	FD	AG	NP	OX	IH	OQ	YT	KV	QM	PM	BY	DA	AE	QZ
Plain......	....	---	---	...	-O	...	NO	....	....	OU	....	....	....	....	UY
	M		M					V	W		N	Q			
	N		O					W	X		O	V			
	O		Q					X	Y		Q	W			
	Q		U					Z	Z		U	X			
								Q	M			Z			

When studying groups 7, 8, 9, and 10 it becomes apparent that Y (8) might easily represent W_p and that V (9) equals Y_p, thus producing the words NOW and YOU. This encourages us to continue our line of reasoning and we may place the letter T in the same vertical line with W and the letter K in the column with Y. In other words, the letter T must be placed in one of the squares numbered 2, 7, or 12, respectively, and the letter K in square 4, 9, or 14. If we further assume that K does not appear in the keyword, it could then be placed in square 14 only, and we can also place L in square 15. Thus:

1	(T)	3	4	5
6	(T)	8	9	10
11	(T)	13	K	L
M	N	O	Q	U
V	W	X	Y	Z

This seems promising and again we substitute our new values in the cryptogram:

Group....	1	2	3	4	5	6	7	8	9	10	11	12	13	14	15
Text.......	BU	FD	AG	NP	OX	IH	OQ	YT	KV	QM	PM	BY	DA	AE	QZ
Group........	....	....	....	....	-0	....	NO	W-	-Y	OU	....	....	....	....	UY
				M			M					N	Q			
				N			O					O	V			
				O			Q					Q	W			
				Q			U					U	X			
				L			T						Z			

At this point it seemed best to attack the cipher letters T (8) and K (9).

It is evident that the plain-text letter represented by K (9) is to be placed in square 11 and the plain-text letter represented by T (8) in either square 4 or 9.

If T is to be put in square 12, the keyword would be at least 12 letters in length and would have to be composed of the letters A, B, C, D, E, F, G, IJ, P, R, S, and T. This is extremely unlikely, as we have 10 consonants and only 3 vowels. It is, therefore, safe to place T in either square 2 or 7, and we may proceed to study the possible cipher letters that may represent K_p.

On the assumption that the keyword is less than 11 letters in length, 3 of the following letters must of necessity belong in squares 11, 12, and 13:

A, B, C, D, E, F, G, H, IJ.

Of these nine letters H or IJ cannot possibly be put in square 11, because they would have to precede K in squares 12 and 13, if they are not part of the keyword.

Let us then place each of the remaining seven letters, one at a time, in square 11 to determine which of them would be most suitable.

A is unlikely as K (9) would then be A_p and the final letter of a two-letter word. B, C, D, and E, after several trials, are also discarded and F considered. The letter F in square 11 suggests the two-letter word IF for T (8) and K (9), and the phrase NOW IF YOU. If this may be assumed to be correct, we can place F, G, and H in squares 11, 12, and 13, respectively, and the letter IJ in either square 4 or 9. Thus:

1	(T)	3	(I)	5
6	(T)	8	(I)	10
F	G	H	K	L
M	N	O	Q	U
V	W	X	Y	Z

And again we substitute:

Group.........	1	2	3	4	5	6	7	8	9	10	11	12	13	14	15
Text...........	BU	FD	AG	NP	OX	IH	OQ	YT	KV	QM	PM	BY	DA	AE	QZ
Plain.............	....	....	....	HO	-K	NO	WI	FY	OU	....	....	....	....	UY	

138

We see that what we thought was the word NOW is really the word KNOW.

As stated above, the letters IJ, P, R, S, and T have been supposed to be part of the keyword. It is not at all likely that only one vowel should occur among four consonants and we are forced to consider the remaining two vowels, A and E, either or both of them may form part of the keyword. We, therefore, remove them from our sequence A, B, C, D, E, and we are enabled to place the remaining three letters, namely B, C, and D, in squares 8, 9, and 10, respectively; putting IJ definitely into square 4, so that we now have the following square table:

I	(T)	3	I	5
6	(T)	B	C	D
F	G	H	K	L
M	N	O	Q	U
V	W	X	Y	Z

Substituting in our cryptogram, we get:

Group	1	2	3	4	5	6	7	8	9	10	11	12	13	14	15
Text	BU	FD	AG	NP	OX	IH	OQ	YT	KV	QM	PM	BY	DA	AE	QZ
Plain	DO	L-	....	....	HO	-K	NO	WI	FY	OU	....	CX	....	....	UY

In group 12 we notice CX$_p$. This digraph is impossible in the English language and we suspect a doublet separated by the letter X. This gives rise to the assumption that DA (13) is C$_p$, and places A with fair certainty in square 7. Since AB rarely terminates a word in English, we have found all the letters contained in the keyword (E, IJ, P, R, S, T) and limited T to square 2. Thus:

I	T	3	I	5
6	A	B	C	D
F	G	H	K	L
M	N	O	Q	U
V	W	X	Y	Z

(At this point the writer was able to anagram the letters of the keyword and had no trouble in assembling them in their correct order, but the analysis will be carried a little further.)

The letters E, P, R, and S remain to be placed in their proper squares; let us, therefore, take each of them in turn and place them in the remaining open squares 1, 3, 5, and 6, and place all possible combinations in our cryptogram as shown:

Group	1	2	3	4	5	6	7	8	9	10	11	12	13	14	15
Text	BU	FD	AG	NP	OX	IH	OQ	YT	KV	QM	PM	BY	DA	AE	QZ
Plain	DO	L...	TA	....	HO	...K	NO	WI	FY	OU	....	CX	C...	....	UY
		LP			MA		PK						CP		
		LR			MT		RK						CR		
		LS			OT		SK						CS		
		LE			UT		EK						CE		

Since groups 11 and 14 give too many combinations, we will disregard them for the moment.

FD (2) becomes LE_p, which is fairly obvious and places E in square 6, making groups 1, 2, and 3, DO, LE, TA, and groups 12, 13, and 14, CX, CE, ED. The latter suggests the word "succeed" which would place S in square 1 and P in square 5, and the only remaining letter, R, in square 3.

The cipher square and cryptogram are, then, as shown below:

```
S   T   R   I   P
E   A   B   C   D
F   G   H   K   L
M   N   O   Q   U
V   W   X   Y   Z
```

```
BU  FD  AG  NP  OX  IH  OQ  YT  KV  QM  PM  BY  DA  AE  QZ
DO  LE  TA  UT  HO  RK  NO  WI  FY  OU  SU  CX  CE  ED  UY
```

"Do let author know if you succeed."

Preparation and use of a Playfair square.—A large square, sub-divided into 25 smaller squares is laid out and the selected keyword, for example, COLUMNAR, is inscribed in the first 8 squares (the keyword consisting of 8 letters), followed by the remaining letters of the alphabet. As there are only 25 squares to be filled, I and J are always put together in one of them. The filled square will then present the following appearance:

```
C   O   L   U   M
N   A   R   B   D
E   F   G   H   IJ
K   P   Q   S   T
V   W   X   Y   Z
```

The plaintext is broken up into pairs of letters, called digraphs. If two like letters, a doublet, occur as one pair, such as EE, DD, FF, etc., an infrequent letter is used to separate them; thus: WALL-BOARDS will be paired WA LX LB OA RD SX. If at the end of the message, an odd letter is left to be enciphered, add the same low-frequency letter to make it a pair, as shown in the example above.

To encipher—

Letters on the same horizontal line.—When two plaintext letters occur on the same horizontal line, each letter is represented by the one immediately to the right of it and the last letter in the line by the one on the extreme left. For example: $ND_p = AN_c$.

Letters in the same vertical column.—The plaintext letters in the same vertical column are represented by the letter immediately below it, and the bottom letter by the letter on the top of the column. For example: $BY_p = HU_c$.

Letters in opposite corners of a rectangle.—Each letter is represented by the letter in the opposite corner of the rectangle and on the same horizontal line with it. For example: $TH_p = SI_c$.

```
Example—Plaintext:  NA    VY    BL    EN    DX
        Ciphertext: AR    WZ    RU    KE    RZ
```

CIPHER BUSTING IN THE SEVENTH CORPS AREA A. A. R. S.*

By Col. STANLEY L. JAMES, *Signal Corps, Signal Officer*

To the more mature members of the Army amateur radio system, the most interesting feature of their training by the Signal Corps is the decipherment of cryptograms, the key word and length of key word for which is unknown except to the originator of the cryptogram.

Prior to the A. A. R. S. operating season of 1936–37, all of these unknown key cryptograms originated in the office of the Chief Signal Officer, and the custom has been to transmit one of these cipher messages on the first Monday of each month. Members were instructed to reply to these messages in the same key with which the original was enciphered. Credit for solution is given by the Chief Signal Officer in his monthly publication P. D. C., by listing therein the amateur station calls, by corps areas, of all who solved each message.

The general impression among members of the Seventh Corps Area system seemed to be that the solution of these cryptograms was too difficult, and therefore, up to September 1936 too little activity was shown. In order to correct this situation, the signal officer, Seventh Corps Area, published monthly in Army Amateur Time, an article on cryptanalysis, confining these articles, for the most part, to the solution of cryptograms enciphered by means of the old Signal Corps Cipher Disk, now known as the Army Amateur Cipher, and designated ARMAC.

*(No. 97, July–September, 1937)

140

In addition to these monthly articles, a Cipher Buster's Certificate was designed, and awarded to each member who solved five unknown key cryptograms during the year 1936–37. The stimulating effect of these certificates, although most gratifying, was anticipated, because if there is anything coveted by a radio amateur, it is a certificate of some kind which he can frame and hang on the wall of his "shack."

In addition to our own efforts, we have been greatly assisted by the office of the Chief Signal Officer during the current season, by the introduction to Army amateurs of single transposition cryptograms, thus breaking the monotony of the old ARMAC substitution cipher.[1] At first the change to transposition was received with considerable consternation, because the Army amateurs had had no instruction in anything but substitution; but as first one member and then another succeeded in solving a transposition cipher, and the solution method was discussed and explained among the members, interest and activity in the whole subject of cryptanalysis became greater than ever before. In order to facilitate the reward for this increased interest, we have increased the available number of unknown key cryptograms by augmenting those transmitted by the Chief Signal Officer monthly by originating one or two each month at Corps area headquarters, thus increasing each member's opportunity to earn a Cipher Buster's Certificate during the operating season. We are now doing a thriving business in certificates, which is another way of saying that the Seventh Corps Area has an ever increasingly large number of cipher busters.

ANALYSIS VERSUS THE PROBABLE WORD *

By HOWELL C. BROWN, WLVS/W6BPU, Pasadena, Calif., *Cryptographer Ninth Corps Area, Army Amateur Radio System*

Some cryptanalysists swear by the "probable" word method and others by the analytical one. In all probability the middle ground is the quickest and safest in the long run. Some cipher busters seem to have the faculty of "guessing" a word that will be found in the text. If they guess right it is the shortest way to find both the period and the key word but, if they are mistaken, they have lost a lot of valuable time and must go back and try others or fall back on analysis. Some of the members have found this out in my Camra in the December Corps Area Bulletin and, after having spent days with probable words, have had to go to analysis and then broken it in a short time.

---

[1] Monoalphabetic substitution with reversed alphabet generally known as the Beaufort system.

*(No. 97, July–September, 1937)

In a very short message about the only possible way is to try for the probable word because we do not have enough letters to make a frequency count of much value. When we have a message of about 50 letters it becomes quite burdensome to try sliding the suspected word along, step by step, and the purpose of this article is to explain an easy and fairly rapid method of doing the same thing. It was originated by a famous French cryptographer, Commandant Bazeries, but has been modified and put in its present form by a member of the American Cryptogram Association who writes under the nom de plume of "Efsee."

We have the following message:

YGFAT   NZAQS   CAAAX   QSGGO   EZAGP   RYAXX

It shows no decided period and is so short that a frequency count even if we could find a possible period, would give us little or no information. Our only recourse is to try for a probable word. Both the message and its solution are based on the cipher known as the Beaufort system which makes use of reversed alphabets, and which was once used by the United States Army. However, by making use of a St. Cyr slide or tableau, it may be used the same way on any cipher of the Vigenère type.

Let's suppose we hope to find the word "bearer." Write the message horizontally and, at the left, the suspected word:

YGFAT   NZAQS   CAAAX   QSGGO   EZAGP   RYAXX

```
B
E
A
R
E
R
```

Our next step is to take B, the first letter of the suspected word and using it as the first letter of the plain text, find what each letter of the cipher text will give as key letter. Next, starting with the second letter of our message, we do the same thing with E. Start with the third letter of the message and do the same thing with A. Continue this until you have used all the letters of the probable word and you will have a work sheet that looks like this:

```
     YGFAT   NZAQS   CAAAX   QSGGO   EZAGP   RYAXX
B    ZHGBV   OABRT   DBBBY   RTHHP   FABHQ   SZBYY
E    KJEX    RDEUW   GEEEB   UWKKS   IDEKT   VCEAA
A    FAT     NZAQS   CAAAX   QSGGO   EZAGP   RYAXX
R    RK      EQRHJ   TRRRS   HJXXF   VQRXG   IPROO
E    X       RDEUW   GEEEB   UWKKS   IDEKT   VCEAA
R            EQRHJ   TRRRS   HJXXF   VQRXG   IPROO
```

It looks as if it took quite a while and does not appear very promising but let's see. We only had to make the decryptment of four lines, BEAR, because the other letters in the trial word were repeated and it was only necessary to copy from the lines already completed.

It is natural that under each A we will find the trial word because with A as message letter the trial word letters remain unchanged. However. in this method. we are not interested in the vertical or horizontal lines but the diagonals. Start with Z in the first or B line and follow the diagonal. It makes no sense. Keep on with the others in order and, starting with the second B in our line the diagonal reads BUSTER. This must be our key word or a part of it anyway. Our next step will be to try it as a key-word and see if we can decipher the cryptogram. Counting from the first letter of the message to the place where the key word starts, we find seven letters, which shows that the period is probably seven and we still lack one letter. We will write our cipher text in seven columns; placing what we have of the key-word over them:

```
B U S T E R —
Y G F A T N Z

A Q S C A A A

X Q S G G O E

Z A G P R Y A
```

The fact that the letters Q, S, and A repeat in columns 1, 2, and 7 would make it appear that we have selected the correct period. Next take the cipher disk or sheet and decipher. This gives us:

```
B U S T E R —
Y G F A T N Z
d o n t l e
A Q S C A A A
b e a r e r
X Q S G G O E
e e a n y d
Z A G P R Y A
c u m e n t
```

It is easy to see that the first line should read: "Don't let", which furnishes another plain letter and, with Z as cipher letter and T as the plain letter, reference to your disk or sheet shows the missing key letter to be "S." The message reads: DONT LET BEARER SEE ANY DOCUMENTS.

If the trial word had been a short one such as THE, we would only find fragments of the key (If that word had been in the message). Unless BEARER had been in the message you would have had a hard time guessing any other probable word and might have continued for a long time before you tried DONT, LET, ANY, DOCUMENTS. I call your attention to this fact to show just how hard it is to guess the probable word. During war a cryptanalyst may be almost certain that the message will have such words as, CORPS, GENERAL, REGIMENT, ATTACK, etc., but a message in civil life, when we know nothing of its origin or about the sender, may resist breaking down for a long time especially if it is very short. If we have several messages enciphered with the same key, it is rather easy to break them down no matter how short they may be but do not be disappointed if a short message resists your efforts entirely. That has happened to the most famous cryptanalysts.

Now let's go back to our message again and repeat a few things. Be sure and do not use the letters of the probable word as key. They are suspected plain-text letters and, instead of sliding the word along through the whole text step by step, we just take each letter and slide it under the message. It will always be the key that shows up when working with the Beaufort cipher.

When looking over these diagonals it is extremely easy to miss a key fragment so keep a close lookout and, if the key does not appear, try any fragments that look as if they might be parts of English words. It might happen that your probable word was not in the message but some of the letters in that word might be there. To illustrate, if we had tried THERE on the above cryptogram, the RE of BEARER would have produced TE of the key. Even with such a small fragment as TE, it might be possible, using it as key and then working on the plain text fragments that appear, to reconstruct the entire key word.

EDGAR ALLEN POE, CRYPTOGRAPHER*

By Lt. Col. WILLIAM F. FRIEDMAN, *Signal Reserve*

It is a curious fact that popular interest in this country in the subject of cryptography received its first stimulus from Edgar Allan Poe. Should a psychologic association test be made, the word "cipher" would doubtless bring from most laymen the immediate response, "Poe" or "The Gold Bug." The fame of Poe rests not a

*EDITOR'S NOTE.—Reprinted, by special permission, from American Literature, vol. VIII, no. 3, November 1936. In the next issue the author will present additional data in amplification of some of the statements contained in the original article, together with the actual cryptograms discussed herein.

*(No. 97, July–September, 1937)

little on his activities with cipher, and much of the esteem in which
this American genius is held today rests in part on the legend of
"Poe the cryptographer."

Several years ago, in an extremely interesting and penetrating
analysis, Joseph Wood Krutch discussed Poe's activities in cryptography, saying:

> Doubtless nothing contributed to a greater extent than did Poe's connection
> with cryptography to the growth of the legend which pictured him as a man at
> once below and above ordinary human nature; but the whole subject is still
> unfortunately wrapped in some obscurity, and it is impossible to be sure
> of the facts as distinguished from his own report of them.[1]

The popular conception of, and the reaction toward, the subject
of cryptography in Poe's time—and to a certain extent today—are
the remnants of a medieval point of view, which regarded it in
somewhat the following light: A cryptogram is a piece of writing to
which a meaning exists but is not immediately perceptible; its
intelligibility is concealed, hence mysterious or occult, and thus supernatural. Therefore anyone practicing the art is of necessity the asso-
ciate of forces governing supernatural phenomena. The mental por-
trait the average layman has even today of the professional cryptographer is that of a long-haired, thick-bespectacled recluse; a cross
between a venerable savant and a necromancer who must perforce
commune daily with dark spirits in order to accomplish his feats of
mental jiu-jitsu.

This impression was doubtless prevalent in Poe's time because authentic information concerning cryptography was extremely limited
and is even today quite meager. One of the interesting anomalies
in the whole field of cryptology is the paucity of sound literature on
the subject. In the most extensive bibliography in print,[2] the number of treatises of real technical merit does not exceed a dozen. Such
a pitiful showing for an art that has been practiced from time im-
memorial cannot be ascribed to a lack of interest in the subject on the
part of the general public, or to a lack of usefulness as a branch of
knowledge. On the contrary, cryptography is employed to a great
degree every day in all countries, in diplomatic, military, naval, busi-

---

[1] Edgar Allan Poe: A Study in Genius (New York, 1926), p. 103. More recently,
Prof. Killis Campbell (in The Mind of Poe and Other Studies Cambridge, Mass., 1933)
says: "What, finally, of the fiber of Poe's mind, of his natural endowments, and of his
intellectual integrity? No one, so far as I know, has ever denied to Poe the possession
of a peculiarly acute and active mind. * * * That he had extraordinary powers of
analysis comes out everywhere—in his critical reviews, in his studies in sensation, in his
ratiocinative and pseudo-scientific stories, in his solving of ciphers and cryptographs"
(pp. 28–29). "Question has likewise been raised in some quarters as to Poe's honesty
and his intellectual integrity. * * * But an even more serious indictment has been
brought against him, to the effect that he at times made a display of learning or affected
an erudition to which he had no claim" (pp. 30–31).

[2] André Lange and E.-A. Soudart. Traité de Cryptographie (Paris: Librairie Félix
Alcan, 1925). The number of items in this list is approximately 100.

146

ness, and social affairs; and as a pastime, it presents many of the elements that constitute the *raison d'être* of the best types of puzzles. Even those who have never delved into it agree that the subject intrigues and tantalizes them. Yet information concerning methods of preparing cryptograms of sound merit is very meager, and that concerning methods of solving them is abysmally lacking to all except a very small circle of professional cryptographers who remain in office only so long as they violate no governmental secrets connected with their work.

It is not strange, then, that in a field wherein popular interest is great but popular knowledge extremely limited many spurious ideas should be current. This state of affairs existed in Poe's day, and consciously or subconsciously Poe saw an opportunity to exploit it for his own purposes. To exhibit deep understanding and thorough knowledge where the stock of knowledge on the part of others is practically nil, would seem to be a pardonable source of gratification to a perfectly normal person; what could be more soothing and reassuring to the victim—according to Krutch's view—of a rather well-developed inferiority complex?

Poe's known cryptographical writings include the article "A Few Words on Secret Writing" which appeared in the July 1841 issue of Graham's Magazine; three supplementary articles appearing in the August, October, and December issues of the same magazine; his tale The Gold Bug; and, if it may be included under the heading of cryptographical writings, a recently discovered letter written to a Mr. Richard Bolton, of Pontotoc, Miss. In none of them can the serious student of the subject find any evidence that Poe was more than a tyro either in the art of cryptography or in its handmaid, the science of cryptographic analysis. Long before his day, men who had made a study of these matters were far more proficient, and their names are all but forgotten.

One of the references that Poe made to cryptography occurs in connection with a review of a book entitled Sketches of Conspicuous Living Characters of France, which appeared in the April 1841 issue of Graham's Magazine. It is as follows:

In the notice of Berryer it is said that, a letter being addressed to the Duchess of Berry to the legitimists of Paris, to inform them of her arrival, it was accompanied by a long note in cipher, the key of which she had forgotten to give. "The penetrating mind of Berryer", says our biographer, "soon discovered it. It was this phrase substitute for the 24 letter of the alphabet—*Le gouvernement provisoire!*"

All this is very well as an anecdote; but we cannot understand the extraordinary penetration required in the matter. The phrase *Le gouvernement provisoire* is French, and the note in cipher was addressed to Frenchmen. The difficulty of deciphering may well be supposed much greater had the key been in a foreign tongue; yet any one who will take the trouble may address us a note, in the same manner as here proposed, and the key-phrase may be in either French, Italian, Spanish, German, Latin, or Greek (or in any of the dialects of these languages), and we pledge ourselves for the solution of the riddle. The experiment may afford our readers some amusement—let them try it.[3]

The way in which Poe puts the matter reminds one very much of the manner in which a conjurer, performing a mystifying trick, extremely simple in itself, surrounds its execution with a great deal of unnecessary stage business to make it appear more complicated and difficult than it really is. A casual inspection of the type of alphabet said to have been employed by the lady of forgetful memory will quickly convince even a novice that the arrangement of letters in the cipher alphabet has absolutely nothing to do with the case. The solution is entirely independent of the arrangement of letters and, of course, Poe knew it. He admits this, in fact, in his essay which he published 3 months later. We might be very much inclined to overlook this particular bit of hokum were it not for the fact that this incident led directly to his writing the essay which appeared in the July number of Graham's.

In the course of this essay Poe repeats, almost verbatum, the remarks made in the April number in connection with the Berryer cryptogram and adds that "this challenge has elicited but a single response, which is embraced in the following letter." He then gives the letter, which encloses two cryptograms composed by means of cipher alphabets of the nature indicated above. Poe solves them, gives the solutions, and says:

In the solution of the first of these ciphers we had little more than ordinary trouble. The second proved to be exceedingly difficult, and it was only by calling every faculty into play that we could read it at all.[4]

Anyone who will take the trouble to go into the matter carefully will, I am sure, be entirely at a loss to account for the difficulty Poe experienced with regard to the second example. The reader will have to take my word for it, of course, but I say that any person who, having devoted but 2 weeks' study to elementary crypto-grams, cannot solve that particular cryptogram in 2 hours at the most, had better turn his attention to other pursuits wherein success will crown his efforts with less expenditure of energy. As a matter of fact the experiment was recently tried upon four persons who had just completed exactly 10 days' study of cryptography. They worked independently, and each accomplished the solution in approximately 35 minutes.

---

[3] J. A. Harrison (ed.), The Complete Works of Edgar Allan Poe (Virginia Edition) [New York, 1902], X, 135–136. Hereafter cited as "Works."
[4] Ibid., XIV, 126.

Over half of "A Few Words on Secret Writing" is devoted to the Berryer form of cryptogram, a type which, despite its utter simplicity, is so impractical that it is employed only by novices, and then only seldom. The actual Berryer cryptogram must, indeed, be considered the concoction of amateurs or of persons whose knowledge of cryptography was extremely limited, for, so far as history records, no such impractical system was ever regularly employed for serious purposes. It is true that Poe comments upon its impracticability, but as to the complexity of the type it is apparent that he thought highly of it.

In this same essay Poe refers to other writings on the subject of cryptography, which, he says, appeared "in one of the weekly papers of this city [Philadelphia]." This paper has been identified as Alexander's Weekly Messenger.[5]

In the discussion of an analogous subject, in one of the weekly papers of this city, about 18 months ago, the writer of this article had occasion to speak of the application of a rigorous method in all forms of thought—of its advantages—of the extension of its use even to what is considered the operation of pure fancy—and thus, subsequently, of the solution of cipher. He even ventured to assert that no cipher, of the character above specified, could be sent to the address of the paper, which he would not be able to resolve. This challenge excited, most unexpectedly, a very lively interest among the numerous readers of the journal. Letters were poured in upon the editor from all parts of the country; and many of the writers of these epistles were so convinced of the impenetrability of their mysteries, as to be at great pains to draw him into wagers on the subject. At the same time, they were not always scrupulous about sticking to the point. The cryptographs were, in numerous instances, altogether beyond the limits defined in the beginning. Foreign languages were employed. Words and sentences were run together without interval. Several alphabets were used in the same cipher. One gentleman, but moderately endowed with conscientiousness, inditing us a puzzle composed of pot-hooks and hangers to which the wildest typography of the office could afford nothing similar, went even so far as to jumble together no less than seven distinct alphabets, without intervals between the letters, or between the lines. Many of the crytographs were dated in Philadelphia, and several of those which urged the subject of a bet were written by gentlemen of this city. Out of perhaps 100 ciphers altogether received, there was only one which we did not immediately succeed in resolving. This one we demonstrated to be an imposition—that is to say, we fully proved it a jargon of random characters, having no meaning whatever. In respect to the epistle of the seven alphabets, we had the pleasure of completely nonplusing its inditer by a prompt and satisfactory translation.

Unfortunately the records that remain of Alexander's Weekly Messenger are exceedingly fragmentary. Despite painstaking research by numerous Poe experts, not a single issue containing any cipher solutions that Poe may have published as a result of his asserted challenge has ever been found, and there seems to be no

---

[5] Krutch, op cit., p. 104.

149

way at the present moment of corroborating Poe's statements.[6] However, we may consider, from Poe's own words, that the cryptogram employing "no less than seven distinct alphabets" represented the most difficult of all those submitted to Poe, and therefore warrants special scrutiny.

Ciphers involving a plurality of different alphabets have been known in the art for a long time. The principle is very clearly described in the oldest tract on cryptography that the world now possesses, that written by Alberti.[7] Multiple alphabet ciphers vary in complexity to a much greater extent than do single alphabet cryptograms, and it is possible to employ in one dispatch a practically unlimited number of distinctly different alphabets. In general it may be said that the greater the number involved, the more difficult becomes the analysis, but the particular manner in which the separate alphabets are employed is an equally important factor in solution. It is very unfortunate that Poe's statements with respect to the seven-alphabet example he solved tell us nothing about the latter factor. Internal evidence contained in his article, especially in his supplementary remarks with reference to a system known as the *chiffre quarré*, indicates that the seven alphabets were employed in one of the simplest possible ways, probably in rotation according to sentence lengths. If such were indeed the case the problem merely resolved itself into the solution of seven separate examples, each of the single alphabet type. But granting that the seven alphabets were used in one of the more intricate ways—let us assume that they were employed in a cyclic manner, changing with successive

---

[6] The following is quoted from Krutch, op. cit.: "Now the first of these articles [in Alexander's Weekly Messenger] was never found by any of the editors of Poe's works and has never been reprinted; but though no complete file of the periodical in question is known to exist some numbers are extant and in one of them is an article on enigmas which does challenge the reader to submit an example of secret writing in which an arbitrary symbol is substituted for each letter of the alphabet. It is not, however, possible to check up on Poe's later statement that in response to this challenge 'Letters were poured in upon the editor from all parts of the country' and were in every case successfully read in spite of the fact that many violated the conditions imposed and one employed seven distinct alphabets in the course of a single communication. Indeed, the fact that Alexander's Weekly Messenger, the paper in question, was exceedingly obscure and very short-lived, coupled with the fact that the second and similar challenge in the very prominent Graham's Magazine certainly brought much less response, makes legitimate a suspicion that Poe's statement embodies a considerable exaggeration" (pp. 103–104). "Just how much of this mysterious power was real and how much pretense it is impossible, as we have said, to determine, and it is extremely unfortunate that the results, if any, of the article in Alexander's Weekly Messenger cannot be traced. It is unfortunate also that the only explanation of his method which he gives, that contained in The Gold Bug, applies only to the simplest sort of cryptogram, and that he nowhere discusses the method employed in solving the more complicated ones" (p. 106).

[7] Leo Baptista Alberti, Trattati in cifra. Vat. Arch., Series Varia Politica, vol. LXXX, folios 173–181. (In the bibliography referred to in footnote 2, this treatise is dated 1480, but I can find no warrant for this. The acknowledged historical authority, Dr. Aloys Meister, in Die Geheimschrift im Dienste der Päpstlichen Kurie (Paderborn, 1906), who prints the Latin treatise in question, assigns no date to the manuscript, stating merely that Alberti died in 1472.)

150

letters of the text—the solution of such a problem still represents a relatively simple case. To give Poe the greatest credit possible, however, it might be considered an achievement for an individual who simply plays with cryptography as a hobby.

In the August number of Graham's, Poe published a cryptogram composed by a Dr. Frailey, of Washington, and sent to him by his well-known friend, F. W. Thomas. Poe says that the solution was forwarded to its author by return mail, and offers *"a year's subscription to the magazine, and also a year's subscription to the Saturday Evening Post, to any person, or rather to the first person, who shall read us this riddle."* [8] He goes on to say:

We have no expectation that it will be read; and, therefore, should the month pass without an answer forthcoming, we will furnish the key to the cipher, and again offer a year's subscription to the magazine, to any person who shall solve it *with the key.*

The September number of the magazine is entirely silent on the subject. In the October number, Poe says:

The cipher submitted through Mr. F. W. Thomas, by Dr. Frailey, of Washington, and deciphered by us, also in return of mail, as stated in our August number, has not yet been read by any of our innumerable readers. We now append its solution * * *.

Poe did not abide by the terms of his August agreement, in which he stated that he would furnish the key and again offer a year's subscription to any person who would solve it with the key. Perhaps his exuberance over his achievement had somewhat died down after the August issue. But an examination of the Frailey cipher should show what there is about it that so excited Poe.

It is unnecessary to illustrate the cryptogram here; one need only indicate that it followed very closely the Berryer type, with the sole modification that a few words and the terminations SION and TION were represented not by letters, but by single symbols. For example, £ stood for IN, and the figure 7 for ON; there were 19 such symbols, all instances of this sort. That they were not the representatives of individual letters was obvious from a mere ocular examination. Compared with the use made of the ordinary letters of the alphabet, the symbols were relatively insignificant. In fact, the solution can practically be accomplished without an analysis of these symbols, the meanings of which can then be merely inserted from the context. What then made the cryptogram seem so intricate to Poe? Let us take a look at the "clear text", and the matter may become apparent:

In one of those peripapetic circumrotations I obviated a rustic whom I subjected to catechetical interrogation respecting the nosocomial characteristic of the edifice to which I was approximate. With a volubility uncongealed by

---

[8] Works, XIV, 134. The italics are Poe's.

the frigorific powers of villatic bashfulness, he ejaculated a voluminous replication from the universal tenor of whose contents I deduce the subsequent
amalgamation of heterogeneous facts. Without dubiety incipient pretension
is apt to terminate in final vulgarity, as parturient mountains have been
fabulated to produce muscupular abortions. The institution the subject of my
remarks, has not been without cause the theme of the ephemeral columns of
quotidian journalism, and enthusiastic encomiations in conversational intercourse.[9]

Despite a long experience with the absurd texts that cryptographic
"inventors" are prone to employ, this, I confess, is quite a gem. It
is a curious thing that persons who offer samples of cryptographic
puzzles of their own "invention" almost invariably contrive to produce a monstrosity of diction like the foregoing. Perhaps it tickles
their sense of humor—the unreasonableness of their language seems
never to occur to them.

If Frailey's cipher was difficult, therefore, it became so not because of any inherent complexity in the method employed, but solely
because the diction was so outrageous. But after the preliminary
stages in solution—that is, after a few of the most important values
had been obtained, which certainly should not consume more than
1 or 2 hours at the utmost—the completion of the puzzle was merely
a matter of patience and the use of an unabridged dictionary. Certainly very little use of the analytical faculties so lauded by Poe
was requisite. The Frailey cipher (naturally, without any information) was presented as a simple test to the same four students
referred to before. In 3 hours all had recovered or reconstructed
the phrase upon which the cipher alphabet was based, which was
"But find this out and I give it up."

The terms in which Poe issued his challenge in regard to the
Frailey cipher are startling enough in themselves, but the esteem in
which he really held the cryptogram is shown and, in addition, an
interesting sidelight on his character is revealed by some correspondence which appeared in the November 15, 1925, issue of the Memphis
Commercial Appeal. A Mr. Richard Bolton, of Pontotoc, Miss., on
November 14, 1841, addressed a letter to Poe, taking him to task in
the following terms:

The November number of your valuable magazine has just arrived. To my
great surprise no notice is taken of my solution of the cryptograph proposed
to your readers in the August number. This I can attribute only to accident
or oversight. As you had thrown the gauntlet which I took up, I must call
upon you as a true man and no craven to render me according to the terms
of the defiance the honors of a field worthily contested and fairly won.

A friend lent me for perusal your magazine for that month. On the 9th of
September, within a month after the arrival of the magazine, my solution was
mailed postage paid, addressed to the editor. Accompanying it were certificates
of two subscribers, Messrs. Glokenan and L. C. Draper (the latter assistant

[9] Ibid., XIV, 138–139.

postmaster) that I had effected the solution unaided by the key and that the September number in which the key was exposed had not arrived.

My solution fully agrees with your published solution except in two words about which I will soon take occasion to remark. I therefore claim to have fully complied with the terms of the challenge and to be entitled to all the rights, privileges, and honors therein expressed.

Poe's prompt reply, couched in the most friendly terms, offered a very clear and unquestionable explanation of what appeared to Bolton as an unwillingness to a division of the honors of victory and a participation in the spoils. The explanation, of course, lay in the fact that the forms of any periodical of fair size must go to press long in advance of issue. Poe then continued as follows:

Upon this hint you will easily see the possibility of your letter not having come to hand in season for acknowledgment in the November number. Otherwise I should have had high gratification in sharing with you then the reputation of a bottle conjurer—for thus the matter seems to stand. In our December number (which has been ready for 10 days) you will find an unqualified acknowledgment of your claims—without even allusion to the slight discrepancies for which I believe the printer is chargeable. I mean to say that you have (I believe) solved the cipher as printed. My solution follows the MS.— both are correct.

Allow me, Dear Sir, now to say that I was never more astonished in my life than at your solution. Will you honestly tell me?—did you not owe it to the accident of the repetition of the word "itagi"? for "those"? This repetition does not appear in the MS.—at least, I am pretty sure that it was interpolated by one of our compositors—a "genius" who takes much interest in these matters—and many unauthorized liberties.

In Dr. Frailey's MS. were many errors—the chief of which I corrected for press—but mere blunders do not much affect the difficulty of cypher solution—as you, no doubt, perceive. I had also to encounter the embarrassment of a miserably cramped and confused penmanship. Here you had the advantage of me—a very important advantage.

Be all this as it may—your solution astonished me. You will accuse me of vanity in so saying—but truth is truth. I make no question that it even astonished yourself—and well it might—for from at least 100,000 readers—a great number of whom, to my certain knowledge, busied themselves in the investigation—you and I are the only ones who have succeeded.

It is with some regret that I must place beside this frank acknowledgment an extract from a letter written by Poe to F. W. Thomas, dated November 26, 1841 (for which I am indebted to Dr. T. O. Mabbott). Bolton's letter, Poe declared,

* * * was dated at a period long after the reception of our Magazine in Pontotoc. * * * He pretends not having seen my solution—but his own contains internal evidence of the fact. Three blunders in mine are copied in his own and two or three corrections of Dr. Frailey's original, by myself, are also faithfully repeated. I had the alternative of denying his claim and thus appearing invidious or of sharing with him an honor which in the eyes of the mob at least, is not much above that of a bottle-conjuror. So I chose the last and have put a finale to this business.

If Poe honestly entertained the suspicion which he directed against Bolton, the course which he followed and the complimentary letter he sent to Bolton, redound to his great credit. But I am sorry to say that after a minute investigation of the whole matter, in which no detail was too insignificant to be overlooked, I must declare that Poe had utterly no foundation for his suspicion. Internal evidence in Bolton's solution, which also appears in the newspaper mentioned, as well as all the attendant circumstances, serve to indicate conclusively that his work was accomplished without the key. Nowhere can one find "three blunders in mine which are copied in his own"; and so far as regards the "two or three corrections of Dr. Frailey's original, by myself", are concerned, who can doubt that Bolton did what every cryptographer does constantly—correct errors from the context? And there were errors—many of them in the cipher text as published by Poe, of which the latter was possibly not aware, though he was aware of the errors in the original. Furthermore, it will be noted that Poe did not, in his letter to Bolton, deny having received the latter's solution mailed on September 9. Now if Bolton mailed his solution on the date indicated, even allowing a whole month for its transit, Poe must have received it by October 9. The key to the cryptogram did not appear in the September number, as Bolton inadvertently stated (a slip of the pen which adds weight to his claim), but appeared in the October number, which could not possibly have arrived before September 9. In fact, as the matter stands, one could, in truth, impute to Poe an unwillingness to share the honors with Bolton, but we may accept in good faith the explanation he offered the latter.

Several inaccurate statements by Poe also occur in connection with his very brief description of a well-known cryptographic method often referred to as the *chiffre quarré*. In the December article in Graham's, speaking of the difficulty of composing impenetrable cryptograms, Poe said:

> We may say, in addition, that the nearest approach to perfection in this matter, is the *chiffre quarré* of the French Academy. This consists of a table somewhat in the form of our ordinary multiplication tables, from which the secret to be conveyed is so written that no letter is ever represented twice by the same character. Out of a thousand individuals 999 would at once pronounce this mode inscrutable. It is yet susceptible, under peculiar circumstances, of prompt and certain solution.[10]

In the first place, even in Poe's day to say that the *chiffre quarré* "is the nearest approach to perfection in this matter" was absurd, for almost any example of it could have been solved within an hour or two by anyone who was worthy of being considered an expert

---

[10] Ibid., XIV, 148.

cryptographer. In the second place, the *chiffre quarré*, which Poe attributed to the French Academy, was first illustrated by Vigenère in 1586. Note that I say described, and not invented, for to all intents and purposes the same method, without actually employing the square table of Vigenère, was occasionally used at least as early as 1560 by certain Italian cryptographers in the employ of the papacy. In the third place, to say of the method that it is one in which "no letter is ever represented twice by the same character" is entirely incorrect. Furthermore, Poe's statement relative to the possibility of solving this type of cryptogram leaves room for doubt as to what he meant to convey by the qualifying phrase "under peculiar circumstances"—if he intended to give the impression that the circumstances are unusual, his statement is erroneous.

Another, almost glaring inaccuracy of Poe's is found in connection with a reference made by him to the Francis Bacon cipher. In the August 1841 number of Graham's Magazine, Poe begins with the following words:

> Our remarks on this head [secret writing] in the July number have excited much interest. The subject is unquestionably one of importance, when we regard cryptography as an exercise for the analytical faculties. In this view, men of the finest abilities have given it much of their attention; and the invention of a perfect cipher was a point to which Lord Chancellor Bacon devoted many months—devoted them in vain, for the cryptograph which he thought worthy of a place in his De Augmentis, is one which can be solved.[11]

Again, in the December number in connection with the question of the so called indecipherable cipher, Poe writes:

> Perhaps no good cipher was ever invented which its originator did not conceive insoluble; yet, so far, no impenetrable cryptograph has been discovered. Our correspondent will be the less startled at this, our assertion, when he bears in mind that he who has been termed "the wisest of mankind"—we mean Lord Verulam—was as confident of the absolute insolubility of his own mode as our present cryptographist is of his. What he said upon the subject in his De Augmentis was, at the day of its publication, considered unanswerable. Yet his cipher has been repeatedly unriddled.[12]

It is rather a late day to take up the cudgel for the Lord Chancellor, but to do him justice I will say in the first place that he certainly did not present his mode of secret writing accompanied by any assertion relative to its indecipherability he merely said that he had invented it while a youth in Paris, and that [45 years afterward] he still thought it worthy of preservation. In the second place, the cryptogram he presented as an example was accompanied not only by a full explanation of the system, but also by the key. Poe's remarks lead one, indeed, to believe that he could not himself have examined Bacon's

[11] Ibid., XIV, 133.
[12] Ibid., XIV, 147–148.

cipher in the De Augmentis, but was writing upon the matter merely from hearsay.

In the course of this discussion only casual reference has been made to The Gold Bug. It is fairly certain that Poe identified himself with its principal character Legrand, whose very name is significant. Regarding the cryptogram in this tale Poe says that it "was of a simple species", that he solved it "readily", and that he had "solved others of an abstruseness 10.000 times greater."

We have seen that so far as the actual record goes it is doubtful whether Poe ever solved any cryptogram that can properly be said to fall outside the class of simple substitution. The Frailey cipher, which was the most difficult of those shown by the record, and about which Poe wrote so enthusiastically, was but a little more complicated than that in The Gold Bug, of which he himself made light. Therefore, to say that he had "solved others of an abstruseness 10,000 times greater" is a considerable exaggeration, even in a tale of pure fancy.

It cannot be denied that Poe was greatly given to exaggeration. It was this foible which led him to make his most famous, and, for him, a most unwarranted, dictum on cryptography namely, that relative to the impossibility of devising the so-called indecipherable cipher. It will be well to give the exact form in which he made the assertion. In A Few Words on Secret Writing, published in Graham's Magazine for July 1841 he stated:

> Few persons can be made to believe that it is not quite an easy thing to invent a method of secret writing which shall baffle investigation. Yet it may be roundly asserted that human ingenuity cannot concoct a cipher which human ingenuity cannot solve."[13]

He repeated the declaration in one of his supplementary articles, and, again, in practically the same form, in The Gold Bug. Even to critical readers without cryptographic training [14] it is apparent that his dictum goes far beyond what he actually demonstrated in any of his cryptographic writings; and to the professional cryptographer it appears about time that Poe's assertion be challenged.

So far as the professional cryptographer is concerned, there has never been any question about the theoretical possibility of constructing at least one or two cipher systems, which are mathematically demonstrable as being absolutely indecipherable. It is far from being the case that the invention of such ciphers had to wait modern advances in cryptographic science; their devising was possible from the very earliest days of secret writing. The difficulty has been to

---

[13] Ibid., XIV. 116.

[14] For example, Krutch, op cit., p. 107, says: "In the course of the articles on cryptography his speculations went far beyond the concrete demonstrations which he affords. 'Human ingenuity', he declared triumphantly, 'could not devise a cypher which human ingenuity could not solve' * * * "

156

make such systems practicable for regular usage by persons having a need for the highest degree of cryptographic security.

A system which is now considered to be one of the very best for practical usage was discovered recently to have been invented by that amazing American genius Thomas Jefferson.[15] There can be no question that had Poe been cognizant of the method proposed by Jefferson he would have pronounced it absolutely inscrutable, for, as compared with the chiffre quarré (of which it will be remembered he said that it was the nearest approach to perfection), Jefferson's system is of a very much greater security. In fact, some of the American patriots of Revolutionary days were far better informed on secure methods of secret writing than was Poe.

It may perhaps be charged that it is unfair to expect of Poe a knowledge of the modern intricacies of a science which, like other sciences, must have undergone rapid development in the past half-century. On the contrary, although it is true that the state of the science is greatly in advance of what it was in Poe's day, long before his time it was much beyond what his remarks lead one to assume. As has already been intimated, 400 years before Poe lived, professional cryptographers were daily employing and solving ciphers of much greater complexity than any which Poe illustrates and terms intricate. The basic principles for solving the type of ciphers Poe discusses were described in detail in papers written by Italian cryptographers before the dawn of the sixteenth century.[16]

The serious student of cryptography can, if he takes the trouble, see in Poe's essay and in his other writings on this subject many things which are not apparent to the layman. Against his will he is driven to the conclusion that Poe was only a dabbler in cryptography. At the same time it is only fair to say that as compared with the vast majority of other persons of his time in this or in foreign countries, his knowledge of the subject, as an amateur, was sufficient to warrant notice. Had he had opportunity to make cryptography a vocation, there is no doubt that he would have gone far in the profession.

THE EVOLUTION OF COMMUNICATION*

By FRANK V. RHODES, *Consulting Engineer, San Francisco, Calif.*

Before man learned to talk, he communicated with others through signs, sounds, and gesticulations. This finally gave way to a recog-

---

[15] *Jefferson's Papers, vol. CCXXXII*, item 41575. Library of Congress, Washington.

[16] Aloys Meister, Die Anfänge der modernen diplomatischen Geheimschriften (Paderborn, 1902).

†Reprinted, by special permission, from issue No. 161, vol. XXVIII, of The Military Engineer. The Mills Building, Washington, D. C.

*(No. 97, July–September, 1937)

nized system of inflected voice utterances, which we call language. It was not until long after spoken language had developed that a means of recording it came into use.

As man developed and moved from place to place, means of communicating with his old home, parents, and friends became necessary, and through the ages various means of communication have been required, and generally have been evolved, to meet the necessities of the times, until, at present, methods have been developed far beyond any dreams of a few years ago. There are now sufficient varied methods of communication to satisfy even unreasonable demands, but still individuals and large organizations are centering their effort upon improving the wonderful means which we have today.

The methods of communication used in ages gone are of much interest, for from them have evolved those in use at present.

Among the ancients.—In 1084 B. C., Agamemnon, in his siege of Troy, placed material for beacon fires on the tops of Mounts Ida, Lemnos, Athos, Cithaeron, the Arachnaean Heights, and other intervening mountains. A man was stationed beside each beacon with instructions to keep his eyes toward Troy. When Troy fell, a fire was kindled on the mountain nearest to the captured city, signaling to the man on the next mountain to start his fire, and so on across the hills to Greece, thus conveying the news. Even ages earlier than the siege of Troy, fire and smoke had been used as signals of communication at a distance. The towers along the Chinese wall were signal towers as well as watch towers.

Theseus, eldest son of the King of Greece, who later became the hero of the Argonautic expedition to secure the Golden Fleece, was, as a boy, sent with a group of other young Athenians as a war indemnity to be sacrificed to the minotaur, the flame-spitting bull of Marathon, which made its home in the labyrinth. The ship carrying these victims was equipped with black sails in token of death, but Theseus had agreed with Aegeus, his father, that if he were victorious in his proposed fight with the minotaur, he would, upon his return, replace all of the black sails with white, emblematic of life. Theseus was victorious over the minotaur but, in his elation, he neglected to replace the black sails with the white, and Aegeus on a high rock overlooking the sea, awaiting the return of his son, saw the black sails returning. This conveyed to him the message that his son was dead and he cast himself into the sea and was drowned. The sea was ever after called the Aegean.

A Persian king, in order to improve on the courier plan which had been in existence prior to his time, placed sentinels all along the route over which he desired messages carried, and instead of a courier running a certain distance and then passing the message to the next, each sentinel remained at his station and shouted the message to the next, and so on until the message reached its destination. The ancient Gauls also used this method. Caesar probably used it in transmitting news of the massacre of the Romans at Orleans, as it reached Auvergne, nearly 150 miles distant, the same day.

Even in very early days, flashes of light were used to convey messages. · The Pharaohs and the Persians used mirrors to flash light for signaling purposes. The shields of the soldiers were used to flash the news of the Battle of Marathon, thus anticipating the heliograph.

The heliograph is still in use. This is an instrument having mirrors which reflect the rays of the sun and cast them to a distant receiving station. A shutter is used to interrupt the beam of light, and thus, by a system of long or short flashes, a message is sent, usually in Morse code. The British Army has used the heliograph in India and Africa, and in some cases has transmitted messages more than 150 miles without their being relayed.

Alexander the Great used a gigantic speaking tube or trumpet, called a stenorophonic tube, which would carry the voice many miles.

Another peculiar signaling system used by the ancients was the clepsydra. A tall glass tube of water, with an opening or faucet at the bottom, would be placed on a hilltop; an identical tube, containing the same amount of water, was placed on a hilltop some distance away. Messages were inscribed at varying heights on each of the tubes. At a signal from the attendant at one tube to the attendant at the other, both would open the faucets. The water, leaving both tubes at an equal rate, was lowered to a given point or message at the same time at both stations. When the water reached the level of the message that was to be conveyed, a second signal would be given, indicating that both faucets were to be shut off. The attendant at the receiving station could then read the desired message at the level of the water.

The Roman and Gallic towers, whose ruins are still seen in France, were originally used as signal towers. Hannibal erected towers in many conquered countries. Colored tunics and spears were used in signaling from them.

Indian signaling.—The American Indians used puffs or rings of smoke for signaling in the daytime, and arrows of fire at night. Puffs of smoke were made by placing a blanket over a fire of damp wood or grass. The blanket would hold the smoke for an interval and would then be withdrawn in order that the smoke might rise in a puff or ring. By repeating this process, the desired number of distinct puffs could be produced. A continuous column of smoke indicated that an enemy was in the vicinity. One puff or ring meant

"Attention"; two puffs indicated that the signaler would sleep at the place of his fire, et cetera.

Signaling with arrows of fire was arranged by dipping the arrow-head in some inflammable substance and igniting it before release from the bow. One fire-arrow discharged vertically into the air signified that the enemy was near; two meant danger; and three, great danger. When many such arrows were fired in rapid succession, it was a call for aid—"enemies are too many." An arrow of fire discharged horizontally across the sky indicated, by the direction of its flight, which way the sender was preparing to travel.

The Incas of Peru at the time of the Spanish conquest had a road system rivaling that of the Romans. Relays of runners were maintained at approximately 5-mile intervals throughout the whole system. By this method of 5-mile relays messages could be carried 150 miles or more in a day. These Inca messages were generally sent by means of the quipo, which was a long cord from which hung, at certain distances, smaller cords of various colors, each having a special meaning. Knots were tied in the smaller cords to indicate the particular message desired.

Early naval signaling.—Prior to the past 100 years, there were many types of signaling or communicating systems in use in various navies of the world. After cannon were introduced on naval ships, their fire was used for signaling as early as the sixteenth century.

Communication between square-rigged ships was carried on by raising and lowering a sail from the yardarm. In the seventeenth century officers of the British Navy worked out a definite signaling system for conveying messages through a code of communication which consisted of varying the position of a single flag. In 1780, Admiral Kempenfeldt introduced the system of using several flags, instead of varying the position of only one flag. From Admiral Kempenfeldt's scheme was evolved the wigwag flag signals now generally in use throughout the world. Admiral Philip Colomb developed a code of light flashes for use during the night.

A system similar to the wigwag was used more than a century ago in France, the signaling being accomplished by large semaphores placed on towers. This was called a "telegraph", even then. Alexandre Dumas, in his Count of Monte Cristo, describes the use of the French semaphore telegraph.

The pony express.—Marco Polo relates that Genghis Khan, ruler of Chinese Tartary, had a courier service similar to the pony express, nearly a thousand years ago. Relay stations were provided about 25 miles apart, and horseback riders, by changing mounts at each station, could deliver messages as far as 300 miles in 1 day.

"Attention"; two puffs indicated that the signaler would sleep at the place of his fire, et cetera.

Signaling with arrows of fire was arranged by dipping the arrowhead in some inflammable substance and igniting it before release from the bow. One fire-arrow discharged vertically into the air signified that the enemy was near; two meant danger; and three, great danger. When many such arrows were fired in rapid succession, it was a call for aid—"enemies are too many." An arrow of fire discharged horizontally across the sky indicated, by the direction of its flight, which way the sender was preparing to travel.

The Incas of Peru at the time of the Spanish conquest had a road system rivaling that of the Romans. Relays of runners were maintained at approximately 5-mile intervals throughout the whole system. By this method of 5-mile relays messages could be carried 150 miles or more in a day. These Inca messages were generally sent by means of the quipo, which was a long cord from which hung, at certain distances, smaller cords of various colors, each having a special meaning. Knots were tied in the smaller cords to indicate the particular message desired.

Early naval signaling.—Prior to the past 100 years, there were many types of signaling or communicating systems in use in various navies of the world. After cannon were introduced on naval ships, their fire was used for signaling as early as the sixteenth century.

Communication between square-rigged ships was carried on by raising and lowering a sail from the yardarm. In the seventeenth century officers of the British Navy worked out a definite signaling system for conveying messages through a code of communication which consisted of varying the position of a single flag. In 1780, Admiral Kempenfeldt introduced the system of using several flags, instead of varying the position of only one flag. From Admiral Kempenfeldt's scheme was evolved the wigwag flag signals now generally in use throughout the world. Admiral Philip Colomb developed a code of light flashes for use during the night.

A system similar to the wigwag was used more than a century ago in France, the signaling being accomplished by large semaphores placed on towers. This was called a "telegraph", even then. Alexandre Dumas, in his Count of Monte Cristo, describes the use of the French semaphore telegraph.

The pony express.—Marco Polo relates that Genghis Khan, ruler of Chinese Tartary, had a courier service similar to the pony express, nearly a thousand years ago. Relay stations were provided about 25 miles apart, and horseback riders, by changing mounts at each station, could deliver messages as far as 300 miles in 1 day.

More than 100 years ago. systems of pony express were in vogue not only in various countries of Europe. but even by newspapers in New York. Richard Haughton, political editor of the New York Journal of Commerce, used a pony express communicating system as early as 1830. By making use of relays of fast horses and a few short railroad lines operating in Massachusetts, Haughton was able to print in New York. by 9 o'clock in the morning, the Boston election returns of the previous day.

In 1832. James W. Webb, editor of the New York Courier and Enquirer. had a pony express system in effect between New York and Washington, which gave much prestige to his paper. In 1833, the Journal of Commerce in New York started a rival pony express, and published news from Washington within 48 hours. In this way the Journal was able to obtain big "scoops" over other publications, and the newspapers in Norfolk. Va., some 230 miles southeast of Washington, received Washington news through the New York Journal of Commerce, which sent it by ocean route from New York faster than the same news from Washington could be sent direct to Norfolk by boat on the Potomac River.

The pony express across the western half of this continent, from the Missouri River to the Pacific coast, reduced the time of communication between coasts by more than 10 days. There were many trials and tribulations in the inauguration of this pony express. and then it lasted only approximately 16 months. as it was replaced in 1861 by a transcontinental telegraph line.

In 1854 Jefferson Davis introduced a bill in Congress asking for an appropriation with which to purchase camels to use for fast transport and communication across the desert wastes of the Southwest. The bill did not pass. In 1855 a Los Angeles newspaper, the Star. had an editorial advocating the use of camels for a 5- or 6-day pony express between Salt Lake City and Los Angeles and 15 or 16 days between the Missouri River and Los Angeles.

Shortly after this the Government appropriated $30,000 to buy camels for fast transport for the Army. Col. David D. Porter was sent to Egypt, where he obtained and brought to the United States 33 camels. On a second trip he brought some 40 more camels. These were all put to work for the Army. and in January 1858. a train of 14 camels walked up Los Angeles' Main Street. So Los Angeles got its camels, but not for the exact use for which it desired to bring them into service.

The Posts.—

> So the posts went with the letters.
> So the posts passed from city to city.
>
> II Chronicles 3: 6 and 10.

Sending a special messenger was the only manner in which letters could be delivered in very ancient times. Such a messenger was required to be familiar with the country and able to defend himself against brigands and wild beasts. He was well paid for his risks. If a slave were sent, and the journey long, there would be doubt as to the delivery of a letter as he might endeavor to escape to his own country.

All of the early rulers had their own courier systems for bringing information from various parts of their countries and for dispatching edicts thereto. No doubt these couriers often carried private messages between individuals, with or without the knowledge of their kings. This gradually developed to the point where influential persons and, later, anyone who would pay for the privilege, were permitted to use the courier systems. It is recorded that in the third century the emperor Diocletian had a definite postal system for his private use.

One of the earliest posts was a courier system maintained in the thirteenth century by the University of Paris for its students. As there were many students from all parts of France, and some from other countries in Europe, it appears that the system was quite extensive. Students turned all their letters over to a designated courier chief who handled their dispatch.

On June 19, 1464, Louis XI of France issued an edict establishing post stations on all of the principal roads of the country, with a courier system between stations. This was for Government use but these royal couriers gradually undertook the carrying of messages for private individuals. This developed to a more or less recognized practice, until the point was reached where, under the reign of Louis XIII, a "comptroller general of the post" was appointed.

It is recorded that, as early as the year 1544, two of the European governments permitted state couriers to carry private dispatches, and within a few years following, they actually legalized the practice and created a monopoly for such, with Government regulations controlling their use.

Richard Fairbanks was probably the first "postmaster" in America. The General Court of the Colony of Massachusetts in 1639 ordered that "all letters from beyond the sea and all letters sent thither, be left with him at his house", and he was allowed a penny for each.

In 1683 William Penn established a weekly pony express mail service between Philadelphia and various nearby towns and communities, followed a little later by regular post routes to the more distant points of the colony and even to some points in Maryland.

On April 4, 1691, the Royal Postmaster General of England appointed Andrew Hamilton as Postmaster General of America, to serve, of course, under the Crown's post office. Apparently he was given much freedom of action. Hamilton visited all of the colonies in arranging for an intercolonial post and received the cooperation of all. The intercolonial post service was started May 1, 1693, with weekly service between Portsmouth, Saybrook, New York, Philadelphia, and some points in Maryland and Virginia. During the winter this service was fortnightly instead of weekly.

In the year 1707 the Crown's General Post in London took over the active control of our post system and retained it until about a year prior to the revolution.

In 1737 Benjamin Franklin was appointed postmaster at Philadelphia, and, not long after, on the death of the Crown's Deputy Postmaster General of the Colonies, Franklin was appointed to that position, being removed in 1744 due to some difficulty with the Governor of Massachusetts.

In the second session of our Continental Congress, in July 1775 it was resolved to have a post-office system of our own and Benjamin Franklin was selected as Postmaster General. He was voted a salary of $1,000 a year.

During the period that our posts were under the Crown, and until 1799, there had been a penalty of death for robbing the mails, but, in the year mentioned, the penalty was changed to flogging. Later the penalty was changed to imprisonment.

Under our first Postmaster General, postage rates were fixed in accordance with the distance carried and the number of "sheets" sent. It cost 6 cents to send one sheet 30 miles; 10 cents for 80 miles; 18¾ cents for 400 miles; and 25 cents for greater distances. Stamps were not in use and the postage charge could be paid either in advance by the sender, or on delivery, by the recipient. However, as early as 1825, Congress had provided for delivering letters in certain cities, with a charge of 2 cents to be paid on delivery. In 1863 a free delivery service was authorized for cities having 50,000 population or more. From time to time after that, modifications were made until at present there are some 2,500 cities in the United States having free delivery of mail.

In England, postage stamps had been used, with great success for some years, so a number of our local city postmasters began issuing them also, to the general satisfaction of the populace. Shortly after this, in 1847, the Postmaster General was authorized to issue stamps. The first were those of 5- and 10-cent denominations, bearing portraits of Franklin and Washington, respectively. During the year ending June 30, 1935, there were over 17,000,000 stamps, stamped envelopes, etc., issued to the post offices of the United States. The annual per capita purchase of postage stamps and other postal services for the same period was about $4.75.

In 1837 there were less than 12,000 post offices in the United States, with total annual revenues of approximately $4,000,000 while in 1935 there were some 45,700 post offices with annual revenues of over $630,000,000. In addition, there are 35,000 rural postal routes covering regularly over 1,300,000 miles.

During the year ending June 30, 1935, the more than 225,000 employees of the postal service handled, in addition to the billions of messages delivered in the United States, some 300,000,000 pieces of mail (exclusive of parcel post) destined to foreign countries. The railway post office car, some 4,000 in number, traveled over 450,000,000 miles in the same year, while air-mail carriers flew over 29,000,000 miles on regularly scheduled air-mail routes.

Electrical communication.—Until some mastery was obtained over the use of electricity in connection with communication, it may be said that, comparatively, all other communication systems were slow.

There is some evidence that both the Hindus and the Egyptians had developed systems of electric communication many centuries ago. In Pre-Adamite Man, a book written by P. B. Randolph long before the telephone was invented, it is stated that there is good evidence that "one of the Cleopatras sent news by a wire to all the cities from Teliopolis to Elephantine, on the Upper Nile."

The first modern suggestion of an electric telegraph was contained in an article signed "C. M." which appeared in Scots Magazine of February 17, 1755. The author was probably Charles Morrison, a Scotch surgeon, who had a reputation for his experiments with electricity. The idea that he described in his article was to have a separate wire for each letter of the alphabet, the wires to be charged in any desired order in accordance with the spelling of the word to be transmitted. The distant end of each of these wires would attract pieces of paper marked with the letter which each wire represented. In this way, any message desired could be spelled out. His idea was never applied. However, it set others to thinking, and one after another various electrical communicating devices were tried.

Harrison Gray Dyar, of New York, was compelled to discontinue his experiments with the electric telegraph and flee the country, as he was being accused of conspiracy to carry on secret communication. His device was a sort of chemical telegraph in which a transmitted electric spark decomposed an acid which had been applied to paper.

A Frenchman, named Ampère (his name now used as a measure of electricity) found that when electricity was sent through a coil of wire, magnetism was increased. He saw the possibilities of using the deflection of a magnetic needle for conveying messages, and he made experiments along those lines. He exhibited a model of such a communicating system in London.

Faraday, in 1831, discovered that the motion of a magnet would generate electricity in a wire (the basis of our modern dynamo). Two German professors, Gauss and Weber, of the University of Göttingen, were experimenting with electrical communication and using a battery as a source of current. They now adapted the generator to an experimental line between their laboratories. Current was generated and passed over the line and through a coil at the further end, moving a magnet to right or left, depending upon the direction of the current flow through the wire.

In Munich, an experimenter named Steinheil improved on the Gauss and Weber system by having a moving needle at the receiving station mark down dots and dashes on a strip of paper. This experimenter was the first to utilize the earth for a return circuit, in place of a second wire.

The first electrical telegraph that was placed in service for use of the public was developed by Charles Wheatstone (a familiar name in the present day electrical industry) and William Fothergill Cooke, both Englishmen. However, it did not make a commercial success. Wheatstone, who was born near Gloucester in the year 1802, obtained a patent on a needle telegraph in 1837 and constructed an experimental line in London. (This was the same year in which Morse was making his models.) With the assistance of one of the railroads, Wheatstone erected a line for a distance of 13 miles, but until its usefulness was demonstrated in assisting in the capture of a murderer, it was slow to receive the patronage of the public.

Morse code telegraphy.—At the time when Wheatstone was experimenting with the telegraph, Morse was also working along very similar lines. Samuel Finley Breece Morse was born in Massachusetts in the year 1791. Returning from France, where he had been studying art, another passenger on the ship *Sully* showed him an electric magnet which he had secured in Europe, from which Morse saw, almost at once, the possibilities of its use in connection with a telegraph. Upon arriving home, he set to work in earnest to develop an electric signaling system. His finances were low and he was required to spend much time in painting. He was given an appointment as a professor of the literature of the arts of design in the University of the City of New York. He set up his crude telegraph apparatus in a room at the college and was soon able to send messages. This was in the year 1835. A Mr. Gale, also a professor at the college was interested in Morse's apparatus and assisted him considerably, later becoming his partner.

By 1837 Morse had greatly improved his apparatus, making use of the electric magnet as a receiving instrument. The same year the national House of Representatives ordered the Secretary of the Treasury to look into the matter of establishing a national system of telegraphs. This urged Morse forward in his experiments in order that he might show the first practical working system. He had much difficulty, however, due to lack of funds.

In September 1837 while he was exhibiting his model telegraph to an English professor in Gale's laboratory, Fred Vail (cousin of Theodore N. Vail) happened in. He was much impressed with the demonstrations and realized immediately what it might mean to the world. Vail asked Morse if he intended to experiment with longer lines, to which Morse replied that he did as soon as he could secure funds. An agreement was reached between the two that if Vail would put in $2,000 with which to make instruments and secure patents, he would be given an interest in the telegraph.

Vail secured $2,000 from his father and started at once, with only the assistance of a boy, to construct a telegraph apparatus to be exhibited to the Postmaster General. The first apparatus that Vail made followed the pattern of that made by Morse, but had a number of improvements, and it was Vail who improved the message code over that designed by Morse, until many feel that the code should have been termed the "Vail code" rather than the "Morse code." It is that code which is in use today. In the latter part of the year 1837, Morse and Vail filed a protecting notice with the Patent Office as to their impending invention.

A patent on the telegraph was issued to Morse in 1840. Congress also appropriated money for building an experimental line between Washington and Baltimore, the line being completed May 23, 1844. It was not put on a commercial basis, however, until April 1, 1845, when service was offered to the public at the rate of "four characters for 1 cent." Under the terms of the agreement by which Congress appropriated money for the experimental line, the Government was given the first right to purchase Morse's invention. It was offered to the Government for $100,000, but the Postmaster General, Cave Johnson, declined the offer.

Telegraph lines continued to be built throughout the eastern portion of this country until, by the year 1851, there were more than 50 telegraph companies operating in the United States, most of them under license to use the Morse patents. In the year 1861, through help of an appropriation by Congress, a line was completed to the Pacific coast. This was the last obstacle of the pony express, and the one which it could not surmount.

The transcontinental telegraph line was no more than completed until there was demand for wire connections with Europe. It was thought, of course, that the most feasible plan would be to go by the way of our Pacific coast up through Canada and Alaska, then across Bering Strait to Asiatic Russia, and through Siberia to Europe, 16,000 miles in all. Our Government appropriated $50,000 for the survey of the route across Bering's Strait. The work of building that line was enthusiastically going forward on both sides of the Pacific, when announcement was made of the successful laying of a trans-Atlantic submarine cable. Although some 850 miles of line had been built on this side of the Pacific, and much work also done on the other side, the project was abandoned.

The telegraph patents and business which the government declined to purchase for $100,000 have grown in worth to where one American telegraph company now has assets of nearly $400,000,000 and has more than 21,000 public offices, handling hundreds of millions of messages annually.

The telephone.—Charles Borseul, in experimenting with the telegraph in 1854, had a theory of how speech could be transmitted, but his theory was never put into successful operation. However, in 1861, Philip Reis, a German, following out Borseul's theory, produced a mechanism that would transmit pitch, but it was never developed to the point where speech could be transmitted.

Alexander Graham Bell, a young teacher of deaf mutes, also a student of acoustics and electricity, had been carrying on experiments with what he termed "harmonic telegraphy." Bell was born in Edinburgh, Scotland, on March 3, 1847. He moved to Canada when he was 23 years of age and, a year later, moved to Boston.

He discovered his principle of the telephone on June 2, 1875, and continued his experiments along the lines of his discovery until March 10, 1876, when he had an instrument that would talk to the extent of transmitting a complete sentence. His principle, and the theory that he was endeavoring to perfect, was, as he stated it:

If I could make a current of electricity vary in intensity precisely as the air varies in density during the production of sound, I should be able to transmit speech telegraphically.

On March 7, 1876, Bell was granted his original telephone patent and in the summer of that year had his apparatus on exhibition at the Centennial Exposition in Philadelphia, where it attracted little or no public attention. Men of science realized by his demonstrations that he had accomplished a wonderful thing, but practical men thought it only an interesting toy.

Bell himself realized what he had accomplished. In order to create interest and to secure financial assistance, he gave lectures accompanied by demonstration, members of his audience being permitted to talk with each other. He did secure some backing, however, and before a year elapsed after the securing of his patent, a number of telephones were in actual service. Bell's experimental telephone of 1876 has increased, during the intervening 60 years to 1936, to more than 17,000,000 telephones in the United States alone.

Theodore N. Vail, for many years the outstanding figure of the telephone industry, could see far beyond the present. He prophesied a common language for this whole earth made necessary by a worldwide telephone system.

One telephone company in the United States now has 275,000 employees who handle 50,000,000 communications each day, and has assets of some $5,000,000,000. Its most valuable asset, however, is its spirit of striving toward the goal where any two persons, anywhere on earth, may, at the limit of speed, which is that of light, be face to face, yet still far apart.

EDGAR ALLAN POE, CRYPTOGRAPHER*

ADDENDUM

By Lt. Col. WILLIAM F. FRIEDMAN, *Signal Reserve*

In the preceding article on this subject comments were made upon Poe's efforts to surround simple cryptographic principles with a veil of mystery, as well as to give an impression of having a more profound knowledge of cryptanalytic theory than he really possessed. The editor of the Bulletin having asked me to add a few details which could not be included in the original article without extend-

---

*EDITOR'S NOTE.—In this addendum the author presents additional data in amplification of some of the statements contained in his original article, "Edgar Allan Poe, Cryptographer", which appeared in the preceding number of the Signal Corps Bulletin.

*(No. 98, October–December, 1937)

ing the latter beyond practical limits, I think it will be best to begin by quoting a paragraph from that article.[1]

Over half of "A Few Words on Secret Writing" is devoted to the Berryer form of cryptogram, a type which, despite its utter simplicity, is so impractical that it is employed only by novices, and then only seldom. The actual Berryer cryptogram must, indeed, be considered the concoction of amateurs or of persons whose knowledge of cryptography was extremely limited, for, so far as history records, no such impractical system was ever regularly employed for serious purposes. It is true that Poe comments upon its impracticability, but as to the complexity of the type, it is apparent that he thought highly of it.

The cipher alphabet to which Poe specifically refers is based upon the key phrase *le gouvernement provisoire* and is as follows:

```
Plain —A B C D E F G H I J L M N O P Q R S T U V X Y Z
Cipher—L E G O U V E R N E M E N T P R O V I S O I R E
```

The foregoing is arranged as an enciphering alphabet, that is, it is arranged for convenience in enciphering. For deciphering, a rearrangement in which the cipher letters are listed alphabetically, is here necessary and is as follows:

```
Cipher—A B C D E F G H I J L M N O P Q R S T U V X Y Z
            B   C   T   A L I D P     H U O E F
            G       X       N R       Q       S
Plain—      J               V         Y
            M
            Z
```

It will be noted that 13 letters here serve the function of an entire alphabet. Certain letters (A, B, C, D, F, H, J, Q, X, Y, Z) cannot appear at all as cipher letters, while certain other letters (E, I, N, O, R, V) have more than one value, a circumstance very likely to lead to difficulty in deciphering a message *even with the key*. For example, consider a message containing the cipher-text sequence ETNOLRETONNNE. In attempting to decipher these letters with the foregoing deciphering alphabet one obtains the following:

```
Cipher—E T N O L R E T O N N N E
        B O I D A H B O D I I I B
        G   N R Q G   R N N N   G
Plain—  J   V   Y J   V       J
        M       M               M
        Z       Z               Z
```

How many minutes would it take an average clerk to decide that the sequence should be translated as MONDAY MORNING? And if the sequence contained an error or two, how long would he have to struggle with its decipherment? The impracticability of such a

---

[1] Signal Corps Bulletin No. 97, p. 45. Hereafter cited as Bulletin No. 97.

cipher for serious purposes is quite apparent. Poe himself comments upon its impracticability, but only after he has devoted many words to praising the method for its security, in which, incidentally, he manages to throw a few compliments in his own direction. Thus:

A key-phrase might easily be constructed in which one character would represent seven, eight, or ten letters. Let us then imagine the word *iiiiiiiii* presenting itself in a cryptograph to an individual *without* the proper key-phrase, or, if this be a supposition somewhat too perplexing, let us suppose it occurring to the person for whom the cipher is designed, and who *has* the key-phrase. What is he to do with such a word as *iiiiiiiii*? In any of the ordinary books upon algebra will be found a very concise *formula* (we have not the necessary type for its insertion here) for ascertaining the number of arrangements in which *m* letters may be placed, taken *n* at a time. But no doubt there are none of our readers ignorant of the innumerable combinations which may be made from these ten *i's*. Yet, unless it occur otherwise by accident, the correspondent receiving the cipher would have to write down all these combinations before attaining the word intended, and even when he had written them he would be inexpressibly perplexed in selecting the word designed from the vast number of other words arising in the course of the permutation.

To obviate, therefore, the exceeding difficulty of deciphering this species of cryptograph, on the part of the possessors of the key-phrase, and to confine the deep intricacy of the puzzle to those for whom the cipher was not designed, it becomes necessary that some *order* should be agreed upon by the parties corresponding—some order in reference to which those characters are to be read which represent more than one letter—and this *order* must be held in view by the writer of the cryptograph. It may be agreed, for example, that the *first* time an *i* occurs in the cipher it is to be understood as representing the character which stands against the *first i* in the key-phrase, that the *second* time an *i* occurs it must be supposed to represent that letter which stands opposed to the *second i* in the key-phrase, etc., etc. Thus the *location* of each cipherical letter must be considered in connection with the character itself in order to determine its exact signification.

We say that some preconcerted *order* of this kind is necessary lest the cipher prove too intricate a lock to yield even to its true key. But it will be evident, upon inspection, that our correspondent at Stonington has inflicted upon us a cryptograph in which *no* order has been preserved, in which many characters respectively stand, at absolute random, for many others. If, therefore, in regard to the gauntlet we threw down in April, he should be half inclined to accuse us of braggadocio, he will yet admit that we have *more* than acted up to our boast. If what we then said was not said *suaviter in modo*, what we now do is at least done *fortiter in re*.[2]

It should be pointed out that if Poe had tried the method he suggests he would at once have seen that it is an unworkable method, for the reason that the text of the message itself would have to be prearranged to conform to the scheme. For example, in the illustrative alphabet based upon the key phrase *le gouvernement provisoire* the cipher letter E stands successively for the plain-text letters B, G, J, M, and Z. Now, if a message started with the word BOG, the

---

[2] *A Few Words On Secret Writing,* Graham's Magazine, July 1841, pp. 37-38. (Italics in original.)

170

cipher group ETE would, on Poe's scheme, be deciphered correctly as BOG; but what if the first word were MOB? It would also be enciphered as ETE, but would be deciphered as BOG. Thus, Poe's scheme for circumventing the difficulties introduced by a multiplicity of plain-text values for one and the same cipher letter is feasible only if the text of a message is prepared *in advance* to meet the requirements of the scheme itself. This is the cryptographic equivalent of "reasoning around a circle."

The reference to "our correspondent at Stonington" in the foregoing extract is in connection with two cryptograms which the latter sent Poe as a result of Poe's challenge in the April 1841 issue of Graham's Magazine, and which Poe discusses in the July number of the same magazine.

Poe solved both messages and said:

In the solution of the first of these ciphers we had little more than ordinary trouble. The second proved to be exceedingly difficult, and it was only by calling every faculty into play that we could read it at all.

In my comments upon this incident, I said: [3]

Anyone who will take the trouble to go into the matter carefully will, I am sure, be entirely at a loss to account for the difficulty Poe experienced with regard to the second example. The reader will have to take my word for it, of course, but I say that any person who, having devoted but 2 weeks' study to elementary cryptograms, cannot solve that particular cryptogram in 2 hours at the most, had better turn his attention to other pursuits wherein success will crown his efforts with less expenditure of energy.

The two cryptograms are appended so that readers may try their own hand at solving them. They are in the exact form in which they were published by Poe. Their solutions will be found on page 87 of this Bulletin.

No. 1

Cauhiif aud frd sdftirf ithot tacd wdde rdchfdr tiu funcfshffheo fdoudf hetmsafhie tuis ied herhchriai fi aeiftdu wn sdaef it iuhfheo hiidohwid wn aen deodsf ths tiu itis hf iaf iuhoheaiin rdffhedr; aer ftd auf it ftif fdoudfiu oissiehoafheo hefdiihodeod taf wdde odeduaiin fdusdr ounsfiouastn. Saen fsdohdf it fdoudf ihufheo idud weiie fi ftd aeohdeff; fisdfhsdf, A fiacdf tdar ief ftacdr aer ftd ouiie iuhffde isie ihft fisd herd hwid oiiiuheo tiihr, atfdu ithot tahu wdheo sdushffdr fi ouil aonhe, hetiusafhie oiiir wd funefshffdr ihft ihffid raeoeu ft af rhfoicdun iiiir hefid iefhi ftd aswiiafiun dshffid fatdin udaotdr hff rdffheafhil. Ounsfiouastn tiidcdu siud suisduin dswuaodf ftifd sirdf it iuhfheo ithot aud uderdudr idohwid iein wn sdaef it fisd desiaefiun wdn ithot sawdf weiie ftd udai fhoehthoafhie it ftd onstduf dssiindr fi hff siffdfiiu.

3 Bulletin No. 97, p. 44.

\

No. 2.

Ofoiioiiaso ortsiii sov eodisoioe afduiostifoi ft iftvi
si tri oistoiv oiniafetsorit ifeov rsri inotiiiiv ridiiot,
irio rivvio eovit atrotfetsoria aioriti iitri tf oitovin
tri aetifei ioreitit sov usttoi oioittstifo dfti afdooitior
trso ifeov tri dfit otftfeov softriedi ft oistoiv
oriofiforiti suittcii · viireiiitifoi ft tri iarfoisiti, iiti
trir uet otiiiotiv uitfti rid io tri eoviieeiiiv rfasueostr
tf rii dftrit tfoeei.

*   *   *   *   *   *   *

For those who are interested in the Frailey cryptogram, in the
solution of which Poe took so much pride, there is shown in figure 1
an exact copy as it appeared in the August 1841 issue of Graham's
Magazine.

The character-for-character decipherment, with notes pointing out
errors that appeared in the message as printed in Graham's Magazine, is given in figure 2 so that the reader may study it in con-

£ 7i A itagi niinbiiit tbitvuiaib9g h auehbiif b ivgiht itau
☞ gvuiitiif 4 t$bt2ihtbo £iiiiadb9 iignit£d i2 ta5ta whbo
ttbibtiiitit9 A iti if X hti 4 ithtt ☞ i ‡ bnniathubii iSt b
eaovuhoSu vtt7diboif * iti nihd6Xht na3ig an choo$ht u‡t-
nvotigg2 iibtvo$if b Eaovu £avg iinoht$h7 niau iti vtheiigbo
iit6 A itagi t7iitig h fifvti iti gvugidviti bubodbub9 A tiiiiadi-
tiavg nbt g iStavi fvuhiiu £thnhiti niiiit8 † bni 4 iiiu£$i ht
d£bo evodbiSa ‡ nbiivihiti uavtib£g ibei —it dbuvo$if ia
niafvti uvgtvnvobi buai9g uii iti £giSv9 i2 gvuiiti A uu
iiubisg ibg tai —it iStavi tbvgi iti itiui A i2 intiuiiibo taovutg
an dvaihfh¶ iavitbog ¶f a ititvghbgight ittauh$h7g ht t7eii-
gb9bo £iiitavigi.

FIGURE 1.

nection with Poe's remarks in his letter to Bolton, as well as in his
letter to F. W. Thomas.[4] Furthermore, I append Bolton's solution
together with his notes.[5] These are offered in substantiation of my
remarks on the matter of Poe's letter to Thomas in regard to Bolton's
solution.

In one of those perpatetic circumrotations I obviated a rustic whom I subjected to catachetical interrogation respecting the homonomial characteristic
of the edifice to which I was approximate. With a volubility uncongealed by
the frigorific powers of villatic bashfulness he ejaculated a voluminous replication from the universal tenor of whose contexts I deduce the subsequent
amalgamation of heterogeneous facts (or fancy). Without dubiety incipient
pretension is apt to terminate in final vulgarity as parturient mountains have
been fabulated to produce muscupular abortions, yet the institution, the subject of my remarks, has not been without cause the theme of the ephemeral

---

[4] Bulletin No. 97, p. 49.
[5] The solution and notes immediately followed the text of Bolton's letter in the November 15, 1925, issue of the Memphis Commercial Appeal. The letter was given on pp.
48-49, Bulletin No. 97.

172

columns of quotidian journals and of enthusiastic encomiations in conversational intercourse.

Notes.⁶—(1) *i*, omitted in the cipher. (2) *t*, omitted in the cipher. (3) *homonomial*—a Greek derivative compound as in homologus and binomial. *Omono-*

£ 7i A itagi niịnbiiịt thitvuiaib9g h auehbiif,b ivgiht itau
IN ONE OF THOSE PERPATETC CIRCUMROTATIONS I OBVIATED A RUSTIC WHOM

☞ gvuiitiif 4 t$bt2ihtbo £iiiiadb9 iignit'£d i2 ta5ta'⚡hbo
SUBJECTED TO CATACHETICAL INTERROGATION RESPECING THE NOSOCO MIAL

ttbibtiiitịt9'A iti if X hti 4 ithtt ☞ iː‡ bnniathubii iSt b
CHARACTERISTC OF THE ED IF ICE TO WHICH I WAS APPROXIMATE WITH A

eaovuhoSu vtt7diboif * iti nihd6Xht na3ig an ẻhoo$ht uːt
VOLUBILITY UNCONGEALED BY THE FRIGORIFIC POWERS OF VILLATIC BASH

nvotig#2 iibtvo$if b Éaovu£avg iinoht$h7 niau iti vtheiigbo
FULNESS HE EJACULATED A VOLUMINOUS REPLICATION FROM THE UNIVERSAL

iit6 A itagi t7iitig h fifvti iti gvugidviti bubodbub9 A tiiiiadi-
TENOR OF WHOSE CONTENTS I DEDUCE THE SUBSEQUENT AMALGAMATION OF HETEROGE

tiavg nbtig iStavi fvuhiiu £thnhiti niiiit8 † bni 4 iiiu£$i ht
NEOUS FACTS WITHOUT DUBIETY INCIPIENT PRETENSIONS APT TO TERMINATE IN

d£bo evodbiSả ‡ nbiivihiti uavtib£g ẻbeẻ —it dbuvo$if ia
FINAL VULGARITY AS PARTURIENT MOUNTAINS HAVE BEEN FABULATED TO

niafvti uvgtvnvobi buai9g uii iti £giSv9 i2 gvuiiti A uu
PRODUCE MUSCUPULAR ABORTIONS YET THE INSTITUTION THE SUBJECT OF MY

iiubisgẻbg tai —it iStavi tbvgi iti itiui A i2 intiuiiibo taovutg
REMARKS HAS NOT BEEN WITHOUT CAUSE THE THEME OF THE EPHEMERAL COLUMNS

an dvaihfhⅡ iavitbog ⁋fả ititvghbgiẻht ittauh$h7g ht t7eii-
OF QUOTIDIAN JOURNALS AND OF ENTHUSIASTIC ENCOMIATIONS IN CONVER

gb9bo £iiitavigi.
SATIONAL INTERCOURSE

1 *h* omitted
2 *h* omitted
3 There should be a space between *t* and *b*
4 *i* omitted
5 There should be no space between *g* and *H*
6 Should be *u*.
7 *h* omitted
8 The *g* is superfluous

9 There should be no space between *t* and *X*
10 There should be no space between *X* and *h*
11 There should be no space between *t* and *t*
12 The *g* should be *t*
13 There should be a space between *g* and *z*
14 The capital *E* should be small letter *e*

15 The *g* should be *u*.
16 The *t* should be *t*
17 The entire word *yet* is omitted by Poe in his solution
18 The *t* should be *t*
19 One *t* is superfluous
20 Small *g* should be capital *A*
21 The *g* is superfluous

The enciphering alphabet:
Plain ABCDEFGHIJKLMNOPQRSTUVWXYZ
Cipher BUTFINDTHISOUTANDIGIVEITUP

X • I   9 • AT   2 • HE   6 • OR
X • OF   1 • AS   3 • WE   7 • ON
X • IF   1 • IS   4 • TO   8 • SION
£ • IT   2 • AN   5 • IO   9 • TION
£ • IN   — • BE
£ • BY

The deciphering alphabet:
Cipher ABCDEFGHIJKLMNOPQRSTUVWXYZ
Plain OA QVDSIE   FLZ   KCBU
      G   P   HM
      R   NY
      T   X
      W

FIGURE 2.

⁶ Bolton's solution and notes are copied exactly as they appear in the Commercial Appeal. Not having the original or a photographic copy thereof, I am not able to vouch for the accuracy of the orthography and punctuation of the printed version as compared with Bolton's original letter. The fact that the not uncommon words *peripatetic* and *homologous* appear as *perpatetic* and *homologus* leads to the suspicion that the compositor and proofreader of the Commercial Appeal are responsible for such errors as are apparent. Bolton's remarks concerning the word *nosocomial* (which the newspaper printed as *nosoconical*) are interesting, but I think he is wrong. The originator of the cipher quite obviously meant the word to be exactly as it deciphers, *viz*, *nosocomial*. The reference numbers to Bolton's notes are as given in the newspaper, but the items to which they apply in his solution were not shown in the solution as printed. However, the reader will have no difficulty in this respect, if he will refer to figure 2.

mos, according to authority, "That have similar laws." May well be used to designate an architectural proportion and thus fairly apply to the characteristics of an edifice. *Nomos* is commonly anglicised into *nominal* whereas *nomos,* from *Nomizo* must be changed into *comial* as you have properly rendered it. But the cipher *whbo,* supposing *w* erroneously used in place of *u,* spells *mial,* not *mical,* as you give it in yours. The character *5* is used but once in the cipher; it may therefore as well be *mo* as *so.* Also by analogy as *4* is to and *5, mo* and *6, or* again—it states also that he used these characters in lieu of various short words to prevent frequent repetitions, but neither *so* nor *os* is used except in *whose* elsewhere in the cipher, while *mo* and *om* are used in *whom, homonomial, from, mountains, encomation.* There was therefore little reason to substitute a character for *so,* but great cause for substituting one for *mo*—especially as in the word homonomial it must occur twice. I am satisfied my translation agrees best with the cipher even though the word *nosoconical* was intended by the author. This word caused me more trouble than all the rest of the cryptograph. (4) *t* omitted in the cipher, translated literally. (5) *c* in the cipher erroneously used instead of *e.* (6) *context.* The general series of discourse Webster. I prefer this to *contents* as more in character with the bombastic words commonly used. The same idea is conveyed by either word. (7) *yet* omitted in your solution. (8) spelled ephemeral. (9) *a* used instead of *A* in the cipher; omitted in your solution.

Incidentally, in Poe's letter to Bolton he asks:

Will you honestly tell me?—did you not owe it to the accident of the repetition of the word "itagi"? for "those"? This repetition does not appear in the ms.—at least, I am pretty sure that it was interpolated by one of our compositors—a "genius" who takes much interest in these matters—and many unauthorized liberties.

Of this it may be said that in the first place, although the group "itagi" appears twice in the message, it represents two different words, "those" and "whose", and secondly that Poe overreached himself in his attempt to minimize Bolton's achievement by stating that this repetition did not appear in the ms. and "was interpolated by one of our compositors." For Poe's own solution shows the presence of "those" and "whose", and since both words are essential to the text and could be represented only by "itagi", "itagi" *must* have been repeated in the ms. I realize that this is a small matter but I point it out only to show how Poe attempts to magnify his own achievement by belittling that of a rival for the honor of being the only one to solve this cryptogram.

Again, Bolton's long argument anent the word *homonomial* is interesting and constitutes one of the internal evidences of independent solution. Poe's own solution [7] gives the word as *nosocomical*—but there is no such word. The word is *nosocomial* and is the adjectival form of *nosocomium,* meaning *hospital. The crypto-*

---

[7] In the solution of this message as printed in the previous article (p. 47, Bulletin No. 97), the word *nosocomial* was spelled correctly, but in Poe's solution, as printed in the October 1841 issue of Graham's Magazine (p. 192), the word was erroneously spelled *nosocomical.*

gram is correct in this particular, for the cipher group "ta5tawhbo", in which the "w" is a misprint and should be "u", has the following equivalents:

```
t a 5  t a u h b o
C O SO C O B I A L  .
H    N N M
N    N N Y
X    X
```

*   *   *   *   *   *   *

The most difficult cryptogram Poe ever solved seems to have been one involving "no less than seven distinct alphabets." In the preceding article (p. 46, Bulletin No. 97) I stated that:

> Ciphers involving a plurality of different alphabets have been known in the art for a long time. The principle is very clearly described in the oldest tract on cryptography that the world now possesses, that written by Alberti.

This early Italian cryptographer, Leo Battista Alberti, died in 1472, leaving to posterity a brief treatise on cryptography which is of great interest not only because it is the oldest extant but also because it contains the first description of the revolving wheel cipher, shown in figure 3. Note that I say "first description", for it is probable that a device of such simple nature would have been thought of in the earliest days of secret writing, which

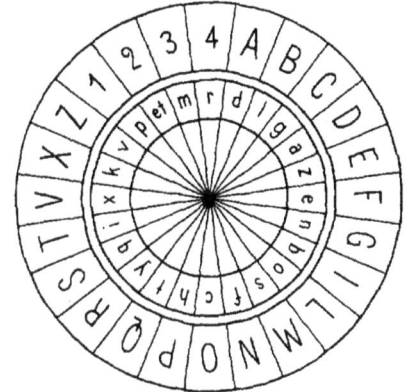

FIGURE 3.

go back to those of ancient history. Indeed, the simple *cipher disk*, as it is commonly termed, has constituted the basis for most of the cipher "inventions" concocted by cryptographers for half a millenium, and even today it apparently comes to amateur cryptographers as the result of what appears to them as being a brilliant flash of imagination. In his description of the device, Alberti clearly portrays the manner in which it can be used for producing polyalphabetic ciphers. Because of its importance in the history of the science, it is of interest to quote Alberti's description. The translation was made at my request by my friend, Charles J. Mendelsohn, Ph. D., professor of history, College of the City of New York. Dr. Mendelsohn is an experienced cryptographer and exceptionally well versed

in the history of cryptography. The translation was made from the
Latin original.[8]

We shall now describe the method of writing which we have devised. It
has these advantages: No cipher that one could use is quicker, none will be
written with more ease, none is more quickly and readily read, none more
secret can be devised if you do not know the keys arranged between me
and my correspondent. I make the assertion that this method will nullify
all the clever and cunning tricks of all the men in the world, all the perseverance of the most careful, and all their painstaking investigation, their skill
and their effort. Industry will not enable any except the initiated to learn
anything that we write in this cipher. Moreover, any scribe you might call
upon will be able to write the cipher at your dictation in ordinary well-known
characters, but will know nothing of what he has written and another will
just as readily read the characters of any message sent to you from some
station abroad. You will understand everything thoroughly, while he whom
you get to read the message aloud to you will not comprehend one syllable.
I am justified in calling this cipher worthy of kings, since they can make use
of it with very little work and without the help of a decipherer initiated into
its mysteries.

But enough on this point. Let us now pursue the subject itself. The following is the extremely secret and convenient method of writing which we
so highly recommend. I make two circles out of copper plates. One, the
larger, is called stationary, the smaller is called movable. The diameter of the
stationary plate is one-ninth greater than that of the movable plate. I divide
the circumference of each circle into 24 equal parts. These parts are called
cells. In the various cells of the larger circle I write the capital letters, one
at a time in red, in the usual order of the letters, A first, B second, C third, and
then the rest, omitting H and K because they are not necessary. Thus we shall
have the 20 capital letters which we have just mentioned. They occupy the
20 cells which are assigned to the fixed and real letters. In addition there are
four cells which will remain empty and are called numeral cells for the reason
that in each of them a small numeral will be inscribed in black—in the first
cell 1, in the second 2, in the third 3, in the fourth 4. In this way all the cells
of the larger circle will be filled with their own letters (and numbers). In
the smaller circle there will be the same number of cells with lines corresponding to those of the larger cells. These will be called movable cells and in each
of them a letter will be inscribed—not a capital, but a small letter in
black, and not in regular order like the stationary characters, but scattered at
random. Thus we may suppose the first of them to be a, the second g, the
third q and so on with the rest until the 24 cells of the circle are full; for
there are 24 characters in the Latin alphabet, the last being et. After completing
these arrangements we place the smaller circle upon the larger so that a
needle driven through the centers of both may serve as the axis of both and
the movable table may be revolved around it. We call this instrument thus
arranged a "formula". The formula must be made in two copies so that you
may keep one and your friend abroad to whom you are going to write may
keep the other. The two formulas must be exactly alike in the position,
number, and arrangement of the characters without any difference whatever.
When all this is finished we shall agree upon an index, for the index is like a

---

[8] Meister, A., *Die Geheimschrift im Dienste der Päpstlichen Kurie*, Paderborn, 1906,
pp. 136–141.

key which opens the entrance to the innermost holy places. The index itself is double: one is made of the stationary capital letters . . .[54] both at will.

We consider the movable index first. Suppose, for example, we agree on the index k in the movable table. As the writer I may set the table of the formula as I wish. Suppose the k is placed under the capital B and the next character under the next. When I write to you I shall first of all write the capital B under which I placed the index k in the formula when I was preparing to write. That will indicate that you abroad when you wish to read my message must turn your formula which is the twin of mine so that k is under B as in mine. From this as a starting point all the other characters of the message will acquire the force and sounds of the stationary characters above them. After writing three or four words I shall change the position of the index in our formula by turning the circle, so that the index k may be, say, under D [*Meister's text reads K. Since, however, we have been instructed to omit K from the larger circle, the reading D has been adopted from another manuscript*]. So in my message I shall write a capital D, and from this point on k will signify no longer B but D, and all the other stationary letters at the top will receive new meanings. You who are away will understand similarly when the capital letter gives you notice that its only meaning is to notify you of the position of the movable circle and to tell you that its position has been changed. You too will now place your index below that character, and in this way you will quite readily read and understand the entire message.

The four movable letters which are below the four top cells containing numerals, whichever they may be, mean nothing, as the saying goes, when used singly and in this case are to be considered nulls. But when joined or when more than one is used they will contribute great advantages to the scheme; of which more presently.

The first setting of the index by means of capital letters is to make us both certain by means of one of the capital letters which of them is the index, and to have an index arranged with you at the start, say B. The very first letter in the message which I write you, will be any small letter that I may pick, say q; accordingly, by turning the tables you will place that letter below the index B in the formula, and q will therefore have the meaning and sound of B. Now we write as we told you when describing the movable index. When the table of the cipher and the arrangement of the cipher are to be changed, then I will write one—but no more—of the characters that are on the smaller circle below the numbers that represent them, say 3 or 4, etc. I shall then substitute this letter in turning the tables for the index B that was agreed upon, and from this point on as demanded by the scheme of writing I shall use the small letters for what was denoted by the larger letters. To deceive more and more those who try to pry into the secret you may arrange with the friend to whom you are going to write that capitals inserted in the text (in general there will be none) will have no meaning. There are many similar possibilities which it would be tedious and superfluous to pursue. In this way it will be possible to indicate the sound and pronunciation of each capital (as you see) by means of the 24 [*small*] letters and on the other hand each of the small letters may be used in the sense of the twenty capital letters, and in addition may denote four numerals by moving the index and circle and changing their position. I come now to the use of the numbers, and nothing could be more admirable.

---

[54] Meister here marks a lacuna in the text. The omission very clearly is substantially as follows: *the other of the small letters on the movable circle, combining.*

The letters representing numerals, as I have pointed out, are small letters used to represent the numbers written above them on the stationary tablet. The numbers in themselves make it possible, by using two or three or four in one service, to represent 336 entire phrases selected at will. For with these numeral letters taken two at a time, for example ps to mean, say 12, or pf for, say, 13, and similar arrangements (which can be made of these four numerals two at a time) 16 phrases may be denoted. But if the same numeral characters are joined in groups of three, for example psf meaning, say, 123, and sfp meaning 231, you will be able to represent 64 phrases. Finally, if the characters are joined in groups of four, for example, sfkp to mean 2431, or fpsk to mean 3124 and so forth, it will be possible to represent up to 256 complete phrases by means of these groupings. Accordingly, the sum of all these complete phrases will be 336. They will be used in the following manner. We shall make up separately a table of 336 lines in which we intend to arrange the various groupings of numerals that have been described, and we shall enter the numerals in the lines, 11 in the first line, 12 in the second, 13 in the third, 14 in the fourth, 21 in the fifth, 22 in the sixth, 23 in the seventh, and so on with the rest as we have done in the table below. In this table, according to agreement, we shall enter in the various lines at the numbers whatever complete phrases we please, for example, corresponding to 12 "We have made ready the ships which we promised and supplied them with troops and grain." Similar complete phrases will be assigned at will to each of the numbers in the table. You must have a copy of this table [tubulac is obviously a misprint for tabulac] with you, and when letters from me reach you abroad, and you find numeral groups in the messages, you will note which numerals are indicated and will look for them in the table of complete phrases and will thereby ascertain what I have written. Nothing is shorter than this system of writing, nor is anything safer, and nothing more set and suitable can be devised for use in ciphers by means of two, three, or four characters. These, too, will not always be the same, but will change and can denote 336 complete phrases—a thing which will amaze everybody. It may be advisable for me to have two tables and for you likewise to have two; in one set the numerals will be arranged in order at the beginnings of the lines conveniently for the reader; in the other set the phrases will be alphabetically arranged under the headings of the letters so that they will not have to be looked up in various places in the table and may be readily at hand for the writer. The headings of the phrases will be arranged as follows: phrases referring to "annona" [i. e., crop] will be placed under the heading a, those referring to conducting "bellum" [i. e., war] under the heading b, those referring to "naves" [i. e., ships] under the heading n, and so on with the rest. These two tables will differ in that the one having the numbers at the beginnings of the lines will have the phrases after them, while in the other there will be no numbers at the beginnings of the lines but a letter conforming to the heading. This will be followed by the phrase and at the end will come the numbers just as they were fitted to the same phrases in the other similar table of phrases of this kind.

When I am going to write to you I seek out the desired phrase in the table, where it is found under the proper letter, then I look for the numbers entered after the phrase. These numbers I then insert in my message according to the formula of the cipher representing them by the letters that denote those numbers. As I have shown, you will get the proper phrases from the numbers.

I hope this little treatise will be safeguarded by my friends and not be allowed to get among the common herd of the unskilled and be profaned. The cipher is worthy of a prince and should be dedicated to the execution of affairs of the greatest moment. Good luck attend you.

178

Tables of numerals

[Here followed three tables composed of the permutations of the digits 1, 2, 3, 4 taken in groups of 2, 3, and 4 at a time.]

It is my wish that this [*cipher*], most convenient and beautiful as it is, and marvelously capable of contributing to the safety of the state and for carrying on affairs of the greatest moment, be dedicated as a consecrated offering to posterity. By using the tables as prescribed, people who are under siege or widely separated will be able to tell one another what is needed without sending letters, but by an arrangement [*metuve appears meaningless here; possibly we should read situve "or position"*] of lights or smoke. If you will understand and consider how valuable this device is you will congratulate me. What, I pray you, is more worthy of admiration than to have a method by which, even against the will of the enemy, and from the greatest distance, you may send word and report on the condition of affairs, saying what you wish done and what the prospects are. Finis.

It is true that Alberti does not state clearly that the device could be used so that the alphabet changes with each letter of the message, in accordance with a key word or key number. But it was only a few years later that the system now called by various names, such as "repeating-key," "multiple-alphabet," "double-key," was used and accurately described by other Italian cryptographers. In particular, the able Italian mathematician and physicist, John Baptista Porta, in his work on cryptography, published in 1563, showed very clearly how such ciphers may be composed, and Dr. Mendelsohn informs me that in a paper which he is preparing for publication he is going to show that Porta has not received credit for proposing multiple-alphabet ciphers with disarranged or mixed sequences. I should like to point out also that Alberti not only is the first writer to have described a polyalphabetic substitution scheme, but also the first one to have described or invented the system now designated as *enciphered code*. For his scheme applying permuted groups of numerals to the members of a list of 336 words and phrases clearly constitutes a small code; *moreover he suggests a two-part arrangement of the contents of the code*, thus deserving the credit for being first to describe (if not to invent) this important feature. These code groups were then to be enciphered, as described, so that the encipherment of the code groups was also polyalphabetic in character.

* * * * * * * *

In the preceding article the *chiffre quarré* (or carré, as it is spelled nowadays) was mentioned in connection with Poe's statement that this method "is the nearest approach to perfection." Poe attributed this cipher to the French Academy. I commented that it was first illustrated by Vigenère in 1586 and that to all intents and purposes the same method, without actually employing the square table, was used at least as early as 1560 by certain Italian cryptographers in the employ of the papacy. Specifically, the Italian cryptographer Matteo

Argenti in his treatise on cryptography shows sets of alphabets arranged according to key words. For example:[9]
No. 4.-Key: Pietro. Alphabet with 18 single letters.

Cipher—h i l m n o p r s t a b c d e f g u

```
       ┌ P r s t u a b c d e f g h i l m n o
       │ I l m n o p r s t u a b c d e f g h
       │ E f g h i l m n o p r s t u a b c d
Plain—┤ T u a b c d e f g h i l m n o p r s
       │ R s t u a b c d e f g h i l m n o p
       └ O p r s t u a b c d e f g h i l m n
```

Example: lhuapaheanslmngtsuumbpaotpebncnealphgsaemagecanud.
Solution: *Si dice per certo che non seguera la guerra contro
Venetiani.*

These alphabets were used in regular keyword succession, and thus
the system corresponds to the so-called Vigenère or repeating-key
cipher. Moreover, Argenti even used a mixed sequence for the cipher
component of cipher alphabets and used this mixed component in keyword fashion, as is shown by the following example:

No. 3.-Key: Argenti. Single figures and letters mixed.

Cipher—2 d o g n l h 3 m 4 a b r 7 z u 8 i 9 e

```
       ┌ A b c d e f g h i l m n o p q r s t u z
       │ R s t u z a b c d e f g h i l m n o p q
       │ G h i l m n o p q r s t u z a b c d e f
Plain—┤ E f g h i l m n o p q r s t u z a b c d
       │ N o p q r s t u z a b c d e f g h i l m
       │ T u z a b c d e f g h i l m n o p q r s
       └ I l m n o p q r s t u z a d c d e f g h
```

Example, using the letters of the keyword in reversed order:
rzr841md844zldnrdo1188eidz22dguz922zu274i98z77olb2.
Solution: *Andara il papa a Bologna se si fara lo guerra contro
Venetiani.*

Although credit for being the inventor of the standard method of
solving this type of cipher is commonly given to Kasiski, a German
cryptographer,[10] who published a work on cryptography in 1863, he
is by no means entitled to this honor. As long back as 1581 John
Battista Argenti seems to have solved ciphers of this type, but he
left no clues as to his method.[11]

[9] This and the next example are taken from Meister, *Die Geheimschrift, etc.*, op. cit.,
p. 85.
[10] Kasiski, F. W., *Die Geheimschriften und die Dechiffrir-Kunst,* Berlin, 1863.
[11] The following is quoted from Meister, *op. cit.*, p. 86:

KEY CIPHER WITH THE LETTERS OF THE ALPHABET

Matteo Argenti transmits to us a key cipher which was laid before him one day by his
employer—by whom is meant the State Secretary—in order that he might study it. He
reports that he deciphered it forthwith without possessing in advance anything on which

However, in 1685 an Englishman, John Falconer, published a small book [12] of great interest, in which he described the chiffre carré and says:

OF SECRET WRITING BY THE KEY CHARACTER

There is an Invention of Secrecy much insisted on (though none of the swiftest) by the Author of the *Secret and Swift Messenger*, and others, beyond any yet mentioned, for Intricacy, wherein each particular *Line, Word, or Letter,* is written by a new Alphabet: but the cited Author himself acknowledges it too tedious for a current Correspondence; which cannot be entertained this way, but at a vast expence of Time and Trouble, to put it in, or take it out of Cypher even by the Key; and secret information, in several Exigencies must be speedy or unprofitable: so that in effect it is unpracticable for the end it is design'd for.

However, lest it should obtain too much credit if supposed undecypherable, its Difficulties shall be considered.

He then takes up various methods of changing the keying, by line, word, and letter, and shows a method for solving each case. It is true that Falconer did not employ the principle now known as "factoring the intervals between repetitions", but the method he indicates, now known as the "probable word method" is a perfectly valid one, even today. Incidentally, credit for this method is commonly given to the French cryptographer, Bazeries, but Falconer anticipated him by 200 years.[13]

* * * * * * *

In the preceding article reference was made to a cipher system invented by Thomas Jefferson. The reader may be interested in knowing what this cipher is like, in view of my comment (p. 53,

to base his manner of solving it. If this statement of Matteo's is correct and he is not merely boasting and attributing to himself a success belonging to his uncle, then this kind of key cipher must have been employed twice for testing the knowledge and keenness of mind of an Argenti. For such a system is found also among the ciphers of Gianbattista Argenti and, to be precise, in the form of a key bearing the date October 8, 1581, with the express remark: Cipher of the illustrious and excellent master; given me for the sake of experimentation on October 8 at the villa. Gianbattista remarks on this point that his chief, Jacomo Boncampagni, had added that it was impossible to solve this kind of cipher without a counter cipher and yet he had accomplished it. And then we see further from the papers of Gianbattista that he made experiments with this method and that after initial failures he had been able to project a cipher in the style for Panicarola which also was actually in use. This letter is cited by Matteo who confesses that he had discovered it among the papers left behind by his uncle. He himself, Matteo, did not employ this key cipher however in the office of the Papal cipher service.

[12] *Cryptomenysis Patefacta: Or the Art of Secret Information Disclosed Without a Key,* London, 1685, p. 17.

[13] In a recent work by two French crytographers (Lange et Soudart, *Traité de Cryptographie,* Paris, 1925) it is stated (p. 173): "Major Bazeries is the inventor of two methods of solving double substitutions, both interesting, more simple, and of more general applicability than those of Kasiski and Kerckhoffs. One of them is based upon assuming a probable word and proceeding with ascertaining the keyword before decrypting the text." An erratum directed toward this paragraph says that the following footnote should be added: "The probable-word method having been already known before M. Bazeries, it would be more correct to say that M. Bazeries has only rediscovered it. This is the method which has been employed in the reading of ancient inscriptions." But the decipherment of ancient inscriptions is a relatively recent event, that of the Egyptian heiroglyphics having been accomplished initially by Young in 1818. I think it would be correct to attribute the first *published* description of the probable-word method to Falconer, in 1685.

Bulletin No. 97) that "there can be no question that had Poe been cognizant of the method * * * he would have pronounced it absolutely inscrutable, for, as compared with the chiffre carré * * * Jefferson's system is of very much greater security."

THE WHEEL CIPHER [14]

Turn a cylinder of white wood of about 2. I. diam. and 6. or 8. I. long. Bore through it's center a hole sufficient to receive an iron spindle or axis of ⅛ or ¼ I. diam. Divide the periphery into 26 equal parts (for the 26 letters of the alphabet) and with a sharp point draw parallel lines through all the points of division from one end to the other of the cylinder and trace those lines with ink to make them plain. Then cut the cylinder crosswise into pieces of about ⅙ of an Inch [diameter] thick. They will resemble backgammon men with plane sides. Number each of them as they are cut off, on one side, that they may [always] be arrangeable in [the same] any order you please. On the periphery of each, & between the black lines, put all the letters of the alphabet, not in their extablished order, but jumbled & without order so that no two shall be alike. Now string them in their numerical order on an iron axis, one end of which has a head and the other a nut and screw, the use of which is to hold them firm in any given position when you chuse it. They are now ready for use, your correspondent having [an exact duplicate of them] a similar cylinder similarly arranged.

Suppose I have to cypher [these words] this phrase 'Your favor of the 22d is received.'

1 turn the 1st wheel till the letter	y. presents itself
turn the 2d and place it',	o. by the side of the y. of the 1st.
turn the 3d and place it',	u. by the side of the o. of the 2d.
turn the 4th and place it',	r. by the side of the u. of the 3d.
turn the 5th and place it',	f. by the side of the r. of the 4th.
turn the 6th and place it',	a. by the side of the f. of the 5th.

and so on till I have got all the words of the phrase arranged in one line. Fix them with the screw. You will observe that the cylinder then presents 25. other lines, not in any regular series, but jumbled & without order or meaning. Copy any one of them in the letter to your correspondent. When he receives it, he takes his cylinder and arranges the wheels so as to present the same jumbled letters in the same order in [a] one line. He then fixes them with his screw and examines the other 25. lines and finds one of them presenting him these words 'Your favor of the 22d is received.' which he writes down. As the others will be jumbled and have no meaning he cannot mistake the true one intended. So proceed with every other portion of your letter. Numbers had better be represented by letters with dots over them as for instance by the 6. vowels and 4. liquids because if the periphery were divided into 36. instead of 26. lines for the numerical as well as alphabetical characters, it would increase the trouble of finding the letters on the wheels. [The cypher may be varied for any number of correspondents by varying

---

[14] Jefferson's Papers, vol. 232, item 41575, Library of Congress, Washington. I have included portions crossed out by Jefferson in the original, because they are of interest as showing how his ideas developed as he was working on the project. These crossed-out portions are shown in brackets. The orthography and punctuation conform exactly with the original, except that Jefferson used capital letters only sparingly, and often a sentence will begin with a small letter. For the sake of clarity the first letter in each sentence has here been capitalized.

the arrangement of the wheels. Every two of those who possess a set of them may have an arrangement private to themselves, and which cannot be understood by the others.]

When the cylinder of wheels is fixed with the jumbled alphabets on their peripheries, by only changing the order of the wheels in the cylinder an immense variety of different cyphers may be produced for different correspondents. For whatever be the number of wheels, if you take all the natural numbers from one to that inclusive, and multiply them successively into one another, their product will be the number of different combinations of which the wheels are susceptible, & consequently of the different cyphers they may form for different correspondents, entirely unintelligible to each other.* For tho' every one possesses the cylinder, and with the alphabets similarly arranged on the wheels, yet if the order be interverted, but one line similar through the whole cylinder can be produced on any two of them.

Suppose the cylinder be 6 I. long (which probably will be a convenient length as it may be spanned in between the middle finger and thumb of the left hand while in use) it will contain 36. wheels, and the sum of it's combinations will be $1 \times 2 \times 3 \times 4 \times 5 \times 6 \times 7 \times 8 \times 9 \times 10 \times 11 \times 12 \times 13 \times 14 \times 15 \times 16 \times 17 \times 18 \times 19 \times 20 \times 21 \times 22 \times 23 \times 24 \times 25 \times 26 \times 27 \times 28 \times 29 \times 30 \times 31 \times 32 \times 33 \times 34 \times 35 \times 36.$

*a.b. b.a.

a.b.c. ⎫ a.c.b. ⎬ 2 b.a.c. ⎫ b.c.a. ⎬ 2 c.a.b. ⎫ c.b.a. ⎭ 2	e.a.b.c.d. e.a.b.d.c. e.a.c.b.d. e.a.c.d.b. e.a.d.b.c. e.a.d.c.b. ⎬ 6	a.e.b.c.d. a.e.b.d.c. a.e.c.b.d. a.e.c.d.b. a.e.d.b.c. a.e.d.c.b. ⎬ 6	a.b.e.c.d. a.b.e.d.c. a.c.e.b.d. a.c.e.d.b. a.d.e.b.c. a.d.e.c.b. b.a.e.c.d. ⎬ 6 etc.	a.b.c.e.d. ⎫ 24	a

d.a.b.c. ⎫ d.a.c.b. d.b.a.c. d.b.c.a. d.c.a.b. d.c.b.a. ⎭ 6	a.d.b.c. ⎫ a.d.c.b. b.d.a.c. b.d.c.a. c.d.a.b. c.d.b.a. ⎭ 6	e.b.a.c.d. e.b.a.d.c. e.b.c.a.d. e.b.c.d.a. e.b.d.a.c. e.b.d.c.a. ⎬ 6	b.e.a.c.d. b.e.a.d.c. b.e.c.a.d. b.e.c.d.a. b.e.d.a.c. b.e.d.c.a. ⎬ 6

a.b.d.c. ⎫ a.c.d.b. b.a.d.c. b.c.d.a. c.a.d.b. c.b.d.a. ⎭	a.b.c.d. ⎫ a.c.b.d. b.a.c.d. b.c.a.d. c.a.b.d. c.b.a.d. ⎭	e.c. etc. 6 e.d. etc. 6 — 24	c.e. etc. 6 d.e. etc. 6 — 24	c.a.e.b.d. 6 d.a.e.b.c. 6 — 24

2 letters can form only 2 series to wit a. b. and b. a.
Add a 3d letter. Then it may be inserted in each of these 2 series either as the 1st, 2d, or 3d letter. Consequently there will be 2x3, series=6 or 1x2x3.
Add a 4th letter. As we have seen that 3 letters will make 6. different series, then a 4th may be inserted in each of these 6 series either as the 1st, 2d, 3d or 4th letter of the series. Consequently there will be 6x4 series=24, or 1x2x3x4.
Add a 5th letter. As 4 give 24 series, the 5th may be inserted in each of these as the 1st, 2d, 3d, 4th, or 5th letter of the series. Consequently there will be 24x5 series= 120=1x2x3x4x5.
Add a 6th letter. As 5 give 120 series, the 6th may be inserted in each of these as the 1st, 2d, 3d, 4th, 5th, or 6th letter of the series. Consequently there will be 120x6 series=720=1x2x3x4x5x6.
And so on to any number.

Many of my readers will recognize Jefferson's device as being practically identical in principle as well as in form with cipher device, type M-94. I will admit that when, in 1922, my friend Professor John Manly brought me a photostatic copy of the foregoing, in Jefferson's own handwriting, with all the corrections Jefferson made as he was describing his invention, I was much startled. For here was another beautiful example of the adage in cryptography that "there is nothing new under the sun." Major Bazeries is credited with having been the inventor of this device, because it was described and pictured in a book written by him in 1901, figure 4 being copied therefrom.[15] But in 1914, Parker Hitt, now Colonel, United States Army, retired, then a captain of Infantry, independently conceived a device employing the same principle. He constructed two devices; one took the form of disks, the other took the form of a set of juxtaposed sliding strips of wood. Colonel Hitt has assured me that he had never seen or heard of Bazeries' cylinder; and it may, of course, be assumed with a high degree of probability that Bazeries had no knowledge of Jefferson's cylinder. In 1917 Captain Hitt brought his device to the attention of Major J. O. Mauborgne, Signal Corps, at that time in charge of the Engineering and Research Division, Office of the Chief Signal Officer. It is to the latter that

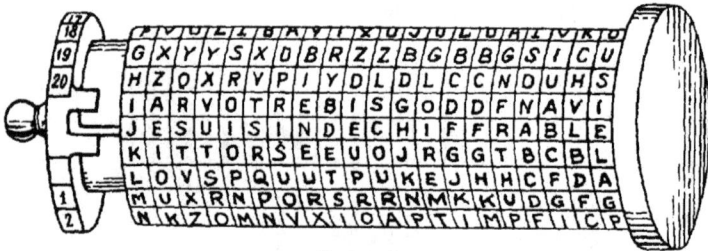

FIGURE 4.

credit should be given not only for the specific embodiment of the Jefferson principle in the present cylindrical form of cipher device type M-94, but also for the preparation of the very thoroughly disarranged alphabets, a feature which was not true of Captain Hitt's embodiment and which makes the solution of messages enciphered by means of the device more difficult.

*   *   *   *   *   *   *

In the previous article I stated that "400 years before Poe lived, professional cryptographers were daily employing and solving ciphers of much greater complexity than any which Poe illustrates and terms intricate. The basic principles for solving the type of ciphers Poe discusses are described in detail in papers written by Italian cryptographers before the dawn of the sixteenth century." Space forbids extensive quotation in substantiation of these statements but I cannot resist presenting the following extracts from another work by Meister.[16]

[15] Bazeries, Commandant, *Les Chiffres Sécrèts Dévoilés*, Paris, 1901.
[16] Meister, A., *Die Anfänge der Modernen Diplomatischen Geheimschrift*, Paderborn, 1902, pp. 20–23.

It is clear, however, that the multiform cryptography of the fifteenth century continued to be elaborated. No one thought of simplifying it; on the contrary, the aim was rather continually to increase the burden of the key and the vocabularies. Often three or six different symbols expressed a single letter of the alphabet, the individual syllables—arranged alphabetically for this purpose, as ba, be, bi, bo, bu, ca, ce, ci, etc.—received special cipher equivalents, and an ever-increasing number of complete words was incorporated into the vocabularies. The wealth of ciphers became so great that it was possible to fill a long alphabetical index with the syllables and words that were to be enciphered. One of these indices is preserved in a volume dating from the middle of the sixteenth century.

* * * * * * *

We have now become acquainted with the internal development of the Venetian ciphers up to the seventeenth century; let us next take a look at their external administration and management. First of all, we shall note that cryptography in Venice was already well organized in the sixteenth century. Up to the year 1542 only one secretary had been appointed, whose duty it was to prepare the cipher despatches and to decipher those coming in. Beginning with 1506 it was Giovanni Soro who, in the course of time, had acquired such a marvelous knowledge of the art of cryptography that he could with ease decipher foreign cryptograms without a knowledge of their keys. His fame spread throughout all Italy, and he was indirectly responsible for elevating the esteem in which the Venetial cryptographic system was held, since courts, and even the Pope himself, at that time applied to the Republic of Venice when they had a cipher despatch which they themselves were unable to decipher. Soro was also of an inventive turn of mind; numerous new cipher-alphabets owe their origin to him.

* * * * * * *

From that time on [1541] Venice had three secretaries educated in the art of cryptography; whether or not the new assistant secretaries were employed exclusively in cryptography, or had other duties to perform and gave assistance to the cryptographic secretary as a side-line, must remain uncertain. Their office was located in the Doge's Palace above the Sala di Segret, and here they worked behind barred doors. When cipher despatches of foreign powers fell into the hands of the Venetians, their translation was ordered at once. No one was allowed to disturb the cryptanalysts, and they were not permitted to leave their office until the solution had been obtained, even though it might take all night. As soon as the solution was obtained it had to be delivered without delay into the hands of the *signorie*. In order to preserve secrecy, it was a matter for gratification if the art of cryptanalysis was bequeathed from one generation to the next in the same family—if the cryptanalysts instructed their sons or their nephews in the art. If the sons succeeded the fathers in the cryptographic service, state secrets simultaneously became family secrets. A violation of these secrets was a capital offense.

On the other hand, new discoveries by private individuals were rewarded, and in this manner a zeal for invention was fired. A certain Marco Raphael received 100 ducats for a method of invisible writing in the year 1525. If the cryptographic secretaries themselves made new discoveries they were publicly praised and received an increase in salary. The usual salary of cryptanalysts was 10, later 12, ducats a month, paid in semiannual installments.

186

[1557.]

Cifra del card. di Burgos[1] con il re Philippo, decifratra alli X febraro 1557 in Bologna.

a	b	c	d	e	f	g	h	i	l	m	n	o	p	q	r	s	t	u	y	z

The cipher symbols and the following syllable tables appear as:

ba	be	bi	bo	bu		pa	pe	pi	po	pu
m	ṁ	-m	m⊦	m𝑓						
						61	62	63	64	65

ca	ce	ci	co	cu		qua	que	qui
16	17	18	19	20				
n	ń	-n	n⊦	n𝑓				
						66	67	68

da	de	di	do	du		ra	re	ri	ro	ru
21	22	23	24	25						
e	é	-e	e⊦	e𝑓		71	72	73	74	75

fa	fe	fi	fo	fu		sa	se	si	so	su
a	à	-a	a⊦	a𝑓						
						76	77	78	79	80

ga	ge	gi	go	gu		ta	te	ti	to	tu
31	32	33	34	35		81	82	83	84	85

ha	he	hi	ho	hu		va	ve	vi	vo	vu
36	37	38	39	40		86	87	88	89	90

ia	ie	ii	io	iu		xa	xe	xi	xo	xu
41	42	43	44	45		91	92	93	94	95

la	le	li	lo	lu		za	ze	zi	zo	zu
5-	5·	-5	5⊦	5𝑓						
46	47	48	49	50		96	97	98	99	—

ma	me	mi	mo	mu		gra	gre	gri	gro	gru
51	52	53	54	55						

na	ne	ni	no	nu		cha	che	chi	cho	chu
56	57	58	59	60						

pra	pre	pri	pro	pru		ff	ll	rr	ss	nn

tra	tre	tri	tro	tru

[1] Franc. Pacecco, card di Burgos, wurde unter Pius IV. Kardinal und starb 1579.

FIGURE 5.

I also cannot resist showing at least one example [17] of a cipher system solved by one of the Argentis in 1557. Note that not only were there equivalents for the single letters, but also there were equivalents for combinations of two and three letters and that in certain cases (ia, ie, ii, io, iu) these combinations had as many as three different equivalents. See figure 5.

Finally, I think it worth while to quote the whole of the treatise by Sicco Simonetta, which is the *oldest* tract on *cryptanalysis* the world possesses. It will be seen that the principles which Poe employed in solving the ciphers he dealt with were well known as early as 1474. The treatise was translated for me from the original Latin by Dr. Mendelsohn, to whom reference has already been made.

SICCO SIMONETTA'S TREATISE ON DECIPHERING [18]

PAVIA, *Monday, July 4th, 1474.*

(1) The first requisite is to see whether the document is in Latin or in the vernacular, and this can be determined in the following manner: See whether the words of the document in question have only five different terminations, or less, or more; if there are only five or less, you are justified in concluding that it is in the vernacular, but if there are more than five, the supposition is that it is in Latin; for all common words in our language end in a vowel, and there are five vowels, a, e, i, o, u. If, on the other hand, the words of the document in question have more than five terminations, you are justified in concluding that it is in Latin, since it is possible for Latin or literary words to end in a vowel, a semi-vowel (l, m, n, r, s, x), and in a mute (b, c, d, f, g, k, q, p, t).

(2) Another rule for determining the same thing, namely, whether the document is in the vernacular or in the Latin or literary language: See whether it contains many or repeated occurrences of words denoted by only one character. In that case it is probable that it is in the vernacular, since in the vernacular words denoted by only one character are very frequent, while in the Latin or literary language they are rare, Latin having only four words denoted by one character or letter, namely, e, a, prepositions, o, an exclamation, and i, a verb in the imperative; and these words, with the exception of the preposition a, rarely occur in letters.

(3) Item. See whether the document in question contains many and repeated occurrences of words of two or three characters or letters; if so you may conclude that it is in the vernacular, since words of this kind are commoner in the vernacular than in Latin.

(4) After you have concluded, according to the preceding rules, that the document in question is in the vernacular, or that it is in the Latin or literary language, you will be certain, if it is in the vernacular, which characters represent vowels (without knowing just which vowel each character represents), since the characters at the ends of words are invariably vowels in the language of all Italy. After determining the vowels in this manner, see which character among those found at the ends of words occurs more often in monosyllabic words of only one letter or character. It is very likely that this character will be e, since e is the copula, and is extremely common in the vernacular, and in addition represents the conjunction e.

---

[17] Meister, *Die Geheimschrift, etc.,* p. 216.
[18] From Meister, *Die Anfänge,* etc., p. 61–3.

(5). Item. Words in the vernacular containing only two letters must be carefully studied, since many of them begin with l, being articles associated with nouns, as lo and la in the singular and le in the plural.

(6) Item. Examine the words consisting of three letters only and see whether any of these occurs frequently in the document, since the word che is very common in the vernacular.

(7) If the document in question appears to be in Latin and not in the vernacular, then examine the characters at the ends of words, and see which of them are most frequent. These will probably be either vowels or s, m, or t, since most Latin words end either in a vowel or in s, m, or t, and only a few end in a mute other than t, exceptions being ab, ad, and quod, which are common enough in letters.

(8) Another rule. See whether the document in question contains any word denoted by a single character; you may conjecture that this word is a, because words of one character, with the exception of the preposition a, are rare in Latin, as has been pointed out above.

(9) Another rule. Examine the characters at the ends of words, which, as has been shown above, frequently represent one of the vowels, or s, m, or t. See whether any of these is found in words of one or two characters. If one of them occurs in a word containing only one character, then that character represents one of the vowels, since there can be no word or syllable without a vowel, and this vowel will be either a, e, i, or o—most likely the preposition a, as has been pointed out above. If the character occurs in a word of two characters, then run over in your mind all words composed of only two letters, and especially those that are common in communications, such as et, ut, ad, si, me, te, and se. And so that none may escape you, I will list here all or almost all the words of two letters. They are: ab, ac, an, and at, da, de, and do, ea, ei, eo, ex, and es, he, hi, id, ii, in, ir, is, and it, me, mi, na, ne, and ni, ob, os, re, se, and si, tu, te, ve, vi, and ut.

(10) Another rule. See whether the document in question contains any words of three characters only, with the first character the same as the last; such a word may well be non, which is of frequent occurrence in documents or sis, or ibi. Other words of three letters must be considered too, such as ala, ama, ana, ara, ede, eme, ere, ehe, ixi, ivi.

(11) Another rule. See whether the document in question contains any word or words in which a character occurs three times in succession; this character will be u, as in uvula.[19]

(12) Another rule. See whether the document in question contains any double character, especially in words of four characters. This character may be l or s, which are frequently doubled, as in esse and ille.

(13) Finally, one more rule, applicable to documents in the vernacular as well as to those in Latin. See whether the document in question contains any character which is always followed by one and the same character. Such a character will represent q, and the character that follows it u, since q is always followed by u; and the character following that which represents u is always a vowel, for q is always followed by u, and after the u we always find another vowel.

The foregoing rules can be circumvented in many ways, as, for example, by writing part of the cipher letter in the vernacular and part in Latin; or by interposing or adding in the document cipher characters that represent no

---

[19] Appears as mula in the ms, and undoubtedly meant to be uuula. The reader should bear in mind that u and v were once undifferentiated in their written form.

letters at all, especially in the case of words of one, two, or three characters or letters; or by writing in two entirely different cipher alphabets; or by representing qu by a single character.

THE EDITOR'S OBSERVATION POST *

JEFFERSON'S CIPHER DEVICE

In the previous issue of the Bulletin, Jefferson's description of his cipher device was given in full on pages 68 and 69 and his original manuscript, which is filed at the Library of Congress, was specifically referred to. Mr. William F. Friedman, of the Office of the Chief Signal Officer, kindly obtained a new photostatic copy of the original manuscript but it was unfortunately received by the editor too late to be inserted in the Bulletin at that time. However, the paper is of such interest that it is felt the Signal Corps Bulletin should bring it to light herewith. (See illustrations on pages 87 and 88.)

*(No. 99, January–March, 1938)

[Handwritten manuscript — Thomas Jefferson's original description of his wheel cipher device. The handwriting is largely illegible in this reproduction.]

The wheel cypher.

Turn a cylinder of white wood of about 2.I. diam. and 6. o 8.I. long. bore through it's center a hole sufficient to receive an iron spindle or axis of ⅓ or ½ I. diam. divide the periphery into 26 equal parts (for the 26. letters of the alphabet) and with a sharp point draw parallel lines through all the points of division from one end to the other, and trace those lines with ink to make them plain. then cut the cylinder crosswise into pieces of about ⅙ of an inch thick. they will resemble backgammon men with plane sides. number them as they are cut off, on one side, that they may be arrangeable in any order ... on the periphery of each, & between the black lines put all the letters of the alphabet not in their established order, but jumbled & without order so that no two shall be alike. now string them in their numerical order on an iron axis, one end of which has a head and the other a nut & screw, the use of which is to hold them firm in any given position when you chuse it. they are now ready for use, your correspondent having ... a similar cylinder similarly arranged.

Suppose I have to cypher this ... 'your favour of the 22d. is recieved'

I turn the 1st. wheel till the letter y. presents itself
then the 2d. and place it's   o. by the side of the y. of the 1st.
then the 3d. and place it's   u. by the side of the o. of the 2d.
then the 4th. and place it's   r. by the side of the u. of the 3d.
then the 7th. and place it's   f. by the side of the r. of the 6th.
then the 8th. and place it's   a. by the side of the f. of the 7th.

and so on till I have got the whole ... you will observe that the cylinder then presents 26. other lines of letters, not in any regular series, but jumbled & without order or meaning. copy any one of them in the letter to your correspondent. when he recieves it, he takes his cylinder and arranges the wheels so as to ... the same jumbled letters in the same order in ... line, he then ... the other 25. lines and finds one of them presenting him these words 'your favor of the 22d. is recieved' which he writes down. as the others will be jumbled & have no meaning he cannot mistake the true one intended. so proceed with every other ... of your letter ... letters with dots over them ... the periphery were divided into 26 instead of 26. lines for the numerical as well as alphabetical characters, it would increase the trouble of finding the letters on the spoke.

the cypher may be varied for any number of correspondents by varying the ... of the wheels, every two of whom the pocket a ... them ... private to themselves, and which can ... by the others.

Thomas Jefferson's original description of his wheel cipher device. Front of item 41575, Jefferson's Papers.

191

Then the cylinder of wheels is fixed with the jumbled alphabets on their peripheries, by only changing the order of the wheels in the cylinder an immense variety of different cyphers may be produced for different correspondents. for whatever be the number of wheels, if you take all the natural numbers from one to that inclusive, & multiply them successively into one another, their product will be the number of different combinations of which the wheels are susceptible, & consequently of the different cyphers they may form for different correspondents, entirely unintelligible to each other. for tho' every one possesses the cylinder, and with the alphabets similarly arranged on the wheels, yet if the order be interverted, but one similar does through the whole cylinder can be produced on any two of them.

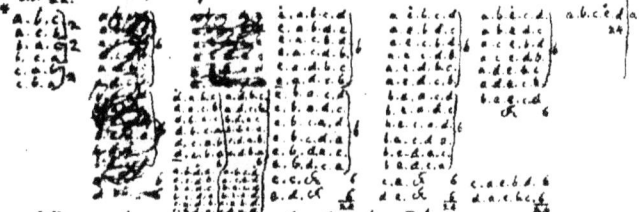

2 letters can form only 2 series, to wit a.b. and b.a.
add a 3d. letter. then it may be inserted in each of these 2 arrangements either as the 2d. or 3d. letter. consequently there will be 2×3 series = 6 or 1×2×3.
add a 4th. letter. as we have seen that 3 letters will make 6 different series then a 4th. may be inserted in each of these 6 series either as the 1st. 2d. 3d. or 4th letter of the series consequently there will be 6×4 series = 24. or 1×2×3×4.
add a 5th letter. as 4. gives 24 series, the 5th may be inserted in each of these as the 2d. 4th or 5th letter of the series. consequently there will be 24×5 series = 120 1×2×3×4×5
add a 6th. letter. as 5 give 120 series, the 6th may be inserted in each of these as the 1st. 2d. 3d. 4th. 5th. or 6th letter of the series. consequently there will be 120×6 series = 720 = 1×2×3×4×5×6.
and so on to any number.
suppose the cylinder be 6.I. long (which probably will be a convenient length as it may be spanned in the hand between the middle finger & thumb of the left hand while in use) it contain 36 wheels. and the sum of it's combinations will be 1×2×3×4×5×6×7×8×9×10×11. ×12×13×14×15×16×17×18×19×20×21×22×23×24×25×26×27×28×29×30×31×32×33×34×35×36.

Reverse side of item 41575, Jefferson's Papers, Vol. CCXXXII, Library of Congress, Washington, D. C.

THE USE OF CODES AND CIPHERS IN THE WORLD WAR AND LESSONS TO BE LEARNED THEREFROM *

By Lt. Col. WILLIAM F. FRIEDMAN, *Signal Reserve*

Col. Parker Hitt, the well-known cryptographer of the American Army, opens his Manual for the Solution of Military Ciphers with the following words:

> The history of war teems with occasions where the interception of dispatches and orders written in plain language has resulted in defeat and disaster for the force whose intentions thus became known at once to the enemy. For this reason, prudent generals have used cipher and code messages from time immemorial.

To cite but one of the many occasions which Colonel Hitt had in mind, perhaps but little known or at least not often recalled these days, wherein the failure to cryptograph but one message profoundly affected the course of one of the most important wars in history, I will go back to our Civil War.

During the Battle of Gettysburg, General Meade decided to withdraw from the field. This decision was made by him on the evening of the second day. He accordingly wrote up the message ordering the retreat, but just as he was about to post it, a cavalry officer arrived with a dispatch which had been taken from a captured Confederate. The dispatch was "in clear" from President Davis to General Lee, informing Lee that it was impossible to assemble another Confederate army to threaten Washington. Meade then knew that Washington could not be threatened and that the only Confederate forces he had to contend with were Lee's. Accordingly, he canceled his order for a Union retreat. If the dispatch from Davis to Lee had been in cipher or code, which would have delayed the decipherment 1 or 2 hours, the order for a Union retreat would have gone forth, and, perhaps, the whole course of the war would have been changed.

There is no necessity, however, to delve into the musty past because of a dearth of material of a more recent vintage. Let me pass over the years intervening between 1865 and 1914 and come at once to the World War.

It would be an impossible task for me to try to present in the course of one article the many interesting details concerning the use of codes and ciphers in the World War. The best one can do is to touch only the high spots and to point out some of the lessons to be learned therefrom. It is not an overstatement, in the opinion of certain

*(No. 101, July–September, 1938)

192

notable persons who themselves are not cryptanalysts, to say that the use of cryptography played a very vital role in the outcome of that war. To cite but one instance, Sir Basil Thomson, who had charge of the Criminal Investigation Department of the British Government, popularly known as Scotland Yard, during the whole of the War and for some years thereafter, has made the statement that the decipherment of but one code message by British cryptographers, the now notorious Zimmermann telegram, did more towards bringing the United States into the War than the sinking of the *Lusitania* had done, and that had not America entered the War when she did, the Allies would have had to surrender.

The Zimmermann telegram was so far-reaching in its consequences that I think a few words about it will not be amiss. This is how the matter is introduced by Burton J. Hendrick in The Life and Letters of Walter H. Page:

One day, in the latter part of February 1917, Page was requested to call upon Mr. Balfour at the Foreign Office. Mr. Balfour quietly handed the Ambassador a sheet of paper—a document that, in its influence upon American policy, proved to be the most sensational that the European War had so far brought forth. This paper contained the message which became famous as the Zimmermann telegram. It disclosed the preparation Germany was making for war with the United States. It was a message from the German Foreign Office in Berlin to Von Eckhardt, the German Minister in the City of Mexico. As Germany had no satisfactory method of communicating with Mexico, this telegram had been sent to Count Bernstorff in Washington, with instructions to forward it by cable to the German Minister in the Mexican Republic. The latter diplomat was directed to enter at once into negotiations with Venustiano Carranza, President of Mexico, and to make an alliance with Mexico for a joint German and Mexican invasion of the United States.

In case this invasion succeeded, Mexico was to obtain Texas, New Mexico, and Arizona—territory which she had lost to the United States as a result of the war of 1846, and which was now to be treated as a kind of Mexican Alsace-Lorraine and be "redeemed." The German plan also contemplated an attempt to detach Japan from her European allies and persuade her to join the German-Mexican alliance. President Carranza, who, as subsequent events disclosed, looked not unfavorably upon his ambitious proposal, was the same Carranza whom President Wilson had supported for the Mexican Presidency among a multitude of revolutionary candidates. Carranza was President of Mexico, indeed, as the result of a succession of events that amounted almost to American intervention.

Just how the British cryptanalysts under Admiral Hall of their Naval Intelligence decoded this message is too long a story to tell at this time. But I will quote a significant passage from General Ludendorff's My War Memories:

The attempt on the part of our Foreign Office to establish military operations with Mexico strengthened public opinion against us in the United States. In spite of my warnings the Foreign Office had used an antiquated and easily decipherable secret code.

194

But if Ludendorff found it easy to criticize the Foreign Office for using an "antiquated" code, he overlooks in his same book the advantages which he derived from poor cryptography on the part of the Russians whom he defeated on the Eastern Front in August 1914. General DuPont says of this:

The maneuver that led up to the Tanneberg victory at the end of August is known. Ludendorff tells it at length in his memories, and covers himself with glory on the basis of it. He cannot be blamed; it is one of the finest operations of the war. But there is one detail which he does not tell, which singularly facilitated his task, and diminishes his bravado. He knew the Russian cipher; all the orders in the army of his adversaries being transmitted by wireless, he deciphered them, and knew what they contained at the same time as their executors. Every night, the intercepted radios were deciphered around 11 o'clock. They were taken to Ludendorff who then drew up his orders, taking them into consideration. When there was some delay, which was rarely the case, he arrived at the cipher bureau anxious to know the cause.

I learned these details personally from the mouth of his cipher officer himself; the public got the revelation of the fact from Falkenhayn who slips it into his memoires incidentally.

Later on I shall discuss further the decipherment of the Russian cryptograms and the effects thereof on the German operations on the Eastern Front.

In order to point out the lessons which can be learned from the use and misuse of cryptography in the World War it is advisable that we learn something about the various cryptographic systems employed by the different combatants. We shall find that all the combatants were guilty of much carelessness, ignorance, and ineptitude in the development of code and cipher systems suitable for the purposes for which they are intended, and in the handling of these systems and of messages cryptographed by their means.

Before coming to a description of the systems themselves, a few words about basic principles may not be amiss. I will assume that the reader knows the essential technical differences between code and cipher methods, and that it is unnecessary to define such common terms as enciphering, deciphering, encoding, decoding, cryptographing, decryptographing, cryptanalysis and cryptanalyst. I do wish, however, to give a definition of the term "signal communication security." This term is used to embrace all means and measures undertaken to nullify as completely as possible the efforts of the enemy in his endeavors to intercept and learn the meaning of the messages transmitted by any of the agencies of signal communication. Now signal communication security can be treated under various phases: visual security, telephone security, radio security, and so on. But the most important of these phases and one which enters to a greater or lesser extent into all the others is cryptographic security. This term is connected with the degree of resistance which cryptographed messages present to unauthorized reading, that is, to their solution.

It may be stated that the degree of cryptographic security afforded by a given system is determined by three things: First, the character of the system itself, that is, its technical soundness; second, the extent to which it is used, which in the case of radio corresponds quite directly with the amount of text that may become available for enemy study; and third, the care with which the system and messages cryptographed by it are handled by using personnel. I shall cite instances which will illustrate the nature and importance of many of these factors, using data from the World War.

The technical soundness of cryptographic systems in general is not dependent solely upon theoretical calculations based upon the number of permutations or combinations afforded by a particular method. Indeed, there are cases in which the permutative possibilities can be expressed in astronomical figures, and yet a single message in an unknown key can be solved in a very short time and sometimes in a purely mechanical way. The number of permutations and combinations a given system affords is relatively unimportant. What is vital, as a rule, is the exact manner in which the elements or processes or steps that constitute the method are applied. For example, take the simple case of what we technically designate monoalphabetic substitution, that is, where a single substitution alphabet is used in replacing the individual letters of a message. Using the 26 letters of our alphabet it is possible to make factorial 26 different substitution alphabets—a number that none of us can really grasp. The possibilities for changing the alphabet are here truly staggering in number. Yet a message of average length written by means of any one of such alphabets can be solved very easily. On the other hand, I could take a set of only 26 of such alphabets and use them in such a way in encipherment, and a very simple way I assure you, that the message could not possibly be read without the key. So it is apparent that the mere number of combinations doesn't mean anything unless qualified in other respects.

So much for preliminary considerations. Let us now take a look at some of the systems employed during the World War. First, those used by the German Army.

At the outbreak of war, the Germans used a cipher system which was known to the French. That is, the basic operations were understood, but, of course, the system was such that it operated in connection with specific secret keywords which could be changed at will. It was a very good system in theory, but in practice it gave rise to such difficulties, when errors in transmission occurred, that there was much traffic in plain text, both in the cases where there were many questions and answers concerning the garbled messages and in the cases where commanders, exasperated by these difficulties, disregarded all rules and sent their original messages in clear. Naturally, these plain-text messages soon enabled the cipher messages to be read and their keys reconstructed, with the result that the entire secrecy of this theoretically very secure cipher system was completely destroyed. This system was in effect from August 6 to November 18, 1914, a period of 3½ months—very important months at that. At this time the French commander in chief wrote to the Minister of War saying:

I have been able to appreciate, like all Army commanders, in the last few days the value of the services rendered by the code section of your cabinet.

There are three lessons to be learned from this situation. First, the factor which was of decisive importance for the solution of the system consisted in the knowledge gained by the French experts as to the general nature of the German telegrams, such as the style, the terminology and structure of reports and orders, common abbreviations, introductory and closing formulas, and so on, all of a highly standardized and stereotyped nature. During the whole war, in fact, as may be pointed out again and again, this stereotyped style formed one of the most valuable sources of data for the cryptanalysts, especially in the solution of code. The first lesson, therefore, is that anything which is of a stereotyped nature is highly detrimental to cryptographic security.

The second lesson to be observed is this: Without adequately trained personnel for cryptographic work, errors and blunders are unavoidable, and these afford direct or indirect clues to solution of the messages. Had the German cryptographic personnel been better trained in the use of the particular cipher system involved, it is certain that there would have been fewer errors, fewer cases of indecipherable messages because of these errors, fewer calls for repetitions, and fewer exchanges in plain text which gave clues as to the meanings of specific messages or cipher groups in specific messages. Secret communication might indeed have remained safe for the necessary period.

Finally, this case calls particular attention to the necessity for having experienced cryptographers devise systems which will be practicable for field use and which can be safely used by enlisted personnel of average intelligence. The particular cipher system in this case was not one which could successfully be employed by such personnel, and it simply broke down under the pressure of war conditions. It is necessary to stress the fact that, although the French cryptanalysts did wonderful work, the numerous blunders made by the Germans really made it possible.

For over 3 months, as I have said before, the French were reading the German cipher telegrams. Then on November 18, 1914, a radical change in the structure and appearance of the German cryptograms took place and for 3 weeks the French cryptanalysts struggled with the messages. Success finally came, again largely due to blunders and carelessness of the Germans. The new system was found to be really simpler than the old one.

Various cipher systems were employed one after the other by the Germans during the first 3 years of the War. They were all more or less simple variations of old principles, and they were used with much carelessness. I need hardly mention that they were all solved soon after they were adopted. Indeed, most of the new keys were solved the day they were placed into effect. As usual, this was rendered easy because of the blunders and carelessness of the using personnel. There were cases, however, in which it was not mere carelessness but downright foolishness which gave the solutions to special keys. I will cite an amusing example which I recently ran across in a little book by a former British intelligence officer, entitled "War, Wireless, and Wangles."

I also recall with gratitude the German wireless chief in Constantinople, who, returning from leave in Germany, had a dinner to celebrate it. After the feast, which must have been a good one, the party repaired to the big wireless station and sent identically the same message of good cheer to all enemy stations round in six different ciphers. Before this happened five of the ciphers were undecipherable by us but we knew the sixth. After the "beano" we knew the lot.

As to what the French and British were using during this time I can pass along very hastily. The French Army used a code for communication between Army headquarters and GHQ, and a rather peculiar transposition cipher for communication between smaller units. The French would have us believe that the Germans never succeeded in solving the latter cipher and it is possible that this is true. However, I am inclined to doubt this, largely for the reason that the French cipher system was by no means indecipherable. If the Germans did not succeed, it must have been because they were not organized to do so, and I am inclined to believe that this was really the case. From the few references that can be found it appears that the Germans had no cryptanalytic units on the Western Front until late in 1916. It must also be true that the German experts who by chance were available for this duty found their work much more difficult because of the fact that radio was purposely restricted from the very beginning both by the French and the British, and because of the fact that cryptanalytic work was begun too late, as the British and the French crytographic regulations had already been affected by experiences gained in observing the mistakes and blunders made by the Germans. In short, the great start which the French in particular had in preparations for cryptographic work not only made it possible for them to keep up, step by step, with the crytographic changes by the Germans, but also to a great extent to apply to their own crytography valuable experience gained from their cryptanalytic work on the German messages. The reverse situation was not the case, for not until about 1917 may it be said that the Germans caught up with their adversaries and then only in cryptographic work. In cryptanalytic work they apparently never quite caught up.

As to the British, they seem to have placed their confidence largely in a modified Playfair cipher. The modification consisted merely in inserting the letters within the square in a haphazard manner rather than in keyword order. Today such a cipher system, no matter if the key were changed twice a day, would not be at all safe, but in those days it seems to have been sufficient. It was only so short a time ago as 1914 that one of the American crytographers, our own Lieutenant Mauborgne (now Chief Signal Officer of the Army), wrote a short study entitled "An Advanced Problem in Cryptography and its Solution," in which, after giving the crytogram which had been prepared by a British Army captain, the author states:

> The students of this school (Army Signal School at Fort Leavenworth then) were practically challenged by Captain Muirhead to discover the meaning of the crytogram, but a solution, so far as the writer knows, has never been forthcoming * * *.

We shall see that the British discarded this cipher in 1917.

In the beginning I alluded to the cryptographic work of the Russians, and a few more words here will not be amiss. Right from the very start military Russian cryptography was a dismal failure and one which, according to some historians, was largely responsible for their terrible disasters on the Eastern Front. Never before in the history of cryptography had it happened that so exceedingly important and complete information about the intentions and order of battle of one side was absolutely betrayed to the other side as a result of a complete disregard of what constitutes good practice in secret communications. In the opinion of the war-time Chief of Intelligence of the German Army, Colonel Nicolai, the decisive injury to the Russian conduct of the war was done by the failure of their cryptographic service. Those of you who would like to know more about the way in which the Russian failures in this work contributed to their defeat should read the very interesting discussion contained in the article by the Swedish cryptographer, Yves Gylden, as printed in several installments in the Signal Corps Bulletin beginning with the issue of November–December 1933. I would like to quote one paragraph from Gylden's article:

> A review of the cryptographic operations on the Eastern Front necessarily emphasizes the dangers connected with the use of radio for communications. A few words on this subject may be in place. The said dangers are very great; that fact cannot be denied. But it would be like throwing out the child with the bath to give up such a valuable, rapid, and simple means of communication as radio for this reason alone. Its value as a means of communication is undenia-

ble, and, strikingly enough, it has been assigned a much greater importance in the armies of the great powers on the continent since the war. Nor was it radio as a means of communication which so often failed, but the cryptographic service, a fact which can never be too greatly emphasized. But if used with a well-organized cryptographic service, fully experienced in cryptanalysis, radio becomes an invaluable means of communication. When used by a personnel ignorant of the principles of cryptanalysis and poorly prepared, it, on the other hand, becomes to the highest degree dangerous for the activities of the armies using it. Common sense alone tells us that the use of a means of communication which leads both to friend and foe must necessarily presuppose exceptionally great knowledge of cryptography and cryptanalysis on the part of the personnel responsible for the operation of that means. Such knowledge must be made compulsory.

Regarding the codes and ciphers used by some of the other belligerents in the World War, the Italians, the Austrians, the Turks, suffice it to say that none of them can be said to have used cryptography with outstanding success and none of them succeeded in avoiding the pitfalls and dangers connected with the subject. I must not, however, fail to say something about cryptography in the A. E. F. It is true that when our troops arrived overseas they were wholly unprepared for cryptographic successes. The only thing we had was the Playfair cipher and the old War Department Telegraph Code, printed in 1915. A code compilation section was established very early, however, and efforts were made to profit by the experiences of the French and the British. At first they were rather hesitant to cooperate, and our section had to do the best it could. How good a job was done in the way of compiling field codes will be clear when I tell you that by the middle of 1918 the French and the British were convinced that our codes were better than theirs and made ready to change their own in favor of our system.

But our great trouble was with the people who used the codes, just as was the case with all the other belligerents. You will say, no doubt, that if all the armies had the same difficulties it might be that the answer to secret communication lies in using something other than code books. Why not cipher systems or cipher devices? But I fear that would be only a partial and an unsatisfactory solution to the problem, for there are difficulties inherent in the use of ciphers also—especially hand-operated ones. Hand-operated cipher systems are indeed much slower, as a rule, than codes; they are no safer, if the codes are properly constructed. Cipher machines and cipher devices present other problems and besides they are still in the developmental stage, although the general principles upon which devices are based have been known for a long time. I must at this point tell you about one case of a cipher device during the World War. Seeing all the difficulties and disadvantages of codes and of hand-operated cipher systems, certain British cryptographers in the latter part of 1917 or very early in 1918 proposed the adoption and use, by all the Allies,

200

of a cipher device to replace field codes then in use. The new device was a simple but apparently very effective modification of one originally devised by Sir Charles Wheatstone, the well-known British scientist of Wheatstone-Bridge fame. The British experts thought so highly of their new device as a cryptographic instrument that one of the arguments advanced against its adoption into usage on the Western Front was to the effect that if one of the devices were captured, the Germans would also adopt it and soon the Allies would no longer be in the fortunate position of being able to solve the German cryptograms, as was theretofore the case. However, this argument did not deter them and they submitted the device to their allies for consideration and criticism. It finally was brought to Washington by special courier. As the adoption of cipher devices for the United States Army was a responsibility of the Chief Signal Officer, the G–2 section of the War Department submitted the proposed device to the Signal Corps for test. Our present Chief Signal Officer, Maj. Gen. J. O. Mauborgne, then major and officer in charge of the Research and Engineering Division, was not so sure of the security of messages enciphered by the device as were the British and French experts. He proposed to have an independent test made, and with that end in view asked that a series of five short messages all in the same key be sent to the Riverbank Laboratories, Geneva, Ill., where a staff of cryptanalysts under my direction was doing certain cryptanalytic work for various branches of the Government, including the War Department. Of course, considering that in actual usage the enemy might have scores or even hundreds of messages at his disposal, the submission of but five short messages (each one had only 35 or 36 letters) for a test of security was, to say the least, hardly fair. But good fortune was with me that day, for with the able assistance of Mrs. Friedman, whose "woman's intuition" played an important part in the successful outcome of what seemed at first a perfectly hopeless task, the messages were solved within 3 hours and their plain texts telegraphed to Washington. Needless to say, the unfavorable report cabled to London put an end to all ideas of adopting the device, which hit the British pretty hard because, as I afterwards learned, they had had thousands of the devices manufactured and ready for distribution. Incidentally, the first of those five test messages we solved read "This cipher is absolutely indecipherable"!

I cite this incident merely to show you that the invention of a good cipher device is a very difficult problem. There is a feverish activity all over the world today looking toward the development of automatic cipher machines, but it will be a long time before we will know how successful such machines will be in practical operation. In the meantime codes and code books for secret communication must be depended upon to a great extent, especially in the lower units in the field.

To get back to the development and use of field codes during the War, up until the early part of 1917 it was thought that code books were impractical for field use. But by June 1917 field codes became general among all the belligerents on the Western Front. It is difficult to say which side first initiated them, and perhaps the development was simultaneous on both sides. At first the majority of such codes were very small and were what we call one-part or alphabetically arranged codes. I believe it was the Germans who first introduced the two-part, or cross-reference code.

To this day such codes still provide the simplest, most practicable means of secret communication for field use. When properly employed, they yield a very high degree of security. But note that I say "when properly employed." This must be emphasized repeatedly, for unless codes are properly used their length of life is very much reduced. By length of life I mean merely this: Given a sufficient amount of traffic, any code can be ultimately solved by the principles of cryptanalysis. Realizing this, we guard against it by replacing one edition of a code by another in which although the same code groups and the same plain-text words and phrases may be present as in the former edition, yet the code groups have now been entirely shifted about so that they no longer have the same plain-text meanings as in the preceding edition. The length of time a given edition may be safely employed—that is, the length of life of the code—therefore depends upon two factors. First, there is the factor of the extent to which the code is employed; that is, the amount of text an enemy may obtain for study of frequencies, and so on. This in turn depends upon two things: First, the restrictions placed upon the distribution of the code, since the wider the distribution the greater the number of messages and the greater the chances for loss or compromise of copies of the code; secondly, the restrictions placed upon the actual usage of the code; that is, what sorts of messages will be encoded in it—secret, confidential, or restricted—and how often such messages are required. The second principal factor in determining the length of life of a code is the care with which the code and messages encoded by it are handled by the using personnel.

There are certain precautions that must be observed in the handling of codes and code messages if we are going to establish and maintain security. These precautions have, I may say, arisen out of the lessons learned during the World War and since that time. They are not merely theoretical considerations, and for each rule that I may bring up I could site many instances where its violation resulted in damage to security.

The subject of restricting code distributions will not concern us here. So far as concerns the using personnel it is merely their duty and responsibility to see that the restrictions placed upon the distribution and upon the individuals to whom codes are to be entrusted are strictly obeyed. But there are other matters which are within the control of using personnel. It may at once be stated that information dangerous to cryptographic security comes from violations of the principles governing the following:

(1) The filing, storage, and safeguarding of all technical paraphernalia pertaining to the code or cipher system employed, that is, the code books, cipher tables, cipher keys, etc.

(2) The classification of messages into the three authorized categories ("secret," "confidential," and "restricted").

(3) The preparation or drafting of the plain text of a message to be transmitted in cryptographic form.

(4) The selection of the particular cryptographic system to be employed in its cryptographing.

(5) The actual cryptographing by means of the system selected.

(6) The handling, filing, and subsequent safeguarding of the literal text of the message.

(7) The preparation of copies of the message for distribution for the information of other persons legitimately concerned with its contents.

(8) The preparation of press releases in which some of the information conveyed by the cryptographed message is, when necessary, communicated to the world at large.

(9) The selection of the particular signal communication agency by which the message is to be transmitted.

(10) The technical procedure followed in transmission, especially in the case of radio.

Aside from the serious military consequences which may follow from the violation of the rules I am about to state, the financial loss attendant upon the compromise of a code book is a serious matter. A code, the preparation of which has cost thousands of dollars and required the services of many persons over a period of many months, may be compromised or rendered worthless by the transmission of a few poorly encoded messages or by carelessness in handling the translation of a single cryptographed message.

I will take up some of the principles listed a few moments ago and give a few details.

The question of physical security of code and cipher documents themselves can be passed over hastily. It is obvious that such things as code books, cipher tables, and the like must be kept in secure safes when not in use, and that periodical accounting to assure their presence is essential. Of course, all kinds of safeguards are advisable against surreptitious photography of such documents, which is much more dangerous than their actual theft.

Next we come to the matter of drafting messages that are to be cryptographed. By all odds the practice most dangerous to cryptographic
security is to fall into the habit of using stereotyped phraseology.
Standardization in content and form in documents such as field orders,
operation instructions, and the like, is necessary, but when such fixity
in expression is carried over into message construction the results are
very detrimental to communication security. It must be assumed that
an alert enemy has made a careful study of our military traffic in plain
language and has become familiar with the words and phrases most
often used to express the most commonly transmitted ideas. Consequently, if the standardization of expression is adhered to in messages
that are to be sent in cryptographic form, the enemy is given a degree
of assistance that can only be appreciated by those who have seen in
actual practice how the solution of cryptograms is facilitated and
sometimes made possible through a knowledge of standardized form
of expression. Many times, after a laborious analysis has been made,
the cryptanalyst has reached the situation when he must, to make further progress, assume or guess a word in the text. If he is dealing
with messages written in stereotypic phraseology, this step is comparatively easy for he "knows" many of the words which will appear;
he does not have to "guess." Hence, it is clear that rearrangement of
words, and deviation from the usual or common form should be practiced as much as possible; it is a good plan never to use the most common expression when an unusual or uncommon one will be just as
clear. Especially important is the avoidance of stereotype in the case
of cipher systems, for in the latter the mechanics of the systems not
only do not permit of the replacement of common expressions by single
code words, but also the use of variants is not possible, as is the case
in code systems. Consequently, the need for avoiding set form and
phraseology is greater when cipher systems are used.

Unnecessary punctuation constitutes a weakness and should be
avoided. A carefully drafted message requires very little punctuation. Superfluous words, unnecessary repetitions, unnecessary references and the like not only increase the lengths of messages but are
also of much assistance in solution. If a message or a part of a message received in secret or confidential code must be quoted in either
plain or secret language in another message or in a letter, the portions
quoted should first be very carefully paraphrased.

The cryptographing is, of course, done at the message center, where
presumably trained cryptographers are assigned the responsibility.
Our regulations, however, require that the cryptographing and decryptographing of secret messages by means of secret codes and ciphers will be performed only under the direct supervision and in the
presence of a commissioned officer.

Of course, there are occasions when there is no time to cryptograph a confidential or even a secret message in the combat zone. The regulations in this case provide that a message may be transmitted in plain language when, in the judgment of the officer concerned, the necessity for getting the information to the addressee without delay is so urgent that this consideration completely outweighs the value that its interception would have for the enemy. The decision to omit cryptographing is at all times the responsibility of the originator or the particular officer concerned and the message must bear the notation "Send in clear" over his signature. Officers will think twice, as a rule, before sending messages in clear if they have to give written authority for each case of plain-language transmission of a message containing secret or confidential information.

It goes without saying that the intermixture of plain language and code or cipher groups in the same message is a highly dangerous practice. Innumerable examples could be cited in the case of messages on all fronts during the World War. Then there is the matter of addresses and signatures of messages and the very important information one can obtain merely from these parts of messages. They should never be cryptographed in the same system as is used in cryptographing the text of the message itself.

Then we come to the question of the handling and filing of the original, literal texts of messages sent in secret or confidential code. Of course, next to having the code book itself, the possession of exact translations of only a few messages will destroy the security of a system almost at once. For this reason, two cardinal principles have been set up to cover this aspect of secret communication:

(1) There should be in existence only a definite, limited number of copies of the plain text of a message crytographed in any secret code or cipher and these copies should be carefully controlled in distribution, handling, and filing.

(2) The plain text should never be filed with the crytogram itself. The further the containers in which the plain-text copies are kept from those in which the cryptograms are kept the better. These containers should never be in the same safe. If only one safe is available, it should be used for the plain-text versions, keeping the cryptograms in a locked filing cabinet.

It is often necessary to make public certain information which has passed through military headquarters in code or cipher. It is obvious that verbatim quotation of extracts from such messages may give important clues to enemy cryptanalytic services. It should be constantly borne in mind that certain kinds of publicity, while necessary in and beneficial to public interest, are much sought after and used to good advantage by enemy intelligence services.

In connection with the amount of traffic an alert enemy may pick up I may call attention to the fact that in the combat zone the less radio is used, the less traffic is intercepted by the enemy. Signal and communication officers should constantly bear this in mind. Another thing in this connection: It is not mere idle curiosity that leads an enemy to set up intercept and goniometric stations even if they cannot solve the intercepted messages. Much valuable information can be obtained as to the grouping of enemy forces and his probable intentions merely by studying the call signs, the directions, and the volume of messages.

Finally, rigid adherence to authorized transmission procedure, especially in the case of radio, contributes very materially to cryptographic security. It facilitates the handling of traffic, since good radio discipline prevents misunderstandings, unnecessary queries, and repetitions. This is important not only because it reduces the amount of information an alert enemy may obtain by constantly listening to the scraps of conversation operators will indulge in under a lax radio discipline and nonadherence to authorized procedure, but also because repetitions give the intercept station every opportunity to obtain absolutely correct messages. When the intercept stations are so far away that the received signals are very weak this is very advantageous to the cryptanalytic service.

Furthermore, rigid adherence to authorized procedure affords a good safeguard against the injection, by enemy transmitters, of false messages in our own circuits. I can only mention this possibility—it forms a whole subject in itself and one concerning which we shall in future hear more and more.

In closing, I think I can best summarize the lessons to be learned from the use of codes and ciphers in the World War by quoting what two very distinguished French crytographers have said. General Cartier, head of the cryptographic service of the French Army during the war declared that "the interception and solution of enemy messages is indisputably superior to all other means for securing intelligence." And General Givierge, head of the same service from about 1923 to 1932 has said:

Cryptograph well or do not cryptograph at all. In transmitting clear text, you give only a piece of information to the enemy, and you know what it is; in cryptographing badly you permit him to read all your correspondence and that of your friends.

THE CRYPTANALYST ACCEPTS A CHALLENGE *

By Lt. Col. WILLIAM F. FRIEDMAN, Signal Reserve, Principal Cryptanalyst, Office of the Chief Signal Officer

The experienced cryptanalyst never willingly accepts challenges to his skill; rarely, if ever, does he go out of his way to look for such challenges. He is usually quite unimpressed when the challenge originates with a person who has only a rudimentary knowledge of cryptography, for the cryptanalyst knows that the novice has never had any practical experience to tell him what would be suitable in the way of a cryptographic system if it must be employed in regular traffic among numerous correspondents. Least of all does the experienced cryptanalyst, A, relish the intercession of a well-meaning friend, B, who engages with a third party, C (usually with some monetary stake between B and C in the background), to demonstrate that A is a marvel and "can break down any old code." One such experience is usually quite sufficient to cure B of any subsequent desire to play up the ability of his friend A at breaking down things—if the friendship doesn't break down altogether.

But occasionally the cryptanalyst may, in a moment of weakness, succumb to a challenge when the attendant circumstances are such as to pique his interest. Challenges contained in articles on cryptography sometimes fall in this category. Many years ago (1917) I encountered two or three such challenges in historically interesting cryptographic works, and took time to find the answers to the problems posed, but I have never thought of them since that time. It is possible that someone has long since published the solutions, but if so, I have not seen them.

With the thought that some of the readers of the Bulletin might find it amusing and interesting to solve the messages forming the subject matter of the challenges, the latter are given below.[2]

---

[2] Readers who wish to demonstrate their prowess may send in their solutions to the editor, who in due course will publish the names and methods employed by those who have successfully solved the problems.

*(No. 103, January–March, 1939)

207

No. 1

THE CHALLENGE OF JOHN DAVYS

The first case is taken from An Essay on the Art of Decyphering, by John Davys, London, 1737. The passage of interest (beginning on page 32) reads as follows:

But, to make fome Amends for the Letter, which I have *thus* intercepted, I fhall fupply its Place with Part of another, which coft me about four Hours clofe Attention to decypher, *Nov. 5. 1734.* It is written in a very particular Manner, the like of which in fome refpects I had never feen. At the firft View it ftrangely furprized me; I had before me a Profpect but of *cold Hunting.* And was *indeed* obliged *Confilium in arenâ capere, to take my Meafures upon the Spot.* As the Cafe was new to me, fo were my Obfervations upon it fuch as, I dare fay, were never ufed before in the Bufinefs of decyphering. But they proved to be exactly right, and fully anfwered my Purpofe.

Extract of a Letter from the Earl of Clanricard *to the Mar-quis of* Ormond.

90	6645737747	83576045	109	655383814976	34
99	677867767358495077	23	70577852	108	26	50495371
8378	36	435476415368	836977	22	40
597278605841 5368	39	764553	91	446577736975	
78	30	5345735169	93	29	108	664568
43724176426957	105	22	104	32	8145795457836944

33

33　70577852　97　109　23　108　74495371　426975456984458²

34　61695175　93　5245　666083　24　824163458348　73

48658469　5378　20　5578854557　4970　49　72656045　111

21　105　40　106　7687　44608387　91　7041735972　30

8354　97　20　99　75785883　105　7669　30　91　111

576971606581686944　102　25　105　37　73　48418469

47787769　76606748　658259814163　105　38　5869457669

426083　22　50775485　39　111　617269574953　34　775481

61486583　24　6754845782　5978　83417469　25　91　666059

102　7663　67787770734469536745　7353　25　107　30　91

816958794567598²　39　8378　26　107　49　584854847544

102　69604557　80847359　83724958　36　847772657987

5049534744785245.

This Extract now appears, juſt as it came to me, with two or three Errors in the Writing, as uſual, and a few old Spellings, which I have not taken upon me to correct. I have produced this Piece, rather than ſome others now in my Hands, for the following Reaſons.

　1. Becauſe, as I have already intimated, it is a *Curioſity*.

　2. Becauſe I am ſure, that I have decyphered it right; for, ſome Time after I had returned it to Mr. *Carte*, he wrote me back Word, that he had found a miſplaced Bit of Paper, by

F　　　　　　　which

which it appeared, that my Interpretation was right to a Tittle.

3. Becaufe, being only a Fragment, and without Date, (tho' *that* may nearly be difcovered by the Contents,) it is not printed in Mr. *Carte*'s Colleftion.

4. Becaufe the fame was afterwards decyphered by a very ingenious Woman, who is capable of becoming a great Proficient in the Art, as I alfo know feveral others of her Sex to be.

But the Truth is, that among thofe who are capable of the Work, very few are * willing to undergo the Fatigue of it. Hence it is the lefs to be wondered at, that fuch ftrange Opinions have gone Abroad concerning an Art fo little known. *Vieta*'s Performance was confidently given out to have been the Effeft of *Magick*; and when *Locatello* publifhed fome *chymical* Secrets in Cypher, it looks as if he had the Fear of the *Holy Office* before his Eyes: For he takes efpecial Care to inform his Reader, that all thofe Paffages (tho' as yet only *written* in Cypher) had been explained to, and allowed by, his Superiors. So that now an innocent Preparation in *Chymiftry* was fecured from all Sufpicion of *Herefie* or *Witchcraft*. However that were, the Generality of Men were not eafily brought to believe, that a Writing might be decyphered by human Means; and I know not, whether all are, even at this Day, convinced of it.

210

No. 2

THE CHALLENGE OF JOHN SCHOOLING

In 1896 there appeared in *Pall Mall Magazine*, in four installments, a rather lengthy article on cryptography, entitled "Secrets in Cipher," by John Holt Schooling. Although a cursory reading shows that the author was more adept at journalism than at cryptography, the article as a whole is still quite valuable even today because of its numerous photographs of cryptographic documents of great historical interest. The last part of the concluding installment is devoted to an explanation of the cipher known as the Russian Nihilists' Cipher, which, judging by the praise Schooling heaps upon it, evidently appealed to him as being the last word in cryptographic security. For the benefit of such readers as may not be familiar with this system, I will condense the explanation which Schooling gives, but will use his own illustration.

A 5 x 5 square divided up into 25 cells forms the basis for the substitution of pairs of digits (1, 2, 3, 4, 5) for the letters of the alphabet. The plain text is first enciphered by means of this square, and then the numerical value of the letters of a keyword are added to the simple substituted pairs of digits representing

	1	2	3	4	5
1	A	B	C	D	E
2	F	G	H	I	K
3	L	M	N	O	P
4	Q	R	S	T	U
5	V	W	X	Y	Z

the plain text. Thus, reproducing Schooling's example, with the keyword Tyrant:

(1)	M	e	e	t	M	e	J	n	P	a	r	i	s	O	n	M	o	n	d	a	y
(2)	32	15	15	44	32	15	24	33	35	11	42	24	43	34	33	32	34	33	14	11	54
(3)	T	y	r	a	n	t	T	y	r	a	n	t	T	y	r	a	n	t	T	y	r
(4)	44	54	42	11	33	44	44	54	42	11	33	44	44	54	42	11	33	44	44	54	42
(5)	76	69	57	55	65	59	68	87	77	22	75	68	87	88	75	43	67	77	58	65	96

NOTE.—Line labeled (1) are the plain-text letters.
(2) are the equivalents of the letters in (1).
(3) are the key letters.
(4) are the equivalents of the key letters in (3).
(5) are the sums of (2) and (4) and yield the cryptogram.

Cipher text:

76	69	57	55	65	59	68
87	77	22	75	68	87	88
75	43	67	77	58	65	96

In passing, I will add that the arrangement of the final cipher text in lines corresponding to the length of the key, as shown directly above, follows Schooling's example in this respect. He says nothing about the desirability of transcribing the text into regular groupings not equal in length to the length of the key, so as to give no clue as to the latter, which is an important feature of any polyalphabetic scheme.

Schooling says of this cipher:

The four illustrations * * * relate to a mode of secret writing * * * which is absolutely undecipherable if the key-word agreed upon by two correspondents be unknown. * * * All the usual aids to solving cipher are useless here, for the same letter of the real message is represented in the cipher by numbers that are different. For example, * * * the *m* of *meet* is represented by 76 the *m* of *me* by 65, the *m* of *Monday* by 43, the first *e* of *meet* by 69, the second *e* of *meet* by 57, the *e* of *me* by 59, etc. It will now be perceived what an admirable cipher this is, for no clue is given by it as to the hidden meaning: in some numerical and other ciphers, the frequency of the sign that stands for the letter *e* will often give a clue, as will also the sign that represents the double *l*, and there are many other details for which the practised decipherer is keenly on the alert: here he is completely baffled, *for the numerical equivalents of the same letter of the alphabet vary indefinitely in the course of a single message*, and this protean nature of the cipher is its most characteristic feature—and yet it is simplicity itself.

*   *   *   *   *   *   *

There are various other ingenious ways of utilizing this lettered square; and as the Russian intellect is quick and subtle, and as many of these prisoners are men of high intelligence, it can readily be perceived what an invaluable thing to these prisoners is this little square, with its twenty-five letters and its five numbers: it is no exaggeration to say that the mental activity and the interest produced by using this square for purposes of communication has saved many a wretched prisoner from madness or from suicide. ·

And now I—the showman—have shown you—the lookers-on—nearly all that I have gathered together about these secret ciphers.

*   *   *   *   *   *   *

The concluding sentences of Parts I, II, and III have each been written in cipher and later on explained. Here is the concluding sentence of part IV, and last, of this account of Secrets in Cipher. It has been written by means of the device illustrated and exactly explained above, but the key-word Tyrant there used has not been used for this concluding sentence; therefore the meaning of the cipher which now follows will never be solved by any one. The "box," which for us has been unlocked to let out the cipher secrets of past centuries, has now closed and firmly shut its fastenings for one hundred years of future time.

JOHN HOLT SCHOOLING.

212

At the bottom of the page, beneath the name John Holt Schooling, appears his challenge message.

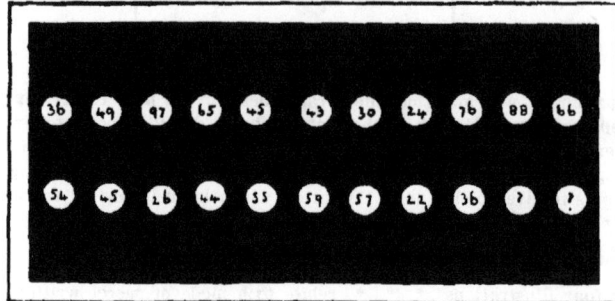

The reader will undoubtedly have difficulty in reading some of the numbers within the white circles of the "box" with which Schooling concludes his article, but that is not to be attributed to poor reproduction by the present printer, for the original article shows illegible digits also. However, in order not to confuse the issue I will append an unmistakable transcription of the secret text. How many of the readers of the Bulletin can forge the instrument that will pick the lock on Schooling's "box"?

```
36  49  97  65  45  43  30  24  76  88  66
54  45  26  44  55  59  57  22  36   ?   ?
```

No. 3

THE CHALLENGE OF WILLIAM BLAIR

In 1802 *The New Cyclopaedia* was published in London, under the editorship of Rees. The article on cipher, rather more extensive than usually found in works of this character, was anonymous but proof is conclusive that it was prepared by a London physician named William Blair. The article is concluded by a cryptographic scheme of Blair's own invention. For reasons which will become apparent in due course I deem it advisable to present a facsimile of the paragraphs that are of interest to us.

How many readers can pick up the gauntlet thrown down by Dr. Blair? In order not to make the matter too difficult, those readers who do not wish to spend too much time on the challenge will find a hint in the last line in fine print on plate III. (This refers to the string of digits at the bottom of the plate.)

Plate III. exhibits a perfectly new plan of secret writing, where there are only three dots (over the line, upon it, and under it), representing eighty-one letters or figures conformably to the alphabet engraved upon the same plate. This method is capable of a surprising variety, but in every variety shall seem to be the same writing; it is also practised by letters and figures, or words, or by all mingled together, without any apparent difference in its form. The reader will never discover anything here besides a simple dot in three positions, and cannot tell whether one, two, three, or more of them, compose each character. The inventor presumes to think that this contrivance is deserving the attention of ingenious men, and might be a very advantageous acquisition in the Foreign Secretary of State's Office; but it would be incompatible with his feelings to submit any such proposal to the judgment of inferior clerks, who, perhaps, know nothing beyond the mechanical use of ciphers, and are totally unqualified to appreciate the merits of a scientific invention. At present he has, therefore, not chosen to divulge the principle of this cipher to any person living.

The following paragraph gives the explanation of the dot-writing on *Plate* III., with the interpretation of the two succeeding examples; and also, in Italic letters, it expresses the author's name, profession, place of residence, and the date of the year: these four different specimens are all deciphered by ONE KEY, which is engraven at the top of *Plate* III., and it would have been easy to have given several hundred more varieties, to be likewise deciphered by the same key.

The art *of* writing in cipher *has been studied by men of the greatest talents and rank in every civilized* country; but among the various *ciphers which* have been *made* public, we *have never seen any that are exempt from considerable objections. Some of them are too laborious for diplomatic uses, or dispatch of business, others are not sufficiently faithful to elude a discovery,*

214

when examined with scrupulous attention; and others are of such a nature as to be inadmissible for practice, except under very peculiar circumstances; besides which, the generality of ciphers are complex and difficult to write, in proportion to their intricacy.

152618035466693599507192735855362202836931217327
245920645394011183947056667685736342011439311439470
659507737799321929697778856580665954453615139932947
850463536419355740796163924393758961981628919963401
283797466464393112515532225949210666463061534649596
867012553226189294071727375269337356163011183949702
235343993242511161775071630646961460473961968493394
786382053824306637295903546799396818814241505284655
220756547484942454669111618027113118121517273648099
499224506544015263914035464505859380163511275721599
689409599920342824626514355849750765645670655570429
894323515122605952011255668674947181394082322661857
130354645074831505668954455121718361510643044352858
374468160666509554768588035938598904122761638443937
172637493458197141736393493717377269394758487244251
627765693867760454758495936935336429399777263844949
353464593385293948775729335036291525573999386940779
9931118017363534144948678911154639395999203246553121
51775790458112182458936847344534606163474393323399122
516173546075738412872248587874759694930001111848494
245569371729875640066726393221836394635544557743938
394007489242618465693354645000756514325445819938674
850858995445512251615937799071574958459393398823224665
246584772837369358599315261817469398744457284123574
43.

bawmkarupfoy.ujozaruhsnyffaxmopets.jhupe.awadzmyglrert.
puhv.kn. usscoxozpewauohjkffyqpd.ubcdp. jsydf kwzpelqgrufxgl
vjrpmcdlw.t.foi. clcyzjfxpablvpdwqozk. ugrjljdru. mg. dhycrpwp

215

wyzjvplsizfhkj. jsmbwebzoaykr. c.ekt. piqeflnxmgjyvdu. ucsgfauz jvzgtmhywmbrpfxglkfzpecfpdex. r. hveh. uwqbwgdgldqkvlwzjhs mlchbtglrpglxveb.pcsvjw.xj jtmgzjd. ugkovcbslqaharuhcw.rulȝq jlsvp. pjlljlcwrzmzprdlppruauedp. jelgljfvvrjquoyh. rp. lobj. symde ezuykqh.zifequlewhjudw.fhg cbseu.rplqbspcdfwqhwiuvqjezyrp. klfgtcnzjf. qmeltekfsdru. gfwi. rpanqrz ayfjcbghzmhua. yeafvawe zkzpykefzm. uuyshtdf klqgtuffxgxwazjxhlwnozyrplqfh. jnafqaljg quvlhaeyzu.r.scsfavk.yhj. kxzyefveckw.zmcpzpm.ahw. zjyhjoqx. uaeeiyyaabgsisoxmhwvmdu. uyduak.veldddwlfqrpqofrzpdfadvw oqwzzpv ruox.lihaealcsnyldj.uhcigluyw. uxonbqusyshiyw.kt.jhc afeljh. pzdiquodlnjgtaclefie. dzuuqaoihoxomlvaqpokwrul. dijyrj.r eljhdqcp.jg. qhj.rub qm.pqvhewqey.jt. zpuepfbagfaih. rjolae.ulee a. ucsj. zjmnulm. pdckbhkxvwkrcbblnorj. a. vfh.jgdkvpfbmqnmoi a.l.ui. nshfdatywizjeoyiukygdl. plbluodkj. ppmp. iappfkaqfjderjw qzooybglnsyvwfxl. khiaj. ae. ucccocucikccncg. jhbitwuiawmzpiiji j.rjmsvujlyaiofdfffodu.uxugm.uiqy.tytcdqdlehrje. aip.zuifeftgjms eh.nc. pg.yhuk.jktk.kkzfo.haoislqn.jqoq.rjhcyeaqaop.zpafdw.pp tyeeagyjofhfozmmushb.yhrjwwz. zjqoedyabi. t. uy. dhaxahy. ift. k uru.

Great care has been taken, in a former part of this article, to exhibit the peculiarities of the English language, and to point out the most approved means of deciphering any secret writing composed alphabetically ; and, "such is the craft of man," says a modern author, "that it is scarcely possible for a letter " in cipher to be written so as not to be deciphered without " any clue but a close application to the letter itself; and that " too, though it were written in a language the decipherer " does not understand." This author has only re-echoed the words of Mr. Falconer, and seems to believe he had even arrived at the ne plus ultra of his art ; but, to shew that the writer of this article entertains a very different opinion, and that he challenges all the scrutinizing powers of man, these few specimens are here adduced. The two former, as has been already stated, contain the same internal sense as the dot-writing, and are explained by the same key. Although the key and explanation may serve to develope the principle on which this cipher is constructed, the writer has nevertheless hazarded making a discovery, by adding this one example more ; wherein the involved sentiment is expressed by points, and which is also decipherable by the same key as the other specimens.

The present mode of corresponding, as well as the preceding, may be conducted with a triformed alphabet, without any suspicion of a cipher being employed. The words represented by the points, in this example, may be found in the paragraph itself ; so that the student will not have to look far for an interpretation of its contents. If, after such an unprecedented challenge, and so many helps toward an explanation, the reader still cannot develop this cipher, he ought to concede that the " craft of man" is inadequate to the task of deciphering it without any clue."

Before the student attempts to decipher the above specimens, or the dot-writing on *Plate* III., it may be proper to inform him that the alphabet by which these paragraphs were composed is wholly unlike any other. The alphabet consists of letters arranged in eighty-one places, forming a square of nine letters which are most wanted in ordinary writing, are there repeated most frequently ; so that it is possible to produce an immense variety in the appearance of the specimens, while that great variety shall make no real difference in their sense or internal meaning. In consequence of such a construction of this alphabet, all the rules for deciphering with which the author is acquainted, are easily and effectually frustrated. The ingenious reader must, therefore, hit upon some new mode of analysing and explaining what is written in the paragraphs alluded to.

A similar method of corresponding admits of such an arrangement of the letters, as to seem like a foreign language : this mode has not any peculiar advantage in practice, but is somewhat remarkable in the appearance of the writing. As for example : *Relieve us speedily, or we perish ; for the enemy has been reinforced, and our provisions are nearly expended,* is thus written :

Sika jygam a fuva quaxo Rolofak adunabi ye, Rasc guema Lovazig-arodi ; Moxati Ho hyka Fagiva myne qui paxo Aukava in Oufa yani moxarico, Pangdo Spulzi Iorixa mugaro ya zangor Alsiva yival Kazeb re linthvath.

In view of the small size to which Blair's plate III had to be reduced for reproduction in the Bulletin (page 36), I append an enlarged transcription of the "Alphabet and Key" which appears in the upper left-hand corner thereof. This should eliminate any ambiguities which might unnecessarily confuse the reader.

Alphabet and Key.

B C S	M T L	I E O
G M T	P U H	O I A
J P U	D A N	H O E
K D Y	F E R	N S I
Q F A	L I S	R T O
V L E	H O T	S U A
W H I	N C U	T A E
X N O	R D A	U E I
Z R .	S F E	A I O

218

WRITING BY CIPHER.

PLATE III.

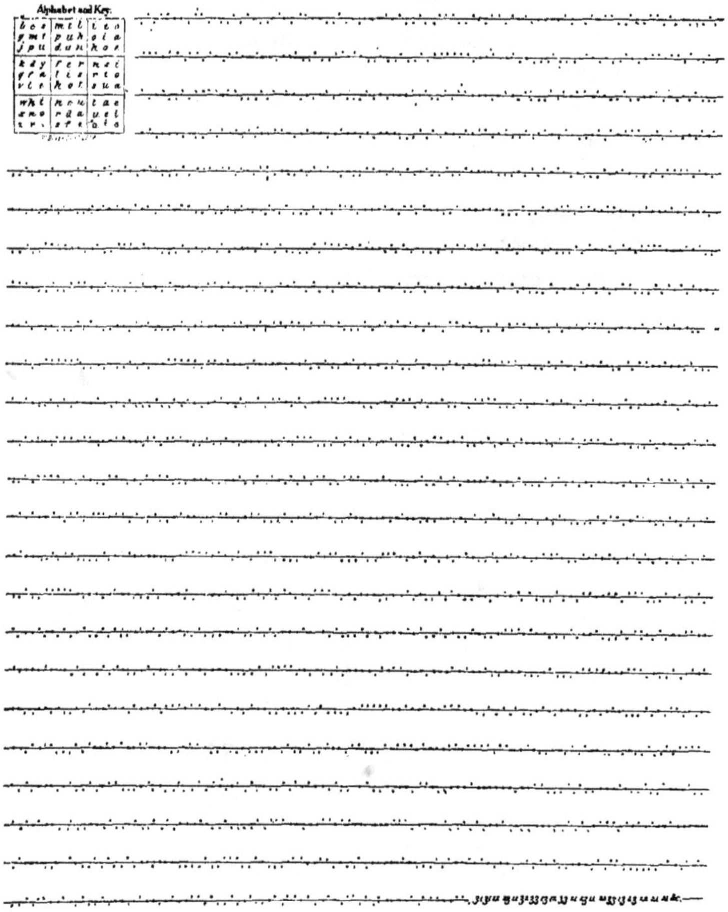

COMMUNICATION SYSTEMS OF THE AMERICAN INDIANS *

By Lt. Col. Lewis F. Acker, Chemical Warfare Service, Pennsylvania National Guard ; Vice President and Director, Society for Pennsylvania Archaeology

In the light of modern progress we accept today as usual the developments of our advanced scientific age. In our acceptance of the past and in our anticipation of future progress, we motivate under the same laws and power of species which have brought forward the human race from the darkness of a humble beginning, through the dawn of realization into the full daylight of human accomplishment. Probably the most significant and true measuring stick for our progress is the gradual and steady advancement of methods of communication between individuals and groups of mankind.

We, of America, have a heritage and laboratory for our investigation like which has been available to no other people in history. Here, in America, has taken place during less than two centuries the conquest of the vast interior of a continent. With the conquest has come the replacement of a race just arrived on the threshold of the Age of Metals. A race with its distinctly different groups of peoples just beginning to learn the advantages and additional powers to be gained by their organization into nations. What might have developed here in America for its red race if the rediscovery of America by the white race of Europe had been postponed for a few centuries can only be measured by the previous steady progress of the red race through the Paleolithic, or Age of Unpolished Stone, and by the ex-

*(No. 103, January–March, 1939)

ceptional accomplishment of this race as it progressed through the Neolithic, or Age of Polished Stone. However, there came the hordes of white invaders from Europe, bringing to the conquest of America a better organized group of peoples 4,000 years farther advanced in their racial development than the red men of America and possessing the weapons and tools only possible as a development of the Age of Iron.

While the methods and equipment of communication of the primitive Americans may appear most basic and, perhaps, insignificant in the light of the advancement by modern peoples with their superior materials and the application of electricity, it is still believed that the story of primitive communications may present an interesting historical conception for the present-day student of this art.

Among the early peoples of America at the time of the coming of the white invader, there was constant warfare first between families and later between communities and tribes. Such courts as existed had jurisdiction only within small communities and groups. To a comparatively large degree might made right. Constant preparedness was the prime essential of the right of the individual or of the group to live and to possess property. This made necessary systems of commonly understood signals of community danger and led onward directly to the design of special secret codes of a fundamental nature for specific and private purposes.

Near every camping place and town site there can still be located today the look-out and signal stations which served as observation posts of these stone age Americans. Here the archaeologist finds the place where a solitary sentinel of that early defense system lighted signal and cooking fires, leaving as evidence of the occupation charred ground and, in the refuse of the camp site, pottery fragments, animal bones, and mussel shells. From these commanding points danger was foreseen. Smoke and fire signals served as agencies to supplement the more natural messenger service and to provide a more advanced and efficient method for recalling the people in time of danger to a central protected position.

For smoke signals fires were built with damp grass, weeds, cedar tops and other such smoke-producing materials well known to these nature wise people. The fire was first allowed to build up during such time as might be required to permit the column of dense smoke to come to the attention of the community or isolated individuals. The signaler would then throw his blanket over the smoldering pile in such a way as to interrupt the ascent of the column of smoke. By withdrawing the blank momentarily be allowed a puff to ascend. The message was then continued by regulating the number, size, and rate of the smoke puffs.

In the case of fire signals a screen was made with a blanket and passed in front of the light according to a similar pattern of spacing. With both fire and smoke signals several fires might be employed simultaneously in order to convey certain types of messages. These types of signals had particular application in rugged terrain and along the coast where they were used as a warning of the approach of ships and landing parties. The narratives of the early explorers make frequent allusions to such beacon fires. War parties returning to their villages made use of such signals in announcing their success in battle, the number of their casualties, and the number of scalps, captives, or ponies, taken as trophies. This gave time for the proper preparations in the distant villages for ceremonial dances and death rites. Such methods also became adapted to purposes other than military and were used by the hunter groups to call the tribe together when herds of buffalo or other game had been located. As a later development from these systems of signaling certain of the plains tribes, including the Sioux, made use of heliograph signals.

Our early travelers on the prairies often noted signal lights thrown high in the air at night. These signals are described by Belden, the white chief of the Santee Sioux, who states that every war party carried bundles of fire arrows. These signal arrows were dipped in combustibles mixed with glue and protected by charred bark. When the signal arrow was to be used a warrior placed it on his bowstring and, pointing the arrow momentarily toward the ground while it was ignited, shot it high in the air. When the arrow had gone a little distance in the air it burst into flames and burned brightly until fallen to the ground. According to the timing of flights of arrows messages were conveyed. By one code a single arrow meant, "the enemy are near," two arrows from the same point meant "danger" and three signal arrows meant "great danger." By the same code a volley of many fire arrows meant "they are too strong" or "we are falling back." If the arrows were shot diagonally they signfied, "in that direction." Changes of signals and any special signals were agreed upon when a war party set out or before it separated during the deployment. During the engagement the fire arrows became useful as incendiary weapons and were used to fire many frontier stations and block-houses Fire arrows were also used to create barriers or barrages of fire in wooded or grassy areas.

Flint and steel were used to strike sparks as signals to establish communication between scouts and small parties creeping up at night on an enemy. The Indian scout sending the message faced the receiver and drew his blanket over his head and arms in such manner as to leave only a small open space on the side away from the enemy. By means of the sparks struck from the flint combat information was passed back. This method, of course, served only to carry information from the front to the rear and any reply or instructions took the form of the natural night calls of some animal or bird.

The use of drum and rattle signals was confined among the primitive peoples of America to ceremonies to mark the changes in phase or cadence of the performance. Due to the ritualistic significance of the turtle as the alpha and omega, the beginning and the end of life itself, the turtle shell rattle was used to signal the opening and the closing of the Big House ceremony so important in the religious and social life of the Algonkian peoples.

Reed instruments were used for signaling principally in tropical America, but whistles of wood were not uncommon in the woodland areas of eastern North America. Whistles of bone, stone, shell, and copper have also been found on these ancient village sites. As the primitive Americans lived close to nature animal totemism was of importance in all clan and tribal functions. The use of animal and bird calls became ritualistic in ceremonies and they were frequently used as signals between concealed or engaged parties. Other signal calls had specific applications and ceremonial significance, such as the journey halloo of an expedition about to set out, the scalp halloo of individual and collective victory and the death halloo of final farewell and spiritual justification. Among certain tribes the arrival of strangers was heralded by a specific and distinctive signal and such individual or party was then met and examined by a reception party before being received into the community. Various calls were used as social signals in games, between lovers, and among children at play.

Motion signals were widely used among the primitive Americans. They were transmitted both on foot and on horse and often with the aid of a blanket or torch. These signals were frequently adaptations of the sign language and often were extremely picturesque in their execution. The basic motion signal was that of discovery which was made by walking or riding in a circle. The circle was used not because of any symbolic significance, but because such movement was most readily discernible by the distant watchers. When the attention of the watchers had been attracted it was followed by the specific sign for enemy or buffalo or other definite thing discovered. The buffalo sign might well serve in certain circumstances for other big game or even in late times for a herd of range cattle. It was made by holding the open blanket at the two corners with the arms outstretched above the head and gracefully swung down to the ground. The enemy signal was made by waving the outstretched blanket back and forth several times above the head or by confused and rapid riding back and forth following the discovery sign. The absence of any explanatory sign after the discovery signal indicated the proximity of a friendly party. The alarm signal was made by throwing the blanket into the air several times in rapid succession. The signal for all clear was given by gently waving the blanket from side to side in front of the body.

Returning war parties or parties of scouts often gave signals of success or failure in terms of captives, trophies, or casualties by robe or blanket signals. The losses were indicated by having the same number of men turn successively to one side and drop to the ground. Other blanket signals of wide usage indicated defiance, advance, halt, and friendship. On those accidental occasions when the discoverer had neither horse nor blanket he might give the alarm from a distance by throwing handfuls of dust high in the air.

During certain seasons of the year in the woodland regions of eastern North America even the more important and frequently used trails became overgrown with brush. In the arid, wind-swept terrain of the midwestern plains trails were quickly and permanently obliterated. In the woodland regions tomahawk blazes on the trees, often in animal totem or other symbolic design, served as signs to mark directions, to show boundaries, to denote warning, to claim possession, and sometimes to identify the maker. Such signs, often in the form of the turtle or other symbolic sign or combination of signs are yet to be found blazed in the bark of primeval trees. In friendly, unwooded terrain small sticks were set into the forks of bushes to mark direction and trail locations. Bent and broken bushes with their resultant leaf contrast served in transmitting similar type signals. In rocky and barren terrain stones were placed on top of larger stones as mute messengers. Among the tribes of the plains the sparse grass was tied at intervals and the tied bunches were then bent to signal the trail and its changes of direction.

The painting of the face of the primitive Americans had definite and purposeful design with message value. In its symbolism the design and colors often lent direct reference to animal totemism, such as the mimicry of the markings of the serpent's skin and of the turtle's shell. These markings proclaimed to the intiated the type of ceremony, degree of mourning, and the hostility or friendliness of the bearer. The many examples of animal totemism found in the signal symbolism of the early Americans reflect directly to their clan and tribal patrons and to mythological conceptions. Every clan and nearly every tribe were related closely, in the belief of their members, to some animal form and often the tribal name was derived from some fancied relationship. Their mythology was that of a free and individualistic people; wandering, hunting, and warring almost at will and owing allegiance to patron gods of good, evil, and neutral characteristics. These were most often symbolized by the creeping, crawling, running, flying, and swimming forms of animal life upon which the tribes were so dependent for food and shelter and, in many cases, felt a strong imaginary kinship. We find today in use by many nations some form of animal life as an emblem, such as our own bald eagle, the British lion, the Chinese dragon, the Russian bear, and many others.

Belts of wampum were frequently passed from tribe to tribe as a signal of record and as a token on occasions of the greatest importance. They were used generally in connection with the sale of property, the making of treaties, the confederation of tribes, and as declarations of war and of peace. These very important messages and ceremonial tokens were especially made for the occasion. They were significantly designed of shell beads of natural white, natural purple, or black and artificial red colors set on backgrounds of skin to convey and record permanently the story of events of the past and plans for the future. Great care was exercised in the construction of wampum belts and they were held in great reverence as archives. In this use of beads of several colors a definite meaning existed for each color and for the way it was used with respect to the other colors in the general design. To the Iroquois and to most other Indian groups white as a color was considered auspicious, and its use in ceremony and ritual grew to represent peace, health, welfare, and prosperity. These ideas were expressed by white wampum when ceremoniously used or set into a record. White strings alone were used commonly with reference to matters of ordinary routine requiring only a slight degree of formality, or merely as preliminary exhibits prior to others of greater import. Black, on the contrary, was considered serious and inauspicious, and had especial reference in ceremony or record to hostility, sorrow, death, condolence, or mourning. A string of black wampum was sent by the tribe as the formal announcement of the death of its chief. Strings of white beads, colored red, were used as a challenge or declaration of war or as an invitation to friends to join in an alliance for war. By suitable combinations of colors various symbolic figures and devices were deftly wrought into the pattern of the belt design. The breadth and length of the belt were determined by the importance of its purpose or record. The chiefs and elders of the people were accustomed to assemble at intervals to rehearse the matters thus mnemonically covered by the several wampum strings, sheaves of strings, and belts in the keeping of the tribe.

Peace and war signals existed between the tribes with very general understanding and interpretation. The broken pipe, a red painted or bloody tomahawk—sometimes having a scalp attached—had general applications as declarations of war as did also the setting up of red painted arrows, together with the totemic symbol of the attacking tribe, along the trails near the enemy's villages. White became the natural peace color of the early Americans and a tuft of white feathers held aloft or placed in the prow of a canoe, or the blowing of the white down feathers of the eagle in the air became accepted as truce signals.

A type method of communication with various tribes in the setting up of a confederation and with the declaration of war is illustrated historically. It concerns the greatest confederation of tribes of the red race against the invaders of the white race. It was organized by Pontiac, the Red Napoleon, chieftain of the "Three Fires" symbolizing the basic confederation of the Ottawas, Ojibwas, and Potawatomies. The war which followed the masterful organization of the various tribes east of the Mississippi River by this great chieftain is of the greatest importance to us because it so nearly destroyed, perhaps for all time, the English settlements of the lands west of the Allegheny Mountains. Had it been successful it would have confined the European occupation of America to the narrow eastern seaboard. Pontiac sent his emissaries to all of the tribes. They carried the wampum belt, proposing union of all red men, and a bloody tomahawk. The date for attack was set for the many tribes by providing a separate bundle of sticks for each tribe, designed so that one stick should be broken ceremoniously each day and so arranged that the last stick would be broken by all of the tribes on the same day as the signal to announce that the time had come for all to rise up and attack the nearest white settlements.

In South America an exact record of accounts was kept for the Emperor and for his subordinate officials in the form of the "Quipus," a system of various colored strings arranged in manner similar to the decimals of our own mathematical system. These recorded and tabulated the production, distribution, and expenditure of the resources of materials and population within the vast empire of the Inca.

The great treeless area of the midwestern plains was occupied by many tribes of distinctly different linguistic stocks all constantly shifting about in the pursuit of buffalo herds. The necessities of this nomadic life resulted in the gradual evolution of a highly developed system of communication by gesture or sign laguage. Sign language barely fell short of the perfection of a common spoken language and its use spread out steadily from the plains to cover, in only slightly less degree, the woodland areas of the Eastern States, the Canadian Northwest and Mexico.

The American Indians lacked an alphabet to make possible a written language. However, in order to fill partially this need they turned once again to their animal totems and to those other animate and inanimate things which to them were representative of ideas and concepts of practical and ceremonial importance. Crude picturization with the use of ideographic symbols served in a crude way to satisfy the need for a communication medium among these primitive American peoples. This comparatively advanced system of communication by pictographs reached its highest advancement in the petroglyph records on rocks along the banks of streams, on rocky islands and as carved on boulders of probable ceremonial significance. At times of ceremonial usage colors might have been applied to the pictographs in order to provide added realism, symbolism, and contrast. The primitive Americans advanced in their pictographic art from the purely imitative to the production of ideographic conceptions for the expression of abstract ideas. As progress was made the pictographs became more and more conventionalized until, in many cases, all semblance of the original was lost and the ideograph became a mere symbol.

One of the masterpieces of communication of the early Americans was the "Walam Olum" or the red bark record of the Lenni-Lenape or Delawares. This was a pictographic chronicle of the genesis and development of their race as recited in the Algonquin tongue in metrical chant in explanation of the symbolism of the pictographs carved in the bark. It passed in ceremony from generation to generation with the deepest reverence. Of only slightly less ceremonial significance were the winter counts or calendars of the Sioux and the Kiowas, relating the events of the successive months, seasons, and years, and recording them in chronicle form. Another form of pictographic record for individuals was the tatooing of the body, a record, however, of value only during the life of the wearer.

An analysis must show that the signals of the American Indians should be classified into two general types; first those designed to supply the deficiency of a written language for placing events and conceptions on record and, second, those designed for private operation involving the necessity for secrecy. The false making of signals was so severely punished as to be scarcely thought of by these early Americans. The utmost precautions were taken in the exact transmission of messages and in keeping their codes secret. The study of the advancement of the primitive Americans in the field of communications must place them on the threshold of civilization and definitely at the end of their period of barbarism.

One Method of Solution of the Schooling "Absolutely Indecipherable" Cryptogram *

By Maj. Gen. J. O. Mauborgne, Chief Signal Officer

As a "has been" cryptanalyst in need of mental recreation, I decided to attack the unknown message prepared by John Holt Schooling in the so-called Modern Numerical Cipher Used by Russian Nihilists, given on page 28 of the Signal Corps Bulletin, volume 103 in the article entitled, "The Cryptanalyst Accepts a Challenge," by Lt. Col. W. F. Friedman, Signal Reserve.

The analysis leading to the solution will be given in considerable detail so that the various mental processes employed may be followed by the tyro. An expert will probably find nothing new in this paper.

Prior to attempting solution of the unknown message, the following preliminary study was made of the system as disclosed on pages 28 to 30 of the article mentioned.

The cipher square comprised 25 letters of the alphabet arranged as follows:

	1	2	3	4	5
1	A	B	C	D	E
2	F	G	H	I	K
3	L	M	N	O	P
4	Q	R	S	T	U
5	V	W	X	Y	Z

FIGURE 1.

*(No. 104, April–June, 1939)

227

The method of encipherment, using the key word "TYRANT," was demonstrated in a short message as follows:

```
(1)  M e e t M e I n P a r i s O n M o n d a y
(2)  32 15 15 44 32 15 24 33 35 11 42 24 43 34 33 32 34 33 14 11 54
(3)  T y r a n t T y r a n t T y r a n t T y r
(4)  44 54 42 11 33 44 44 54 42 11 33 44 44 54 42 11 33 44 44 54 42
(5)  76 69 57 55 65 59 68 87 77 22 75 68 87 88 75 43 67 77 58 65 96
```

Line (1) gives the plain text of the message.

Line (2) gives the numerical values for each letter immediately above as determined from the cipher square (fig. 1).

Line (3) is the subscribed key word "Tyrant" used as often as necessary.

Line (4) gives the numerical values for each letter of the key word above as determined from the cipher square (fig. 1), which values are to be added to figures of line (2), to give

Line (5) the enciphered text of the message, which might have been written for transmission according to Schooling as:

```
76  69  57  55  65  59  68
87  77  22  75  68  87  88
75  43  67  77  58  65  96
```

For easier reference, figure 1 might also have been written:

```
A  B  C  D  E  F  G  H  I  K  L  M  N  O  P  Q  R  S  T  U  V  W  X  Y  Z
11 12 13 14 15 21 22 23 24 25 31 32 33 34 35 41 42 43 44 45 51 52 53 54 55
```

First conclusion.—With the few groups of figures used, the combinations produced by adding figures representing plain text letters to those representing letters of a repeated key word must be comparatively few. If a cipher of this kind were constantly encountered, it would expedite solution to prepare a table showing all of the added numerical values of every letter with every other letter in turn, e. g.:

$$AA=11+11=22$$
$$AB=11+12=23$$
$$AC=11+13=24$$
$$AD=11+14=25$$
$$AE=11+15=26$$
$$AF=11+21=32$$
$$AG=11+22=33 \text{ etc.}$$

after which the results might be grouped, showing all two-letter combinations having the same numerical value, such as 97=WU, XT, YS, ZR; 30=EE, etc. In other words, such a table would enable an immediate list of possible two-letter combinations corresponding to a given two-digit number representing the combination of a plain text letter with a letter of the key. Obviously, in a combination such as 76, corresponding to T and M, it would be impossible to tell whether the T or the M is the plain text letter without trial.

Where only one message is involved, it would save time merely to take each of the figure combinations of the cipher message and determine by computation what pairs of letters only can correspond to each. This will limit the examination of unnecessary pairs of letters and save much work. Examples will be given later.

Furthermore, it occurred to me that there might be considerable merit in giving numerical frequency weights to each letter of the pairs so determined and then to add the separate frequency values to give a total value equivalent to the combined frequencies of the pair, as a further method of narrowing the search for the correct pairs of letters which correspond to any given two-digit number found in the cipher text.

In order to do this, the following table of frequencies based on a total word count of 10,000 letters of literary English (Hitt) was used in evaluating the frequency of the various pairs.

TABLE 1

A	778	H	595	O	807	U	308
B	141	I[1]	667	P	223	V	112
C	296	J	51	Q	8	W	176
D	402	K	74	R	651	X	27
E	1277	L	372	S	622	Y	196
F	197	M	288	T	855	Z	17
G	174	N	686				

[1] Since I and J in this Nihilist cipher system are both represented by I, perhaps I should have been given the weight of 718 (I plus J) but this was not thought of until solution had been accomplished.

It was decided to try out the two methods just given on the sample message which demonstrated the method of encipherment given by Schooling.

Several of the examples taken from the work sheets are reproduced herewith to show the method of determining all the pairs of letters which can correspond to a given pair of digits of the cipher text.

76

V	W	X	Y	Z	Q	R	S	T	U
51	52	53	54	55	41	42	43	44	45
25	24	23	22	21	35	34	33	32	31
K	I	H	G	F	P	O	N	M	L

76 = VK WI XH YG ZF QP RO SN TM UL

230

O	T	U	Y	Z
34	44	45	54	55
35	25	24	15	14
P	K	I	E	D

69=OP TK UI YE ZD

22

A
11

11
A

22=AA *Only*

All other two-figure groups of the sample cipher message were similarly examined and a table was then prepared as follows, showing all the results, so that comparison could be made with the clear text, the letters of the code word and the cipher text figures:

(Table 2 is reproduced on the following page.)

TABLE 2

M	e	e	t	M	e	I	n	P	a	r	i	s	O	n	M	o	n	d
T	y	r	a	n	t	T	y	r	a	n	t	T	y	r	a	n	t	T

POSSIBLE PAIRS

76	69	57	55	65	59	68	87	77	22	75	68	87	88	75	43	67	77	58
VK	GP	BU	AT	FT	DU	EX	WP	WK	AA	VI	XE	WP	TT	QO	LB	WE	WK	SE
WI	TK	CT	BS	GS	ET	DY	XO	XI		WH	YD	XO	SU	RN	MA	XD	XI	TD
XH	UI	DS	CR	HR	IP	CZ	YN	YH		XG	ZC	YN	OY	SM	FG	YC	YH	UC
YG	YE	ER	DQ	IQ	KO	SK	ZM	ZG		YF	SK	ZM	NZ	TL		ZB	ZG	NK
ZF	ZD	GP	FO	AY		TI	RU	RP		QO	TI	RU		YF		RK	RP	OI
QP		HO	GN	BX		UH	ST	SO		RN	UH	ST		XG		SI	SO	PH
RO		IN	HM	CW		NP		TN		SM	NP			WH		TH	TN	
SN		KM	IL	DV		OO		UM		TL	OO			VI		UG	UM	
TM				LO												ON		
UL				MN												PM		

The underlined pairs correspond to the letters of the clear text and of the key text above them but do not indicate which letter of the pair is the clear text letter or which the key text letter. Pairs are not arranged in order of joint frequency.

The various columns were then examined for the joint frequencies of the various pairs of letters corresponding to each pair of cipher figures, as in the example which follows, using the frequency values in the Hitt table shown above:

$$
\begin{array}{ll}
& 76 \\
VK=112+\ 74= & 186\ (10) \\
WI=176+667= & 843\ (4) \\
XH=\ 27+595= & 622\ (6) \\
YG=196+174= & 370\ (7) \\
ZF=\ 17+197= & 214\ (9) \\
QP=\ \ \ 8+223= & 231\ (8) \\
RO=651+807=& 1458\ (1) \\
SN=622+686=& 1308\ (2) \\
\underline{TM}=855+288=& 1143\ (3) \\
UL=308+372= & 680\ (5)
\end{array}
$$

Figures in parentheses were placed opposite the various pairs to indicate frequency order for later tabulation and selection of pairs in numerical order for trial.

By the same method the following tables were built up to determine the order of frequency for all pairs of table 2 in which the indicators tabulated below were finally entered:

76	69	57	55	65	59	68
VK(10)	OP(2)	BU(6)	AT(1)	FT(3)	DU(4)	EX(3)
WI(4)	TK(4)	CT(4)	BS(7)	GS(7)	ET(1)	DY(7)
XH(6)	UI(3)	DS(5)	CR(4)	HR(1)	IP(2)	CZ(8)
YG(7)	YE(1)	ER(1)	DQ(8)	IQ(4)	KO(3)	SK(6)
ZF(9)	ZD(5)	GP(7)	FO(3)	AY(6)		TI(2)
QP(8)		HO(2)	GN(6)	BX(10)		UH(5)
RO(1)		IN(3)	HM(5)	CW(9)		NP(4)
SN(2)		KM(8)	IL(2)	DV(8)		OO(1)
TM(3)				LO(2)		
UL(5)				MN(5)		

87	77	22	75	68	87	88
WP(5)	WK(7)	AA(1)	VI(5)	EX(3)	WP(5)	TT(1)
XO(4)	XI(5)		WH(6)	DY(7)	XO(4)	SU(3)
YN(3)	YH(4)		XG(8)	CZ(8)	YN(3)	OY(2)
ZM(6)	ZG(8)		YF(7)	SK(6)	ZM(6)	NZ(4)
RU(2)	RP(3)		QO(4)	TI(2)	RU(2)	
ST(1)	SO(2)		RN(1)	UH(5)	ST(1)	
	TN(1)		SM(3)	NP(4)		
	UM(6)		TL(2)	OO(1)		

233

75	43	67	77	58	65	96
VI(5)	LB(2)	WE(2)	WK(7)	SE(1)	FT(3)	VU(4)
WH(6)	MA(1)	XD(9)	XI(5)	TD(3)	GS(7)	WT(1)
XG(8)	FG(3)	YC(7)	YH(4)	UC(6)	HR(1)	XS(3)
YF(7)		ZB(10)	ZG(8)	NK(5)	IQ(4)	YR(2)
QO(4)		RK(5)	RP(3)	OI(2)	AY(6)	ZQ(5)
RN(1)		SI(4)	SO(2)	PH(4)	BX(10)	
SM(3)		TH(3)	TN(1)		CW(9)	
TL(2)		UG(8)	UM(6)		DV(8)	
		ON(1)			LO(2)	
		PM(6)			MN(5)	

The outcome of this examination was rather surprising. It could not have been expected, without considerable previous experience, that in 11 out of 21 columns, the pairs showing highest joint frequency would have been the actual pairs used in the encipherment of the message. Of the remaining 10 cipher pairs, 4 required use of the pairs of letters having the second highest frequency, 4 required use of the pair that showed the third highest frequency, while 1 fifth and 1 sixth place frequency also were required.

Conclusions drawn, subject to check and recheck, are: We may expect that in messages approximately 21 letters long:

a. About half of the cipher groups will be represented by the pairs of letters having the highest joint frequency;

b. About one-third of the groups will be second and third highest frequency groups;

c. The remainder will be represented by fourth, fifth or sixth highest frequencies.

This principle would appear to be valuable in connection with the solution of this type of cipher.

The foregoing analysis demonstrates the well-known great value of being able to analyze and understand the system by which an unknown message has been enciphered.

THE UNKNOWN MESSAGE

At this stage it was felt that sufficient work had been done to develop a promising method of attack on the following "absolutely indecipherable" message presented by Schooling. The message read:

36 49 97 65 45 43 30 24 76 88 66 54 45 26 44 55 59 57 22 36

234

Prior to attempting solution, the following assumptions were made:

a. The writer of the cipher message probably *did not:*

(1) Use a cipher square different in letter arrangement from that shown in the example. (Suppose he had used a mixed alphabet, what complications, if any, would have been involved?)

(2) Employ a key phrase instead of a single key word only.

(3) Use a random-mixed running key instead of a key word.

b. English was used for both message and key.

c. Method of encipherment is exactly as Schooling demonstrated.

d. Since the message is almost identical in length with the example, half of the cipher groups will be represented by the pairs of letters corresponding to that group which show the highest joint frequency; about one-third of the groups will consist of second or third highest frequency letter groups; and the remaining cipher groups will be represented by fourth, fifth, or sixth highest frequency letter groups.

Decision.—To attack the unknown cipher message using the system so far demonstrated and then apply the probable pairs in order of joint frequency to the corresponding cipher groups, until the length of the key word is determined; recover the key word by trial and error procedure, and, having found the frequency orders of the letters of the key word from the frequency order indicators attached to the letters of the key word, find the corresponding letters of the text in each case.

Procedure as shown by work sheets.—1. Find possible pairs of letters corresponding to each cipher group. Either letter of a pair may be a letter of the key word.

```
36=11A 12B 13C 14D 15E
   25K 24I 23H 22G 21F

 = AK  BI  CH  DG  EF

49=14D 15E 24I
   35P 34O 25K

 = DP  EO  IK

97=52W 53X 54Y 55Z
   45U 44T 43S 42R

 = WU  XT  YS  ZR

65=21F 22G 23H 24I 11A 12B 13C 14D 31L 32M
   44T 43S 42R 41Q 54Y 53X 52W 51V 34O 33N

 = FT  GS  HR  IQ  AY  BX  CW  DV  LO  MN

45=11A 12B 13C 14D 21F 22G
   34O 33N 32M 31L 24I 23H

 = OA  BN  CM  DL  FI  GH
```

```
43 = 11A 12B 21F
     32M 31L 22G

   = AM  BL  FG

30 = 15E = EE
     15E

24 = 11A 12B = AC  BB
     13C 12B

76 = 51V 52W 53X 54Y 55Z 41Q 42R 43S 44T 45U
     25K 24I 23H 22G 21F 35P 340 33N 32M 31L

   = VK  WI  XH  YG  ZF  QP  RO  SN  TM  UL

88 = 33N 340 35P 43S 44T
     55Z 54Y 53X 45U 44T

   = NZ  OY  PX  SU  TT

66 = 33N 32M 31L 21F 22G 23H 24I 25K 51V 52W 53X 54Y 55Z
     33N 340 35P 45U 44T 43S 42R 41Q 15E 14D 13C 12B 11A

   = MN  MO  LP  FU  GT  HS  IR  KQ  VE  WD  XC  YB  ZA

54 = 11A 12B 13C 21F 22G 23H
     43S 42R 41Q 33N 32M 31L

   = AS  BR  CQ  FN  GM  HL

45 = (See above)

26 = 11A 12B 13C
     15E 14D 13C

   = AE  BG  CC

44 = 11A 12B 13C
     33N 32M 31L

   = AN  BM  CL

55 = 11A 12B 13C 14D 21F 22G 23H 24I
     44T 43S 42R 41Q 340 33N 32M 31L

   = AT  BS  CR  DQ  FO  GN  HM  IL

59 = 14D 15E 24I 25K
     45U 44T 35P 340

   = DU  ET  IP  KO

57 = 12B 13C 14D 15E 22G 23H 24I 25K
     45U 44T 53S 42R 35P 340 33N 32M

   = BU  CT  DS  ER  GP  HO  IN  KM

22 = 11A = AA
     11A

36 = (See above)
```

478603 O - 42 - 16

2. Joint frequency for each of the above pairs was then computed and relative standing determined for pairs corresponding to each cipher group as shown below. (Individual value of each letter as determined from Hitt's table, page 29 supra, has been omitted.) Joint frequency order is given by number in parentheses.

36	49	97	65	45
AK 852(3)	DP 625(3)	WU 484(4)	FT 1052(3)	OA 1585(1)
BI 807(4)	EO 2084(1)	XT 882(1)	GS 796(6)	BN 827(3)
CH 891(2)	IK 741(2)	YS 818(2)	HR 1246(1)	CM 384(6)
DG 576(5)		ZR 668(3)	IQ 675(7)	DL 774(4)
EF 1474(1)			AY 974(4)	FI 864(2)
			BX 168(10)	GH 769(5)
			CW 472(9)	
			DV 514(8)	
			LO 1179(2)	
			MN 974(5)	

43	30	24	76	88
AM 1066(1)	EE (1)	AC 1074(1)	VK 186(10)	NZ 703(4)
BL 513(2)		BB 282(2)	WI 843(4)	OY 1003(2)
FG 371(3)			XH 622(6)	PX 250(5)
			YG 370(7)	SU 930(3)
			ZF 214(9)	TT 1710(1)
			QP 231(8)	
			RO 1458(1)	
			SN 1308(2)	
			TM 1143(3)	
			UL 680(5)	

66	54	45	26	44
NN 1372(2)	AS 1400(1)	(See above.)	AE 2055(1)	AN 1464(1)
MO 1095(5)	BR 792(4)		BD 543(3)	BM 429(3)
LP 595(8)	CQ 304(6)		CC 592(2)	LC 668(2)
FU 505(10)	FN 883(3)			
GT 1029(6)	GM 462(5)			
HS 1217(4)	HL 967(2)			
IR 1318(3)				
KQ 82(13)				
VE 1389(1)				
WD 578(9)				
XC 323(12)				
YB 337(11)				
ZA 795(7)				

55	59	57	22	36
AT 1633(1)	DU 710(4)	BU 449(6)	AA(1)	(See above.)
BS 763(7)	ET 2132(1)	CT 1151(4)		
CR 947(4)	IP 890(2)	DS 1024(5)		
DQ 410(8)	KO 881(3)	ER 1928(1)		
FO 1004(3)		GP 397(7)		
GN 860(6)		HO 1402(2)		
HM 883(5)		IN 1353(3)		
IL 1039(2)		KM 362(8)		

A table derived from the above, showing letter groups corresponding to each cipher group *in order of priority* was prepared for ready reference.

TABLE 3

Order	36	49	97	65	45	43	30	24	76	88	66	54	45	26	44	55	59	57	22	36
(1)	EF	EO	XT	HR	OA	AM	EE	AC	RO	TT	VE	AS	OA	AE	AN	AT	ET	ER	AA	EF
(2)	CH	IK	YS	LO	FI	BL		BB	SN	OY	NN	HL	FI	CC	LC	IL	IP	HO		CH
(3)	AK	DP	ZR	FT	BN	FG			TM	SU	IR	FN	BN	BD	DM	FO	KO	IN		AK
(4)	BI		WU	AY	DL				WI	NZ	HS	BR	DL			CR	DU	CT		BI
(5)	DG			MN	GH				UL	PX	MO	GM	GH			HM		DS		DG
(6)				GS	CM				XH		GT	CQ	CM			GN		BU		
(7)				IQ					YG		ZA					BS		GP		
(8)				DV					QP		LP					DQ		KM		
(9)				CW					ZF		WD									
(10)				BX					VK		FU									
(11)											YB									
(12)											XC									
(13)											KQ									

3. *Determination of length of key words.*—All highest joint frequency pairs were then written as follows on the assumption that about 50 percent would appear in final key and corresponding plain text:

TABLE 4

36	49	97	65	45	43	30	24	76	88	66	54	45	26	44	55	59	57	22	36
E^1	E^1	X^1	H^1	O^1	A^1	E^1	A^1	R^1	T^1	V^1	A^1	O^1	A^1	A^1	A^1	E^1	E^1	A^1	E^1
F^1	O^1	T^1	R^1	A^1	M^1	E^1	C^1	O^1	T^1	E^1	S^1	A^1	E^1	N^1	T^1	T^1	R^1	A^1	F^1

Under 30 and 22, E and A, respectively, must be letters of the key, since there are no alternative pairs. Under the same cipher groups we have determined E and A to be letters of the plain text.

The two groups TRA appearing in the lower line at once attract the eye. Their similarity at once suggests that they may be letters of the key word indicative of length of key word. Counting from T of TRA, inclusive, to the next T, inclusive, before the following TRA, we get a count of 14. The key word therefore may be either 14, or more probably, 7 letters long. Assuming length as 7 letters, we put vertical dotted lines after every seventh letter as in above diagram (table 4).

4. *Recovery of key word.*—Since there is no question that E is the seventh letter of the key word, then we know at once that A under 26 is a letter of the plain text.

Looking at the first TRA, RA appears to be correct but the X above the T seems improbable of combination either with HO or RA. HO suggests WHO, so we begin to believe that a key word seven letters long and ending in E would not have WHO in the middle of it but rather that it forms a whole word or part of a word of the plain text, so we leave HO above the line and RA below the line. Next we try W⁴ above the line under 97 and try its corresponding letter U⁴ below the line as shown below:

TABLE 5

36	49	97	65	45	43	30	24	76	88	66	54	45	26	44	55	59	57	22	36
H²		W⁴			F³														
E¹	E¹	X³	H¹	O¹	A¹	E¹	A¹	R¹	T¹	V¹	A¹	O¹	A¹	A¹	A¹	E¹	E¹	A¹	E¹
F¹	O¹	T¹	R¹	A¹	M¹	E¹	C¹	O¹	T¹	E¹	S¹	A¹	E¹	N¹	T¹	T¹	R¹	A¹	F¹
C³		U⁴			G³														

Then we proceed to underline the second RA as part of the key word under 57 and 22. We are sure that that A is in the key word. This gives the plain text EA for cipher groups 57 and 22.

Returning to the first group of seven letters, we find an O as the second letter below the line with an equivalent plain text letter E. The corresponding letter below the line under 76 of the corresponding second cipher group of the next seven letters is also O. These O's might well be in the key word because F O U R A M E becomes suspiciously close to presenting a solution. Glancing at the lower line under 24, the letter C suggests itself as the first letter of the code word, rather than the F found under the initial 36 which has an equivalent plain text letter E. It is unlikely that EE form the first two letters of the first plain text word. On a chance that C may be the first letter of the key word, we find the group CH with a joint frequency of 2 as probable, so putting C below the line and H above the line, we get for the key word C O U R A M E and above it we find H E W H O A E. It seems we are near the solution. The key word suggested by inspection is C O U R A G E. Looking up our 43 column in table 3, we find the third highest frequency group FG, so we place the G below the line and the F above it. We check the text so far,

HE WHO FEAR

CO URA GECO

We have found the key word!

5. *Decipherment of the unknown message.*—What remains is simple. We now write and repeat the key word below the line, noting the joint frequency standing of each key word letter for each cipher group number so as to be able to find the corresponding plain text letter of the same frequency standing to put above the line, with the following result:

TABLE 6

36	49	97	65	45	43	30	24	76	88	66	54	45	26	44	55	59	57	22	36
H²	E¹	W⁴	H¹	O¹	F³	E¹	A¹	R¹	S³	I³	S¹	H⁵	A¹	L³	F³	D⁴	E¹	A¹	D⁵
C²	O¹	U⁴	R¹	A¹	G³	E¹	C¹	O¹	U³	R³	A¹	G⁵	E¹	C³	O³	U⁴	R¹	A¹	G⁵

So the "absolutely indecipherable" cipher message is solved—and by a frequency method, in spite of the statements of Schooling to the contrary! It reads: "HE WHO FEARS IS HALF DEAD."

Time required for solution was 2 hours and 49 minutes.

It is interesting to note how closely the frequency percentages of the cipher pairs used agree with those found in the examination of the sample message which had only one more letter. We find in the unknown message the following results:

	Percent
First order pairs	50
Second and third order pairs	30
Fourth and fifth order pairs	20

whereas in the sample message we found:

First order pairs	52. 4
Second and third order pairs	33. 3
Fifth and sixth order pairs	14. 3

AFTERTHOUGHTS

It occurred to me that some of our enthusiastic cryptanalysts might be interested in spending some spare time examining some unknown messages in a modified form of the "Nihilist Cipher" which I have devised, and, by such examination, arrive at methods of procedure which might extend our knowledge of cryptanalytic processes to be used in attacking this and similar cipher systems. For obvious reasons, neither the "Nihilist Cipher" nor my modification of it are suitable for military field use.

The four messages given below are all enciphered by the same modified system, determination of which we leave to the nimble wits of the reader. The form of cipher square and the method of numerically adding the equivalents of the cipher key to those of the plain text are used as in the Schooling disclosure. The language is English. Message No. 1 is in a different key from that used for messages numbered 2, 3, and 4, which are military messages, all in the same key, but from different sources.

All of these messages are decipherable—No. 1 with great difficulty because of being a single example, whereas messages 2, 3, and 4, because of possibility of comparison, should be found to be only moderately difficult for advanced students of cryptanalysis.

It is to be hoped that there will be sent to the office of the Chief Signal Officer solutions of all messages, accompanied by statements as to methods used, disclosure of the modification made in the system of encipherment, the keys employed (which require nothing but the exercise of memory on the part of the cryptographer) and the actual time used for solution.

Message No. 1

85	36	57	66	53	59	88	98	38	86	48	54	98	49	56	45	66	54	64	70
35	98	45	58	64	26	54	75	75	57	96	57	44	77	30	54	88	36	45	85
38	32	52	73	78	85	56	36	31	56	79	98	46	56	46	79	27	54	26	88
69	48	48	64																

Message No. 2

46	78	55	66	46	85	87	78	54	55	55	74	65	55	75	52	22	48	85	39
55	76	57	38	67	26	43	59	64	28	57	22	43	55	89	66	84	32	34	57
32	66	24	35	54	58	85	36	36	86	37	55	46	45	66	86	68	86	73	33
99	65	86	48	77	23	46	68	59	44										

Message No. 3

47	55	63	76	64	68	87	78	54	55	59	65	43	67	88	56	43	29	52	59
59	64	46	36	38	40	35	26	84	55	68	26	53	52	78	58	64	65	27	56
52	55	57	32	55	57	85	79	54	87	28	95	30	44	98	107	74	68	73	37
107	54	86	60	86	55	28	77	40	51	85	96	63	28	55	59	50	77	78	56
78																			

Message No. 4

25	68	54	35	64	64	73	88	64	22	86	74	45	77	66	64	26	57	92	39
57	67	26	56	40	57	66	30	66	28	68	33	34	65	65	69	74	65	27	57
54	79	46	25	32	59	56	76	32	77	36	78	57	44	97	77	75	78		

Solutions to "Challenge Messages" *

By Lt. Col. William F. Friedman, Signal Reserve; Principal Cryptanalyst, Office Chief Signal Officer

In the preceding issue of the Bulletin, I presented several so-called "challenge messages" issued years ago by certain cryptographers, the solutions to which, so far as I am aware, have never been published. No doubt many readers of the Bulletin solved all or nearly all the messages submitted, as these examples are after all very simple in their nature. Only the Blair messages should have given any trouble and if so it is attributable almost entirely to the fact that they contain so many errors. It was for this reason that it was deemed advisable to present the Blair messages in facsimile, so that such readers as might be coerced into making an attempt to solve them could not subsequently attribute their difficulties to carelessness on my part or on the part of the editor of the Bulletin, who probably feels the onus of his responsibility sufficiently in other directions to have no desire to suffer any additional blame for his indiscretions in presenting faulty cryptographic puzzles for the instruction and amusement of his readers.

1. THE DAVYS MESSAGE

a. Brief examination of the text of the message shows that there are a few isolated numbers (such as 90, 109, 34, in the first line of

*(No. 104, April–June, 1939)

text) and many "strings" of figures, the latter in every case containing an even number of digits. Let us mark off these strings of digits in pairs, and make a frequency distribution of the text. It is as shown in figure 1.

2d Digit

1st Digit	0	1	2	3	4	5	6	7	8	9
1										
2	II	I	III	II	II	III	II			I
3	IIII		I	I	III		II	I	I	III
4	II	5̄ III	III	II		5̄ II	5̄ 5̄ 5̄ II		III	5̄ I	5̄ 5̄
5	III	II	IIII	5̄ 5̄ 5̄ II	5̄ 5̄ II I			5̄ 5̄ 5̄	5̄ II	5̄ I
6	5̄ III III			III		5̄ II III	III	5̄ II	III	5̄ 5̄ 5̄ 5̄
7	5̄ I	III	5̄ I	5̄ 5̄ II		5̄ I	5̄ 5̄ 5̄	5̄ III	5̄ 5̄ III	III
8	I	5̄ I	5̄	5̄ 5̄ 5̄ 5̄	II		III			
9	I	5̄		II			II		II	
10			III		I	5̄	I	II	III	II
11		III								

FIGURE 1.

b. The tallies are seen to be more or less concentrated in the central section of the square, from about 40 to 90. Remembering that we are dealing with text of a vintage of 1790, when our alphabet consisted of but 24 letters (I and J, U and V were regarded as similar), when we try to "fit the distribution to the normal" we find that beginning with the number 41 and ending with the number 64 the high-frequency letters fall at the proper places, and so do the low-frequency letters. Going right on with 65=A and ending with 88, we find a second distribution that also fits the normal alphabet (note figure 2).

c. When we substitute these values in the text we immediately get good words.

d. What about the numbers from 20 to 40? Study of lines 3, 4, and 5 will soon convince one that these numbers are without question nulls. So they may be crossed out and disregarded.

e. There are now left the numbers from 90 to 111, which are apparently the equivalents of words. Possibly the numbers and the words are in parallel sequence, that is, the words progress in alphabetic

2d Digit

1st Digit	0	1	2	3	4	5	6	7	8	9
1										
2	II	I	III	II	II	III	II			I
3	IIII		I	I	III		II	I	I	III
4	II	5̄ III	III	II		5̄ II	5̄ 5̄ 5̄ II		III	5̄ I	5̄ 5̄
5	III	II	III	5̄ 5̄ 5̄ II	5̄ 5̄ II			5̄ 5̄ 5̄	5̄ II	5̄ I
6	5̄ III III			III		5̄ II III	III	5̄ II	III	5̄ 5̄ 5̄ 5̄
7	5̄ I	III	5̄ I	5̄ 5̄ II		5̄ I	5̄ 5̄ 5̄	5̄ III	5̄ 5̄ III	III
8	I	5̄ I	5̄	5̄ 5̄ 5̄ 5̄	II		III			
9	I	5̄	II				II		II	
10			III		I	5̄	I	II	III	II
11		III								

FIGURE 2.

order and the numbers in numerical order. If so, then the number 91 should stand for a word near the beginning of the dictionary, such as "and." Try it and see how it fits in every place it occurs. Proceeding in this manner the meanings of practically all these values may be ascertained and it is found that the alphabetic arrangement is disturbed only in one or two places: The number 93 seems to be "of," the number 111 seems to be "not," but these values are not in alphabetic order. We shall have to be satisfied with this, however, as the message makes fairly good sense—the latter part much better than the former. The following is offered as a solution, not perfect perhaps, but adequate to the occasion:

(Solution is reproduced on following two pages.)

1.   90   6645737747   83576045   109   655383814976   34
    ALTHOUGH   B E I N G   T R U E   THAT   A N T R I M   NULL

2.   99   677867767358495077   23   70577852   108   26   50495371
    HAS   C O M M I S I O N   NULL   F R O M   H.M.   NULL   K I N G

3.   8378   36   435476415368   836977   22   40
    T O   NULL   C O M A N D   T E N   NULL   NULL

4.   5972786058415368   39   764553   91   446577736975
    T H O U S A N D   NULL   M E N   AND   D A N I E L

5.   78   30   5345735169   93   29   108   664568
    O   NULL   N E I L E   OF   NULL   H.M.   B E D

6.   43724176426957   105   22   104   32   8145795457836944
    C H A M B E R   IT   NULL   IS   NULL   R E P O R T E D

7.   33   70577852   97   109   23   108   74495371   42697545
    NULL   F R O M   ENGLAND   THAT   NULL   H.M.   K I N G   B E L E

8.   34   61695175   93   5245   666083   24   824163458348   73
    NULL   W E L L   OF   M E   B U T   NULL   S A Y E T H   I

9.   48658469   5378   20   5578854557   4970   49   72656045   111
    H A V E   N O   NULL   P O W E R   I F   I   H A V E   NOT

10.   21   105   40   106   7687   44608387   91   7041735972   30
    NULL   IT   NULL   JUST   M Y   D U T Y   AND   F A I T H   NUL

11.   8354   97   20   99   75785883   105   7669   30   91
    T O   ENGLAND   NULL   HAVE   L O S T   IT   M E   NULL   AND

12.   576971606581686944   102   25   105   37   73   48418469
    R E G U A R D E D   FOR   NULL   IT   NULL   I   H A V E

13. 47787769   76606748   658259814163   105   38   5869457669
    G O N E   M U C H   A S T R A Y   IT   NULL   S E E M S

14. 426083   22   50775485   39   111   617269574953   34   775481
    B U T   NULL   K N O W   NULL   NOT   W H E R I N   NULL   N O R

15. 61486583   24   6754845782   5978   83417469   25   91   666059
    W H A T   NULL   C O U R S   T O   T A K E   NULL   AND   B U T

16. 102   7663   67787770734469536745   7353   25   107   30   91
    FOR   M Y   C O N F I D E N C E   I N   NULL   THE KING   NULL   AND

17. 8169587945675982   39   8378   26   107   49   584854847544
    R E S P E C T S   NULL   T O   NULL   THE KING   I   S H O U L D

18. 102   69604557   80847359   83724958   36   847772657987
    FOR   E V E R   Q U I T   T H I S   NULL   U N H A P Y

19. 5049534744785245.
    K I N G D O M E

2. THE SCHOOLING MESSAGE

a. The Schooling challenge message belongs to the type known as "repeating-key cipher." It will help a great deal if we can ascertain the length of the key to the message, for then we can deal with it in the usual manner of repeating-key ciphers, which is to look for and factor the intervals between repetitions of digraphs, trigraphs, and longer polygraphs. But unfortunately the message is very short (only 20 letters) and it is possible that the key Schooling used is fairly long, in comparison with the length of the message, so that there may be no opportunity for repetition within the same cipher alphabets. If the key is 20 letters in length we have only one complete cycle to deal with; if it is 10 letters in length, we have two complete cycles, and so on. However, let us study the text and see whether there are any repetitions at all. Only two cases are found: 36 occurs twice and 45 occurs twice. The interval between the two 36's is 20; that between the two 45's is 8. They possess the common factors 2 and 4. A 2-letter key sounds hardly reasonable; one of 4 letters not much better, in view of all Schooling says about his challenge remaining unsolvable forever. Probably both of these single-letter repetitions are of the "accidental" and not the "causal" type. But perhaps we can obtain a clue as to the length of the key by taking advantage of certain principles consequent upon the mechanics of the system.

b. If examination be made, it will be noted that the maximum difference between the cipher equivalents of any two plain-text letters enciphered by any given keyletter cannot exceed 44. For example, with keyletter R, A_p is represented by $11+42=53$; Z_p is represented by $55+42=97$; $97-53=44$. *This relationship holds for every keyletter.* Consequently, if we transcribe the message according to various assumed key lengths it is possible that we may find that only certain key lengths will yield diagrams in which this principle of not exceeding 44 is not violated. Accordingly, we transcribe the message according to hypothetical key lengths of 4 to 10 letters. Thus:

KEY OF 4 LETTERS

1	2	3	4
36	49	97	65
45	43	30	24
76	88	66	54
45	26	44	55
59	57	22	36

KEY OF 5 LETTERS

1	2	3	4	5
36	49	97	65	45
43	30	24	76	88
66	54	45	26	44
55	59	57	22	36

KEY OF 6 LETTERS

1	2	3	4	5	6
36	49	97	65	45	43
30	24	76	88	66	54
45	26	44	55	59	57
22	36				

KEY OF 7 LETTERS

1	2	3	4	5	6	7
36	49	97	65	45	43	30
24	76	88	66	54	45	26
44	55	59	57	22	36	

KEY OF 8 LETTERS

1	2	3	4	5	6	7	8
36	49	97	65	45	43	30	24
76	88	66	54	45	26	44	55
59	57	22	36				

KEY OF 9 LETTERS									KEY OF 10 LETTERS									
1	2	3	4	5	6	7	8	9	1	2	3	4	5	6	7	8	9	10
36	49	97	65	45	43	30	24	76	36	49	97	65	45	43	30	24	76	88
88	66	54	45	26	44	55	59	57	66	54	45	26	44	55	59	57	22	36
22	36																	

c. Consider the first transcription, that based upon the assumption of a key of four letters. If this were correct, then the numbers in the respective columns would belong to the same cipher alphabet. Consider column 3 in that transcription: It contains numbers ranging from 22 to 97, a difference of $97-22=75$. This means that the key can *not* be four letters in length, for, according to subparagraph *b* above, in no case can this difference exceed 44. Continuing in this manner, it is found *that there is one and only one transcription in which there are no violations of this principle that two numbers in the same column must not differ by more than 44.* It is that for a key of seven letters.

d. Further analysis of the mechanics of the system will soon disclose another principle applicable to it: Certain cipher equivalents can represent only one possible combination of plain text and keyletter; for example, the cipher equivalent 22 can only be the result of enciphering A_p by A_k; no other combination will yield 22. Likewise, certain cipher equivalents can represent only two possible combinations; for example, 33 can represent only the result of enciphering A by G (or G by A) and B by F (or F by B). The following table shows all possible combinations for this system:

TABLE 1.—*Table of possible plain-text/key values for schooling cipher*

02	VV			
03	VW			
04	VX	WW		
05	VY	WX		
06	VY	WY	XX	
07	WZ	XY		
08	XZ	YY		
09	YZ			
10	ZZ			
22	AA			
23	AB			
24	AC	BB		
25	AD	BC		
26	AE	BD	CC	
27	BE	CD		
28	CE	DD		
29	DE			
30	EE			
32	AF			
33	AG	BF		
34	AH	BG	CF	
35	AI	BH	CG	DF

TABLE 1.—*Table of possible plain-text/key values for schooling cipher*—·Con.

36	AK	BI	CH	DG	EF							
37	BK	CI	DH	EG								
38	CK	DI	EH									
39	DK	EI										
40	EK											
42	AL	FF										
43	AM	FG										
44	AN	BM	CL	FH	GG							
45	AO	BN	CM	DL	FI	GH						
46	AP	BO	CN	DM	EL	FK	GI	HH				
47	BP	CO	DN	EM	GK	HI						
48	CP	DO	EN	HK	II							
49	DP	EO	IK									
50	EP	KK										
52	AQ	FL										
53	AR	BQ	FM	GL								
54	AS	BR	CQ	FN	GM	HL						
55	AT	BS	CR	DQ	FO	GN	HM	IL				
56	AU	BT	CS	DR	EQ	FP	GO	HN	IM	KL		
57	BU	CT	DS	ER	GP	HO	IN	KM				
58	CU	DT	ES	HP	IO	KN						
59	DU	ET	IP	KO								
60	EU	KP										
62	AV	FQ	LL									
63	AW	BV	FR	GQ	LM							
64	AX	BW	CV	FS	GR	HQ	LN	MM				
65	AY	BX	CW	DV	FT	GS	HR	IQ	LO	MN		
66	AZ	BY	CX	DW	EV	FU	GT	HS	IR	KQ	LP	MO	NN
67	BZ	CY	DX	EW	GU	HT	IS	KR	MP	NO		
68	CZ	DY	EX	HU	IT	KS	NP	OO				
69	DZ	EY	IU	KT	OP							
70	EZ	KU	PP									
72	FV	LQ										
73	FW	GV	LR	MQ								
74	FX	GW	HV	LS	MR	NQ						
75	FY	GX	HW	IV	LT	MS	NR	OQ				
76	FZ	GY	HX	IW	KV	LU	MT	NS	OR	PQ		
77	GZ	HY	IX	KW	MU	NT	OS	PR				
78	HZ	IY	KX	NU	OT	PS						
79	IZ	KY	OU	PT								
80	KZ	PU										
82	LV	QQ										
83	LW	MV	PR									
84	LX	MW	NV	QS	RR							
85	LY	MX	NW	OV	QT	RS						
86	LZ	MY	NX	OW	PV	QU	RT	SS				
87	MZ	NY	OX	PW	RU	ST						
88	NZ	OY	PX	SU	TT							
89	OZ	PY	TU									
90	PZ	UU										
92	QV											

TABLE 1.—*Table of possible plain-text/key values for schooling cipher—*Con.

93	QW	RV		
94	QX	RW	SV	
95	QY	RX	SW	TV
96	QZ	RY	SX	TW	UV
97	RZ	SY	TX	WU
98	SZ	TY	UX	
99	TZ	UY		
00	UZ			

e. We are now ready to study in detail the transcription into seven columns:

KEY OF 7 LETTERS

1	2	3	4	5	6	7
36	49	97	65	45	43	30
24	76	88	66	54	45	26
44	55	59	57	22	36	

We are fortunate in finding two numbers which in table 1 show only one combination possible: The number 22 in column 5 can only represent the combination AA (A_p enciphered by A_k); the number 30 in column 7 can only represent the combination EE (E_p enciphered by E_k). We may therefore immediately decipher these two columns:

KEY OF 7 LETTERS

Column	1	2	3	4	5	6	7
Key					A		E
Cipher	36	49	97	65	45	43	30
Plain					0		E
Cipher	24	76	88	66	54	45	26
Plain					S		A
Cipher	44	55	59	57	22	36	
Plain					A		

Next we try to find a column that has a number which has only two combinations in table 1. Column 1, containing the number 24, answers this specification; so does column 6, containing the number 43. Since column 6 has letters already deciphered on either side, it seems advisable to work with in preference to column 1.

f. The number 43 has only the possible combination AM and FG; that is, A_p enciphered by M_k or M_p enciphered by A_k will yield 43, and F_p enciphered by G_k or G_p enciphered by F_k will yield 43. Now if we consider all three numbers in column 6, then whatever is correct for the keyletter for that column must yield a possible plain text letter for each number in the column. For example, if A is the keyletter, than 43, 45, and 36 must all yield plain text letters. In this case, with keyletter A, $43=M_p$, $45=O_p$, and $36=K$. But not only do these plain-text letters yield poor combinations in the diagram, but also if A is the keyletter for column 6, the key would end in ...AAE, which is impossible. We conclude that A cannot be the keyletter for column 6. Try M, which yields A_p for 43, C_p for 45, and an impossibility for 36. The keyletter is not M. There is left only the combination FG. Try F, it yields G_p for 43, I_p for 45, and E_p for 36. These do not yield such good combinations as does G for the keyletter, which yields the following:

Column	1	2	3	4	5	6	7
Key					A	G	E
Cipher	36	49	97	65	45	43	30
Plain					O	F	E
Cipher	24	76	88	66	54	45	26
Plain					S	H	A
Cipher	44	55	59	57	22	36	
Plain					A	D	

g. The key appears to be a seven-letter word ending in AGE. The imagination soon yields the word COURAGE and trial of this word gives the solution:

Column	1	2	3	4	5	6	7
Key	C	O	U	R	A	G	E
Cipher	36	49	97	65	45	43	30
Plain	H	E	W	H	O	F	E
Cipher	24	76	88	66	54	45	26
Plain	A	R	S	I	S	H	A
Cipher	44	55	59	57	22	36	
Plain	L	F	D	E	A	D	

Plain text: HE WHO FEARS IS HALF DEAD.

3. THE BLAIR MESSAGES

a. Blair states (on his p. 113, middle paragraph) that "the following paragraph gives the explanation of the dot writing on plate III," and in the next paragraph gives what is presumed to be the plain text of the message of plate III, as well as of the cipher messages on his pages 114 and 115. Hence, let us turn our attention at once to plate III. It shows at the upper left an "Alphabet and Key" and 24 lines with dots on the lines, above the lines, and below the lines. As though he entertains considerable doubts as to the ingenuity or skill of his readers, Blair gives a hint as to the system used by showing at the end of the last line of plate III a series of 1's, 2's, and 3's, but with no particularly recognizable grouping. His hint is, however, really not necessary. Since the dots seems to be the significant elements of the text, and they are of only three sorts (on, above, below the line), we begin by translating the "text" into the digits

1, 2, and 3. The first 48 dots in the first line of "text" yields the following (fig. 3):

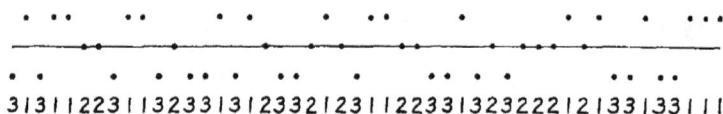

3131122311323313123321231122331323222121331331111

FIGURE 3.

b. Since the "Alphabet and Key" contains 81 cells grouped in a square 9 x 9, it is obvious that if only 3 elements are used in a scheme of indicating specific cells by coordinates, we must use these elements in groups of four. That is, the series of digits 1, 2, 3 must be grouped in 4's, as follows:

```
3131   1223   1132   3313   1233   2123   1122   3313
2322   2121   3313   3111
```

FIGURE 4.

Let us apply the digits 1, 2, 3 to the "Alphabet and Key" in the simplest fashion, as in figure 4. A cipher group such as 3 1 3 1 we shall take to mean "horizontal section 3, line 1 thereof; vertical section 3, column 1 thereof." This gives the letter T. Applying this scheme to the "text" we obtain the following:

```
3131   1223   1132   3313   1233   2123   1122   3313
 T      H      E      .      A      R      T
2322   2121   3313
 O      F      .
```

Here we have the start of the message which Blair himself gives: "The art of writing in cipher has been studied . . .," etc. We shall not take the trouble to check all the dots on plate III.

251

c. Blair states that the foregoing plain text for the dot writing on plate III is also the plain text for his example using numbers (message on his p. 114) and for his example using letters (message at bottom of p. 114 and top of p. 115). `Let us see if we can prove his assertion. The message on page 114 begins: 1 5 2 6 1 8 0 3 5 4 ˋ6 6 6 9 3 5 9 9 5 0 7 1 9 2 7 3 5, etc. If the "Alphabet and Key" on plate III applies to this also, then we must have different coordinate indicators than the three digits 1, 2, 3. There are nine rows and nine columns in the key. Let us number them in normal fashion as

ALPHABET AND KEY

	1	2	3	4	5	6	7	8	9
1	B	C	S	M	T	L	I	E	O
2	G	M	T	P	U	H	O	I	A
3	J	P	U	D	A	N	H	O	E
4	K	D	Y	F	E	R	N	S	I
5	Q	F	A	L	I	S	R	T	O
6	V	L	E	H	O	T	S	U	A
7	W	H	I	N	C	U	T	A	E
8	X	N	O	R	D	A	U	E	I
9	Z	R	.	S	F	E	A	I	O

FIGURE 5.

in figure 5. If we divide the text into pairs of figures, casting all zeros out, and apply the key of figure 5 we have:

```
15   26   18   (0)   35   46   66   93   59   95   (0)   71   92   73   . . .
 T    H    E          A    R    T    .    O    F          W    R    I   . . .
```

Here again is the same message beginning "The art of writing . . .," etc.

d. If the message in letters (bottom of Blair's p. 114) also begins "The art of writing," then the first few letters of the text should be divided up and assigned equivalents as follows:

```
BA   WM   KA   RU   PF   OY   .U   JO   ZA   RU   HS   NY . . .
 T    H    E         A    R    T    .    O    F    .    W . . .
```

But at once we see an inconsistency: RU stands for "period" in one place and F in another. But as we scan the whole message the impression is unmistakable that RU represents "period", which in this case serves as a word separator. If we assume an error in the text, for example the omission of a pair of cipher letters between the OY and the .U, we can make the RU's fit.   Thus:

```
BA  WM  KA  RU  PF  OY  ??  .U  JO  ZA  RU
T   H   E   .   A   R   T   .   O   F   .
```

Continuing in this manner for a little ways in the text, checking our grouping by means of the occasional RU's, we find that the various plain-text letters seem to have different equivalents, suggesting that all the letters of the alphabet have been used as coordinate indicators for the key.   It then becomes a question of juggling the coordinate-indicating letters to make them fit the values given by the plain text—and also straightening out many errors which are in the text. Only a half dozen letters were placed as coordinates when it became clear that the letters within the first three columns of the interior square were used in the same order as coordinates.   The result is shown in figure 6.

ALPHABET AND KEY

			B	G	J	K	Q	V	W	X	Z
			C	M	P	D	F	L	H	N	R
			S	T	U	Y	A	E	I	O	.
B	C	S	B	C	S	M	T	L	I	E	O
G	M	T	G	M	T	P	U	H	O	I	A
J	P	U	J	P	U	D	A	N	H	O	E
K	D	Y	K	D	Y	F	E	R	N	S	I
Q	F	A	Q	F	A	L	I	S	R	T	O
V	L	E	V	L	E	H	O	T	S	U	A
W	H	I	W	H	I	N	C	U	T	A	E
X	N	O	X	N	O	R	D	A	U	E	I
Z	R	.	Z	R	.	S	F	E	A	I	O

FIGURE 6.

ε. As for the message (on the lower half of Blair's p. 115), if we count the intervals between letters having a dot underneath, we find the following:

```
G R E A T     C A R E    H A S      B E E N      T A K E N
  .   .          .   .      .          .            .     .
  2   1          3   2      2          3            3     1
```

Applying the simple key of figure 4, and making the necessary corrections (for errors either on Blair's part or on the part of the printer), we have the message: "Such is the craft of man that it is scarcely possible . . ., etc.," exactly as Blair quotes it within the paragraph with the dots under the letters (bottom of Blair's p. 115).

f. As for the italicized letters of the text (at the bottom of Blair's p. 113 and the top of p. 114), if we count the intervals between the italicized letters, and apply the simple key of figure 5, *making the many necessary corrections for errors,* we have the "author's name, profession, place of residence, and the date of the year," which turn out to be as follows:

WILLIAM BLAIR, A SURGEON. GRUSCEL (?) STREET, BLOOMS-BURY SQUARE, LONDON. (The message ends with the letters BXSWH, and if these indicate the date I am unable to interpret them)

g. By the time we have arrived at this point we feel almost exhausted from the struggle with the errors in Blair's messages and are ready to cry quits. But we still have his last message to study, the one on his page 117. He gives us the plain text and its encipherment. Let us first try to put the two together so as to get as much consistency as possible out of the material. In the first place, counting solely the letters in the alleged plain text we find a total of 88. The number of letters in the alleged cipher text is 164. If we had what we might expect, a two-letter cipher in which each plain-text letter is replaced by a two-letter combination, there should be at least 176 letters in the cipher text. So we are either wrong in our assumption or else some of the cipher text has been omitted or, again some of the plain text may have failed to have been enciphered by carelessness on Blair's part. However, let us do as much as we can in the way of putting the cipher text and the plain text together merely by taking advantage of such repetitions as are present. The arrangement shown in figure 7 seems to be the best that can be done. Note the number of "checks" there are, shown by indicating above each pair of letters the number of times it occurs with the value shown beneath it. It appears that for the most part all the combinations are vowel-consonant pairs and that it is immaterial whether the order of the letters is C–V or V–C. The majority are, however, of the type C–V. Only a very few cases of V–V or C–C combinations are found, and these are probably errors. The reader is asked to note the number of errors we must assume to have been perpetrated by Blair. An attempt is made to build up the coordinates that will give the values we may be fairly sure of, using the same "Alphabet and Key" as before. Many letters fall into positions yielding excellent checks—but by this time our patience is really exhausted and we cry: "Enough! There is no use in wasting more time on such stuff!" It is possible that someone with more leisure at his disposal than I have may be able to reconstruct the particular alphabet and key that Blair used for his last example, and if so, let him have the fun of finishing the job.

254

$\frac{2}{SI}$ $\frac{5}{KA}$ JY $\frac{3}{GA}$ $\frac{2}{MA}$ FU $\frac{7}{VA}$ QUA $\frac{2}{XO}$ $\frac{3}{RO}$ $\frac{2}{LO}$
R   E   L   I   E   V   E   U   S   S   P

$\frac{3}{FA}$ $\frac{5}{KA}$ DU NA BI YE RA SC GUE $\frac{2}{MA}$ $\frac{2}{LO}$
E   E   D   I   L   Y   O   R   W   E   P

$\frac{7}{VA}$ $\frac{2}{ZI}$ $\frac{3}{GA}$ $\frac{3}{RO}$ DI $\frac{2}{MO}$ $\frac{3}{XA}$ TI HO HY $\frac{5}{KA}$ $\frac{3}{FA}$
E   R   I   S   H   F   O   R   T   H   E   E

GI $\frac{7}{VA}$ MY NE QUI $\frac{2}{PA}$ $\frac{2}{XO}$ AU $\frac{5}{KA}$ $\frac{7}{VA}$ $\frac{2}{IN}$ OU
N   E   M   Y   H   A   S   B   E   E   N   R

$\frac{3}{FA}$ $\frac{2}{YA}$ NI $\frac{2}{MO}$ $\frac{3}{XA}$ $\frac{2}{RI}$ CO $\frac{2}{PA}$ $\frac{2}{NG}$ DO SP
E   I   N   F   O   R   C   (ED)   A   N   D   O

UL $\frac{2}{ZI}$ IO $\frac{2}{RI}$ $\frac{3}{XA}$ MU $\frac{3}{GA}$ $\frac{3}{RO}$ $\frac{2}{YA}$ ZA $\frac{2}{NG}$ OR
U   R   P   R   O   V   I   S   I   O   N   S

AL $\frac{2}{SI}$ $\frac{7}{VA}$ YI $\frac{7}{VA}$ L $\frac{5}{KA}$ ZE BR EL $\frac{2}{IN}$ $\frac{2}{TH}$
A   R   E   N   E   A(RLY)   E   X   P   E   N   D

$\frac{7}{VA}$ $\frac{2}{TH}$
E   D

FIGURE 7.

The Morse Code proved too tricky for Continental operators.

The Continental Code *

By Capt. T. T. Teague, Signal Corps

It is believed that a consideration of the Continental Telegraph Code should be based on a prior consideration of the Morse Code of which it is a modification.

The Morse Code was contrived by the inventor of the telegraph, Prof. Samuel Finley Breeze Morse. It is a three element code; the letters of the alphabet being made up of dots, dashes, and spaces; the latter as constituent integral units.

The complete Morse Code is as follows:

A	. —	N	— .	&	. . . .
B	— . . .	O	. .	1	. — — .
C	. . .	P	. . . . .	2	. . — . .
D	— . .	Q	. . — .	3	. . . — .
E	.	R	. . .	4	. . . . —
F	. — .	S	. . .	5	— — —
G	— — .	T	—	6	. . . . . .
H	. . . .	U	. . —	7	— — . .
I	. .	V	. . . —	8	— . . . .
J	— . — .	W	. — —	9	— . . —
K	— . —	X	. — . .	0	— —
L	—	Y	. . . .		
M	— —	Z	. . . .		

Period .	. . — — . .	Brackets	BX	
Comma ,	. — . —	Dollar sign $	SX	
Semicolon ;	SI	Apostrophe '	8	
Colon :	KO	Decimal	DOT	
Interrogation ?	— . . — .	Percent sign %	OSO	
Exclamation !	— — — .	Inner quotations start	QX	
Hyphen -	HX	Inner quotations end	QY	
Dash —	DX	Underline start __	UX	
Parenthesis start (	PN	Underline end	UJ	
Parenthesis end)	PY	Capital letter	CX	
Quotation start "	QN	Small letter	I5	
Quotation end "	QJ	Not code	E5	
Paragraph	— — — —	Pounds sterling	LX	
Fraction bar /	E	Shillings	UT	
Colon dash :—	KX	Pence	D	
Colon quote :"	KQ			

As first made up the punctuation section was not as exhaustively complete as shown above—but provision for all punctuations was soon

*(No. 104, April-June, 1939)

made. They were needed as the mail service was not what we are now accustomed to and the telegraph service wished to boast that it was possible to live up to the Greek—graph, to write; tele, at a distance—and reproduce, exactly, anything that could be written or printed. To convey the true meaning in press work this was necessary, and there are many stories of the accurate telegraphing, in proper form, of statements of account and financial statements of mercantile firms.

At first glance there seems to be little rhyme or reason involved in its fabrication but upon more careful analysis we will find that it is quite scientifically put together to best accomplish its purpose.

We will give the value of the duration of time of the dot as unity or one. The value of the dash, in comparison, is usually set at three or, in other words, the dash is supposed to be three times as long as the dot. This seems like a rank approximation as one can easily realize that a dot can be made with a key in a pretty slim amount of time and three times this amount wouldn't make much of a dash. But as a matter of fact our measuring scheme isn't quite such an approximation after all. With excellent transmission, monitored. if we measure with a micrometer the length of the inked dot and the inked dash as electrically and mechanically recorded on the uniformly running paper tape we will find that the latter is in reality very close to three times as long as the former. With the same transmission it could be shown that, in the case of a dot the circuit remains closed about $\frac{1}{24}$ second and for the dash $\frac{1}{8}$ second.

The incidental spaces separating the dots and dashes is given a value equal to the dot, or one. The element space is given a value of three but there should be no interletter space with a value in excess of three as it is merely necessary to suggest the idea of the element space to the brain and not to accentuate it by increased length so any contemplated adjacent incidental spaces are merged with the element space.

Now let us evaluate the alphabet of this code:

A	.—	=5[1]	J	—.—.	=11	S	...	=5
B	—...	=9	K	—.—	=9	T	—	=3
C	.. .	=7[2]	L	——	=5	U	..—	=7
D	—..	=7	M	——	=7	V	...—	=9
E	.	=1	N	—.	=5	W	.——	=9
F	.—.	=7	O	. .	=5	X	.—..	=9
G	——.	=9	P	.....	=9	Y	.. ..	=9
H	....	=7	Q	..—.	=9	Z	... .	=9
I	..	=3	R	. ..	=7			

[1] Equals (dot, 1; incidental space, 1; dash 3; total 5).
[2] Equals (dot, 1; incidental space, 1; dot 1; element space, 3; dot, 1; total 7).

(The letter L and the figure 0 (zero) are dashes of length values of 5 and 7, respectively.)

To diverge for a moment to cryptanalysis we will consider a normal English frequency table—Edgar Allan Poe, Vesin de Romanini, Hitt, Freidman—say, Hitt (Parker Hitt, Colonel, Signal Corps, retired—the father of military cryptography in our Army):

E T O A N I R S H D L U C M P F Y W G B V K J X Z Q

We could take the telegraph frequency table but we must remember that Professor Morse couldn't consider a telegraph frequency table because one couldn't exist until he got his telegraph invented.

Let us see how the values run:

E	T	O	A	N	I	R	S	H	D	L	U	C	M	P	F	Y	W	G	B	V	K	J	X	Z	Q
1	3	5	5	5	3	7	5	7	7	5	7	7	7	9	7	9	9	9	9	9	11	9	9	9

We can guess that Professor Morse knew what he was about, eh!

As soon as the electric telegraph was invented the other nations of the earth started to use it—and they took along the Morse Code, too. But in use it proved to be a wee bit too fast for them to attain both accuracy and speed with it.

Consider a couple of fairly trick words—"ceiling" or the proper name "Reilly." In the latter there is a faint difference between the interspacing of the elements of the letter "R" and the intraspacing between the letters "e" and "i." With these letters following one another as they do in this word there is some chance for confusion. The "r" may easily become "ei" and the "ei" become "r." Many other examples could be shown.

An interesting commentary upon the difference between the mental traits of Americans and those of other nationalities lies in the fact that at no time was a change in the Morse Code seriously contemplated in this country (we thought it was O. K. and could get accuracy and world's record speed with it and plenty of operators to work it). In the eastern hemisphere it was different. None of those foreign nations thought it was satisfactory as it was originally compiled, and all of them changed it.

In this country the telegraph service has always been a private commercial enterprise, i. e., the Western Union Telegraph and Postal Telegraph Companies. In all other countries the telegraph is a government service, usually under a "Bureau of Posts," i. e., Post Office Department. (Of course, in our Philippine Islands the telegraph is an insular government service—Bureau of Posts—and in Alaska, War Department—the Signal Corps Alaska Communication Service.)

The item that limited the desired expansion of the telegraph service—anywhere—was circuits. There was no wire of any appreciable length until the telegraph was invented. There had been no demand for it and nobody knew how to make it. As a consequence, short pieces were made in foundries and welded together when long lengths were required. When France, for example, adopted the wire telegraph, the service would center at its capital city, Paris, with at first short lines radiating in a few directions to suburbs. In Germany, it would be Berlin and a like small surburban area would be served. In each of these countries, the telegraph being a government service and the Morse Code unsatisfactory for their use, it was officially modified and thus there was in France an official French modification and in Germany an official German variation of the code and, of course, they were different.

Gradually the areas served about Paris and Berlin became more extensive and ultimately there obtained an international circuit between the two countries. The difference in language caused no difficulty as telegraphic communication is letter by letter, but the differences in the modified codes did greatly reduce the speed in operation until the French operators learned thoroughly the German variation and vice versa.

To eliminate this intolerable feature a convention was held in Europe where the international telegraphic difficulty existed. Officially appointed delegates proceeded from their various countries to one point and in convention they talked and conferred, orated, argued, voted and finally agreed on a modification to supersede all extant modifications. This code was called the International Morse Code and our original code was called by them the American Morse Code for the purpose of distinction. This convention it so happens was held in Russia—St. Petersburg (Leningrad) in 1875—but the Russians still retain their own telegraph code due to their alphabet being so different in individual letters. Of course there were many other subjects beside this code that were considered with a view to improvement.

Inasmuch as the submarine cable traffic was not of comparatively great weight and the few cables then linking England with other countries were English owned and operated, it was not imperative that England, isolated to the degree she was, be in any great rush to adopt and put into use the new code. In England, therefore, they referred to it as the Continental Code—the one in use on the continent. We, speaking the same language, adopted the name from them.

With Senatore Guglielmo Marconi's invention of the radiotelegraph (wireless, it was then called) we quickly adopted its use. Our merchant marine boasted but one regular line of steamships—the American Line—crossing the Atlantic Ocean to Europe on a schedule. We had many coastwise lines. Most of them equipped their steamers with radiotelegraph apparatus and on the Atlantic coast we had one large radio company, the United Wireless Co.; one small company, the Massie Wireless Co. and an American branch of the parent European company, the Marconi Wireless Telegraph Co. of America. Later the Germany company, Telefunken Gasellshaft, was represented here. But all the American radio operators were Morse Code men—ex-Western Union, Postal Telegraph, railroad, stock exchange, Associated Press, etc.—most of whom did not know that there was a Continental Code and they used the Morse Code in their radio work.

When an American ship worked or relayed for a foreign ship, for instance, each realized the difference in the code the other chap was using. But they got along. An efficient Morse man copying a radio signal from a European could learn to handle the Continental Code accurately, and at the speed offered, in, usually, a matter of minutes! It doesn't work the other way around, however, as one can readily see by a comparison of the two codes.

Here is the Continental Code:

A	.—	J	.———	S	...	2	..———
B	—...	K	—.—	T	—	3	...——
C	—.—.	L	.—..	U	..—	4	....—
D	—..	M	——	V	...—	5	.....
E	.	N	—.	W	.——	6	—....
F	..—.	O	———	X	—..—	7	——...
G	——.	P	.——.	Y	—.——	8	———..
H	....	Q	——.—	Z	——..	9	————.
I	..	R	.—.	1	.————	0	—————

Period .	......	Parenthesis ()	—.——.—
Comma ,	.—.—.—	Quotation "	.—..—.
Semicolon ;	—.—.—.	Underline _	..——.—
Colon :	———...	Fraction bar /	—..—.
Interrogation ?	..——..	Paragraph	—....—
Exclamation !	——..——	Decimal .	DOT
Hyphen -	—....—	Dollar sign $	DL
Apostrophe '	.————.	Percent %	PC

Inspection shows it to be not as complete as to punctuation as is the Morse. Complicated boxes are no longer telegraphed—they can be mailed more cheaply and thereby delivered to their destination in sufficient time.

It is also seen to be a two-element code, the dot and the dash making up the letters, etc. The element space appears only in one punctuation mark—the period—but it is a long signal and one has plenty of time to consider the whole train of dots and spaces and punctually strike the period on one's tyepwriter. The odd length dashes of the Morse letter "L" and figure "0" have also been eliminated.

Evaluated, it stands as follows:

A	.—	=5	J	.———	=13	S	...	=5
B	—...	=9	K	—.—	=9	T	—	=3
C	—.—.	=11	L	.—..	=9	U	..—	=7
D	—..	=7	M	——	=7	V	...—	=9
E	.	=1	N	—.	=5	W	.——	=9
F	..—.	=9	O	———	=11	X	—..—	=11
G	——.	=9	P	.——.	=11	Y	—.——	=13
H	....	=7	Q	——.—	=13	Z	——..	=11
I	..	=3	R	.—.	=7			

According to the telegraph frequency table (Hitt), comparative weights are:

	E	O	A	N	I	R	S	T	D	L	H	U	C	M	P	Y
Continental	1	11	5	5	3	7	5	3	7	9	7	7	11	7	11	13
Morse	1	5	5	5	3	7	5	3	7	5	7	7	7	7	9	9

	F	G	W	B	V	K	X	J	Q	Z
	9	9	9	9	9	9	11	13	13	11
	7	9	9	9	9	9	9	9	11	9

According to the normal frequency table comparative weights are:

	E	T	O	A	N	I	R	S	H	D	L	U	C	M	P	F
Continental	1	3	11	5	5	3	7	5	7	7	9	7	11	7	11	9
Morse	1	3	5	5	5	3	7	5	7	7	5	7	7	7	9	7

	Y	W	G	B	V	K	J	X	Z	Q
	13	9	9	9	9	9	13	11	11	13
	9	9	9	9	9	9	9	9	9	9

(The 13 count appears for the first time in the Continental.)

It is evident from the above that the Continental is a plainer code to some people. Instead of, to them, a Morse letter of confusing make up they now have more clarity and more time to identify and record each character. On the other hand, the Morse is the faster code, i. e., with two "both code" men of equal speed in the respective codes, one transmitting either telegrams or press in Morse and the other in Continental, the man sending Morse would unquestionably pull ahead of the other sending Continental and would handle much more traffic or press in a day's work. If it were necessary to handle press, as per copy (all punctuations), then the Morse man would increase the lead. This is apparent from only a casual inspection of the two sets of punctuations. That the Morse is more flexible is also apparent from a comparison of their respective punctuation facilities.

As there is no frequency table possible as to figures, we may compare them in numerical order:

	MORSE			CONTINENTAL	
1	.－－.	11	.－－－－		17
2	..－..	11	..－－－		15
3	...－.	11	...－－		13
4	....－	11	....－		11
5	－－－	11	.....		9
6	......	11	－....		11
7	－－..	11	－－...		13
8	－....	11	－－－..		15
9	－..－	11	－－－－.		17
0	－－－	7	－－－－－		19

There is a short form for Continental numerals which is employed to some extent:

1	.－	6	－....
2	..－	7	－...
3	...－	8	－..
4	....－	9	－.
5	.....	0	－－－

In a comparatively short time after the world started to equip its ships with radiotelegraph sets another convention was held in Europe— in Switzerland. At Berne it was decided that, in the interest of accuracy and safety, the marine stations and the land stations with which they communicated must use the Continental Code. In the services, the Navy (and Marine Corps, being under the Navy Department) was the first to adopt the Continental owing to the fact that they had occasion to communicate by radio with sundry foreign craft already employing it. The Army followed suit in a comparatively short time to afford smoothness in Army and Navy intercommunications in joint maneuvers or in time of war. It was officially designated, at one time, the General Service Code, due to the fact that it could replace all other codes then in use.

It may be officially designated as the General Service Code at one place and time, and as the International Morse Code (technically, the most correct designation) somewhere else all the time, but to the operator who pounds it out with a key or a bug, fights it through atmospherics, and puts it down with a stick or a mill, it will probably always be the Continental Code.

Editor's Observation Post *

SOLUTIONS TO CIPHERS

In the January–March 1939 issue of the Bulletin a series of ciphers were published and readers invited to submit their solutions to the editor. The statement was made that the names of those submitting solutions, together with the methods employed by each, would appear in a subsequent number. Unfortunately space limitations do not permit the printing of those solutions received as, in practically all instances, they are rather long and involved. Lieutenant Colonel Friedman has, however, reviewed all the replies received and in a letter to the editor has the following comment to make in substance:

The number of solutions to the cryptograms set forth in my article, The Cryptanalyst Accepts a Challenge, which appeared in the January–March 1939 issue of the Bulletin, was rather disappointing. In all, only seven readers accepted the gauntlet and but two of them submitted solutions to anything more than the Schooling cryptogram, which was the easiest of the set.

The names of those who submitted a solution to the Schooling cryptogram include—

Staff Sgt. Sydney R. Cleghorne, Three Hundred and Sixty-ninth Inf., New York National Guard.

Second Lt. James H. Davitt, Signal-Reserve.

Maj. Jackson K. Fairchild, Signal-Reserve.

Maj. Paul C. Gripper, Signal Corps.

Second Lt. S. T. Martin, Jr., Signal-Reserve.

Master Sgt. Charles Murray, Second Signal Service Company.

Capt. Lee R. Williams, Twenty-fifth Infantry.

Perhaps the most succinct but nevertheless quite adequate of the solutions to the Schooling challenge was that offered by Captain Williams, who has had, so far as I am aware, no formal instruction in cryptanalysis. It conforms to the solution presented by myself in the April–June Bulletin, as indeed do all the other solutions, but is, I am pleased to admit, more terse and to the point than is my own. The solution submitted by Sergeant Cleghorne is also very brief, but to the point.

*(No. 105, July–September, 1939)

The two readers who submitted a solution for the Davys cryptogram are—

Second Lt. S. T. Martin, Jr., Signal-Reserve.

Master Sgt. Charles Murray, Second Signal Service Company.

Finally, the sole reader who submitted solutions to the Blair cryptograms is Second Lieutenant Martin, but even he did not solve all of them.

But I can hardly find fault with the many readers who doubtless tried their skill on the Blair messages and gave up, for not only is the method Blair proposes a cryptographic monstrosity, but also his examples are so replete with errors as to disgust the serious student long before he has come to the last of them.

A discussion of a work by Porta,
one of the master cryptographers
of the Renaissance.

The Earliest Solution of a Multiple Alphabet
Cipher Written With the Use of a Key *

By Charles J. Mendelsohn, Ph. D., formerly Captain, M. I. D., G. S.

In Kerckhoff's Cryptographie Militaire (Paris, 1883), page 34, we
find the following passage:

> Except for a short study written in 1863 by the German Major Kasiski, I
> know of no published attempt at the decipherment of a multiple alphabet cipher.
> Everything that appears in the works of Porta, Cospi, Breithaupt, 'S Gravesande,
> Thicknesse, Klueber, Lacroix, Vesin, Joliet, and others applies only to single
> alphabet ciphers. Moreover these authors have never even dreamed of de-
> ciphering any cryptograms except those in which the separation of the words
> is openly indicated.

Lange et Soudart, in their Traité de Cryptographie (Nouvelle Édi-
tion, Paris, 1935), page 166, repeat this statement, almost verbatim.

The passage contains several errors. Omitting for the moment
Porta, who is to form the main subject of the present paper, we note
several writers on cryptography who considered the decipherment of
continuous writing as well as of multiple alphabet ciphers before the
appearance of Kasiski's study.

Of the authors expressly mentioned in the paragraph just quoted,
Thicknesse, in his Treatise on the Art of Decyphering, etc. (London,
1772), has dealt with both the subjects under discussion. On pages
58, ff. he discusses the decipherment of the multiple-alphabet cipher
named after Count Gronsfeld. True, he has lifted his discussion
word for word and without credit from Falconer (who will presently be discussed), but it is manifestly unfair to say that he has
nothing on the subject. 'S Gravesande's Introductio ad Philosophiam
(Leyden, 1737), paragraphs 1001, ff., solves a single alphabet cipher
written continuously. The cipher in question turns out to be one
solved by Giovanni Battista Porta in his De Furtivis Literarum
Notis (Naples, 1563), book III, chapter X, whom 'S Gravesande
fails to mention. His solution is more elaborate than Porta's.

J. F. (i. e. Falconer), whose Cryptomenysis Patefacta, published
(in English, despite the title) in London in 1685, is a work well
worthy of any cryptographer's attention, has an extended discussion
of the solution of multiple alphabet ciphers (pp. 17–33) concluding
with the material on the Gronsfeld cipher later lifted by Thicknesse,
but containing much more, and more valuable, material on the sub-

*(No. 106, October–December, 1939)

ject. Falconer deals also (pp. 15–16) with the matter of continuous writing.

An unpublished work on multiple alphabet ciphers may be mentioned here for completeness' sake. It is a treatise found in the Archives Générales at Brussels, dating from some time between 1676 and 1774, and entitled "Traité de l'Art de Déchiffrer." It was described in the Revue des Bibliothèques et Archives de Belgique, volume 6 (1908), pages 1–19, by H. Seligmann, who gives a summary of the method of solution proposed. This method consists essentially of trying out words and parts of words until sense appears in both the cipher text and the key.

The Rev. Mr. (William) Smith, at Cambridge, England, in 1745, published his A Natural History of Nevis . . . with . . . An Introduction to the Art of Decyphering. Pages 269–278 of this work contain the solution of a continuously written monoalphabetic cipher.

J. B. Andres' anonymously published Steganographie oder die Geheimschreibekunst (Nuernberg, 1799) considers the solution of a multiple alphabet cipher written with the use of a key on pages 27–46. Even though the method described is scarcely to be recommended unless the solver starts his work early in life and has good prospects of living to a ripe old age, Andres does contribute a discussion of the subject long before 1863.

A second anonymous little German book, Die Kunst Geheime Schriften zu Entziffern (Leipzig, 1808), treats of solving single alphabet substitution ciphers without word division on pages 95–98.

Finally we may mention Poe's well-known discussion of the continuously written cipher of the Gold Bug, written in 1843.

After this brief résumé of what others have done, we proceed to take up the contributions of Porta. Book III, chapter X, of the De Furtivis Literarum Notis has already been mentioned in connection with 'S Gravesande. This chapter is entitled "An example of how continuous writing may be deciphered," and contains a page and three-quarters of suggestions on the subject. The following chapter —an extremely short one—goes a bit further, and gives some suggestions on how to proceed with a message in which the words are wrongly divided. Chapter XVIII of the same book (p. 192) is headed, "How to separate the parts of a disk cipher when the writing is continuous," and chapter XIX (p. 193) proceeds (none too satisfactorily, it must be admitted) to exemplify the rules. Book II, chapter IX (p. 172) bears the heading, "How to separate the parts of a message when the writing is continuous," and offers many useful hints such, for example, as the identification of particles, which, once identified and marked off from the words on either side, will indicate the beginnings and endings of other words.

Porta does not rest content, however, with remarks on the difficulties accompanying the absence of word division, but, despite any assertions to the contrary, gives directions for the solution of multiple alphabet ciphers. The first devices of this class that he describes are his multiple disk ciphers (book II, chs. VII–X; pp. 70, ff.). These ciphers are a development of the method of Trithemius (Polygraphia, Cologne, 1571, pp. 70, ff; in the original edition of the Polygraphia, Oppenheim, 1518, which has no page numbers, the matter appears at folio B, III of the section entitled "Clavis Polygraphiae"). Whereas, however, Trithemius' method in its simplest form consists merely of a series of normal alphabets as in the so-called Vigenère Table, used in regular succession without a key word, Porta uses his alphabets similarly, but employs arbitrary characters the normal sequence of which is known only to those in possession of the cipher disk. In other words, the alphabets are equivalent to a Vigenère Table in which the primary or basic alphabet is not normal but mixed. Elaborations given by Porta consist in writing without word division, in the use of nulls, and in variations secured by the employment of certain extra characters the details of which need not here concern us.

Far from omitting a discussion of the decipherment of these, Porta discusses their solution in detail (book III, chs. XV–XXII), and solves three messages set up by himself (chs. XVII, XIX, XXII). These solutions, while they cannot be called entirely satisfactory, contain many useful suggestions. Details are omitted here, since our object is to discuss the solution of a multiple alphabet cipher written with the use of a key.

We can point to two early claims of the decipherment of such ciphers in which details are lacking. Porta (book II, ch. XVI, p. 102) warns against the use of proverbs as keys for multiple alphabet ciphers on the ground that they are easily guessed, and cites one of his own exploits of this nature—the earliest recorded claim, so far as I know, of the solution of such a cipher—concerning which he tells us:

It will not be amiss to mention that, to the amazement of the writer (of the message), I deciphered a message of this kind, sent some time ago by some amateur who was then employed at Rome, in the very hour in which I received it. The reason for my success may have been that the key of the message consisted of the proverb OMNIA VINCIT AMOR, since this proverbial statement is familiar to almost every one.

This anecdote, though it does contain a hint that may prove useful in the work of solution, does not in itself provide a method of solution or a claim to the possession of such a method.

Aloys Meister in his Die Geheimschrift im Dienste der Paepst-
lichen Kurie (Paderborn, 1906), pages 294–295, cites a claim of
Giambattista Argenti, papal secretary for ciphers 1585–1591, to
having solved a cipher written in that early form of multiple alphabet cipher which is commonly (but, parenthetically, quite mistakenly) called the Alphabets of Porta. This cipher is given in Meister's text as follows: q a e t e p e e e a c s z m d d f i c t
z a d q g b p l e a q t a c u i. (The c occurring at letter 34
should read i.) The solution is, Arma virumque cano Troie qui
primus ab oris. The key is given as In principio; it should be In
principio erat verbum.

There is every reason to believe that this cipher was solved by
guesswork. Surely a message consisting of the opening line of
Vergil's Aeneid and a key consisting of the first words of the Gospel
of St. John constitute ideal material for that kind of solution. No
method of otherwise solving the cryptogram is even hinted at. The
key contains 21 letters and the message only 36, so that there is not
even one full repetition of the key. Within the cipher itself there
is only one repetition, and that of two letters—e a (letters 9–10 and
29–30). This repetition, moreover, is of no value whatever to the
decipherer—rather a hindrance, since the two occurrences of e a
represent different clear-text equivalents, m q and u s respectively.
In other words there are really no cipher repetitions at all, and if
this message was solved by any process other than guesswork the
feat was accomplished in some way entirely unknown to modern
cryptographers.*

It is true, too, that Porta makes the direct statement that multiple
alphabet ciphers written with the use of a key will defy any attempt
at solution. The chapter in which he describes the method commonly
called the Alphabets of Porta—though Porta makes no claim to having invented them—is headed (book II. ch. XVI, p. 99) "another
method of using a key without which the message cannot be solved";
and Porta proceeds to say: "The more one attempts to explain its
perplexities, the more uncertainly one drifts about in deciphering it."

---

*Despite what certainly appears to be a rather slighting characterization of this
solution (Dr. Mendelsohn uses the harsh word "guesswork" twice in this paragraph). I
think this sort of characterization is hardly what he intended. No one better appreciated
the value of the probable-word method of solution in practical cryptanalysis than did
Dr. Mendelsohn. He and I exchanged many pleasant words in discussing this Argenti
solution. he claiming it to have been the result of what he called "pure guesswork" and
I defending the solution as one that was perfectly legitimate, consisting of assuming a
word in either the key text or the message text and checking one against the other. This
sort of solution, it is true, has no direct bearing upon the method of solution based upon
the principle of factoring the intervals between repetitions in the cipher text, but I hesitate to call it "guesswork" if the impression is left that such a solution is unworthy of
the cryptanalyst.—W. F. F.

This statement is repeated word for word in the second edition of the De Furtivis Literarum Notis (Naples, 1602; book IV, ch. XVI, p. 119). At the same time, however, this second edition contains a chapter (book IV, ch. XVII, p. 122) which does not appear in the first edition, and which bears the heading, "How a message prepared with a key may be solved and read without the key." So far as I have been able to ascertain, this chapter is nowhere mentioned in works on cryptography, old or new. It merits attention as the earliest published attempt to show how to solve the type of cipher in question. It merits it the more since Porta is certainly, at least so far as published work goes, one of the master cryptographers of the Renaissance. Except in one point—but that is an important one—I fear this chapter will not add to Porta's fame as a decipherer. It suffers from a fault that crops up now and again in his decipherments—the fact that he is deciphering a cryptogram which he has himself composed; and there are other grievous faults in this solution, as will appear later. None the less, what Porta writes deserves to be weighed and considered.

The second edition of Porta's work, in the chapter in question as well as in others, has suffered from execrable proofreading. I have accordingly, in the translation of the chapter which I shall now give, been at pains to restore the text at several points, and have indicated emendations in footnotes. In giving the cipher message I have, for convenience, numbered the letters with Arabic and the words with Roman numerals. I have likewise numbered the paragraphs to facilitate reference in the comments which I have given following the text.

"(1) We are now attempting an arduous and difficult task; for all cryptographers have hitherto considered this method of writing not merely extremely difficult but actually impossible to solve. I have always believed, however, that anything locked up by the use of a system may be opened by using the same system. It must, however, be noted that in the present case the acumen of the decipherer can do more to hit the mark than the rules which we apply. In order more clearly to understand the rules for deciphering, we shall present a larger enciphering table [than that previously given in the so-called Alphabets of Porta], so that we may more clearly perceive the methods of combining the letters. The earlier table was presented in summary form, but we are now going to expand it.

269

```
A  a b c d e f g h i l m n o p q r s t u x
   b c d e f g h i l m n o p q r s t u x a

B  a b c d e f g h i l m n o p q r s t u x
   c d e f g h i l m n o p q r s t u x a b

C  a b c d e f g h i l m n o p q r s t u x
   d e f g h i l m n o p q r s t u x a b c

D  a b c d e f g h i l m n o p q r s t u x
   e f g h i l m n o p q r s t u x a b c d

E  a b c d e f g h i l m n o p q r s t u x
   f g h i l m n o p q r s t u x a b c d e

F  a b c d e f g h i l m n o p q r s t u x
   g h i l m n o p q r s t u x a b c d e f

G  a b c d e f g h i l m n o p q r s t u x
   h i l m n o p q r s t u x a b c d e f g

H  a b c d e f g h i l m n o p q r s t u x
   i l m n o p q r s t u x a b c d e f g h

I  a b c d e f g h i l m n o p q r s t u x
   l m n o p q r s t u x a b c d e f g h i

L  a b c d e f g h i l m n o p q r s t u x
   m n o p q r s t u x a b c d e f g h i l

M  a b c d e f g h i l m n o p q r s t u x
   n o p q r s t u x a b c d e f g h i l m

N  a b c d e f g h i l m n o p q r s t u x
   o p q r s t u x a b c d e f g h i l m n

O  a b c d e f g h i l m n o p q r s t u x
   p q r s t u x a b c d e f g h i l m n o

P  a b c d e f g h i l m n o p q r s t u x
   q r s t u x a b c d e f g h i l m n o p

Q  a b c d e f g h i l m n o p q r s t u x
   r s t u x a b c d e f g h i l m n o p q

R  a b c d e f g h i l m n o p q r s t u x
   s t u x a b c d e f g h i l m n o p q r

S  a b c d e f g h i l m n o p q r s t u x
   t u x a b c d e f g h i l m n o p q r s

T  a b c d e f g h i l m n o p q r s t u x
   u x a b c d e f g h i l m n o p q r s t

U  a b c d e f g h i l m n o p q r s t u x
   x a b c d e f g h i l m n o p q r s t u

X  a b c d e f g h i l m n o p q r s t u x
   a b c d e f g h i l m n o p q r s t u x
```

[NOTE.—To encipher with this table, the key letter is found at the left. The clear text letter is then taken from the upper line opposite the key letter and

270

enciphered by the letter beneath it. Thus, in the key of P, D is enciphered by T. The table differs from the usual "Alphabets of Porta" table in that (1) there is a different alphabet for each letter of the key instead of one alphabet for a pair of key letters—A and B, C and D, etc.; and (2) these alphabets have an independent cipher equivalent for each letter of the clear text, while in the earlier table the equivalents are reciprocal—if clear text A in the earlier table is denoted, for example by cipher M, then clear text M is denoted by cipher A. The present table is the equivalent of the common so-called "Vigenère Table," except that the alphabet in which the clear text and the cipher equivalents are the same (A, clear=A, cipher, etc.) is placed last instead of first.]

"(2) In order that the table just given may more readily be used in deciphering, we shall expand it in such a way that each letter in a cryptographic text may appear in all the ways in which it is possible for it to occur. We shall accomplish this by associating each letter with successive pairs of other letters, one [1] letter of each pair denoting the clear text equivalent of the cipher letter, the other [1] the corresponding key letter. We might dispense with this table, since it is possible to find these same combinations in the preceding table, but since it is more difficult and perhaps more impossible [sic!] we have expanded the table to facilitate matters and [2] have inserted it here.

A	B	C	D	E	F	G	H	I	L	M	N	O	P	Q	R	S	T	U	X
ax	aa	ab	ac	ad	ae	af	ag	ah	ai	al	am	an	ao	ap	aq	ar	as	at	au
bu	bx	ba	bb	bc	bd	be	bf	bg	bh	bi	bl	bm	bn	bo	bp	bq	br	bs	bt
ct	cu	cx	ca	cb	cc	cd	ce	cf	cg	ch	ci	cl	cm	cn	co	cp	cq	cr	cs
ds	dt	du	dx	da	db	dc	dd	de	df	dg	dh	di	dl	dm	dn	do	dp	dq	dr
er	es	et	eu	ex	ea	eb	ec	ed	ee	ef	eg	eh	ei	el	em	en	eo	ep	eq
fq	fr	fs	ft	fu	fx	fa	fb	fo	fd	fe	ff	fg	fh	fi	fl	fm	fn	fo	fp
gp	gq	gr	gs	gt	gu	gx	ga	gb	gc	gd	ge	gf	gg	gh	gi	gl	gm	gn	go
ho	hp	hg	hr	hs	ht	hu	hx	ha	hb	hc	hd	he	hf	hg	hh	hi	hl	hm	hn
in	io	ip	iq	ir	is	it	iu	ix	ia	ib	ic	id	ie	if	ig	ih	ii	il	im
lm	ln	lo	lp	lq	lr	ls	lt	lu	lx	la	lb	lc	ld	le	lf	lg	lh	li	ll
ml	mm	mn	mo	mp	mq	mr	ms	mt	mu	mx	ma	mb	mc	md	me	mf	mg	mh	mi
ni	nl	nm	nn	no	np	nq	nr	ns	nt	nu	nx	na	nb	nc	nd	ne	nf	ng	nh
oh	oi	ol	om	on	oo	op	oq	or	os	ot	ou	ox	oa	ob	oc	od	oe	of	og
pg	ph	pi	pl	pm	pn	po	pp	pq	pr	ps	pt	pu	px	pa	pb	pc	pd	pe	pf
qf	qg	qh	qi	ql	qm	qn	qo	qp	qq	qr	qs	qt	qu	qx	qa	qb	qc	qd	qe
re	rf	rg	rh	ri	rl	rm	rn	ro	rp	rq	rr	rs	rt	ru	rx	ra	rb	rc	rd
sd	se	sf	sg	sh	si	sl	sm	sn	so	sp	sq	sr	ss	st	su	sx	sa	sb	sc
tc	td	te	ef	tg	th	ti	tl	tm	tn	to	tp	tq	tr	ts	tt	tu	tx	ta	tb
ub	uc	ud	ue	uf	ug	uh	ui	ul	um	un	uo	up	uq	ur	us	ut	uu	ux	ua
xa	xb	xc	xd	xe	xf	xg	xh	xi	xl	xm	xn	xo	xp	xq	xr	xs	xt	xu	xx

[NOTE.—In this table the capital letters at the heads of the columns represent the cipher text. The first letter of each pair of letters denotes the clear text,

---

[1] I read "alteram" for "altera."
[2] I read "et" for "ex."

271

the second the key. Thus, if we have **Q** in the cipher text, we know that it may have arisen from clear text A in the key P, from clear text B in the key O, etc. As Porta says, the same information can be obtained from the preceding table.]

"(3) We proceed to give the rules for deciphering: It is necessary to investigate with the greatest care [3] whether the same letter occurs two, three, four, or five times in succession in the cryptogram. Five in succession will never occur, or very rarely indeed. Then letters in direct or reverse alphabetical order must be examined—direct, as, for example, ABCD, reverse, as DCBA; and this applies to letters in uninterrupted alphabetical order, such as ABCD, as well as to those with [equal] intervals between the letters, such as ACEG, and [to letters with such intervals] in reverse order, such as GECA. It is from such occurrences that the rules for deciphering are derived. To avoid confusion and to proceed clearly we shall note several rules.

"(4) In deciphering a cryptogram the same letter may occur several times in succession, or letters may occur in direct or reverse alphabetical order. A [cipher] letter may be repeated when the letters of the key and those of the clear text are the same. Thus, for example, AAA in the key of AAA will give BBB; and if BBB is found [in the cryptogram] the letter of the clear text as well as that of the key will [alphabetically] immediately precede the letter of the cipher text.

"(5) A letter will be repeated likewise if the letters of the clear text and those of the key are in alphabetical order, but with the letters of the clear text in direct and those of the key in reverse sequence—for example, ABC of the clear text with the key CBA gives DDD.

"(6) So also a repetition of the same letter will result if the letters of the clear text are in alphabetical order while those of the key are in reverse alphabetical order but with [equal] intervals of one, two, or three letters between. Thus, if the clear text is ACE and the key ECA, FFF will result [in the cipher text]. With intervals of two letters, if the letters of the clear text are ADG and those of the key GDA, HHH will result. The cipher letter will be that which [alphabetically] follows the first letter of the key; here we have F which follows E, and H which follows G.

"(7) In case the letters of the clear text and those of the key are different but both are in alphabetical order, then, for example, clear text ABC with the key DEF will give EGI as the cipher text; and clear text ABC with the key EFG will give FHL.[4] The cipher text has a one-letter interval between each two letters and [its first letter] follows the first letter of the key, which is E,[5] giving the cipher text FHL.[1]

[3] I read "diligentia" for "diligenda."
[4] Misprinted FHI in the text.
[5] Misprinted D in the text.

"(8) The case is similar if the letters both of the clear text and of the key are in reverse alphabetical order. Thus, clear text CBA with the key FED gives IGE, the letters of which are likewise in reverse order.

"(9) The result will be the same if the key runs in direct alphabetical order while the clear text is in reverse order, or if the clear text is in direct order with the key in reverse.

"(10) Having given these rules, let us present an intercepted message, so that we may proceed to decipher a cryptogram.[6]

	I								II			III				IV		
1	2	3	4	5	6	7	8	9	10	11	12	13	14	15	16	17	18
M	M	M	B	T	X	C	O	P	X	B	D	F	B	V	G	S	T

	V						VI			VII		VIII		
19	20	21	22	23	24	25	26	27	28	29	30	31	32
I	N	X	G	T	N	G	T	C	C	C	C	T	A

	IX				X				XI			
33	34	35	36	37	38	39	40	41	42	43	44	45	46
A	M	H	C	M	A	H	T	B	X	T	M	O	Q

	XII				XIII						XIV		
47	48	49	50	51	52	53	54	55	56	57	58	59	60	61
S	L	Q	P	R	M	M	M	B	T	T	H	M	H	V

	XV					XVI			XVII		XVIII			
62	63	64	65	66	67	68	69	70	71	72	73	74	75	76	77
A	C	E	O	H	G	L	L	L	L	I	V	X	I	O	G

"(11) Finding three letters alike in the first word I consult the rule concerning repeated letters, and find that when the key is in straight alphabetical order and the clear text is in reverse alphabetical order a repetition of letters is produced in the cipher text. Accordingly, in the expanded table I consult the column beneath the letter M, and look there [7] for three letters of clear text in reverse alphabetical order with [the letters of] the key [corresponding to them] in regular order, and such that both sets of letters may go to the formation of an actual word; and near the bottom of the column I find STU in direct order and NOP in reverse order [i. e., PON]. Accordingly I note down these values beneath their corresponding [cipher] letters as doubtful and uncertain until I can remove my doubts by the use of other rules.

---

[6] Porta's later comment shows that the message is intended to show word division. In his text it does so only in part. I have separated the words throughout the message. For convenience of reference I have numbered the words in roman and the letters in arabic numerals. In the printed text letter No. 21 is misprinted R, No. 32 appears as G, No. 41 as O, and No. 73 as N.

[7] The text is corrupt, but the meaning is clear. Perhaps "requirendo" should be "requirens." For "ubi" I read "ibi."

"(12) Next, at the end of the sixth word and the beginning of the seventh[8] I find the same letter four times in succession—CCCC—and this may be of great help to us. In the table, under C, I find HILM, and opposite that group QPON, and I note that these two groups of letters cannot go to form real words, since P followed by O does not make any actual words. [See the commentary on this paragraph below.] At the end of the column I find STUX with CDEF opposite, and I am justified in believing that these letters may form actual words.

"(13) In the third place, I see M three times in the thirteenth word, thus: MMM. I conclude that the group may denote STU, PON, and, since I have now found this twice,[9] I believe it may well be part of the key.

"(14) In the sixteenth word[10] I find LLL with a fourth L at the beginning of the seventeenth.[11] In the expanded table, at the bottom of the table headed by L, I find RSTU with PONM[12] opposite, and, since I am continually finding STU, I consider it certain that it is the beginning of the key.

"(15) Finally, at the end of the fourteenth word[13] and the beginning of the fifteenth[14] I find four successive letters in alphabetical order, separated from one another by a one-letter alphabetical interval, VACE. In accordance with rule 3, I can say [that we have] STU. Since this combination has been repeated several times, there is reason to believe that it belongs to the key, and, since three occurrences of STU are at the beginning of a word, the remaining letter, R, will be at the end of the preceding word, and we shall have R STU.[15]

"(16) Accordingly I look in the first[16] table, and, with the key R, I find that cipher letter U has a C above it. Then, since for key S cipher A, I find D and key T, cipher C gives E, while key V cipher E gives F, the four letters will read CDEF. Hence C will belong to the fourteenth[17] word and F to the fifteenth,[18] and since C is a letter of the fourteenth[17] word and comes at the end of the word, we can have nothing except SIC, HIC, DIC, and [corresponding to this] DEF will indicate DEFENDO, DEFECTUS or DEFICIT.

---

[8] The groups CCCC extends through the two-letter seventh word to include the first letter of the eighth. On the other errors in the paragraph, see the commentary below.

[9] Cf. above, par. 11.

[10]. The text reads "fifteenth."

[11] The text reads "sixteenth."

[12] The text reads MNOP.

[13] The text reads "thirteenth."

[14] The text reads "fourteenth."

[15] Obviously Porta's intention was to show a space between R and S, but the text fails to do so.

[16] There is no apparent reason for looking in the "first" rather than in the "expanded" table.

[17] The text reads "thirteenth" and has "tertiadecima" for "tertiadecimae."

[18] The text reads "fourteenth."

"(17) *Since there are 17 letters between the 3 letters* MMM *and the 4 letters* LLLL, *and 51* [19] *between* [20] *the first 3* MMM *and the same 3 letters repeated in the thirteenth* [21] *word, I conclude that the key has been given 3 times, and decide correctly that it consists of 17 letters.* [Italics mine.]

"(18) I make a guess that the key may read STUDENS SIC DEFICIO. Substituting these letters as the key for the letters of the cryptogram [I see] that in some cases actual words result while elsewhere they do not. I then write STUDIUM SIC DEFICIO, and obtain some real words while in other cases none come to light. Finally, by writing STUDIUM HIC DEFICIT I find the whole cryptogram is deciphered as follows:[22]

	I								II			III				IV		
	1	2	3	4	5	6	7	8	9	10	11	12	13	14	15	16	17	18
	P	O	N	T	I	A	N	E,	E	S	T	U	X	O	R	T	U	A

	V						VI			VII		VIII		
	19	20	21	22	23	24	25	26	27	28	29	30	31	32
	M	O	R	T	U	A,	V	I	X	U	T	S	I	T

	IX					X				XI				
	33	34	35	36	37	38	39	40	41	42	43	44	45	46
	N	O	M	E	N	S	U	U	M,	N	I	H	I	L

	XII					XIII							XIV		
	47	48	49	50	51	52	53	54	55	56	57	58	59	60	61
	M	A	N	E	T,	P	O	N	T	I	U	S	C	U	R

	XV						XVI			XVII		XVIII				
	62	63	64	65	66	67	68	69	70	1	72	73	74	75	76	77
	S	T	U	D	E	T	N	O	N	M	E	L	A	T	E	T "

COMMENTARY

PARAGRAPHS 4–6. Latin words never contain the same letter three times in succession, and almost never begin or end in doubled letters. The occurrence of the same letter three times in succession would be an unusual event, and such an event is certainly not to be expected in the clear text and in the key at the same time. Moreover, if it did happen, Porta's statement that the same letter occurring three times in succession in both clear text and key will produce a cipher text consisting of the next letter of the alphabet three times in succession is true only if the letter in clear text and key is A. Even if

[19] The text has SI instead of LI.
[20] Omitting "a" of the text.
[21] The text reads "twelfth."
[22] I have again numbered the words and the letters.

Porta's hypothesis were likely and his conclusions up to this point correct, his ultimate conclusion—that the occurrence of the same letter three times in succession in the cipher text indicates the existence of the conditions described in clear text and key—is incorrect; and it remains incorrect even when he modifies it, as he does in the next two paragraphs.

What paragraphs 4–6 tell us is, in effect, that if we find the same letter several times in succession in the cipher text we are to conclude one of three things: (1) The clear text and the key both consist of repetitions of a single letter—the same letter in the clear text as in the key; (2) the clear text and the key contain letters in alphabetical order, with the sequence direct in one case and reversed in the other; or, (3) as in (2), but with equal intervals between the letters.

If it is a poor rule that will not work both ways, these are very poor rules indeed. It is quite true that the conditions described will produce repeated letters in the cipher text. It is, however, equally true that these repetitions may come about in other ways. Thus the clear text ARTI with the key DIGR—both groups of letters unexceptionable in Latin—will yield the cipher text EEEE. It is not difficult to find other examples, especially of three-letter repetitions. Clear text QUA with the key SOM gives cipher NNN; clear text QUO with the key ASC gives cipher RRR, etc. In fact Porta might have found in the very cryptogram under consideration two cases in which his reasoning does not apply: cipher text AA (letters 32 and 33) represents clear text TN and key CI, and cipher text TT (letters 56 and 57) is derived from IU in both clear text and key.

The only test is whether any given arrangement of clear text and key yielding a cipher text composed of repetitions of a single letter consists of letters in an order allowed by the Latin language. Any sequence of letters fulfilling that requirement may be correct. Porta has fallen into the old fallacy of concluding that since all monkeys are animals all animals are monkeys.

The statement of paragraph 6, that under the conditions given the cipher text will consist of repetitions of the letter alphabetically one beyond the first letter of the key, is true only if the first clear text letter is A. If this first letter is B, the first letter of the cipher text will be alphabetically *two* letters beyond it, if C, *three* beyond, etc.

PARAGRAPHS 7–8. The encipherments given are correct and exhibit the phenomena mentioned. The statement, however, that the first letter of the cipher text will be alphabetically one letter beyond the first letter of the key is just as erroneous here as it was in paragraph 6; and in paragraph 8, where the clear text does not begin with A, we find no remark concerning the first letter of the cipher text. Clear text FGH with the key LMN gives a cipher text that begins not with M, as Porta's rule would require, but with R. Moreover, as was pointed out in connection with paragraph 6, a cipher text of the nature described by no means justifies the conclusion that the clear text and the key were of the kind indicated: cipher text RTX, for example, will result from clear text FGH with the key LMN, but it will result equally well from other combinations, e. g., from clear text EOR with the key MED.

PARAGRAPH 9. This is intended as a general statement applying to paragraphs 5–8.

PARAGRAPH 11. Porta assumes without further proof that PON belongs to the clear text and STU to the key, while the case might just as well be reversed. Fundamentally the whole argument rests on the mistaken reasoning of paragraphs 4–8.

PARAGRAPH 12. This whole passage is quite unworthy of Porta. In the first place, the letters opposite HILM in the C column of the table are QPON as I have given them. Porta's eye must have deceived him, for he gives MNOP—the wrong letters, and in the wrong order. He then says that the letters STUX at the end of the C column have CDEF opposite them, while actually the letters are FEDC. What Porta should have noted is the possibility of clear text STUX with key FEDC, or, in reverse order, clear text XUTS with the key CDEF.

PARAGRAPH 14. Porta seems to forget that the two-letter groups of his "expanded table" have the clear text letter first and the key letter after it. The error is less important than it might be since the arrangement is reciprocal: E, for example, in the key H, is denoted by O, and H in the key E is likewise denoted by O. The statement that the text has PONM and the key RSTU is erroneous, and shows blind trust in a rule without troubling to check the result. The *first* of the four cipher L's results from clear text N in the key T. Compare the commentary on the paragraph 17, below.

PARAGRAPH 15. This paragraph contains a very careless error, and one that betrays the fact that Porta is working with a made-to-order message. He *knows* that STU is part of the key because he has composed the message himself, key and all. As a consequence he overlooks the fact that this particular occurrence of STU does not belong to the key but is part of the text. His cipher text shows the words separated, and even though he mistakenly assigns STU in this passage to the key he takes advantage of the correct word division.

PARAGRAPH 16. The confusion between key and clear text noted in connection with paragraph 15 continues here. Furthermore the word ending in C might be Fac or Lac as well as either of the three words mentioned.

PARAGRAPH 17. *In spite of the confusion presently to be noted, this paragraph is of great importance as the first intimation in cryptographic*

277

literature—and first by over 200 years—of a method for determining the length of the key. There are not 17 letters between MMM and LLLL, but 16; the first of the four L's is an unfortunate accident, and the actual repetition of the key starts with the second L.

Porta has based his solution, as he himself says (par. 3), on the occurrence of the same letter two or more times in succession in the cipher text. Since his conclusions based on such occurrences are invalid, the solution of the cipher is really not a solution. What has happened is that the hand that built up has also torn down—torn down, however, with advance knowledge of the entire structure on which it was working. The message is a trick message to begin with, composed in such a way as to yield the repetitions on which the author intended to base his reasoning. The chances of finding such a large number of successive repetitions in an ordinary 77-letter cipher text would be very slim indeed.

It seems worthy of note that Porta has not, in connection with his discussion of the present cipher, taken up the method of attempting to guess a word, though he has elsewhere (book III, Ch. VIII, p. 165) discussed such a procedure at length. He says:

Much light will be shed on the subject if the knowledge of the surrounding circumstances (which we have said it is valuable for the interpreter to know) is taken into consideration. At the very start, and before taking up the writing, it may be possible in this way to arrive at some conclusions by means of guesswork. For example, from the fact that spies have intercepted a letter from the hand of a soldier the conclusion will be drawn that military affairs are discussed [in the message]. This renders it probable that the word "belli" [war] is contained in the letter, and that four letters of that word [20] or the five, six, or more of which the word is composed, will not fail to be present if the language is known to be Latin. If the language is the vernacular the proper word must be sought out.

Still, Porta's effort contains a distinct contribution to the history of deciphering. The discovery of the method for determining the length of the key—the method based on the intervals separating two occurrences of the same group of cipher letters—is generally credited to Kasiski's Die Geheimschriften und die Dechiffrierkunst (Berlin, 1863), pages 61, ff. It is interesting, in this connection, to quote Kasiski's procedure:

First of all we must try to ascertain the number of letters composing the key. For this purpose we locate all repetitions of two or more letters in the cryptogram, calculate the distance separating the repetitions from one another, note beneath the cryptogram the repetitions with the number of letters separating them, and endeavor to break up this number into its factors * * *. The factor most frequently found indicates the number of letters in the key.

---

[20] NOTE.—The other letters vary according to the form used.

I would not go so far as to say that Porta, writing more than 250 years earlier, had anticipated this method. Certainly, however, he had an inkling of it when he wrote:

Since there are 17 letters between the first three MMM and the same three letters repeated in the thirteenth word, I decide that the key has been given three times, and conclude correctly that it consists of 17 letters.

The errors in the argument are discussed above, but a modicum of truth remains. If Porta had taken an everyday message instead of a trick composition of his own and applied the reasoning of this paragraph, he might have demolished the "chiffre indechiffrable" before it ever acquired its exaggerated reputation.

A famous novelist turns
to cryptography

Jules Verne as Cryptographer *

By Lt. Col. William F. Friedman, Signal Reserve

We may suppose, with some degree of assurance that Jules Verne, unlike Edgar Allan Poe, by no means regarded cryptography as one of the many fields of abstruse science in which he had attained proficiency or of which he claimed more than a layman's knowledge.[1]

---

[1] See an article by the present author, entitled "Edgar Allan Poe, Cryptographer," in American Literature, vol. VIII, No. 3, November 1936. This article was reprinted in the SCB No. 97 (July–Sept., 1937) ; an addendum thereto will be found in the SCB No. 98 (Oct.–Dec., 1937).

*(No. 108, April–June, 1940)

For Verne never assumes the air of omniscience to be found in some of Poe's more serious work, for example, in his article "A Few Words on Secret Writing." On the other hand it is undoubtedly true that Verne is indebted to Poe for certain of his devices, especially that in which the unraveling of a cryptogram forms a more or less vital element in the romance which he unfolds.

Three of Verne's stories forming the series known as Extraordinary Journeys, employ this device. They are, in chronological order, A Journey to the Center of the Earth (1864), The Giant Raft or 800 Leagues on the Amazon (1881), and Mathias Sandorf (1885). All three stories use different types of cryptograms. In only one of them does Verne attempt, in the character of one of his heroes, to solve the cryptogram by straightforward cryptanalytic methods, as Poe did in The Gold Bug, and it is with considerable regret that I find it necessary to say that in this one attempt he failed to do justice to his own ingenious mind. And, furthermore, the solutions which he obtains in the other two cases come very close to violating one of the tenets of the code of ethics imposed upon themselves in these days by all good detective story writers—never (to use a current idiom) "put over a fast one on the reader." That is, no "trick solution" is admissible.

1. THE CRYPTOGRAM IN A JOURNEY TO THE CENTER OF THE EARTH

In this romantic tale a German savant, Professor Lidenbrock, discovers in an Icelandic manuscript he has picked up in an old bookshop a piece of parchment on which appear "in transverse lines, cabalistic characters," and Verne, through the mouth of the professor's nephew, who is telling the story, says:

Here is the exact facsimile of it. I insist upon presenting these singular characters, for they lead Professor Lidenbrock and his nephew to undertake the strangest expedition of the nineteenth century:

FIGURE 1.

The Professor looked for a few moments at this series of characters; then he said, raising his spectacles:

"They are Runic characters; these type are absolutely identical with those of Snorre Turleson's manuscript! But—what can that signify?"

As the Runic seemed to me to be an invention of savants to mystify the poor world, I was not sorry to see that my uncle did not comprehend it at all. At least so it seemed to me, from the movement of his fingers, which commenced to tremble terribly.

"It is, however, old Icelandic!" he murmured between his teeth * * *.

Evidently a Runic inscription. "But there is a secret, and I will discover it—or else!" A violent gesture finished his thought.

"Put yourself there," he added, indicating the table with his fist, "and write."

I was ready in an instant.

"Now, I am going to dictate to you each letter of our alphabet corresponding to one of these Icelandic characters. We will see what that will give. But, by St. Michael, take good care that you don't make a mistake!"

The dictation commenced. I did my best; each letter was called one after the other, and formed the incomprehensible succession of the following words:⁻

mm.rnlls	esreuel	seecJde
sgtssmf	untelef	niedrke
kt,samn	atrateS	Saodrrn
emtnaeI	nuaect	rrilSa
Atvaar	.nscrc	ieaabs
ccdrmi	eeutul	frantu
dt,iac	oselbo	KediiI

When this work was finished, my uncle eagerly took up the sheet upon which I had just written, and attentively examined it for a long time.

"What does that mean?" he repeated mechanically.

Upon my word, I would not have been able to tell him. Besides, he did not question me for that purpose, and he continued to talk to himself, saying:

"That's what we call a cryptogram, in which the sense is concealed under letters purposely jumbled, and which properly arranged would form an intelligible sentence!"

Because the message on the parchment was written by one Arne Saknussemm, an Icelandic savant and celebrated alchemist of the seventeenth century, the professor concludes that the plain language of the cryptogram is Latin. His reasoning is quite clear, as can be noted in what follows.

*   *   *   *   *   *   *

"And first of all," said my uncle, "we must find the language of this 'cipher.' That ought not to be difficult."

At these words I quickly raised my head. My uncle continued his soliloquy as follows:

"Nothing is easier. There are in this document 132 letters, which give 79 consonants to 53 vowels. Now, it is nearly according to this proportion that the words of Southern languages are formed, whilst the idioms of the North are infinitely richer in consonants. A Southern language must then be in question.

"But what language is it?"

---

² The first two characters of the initial group are *m m*, to correspond with the symbol ⋈. This makes the first group contain 8 characters, whereas the other groups down to about halfway in the message regularly contain only 7 characters, and the rest of the groups, only 6. In some editions this first group is made to contain only 7 characters by dropping out one of the *m*'s. Verne evidently intended the double *m* to act as a single character.

That is what I expected of my savant, in whom I discovered, however, a profound analyst.

"This Saknussemm," he replied, "was a learned man; but as soon as he wrote in a language other than his mother tongue, he would choose by preference the language in vogue among the cultivated minds of the seventeenth century—I mean Latin. If I am mistaken, I can try Spanish, French, Italian, Greek, or Hebrew. But the savants of the seventeenth century generally wrote in Latin. I have then the right to say, *a priori*, that this is in Latin."

I jumped in my chair. My recollections of Latin revolted against the pretension that this succession of bizarre words could belong to the smooth language of Virgil.

"Yes! in Latin," continued my uncle, "but in jumbled Latin."

"So much the better!" I thought. "Uncle, if you unravel it you are sharp."

"Let us examine it carefully," he said, taking up again the sheet on which I had written. "Here is a series of 132 letters presented in an apparent disorder. There are words in which the consonants are met alone, like the first 'mrnlls',[1] others in which, on the contrary, the vowels abound, the fifth, for example, 'unteief,' or the next to the last, 'oseibo.' Now, this arrangement has evidently not been combined; it is determined *mathematically* by the unknown rule which governed the succession of these letters. It seems certain to me that the original sentence was written regularly, then turned about in accordance with the law which we must discover. Whoever possesses the key to this 'cipher' could read it fluently. But what is this key?"

* * * * * * *

The professor decides to try an experiment.

"Let us see," said he; "the first suggestion which would occur to one, for mixing up the letters of a sentence, it seems to me, is to write the words vertically instead of horizontally."

* * * * * * *

While making his great experiment, the eyes of Professor Lidenbrock flashed like lightning through his spectacles, his fingers trembled when he took up the old parchment again, he was very much affected. Finally, he coughed violently, and, in a grave tone, reading out successively the first and then the second letter, of each word, he dictated to me the following series:

        mmessunkaSenrA.icefdoK.segnittamurtn
        ecertserrette,rctaivsadua,ednecsedsadne
        lacartniiiluJsiratracSarbmutabiledmek
        meretarcsilucoYsleffenSnI

In finishing these letters, named one by one, which presented no sense to my mind, I was moved, I will confess; I then expected that the Professor would pompously roll out from his lips a sentence of most magnificent Latin.

But who could have forseen it? A violent blow from his fist shook the table. The ink jumped out of the stand, and my pen fell out of my hands.

"That's not it," cried my uncle. "That's not common sense!"

Then, shooting across the room like a cannon ball, and rushing down the staircase like an avalanche, he rushed into Konigstrasse, and fled with all his might.

* * * * * * *

---

[1] This should be *mmrnlls*, since Verne treats the double *m* as a single character.

The nephew then decides to try his own ingenuity on the parchment.

I endeavored to group these letters so as to form words. Impossible. By joining them by twos, threes, or fives or sixes, absolutely nothing intelligible was obtained; there were the fourteenth, fifteenth, and sixteenth [4] letters which formed the English word "ice," the eighty-fourth, the eighty-fifth, and the eighty-sixth formed the word "sir." Finally, in the body of the document, and on the third line, I observed the Latin words "rota," "mutabile," "ira," "nec," "atra."

"The deuce!" I thought, "these last words would seem to justify my uncle as to the language of the document." And also on the fourth line I perceive, besides, the word 'luco,' which is translated by 'sacred wood.' It is true that on the third we read the word 'tabiled,' of perfect Hebrew form, and on the last, the words 'mer,' 'arc,' which are purely French.

Here was something over which to lose one's head. Four different idioms in this absurd phrase! What relation could there exist between the words "ice, sir, anger, cruel, sacred wood, changing, mother, bow, or sea?" The first and the last alone readily go together; there was nothing astonishing that, in a document written in Iceland, a "sea of ice" should be spoken of. But to understand the rest of the cryptogram from that was another thing.

I debated then with myself against an insoluble difficulty; my brain became heated; my eyes were fixed upon the sheet of paper; the 132 letters seemed to jump around me like those silver drops which glide in the air around our heads when we have an attack of vertigo.

I was a prey to a sort of hallucination; I was stifled; I wanted air. Mechanically, I fanned myself with the sheet of paper, the two sides of which presented themselves successively to my gaze.

What was my surprise, when in one of these rapid movements, at the moment that the back of the sheet turned towards me, I thought I saw some perfectly legible words appear—Latin words, among others "craterem" and "terrestre"!

Suddenly, a light broke in upon my mind; from these few indications I saw the truth; I had discovered the law of the cipher. To read this document it was not even necessary to read it through the leaf reversed! No. Just as it was, just at it had been dictated to me, so it could be spelled out readily. All the ingenious combinations of the professor were realized; he was right as to the disposition of the letters, right as to the language of the document! There was a "something" needed to be able to read this Latin phrase from one end to the other, and this "something" chance had just given me!

The extent of my emotion may be understood! My eyes were affected. I could not make use of them. I had thrown the sheet of paper on the table. It was sufficient for me to cast one look at it to become possessor of the secret.

Finally I succeeded in calming my imagination. I compelled myself to walk around the room twice to quiet my nerves, and I returned to bury myself in the enormous armchair.

'Let us read," I cried to myself, after having filled my lungs with a fresh supply of air.

I leaned over the table; I placed my finger successively on each letter, and, without stopping, without hesitating a moment, I pronounced the entire sentence in a loud voice.

*　　　*　　　*　　　*　　　*　　　*　　　*

---

[4] The double *m* is counted as one character; the period is omitted in the count.

283

The professor returns but his nephew is reluctant to disclose the secret for fear he will have to accompany his uncle on a perilous journey. During the course of this wrestling with the problem Verne presents some calculations dealing with the chances of finding the solution by trying out all possible combinations. The nephew feels reassured that nothing will come of these experiments, for—

I knew very well that if he succeeded in arranging these letters according to all the relative positions which they could occupy, the sentence would eventually be found. But I also knew that 20 letters alone can form two quintillion, four hundred and thirty-two quadrillion, nine hundred and two trillion, eight billion, one hundred and seventy-six million, six hundred and forty thousand combinations. Now there were 132 letters in the sentence which would give a number of different sentences composed of at least 133 figures— a number which is almost impossible to enumerate, and which is entirely beyond comprehension.

I was reassured as to this heroic method of solving the problem.

And well he might be—for that is hardly the way in which a cryptanalyst would approach the matter!

Finally, the nephew acquaints the professor with his discovery and discloses the solution to the mystery of the cipher.

"Ah! You ingenious Saknussemm!" he cried, "you first wrote your sentence reversed!"

And rushing at the sheet of paper, his eye disturbed, his voice trembling with emotion, he read the whole document, going backward from the last letter to the first.

It was composed as follows:

In Sneffels Yoculis craterem kem delibat umbra Scartaris Julii intra calendas descende, audas viator, et terrestre centrum attinges. Kod feci. Arne Saknussemm.

Which bad Latin may be thus translated:

Descend, bold traveller, into the crater of the Yokul of Sneffels which the shadow of Scartaris caresses before the calends of July, and thou shalt reach the centre of the earth. Which I have done. Arne Saknussemm.

*   *   *   *   *   *   *

In analyzing the elements of Verne's solution of this cryptogram, the first thing noted is that Verne was obviously aware of the cryptographic aspects which the writing by means of runes assumes for the uninitiated. Indeed, characters very similar to them even today constitute a form of cipher writing frequently adopted by novices in the art of cryptography. The uninitiated believe that by the use of symbols which do not at all resemble the letters of our established orthography they have imparted an air of impenetrable mystery to their cryptograms. But Verne knows more than this: he tells us, indeed, a few interesting facts about the strange symbols. "They are Runic characters," he says through his mouthpiece, Professor Lidenbrock,

"Old Icelandic—evidently a Runic inscription." Then he proceeds to give for each character of the cabalistic writing the letter of our alphabet to which it corresponds. Now Verne does not concoct these equivalents out of his fertile imagination; he actually takes pains to be scientifically accurate in his work, for if the reader will consult any standard treatise on runes, which represent the oldest form of Germanic writing and which were used for purposes of writing throughout a vast area of northern Europe from the third to the fourteenth century, he will find that Verne is substantially correct in his assignment of letter values to the runic symbols. Incidentally, considering the carelessness of the authors and especially the publishers of romantic tales in which cryptograms play an important role, it is gratifying to find that Verne's runic inscription and his transliteration of it into characters is comparatively free from errors, for I have found but four of them in the whole cryptogram. That is, if one confirms the transliteration Verne gives of the runes into letters, one finds that in only four cases has he made an error in the rune—the letters themselves are entirely correct.

The professor realizes, as soon as he has transliterated the runes into letters, that the writing confronting him is a cryptogram. "That's what we call a cryptogram, in which the sense is concealed under letters purposely jumbled and which properly arranged would form an intelligible sentence." From the cryptanalytic point of view, it is to be noted that the reasoning here is a bit hasty, for until he has ascertained the type of cryptogram the professor has no warrant for saying that "the sense is concealed under letters purposely jumbled" and that if "properly arranged (they) would form an intelligible sentence." This description applies only to the primary class of ciphers designated as *transposition*, in which the letters of the plain text are all present but have merely been rearranged according to some scheme previously agreed upon between correspondents. The other primary class of ciphers is that designated as *substitution*, in which other letters, or characters, have been substituted for the letters of the original message. Had Verne merely mentioned that in a cipher in which the letters have only been shifted about the normal proportions of vowels and consonants as found in ordinary plain language still hold true, and that these normal proportions exist in the cryptogram, he would have given a technically adequate reason for saying that the "sense is concealed under the letters purposely jumbled." Incidentally, the first step that the professor took was one of substitution, for he replaced each rune by a letter of the alphabet, and, as we have noted above, the runes in this case serve merely as substitutive symbols for the letters of the underlying message.

When we come to Verne's analysis leading to the conclusion that the language of the cryptogram is that of a southern European land and specifically Latin, we find some excellent and valid reasoning. It is evident that Verne really knew a good deal about the proportions that normally exist between the vowels and consonants of various languages. However, just why Verne jumps to the conclusion that it is in "jumbled Latin" remains obscure. Certainly there is nothing to justify such an assumption at this stage in the analysis. Likewise obscure is the reasoning which follows this unwarranted conclusion. "Now, this arrangement has evidently not been combined; [5] it is determined *mathematically* by the unknown rule which governed the succession of these letters. It seems certain to me that the original sentence was written regularly, then turned about in accordance with a law which we must discover." It is too bad that Verne did not place this matter before that in which he sets forth the reason for concluding that the message is in Latin, for had he done so he would have been able to show how he reached the conclusion that the cryptogram is a transposition and not a substitution cipher, a step which logically precedes that of deducing that the cryptogram was written in Latin.

When the professor decides to experiment with various regular types of rearrangements of letters he is on firm ground, for it is only too true, as many a cryptanalyst will ruefully admit, that in transposition ciphers solution is often a matter of trial and error. (Most cryptanalysts detest them because their solution affords few opportunities for the use of the scientific tools he can apply in the case of substitution ciphers.) The first experiment the professor makes is a logical one. "Let us see," he says, "the first suggestion which would occur to one, for mixing the letters of a sentence, it seems to me, is to write the words vertically instead of horizontally." And since the text of the cryptogram is written in groups of six and seven characters, he decides to reverse the operation he conceives to have been performed originally and writes the 1st, 2d, . . . letter of each group successively. The result is what is shown on p. 73—still unintelligible text.

We may forgive Verne for his drama in causing the professor to fly from his study in chagrin, rage, and puzzlement. He could, of course, as readily have led the professor to the solution, just as he led the professor's nephew to it. In fact, it would have been easier—and it would not have looked, as it now does, like "pulling a rabbit out of a hat." Moreover, Verne made a slip in his explanation of how the professor's nephew stumbled upon the solution. For he has the nephew fanning

[5] The meaning of this first sentence is problematical, even in the French text. Perhaps Verne means that the arrangement is not the result of a combination, using the latter word in the same way as we do in referring to the "combination" to the lock on a vault door.

286

himself with the sheet of paper upon which the cryptogram had been transcribed as dictated by the professor, "when in one of these rapid movements, at the moment that the back of the sheet turned toward me, I thought I saw perfectly legible words appear—Latin words, among others 'craterem' and 'terrestre'!"

If the reader will try the experiment, writing the letters "meretarc" on a transparent piece of paper and viewing the writing from the back of the sheet he will see that far from causing the letters to become perfectly legible and disclosing the word "craterem," the writing when viewed from the back of the sheet upon which it is written becomes if anything more cabalistic in appearance than ever. Indeed, a very simple type of cipher writing is that called "mirror writing," which consists in forming the characters in such a manner as to make the writing unintelligible and mystifying—until it is held before a mirror. (Mirror-writing is a trick often practiced by children.)

Verne could just as easily have given the professor credit for a little more intelligence than he does when it comes to this last step in the interpretation of the cryptogram. After all, a man of the scholarship he attributes to the professor would surely have seen through this last and simplest phase of the disguise assumed by the message in cryptographic form, especially since he had enough intelligence to accomplish the first and much more difficult part of the solution, namely, the transcription of the original groups of letters into the final form shown. Casual inspection of "reversed writing" is all that is necessary to uncover the mystery.

It is noteworthy to add that Verne apparently had a weakness for this type of transposition, reversed writing, for two of the three cryptograms encountered in his stories involve this form of disguise.

2. THE CRYPTOGRAM IN MATHIAS SANDORF

In this tale Verne introduces a cryptogram which has been enciphered by means of a very old cryptographic device termed a "rotating grille." This consists of a small square sheet of thin metal or cardboard divided up into smaller squares, in some of which apertures have been cut at definite locations. An example of a grille is shown in figure 2. This is a grille with 6 squares per side, making an area of 36 small squares. Nine of these small squares have been cut out, so that they present openings or apertures through which letters may be written on an underlying surface. If this grille is superimposed upon a piece of cross-section paper the cells of which are identical in their dimensions with those of the apertures of the grille, these apertures will disclose 9 cells of the underlying cross-section paper and in these cells the first 9 letters of the message to be conveyed may be written. If the grille is then turned 90° and again placed over the cross-section paper at exactly the same spot, 9 more cells will be disclosed by the apertures in the grille and 9 more letters of the message may be written in those cells. Twice more the grille may be turned and the same procedure executed, whereupon every one of the 36 cells of the underlying cross-section paper will have been disclosed and each of these 36 cells will be occupied by a letter. When the grille is removed, there will be 36 letters in a disarranged sequence on the piece of underlying cross-section paper. These letters may now be transcribed in groups or in an unbroken sequence, taking them in the normal order (left to right and top to bottom) from the square. All the original letters of the message are there, in unchanged form, but because their original order has been changed they will be unintelligible, that is, we will have produced a cryptogram. If the

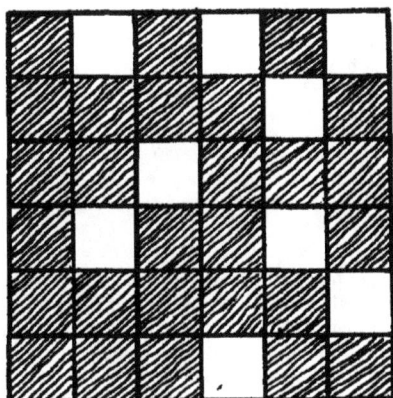

FIGURE 2.

message is longer than 36 letters, another 6 by 6 area of the cross-section paper is treated the same way, with the same grille, making another cipher square of 36 letters. Thus, a long message would be enciphered in successive sets of 36 letters until completed.

In case there are not enough letters to fill up the last square of 36 letters, meaningless or null letters are used to complete the square. A person not having the grille will be unable to read such a message—so the theory runs. The recipient of such a cryptogram, having an identical grille, writes out the cryptogram on a 6 by 6 piece of cross-section paper in the normal order of writing, and applies the grille to the 36 letter squares in the same fashion. But he takes the letters out of the squares in the order disclosed by the apertures in the grille, turning the latter in the same direction as it was turned in encipherment, the direction being previously agreed upon between the correspondents.

Now the solution of a cryptogram prepared by means of an unknown grille is by no means a simple matter, but it can be done. Verne was perhaps aware that a solution is possible, but he did not try it in Mathias Sandorf, and I am quite sure that he was technically on the right side in not trying, for the exposition would be much beyond the understanding of the casual reader of romantic detective stories.

However, let us see how Verne got around the problem he set for himself when he introduced this sort of cryptogram in Mathias Sandorf. A few brief extracts from the story are necessary.

"A message?" exclaimed Sarcany. "Wait, Zirone! This warrants a reprieve!" He stopped the hand of his companion as it was about to close on the neck of the carrier pigeon. Then taking the small bag which was attached to its wing he opened it and withdrew a message written in cipher language.

The message contained only 18 words, disposed in three vertical columns, as follows:

```
l h n a l z      z a e m e n      r u i o p n
a r n u r o      t r v r e e      m t q s s l
o d x h n p      e s t l e v      e e u a r t
a e e e i l      e n n i o s      n o u p v g
s p e s d r      e r s s u r      o u i t s e
e e d g n c      t o e e d t      a r t u e e
```

There was neither a point of origin nor a point of destination indicated on the message. Would it be possible to understand the meaning of these 18 words, without knowing the cipher?

*   *   *   *   *   *   *

"From a careful examination of this dispatch," said Sarcany, "it is clear to me that the key is based neither upon a number nor upon a conventional alphabet which would assign to each of the letters a significance other than its true one. Yes, in this message an *s* is an *s*, a *p* is a *p*, but the letters have been arranged in an order which can only be reconstructed by means of a grille!"

"Perhaps," said Toronthal, "but without the grille it is impossible to reconstruct the message."

*   *   *   *   *   *   *

In the fourth drawer which Sarcany examined, among some papers he had not encountered before he found a sort of a card irregularly perforated. This card attracted his attention immediately. "The grille!" he said.

He was not mistaken.

This grille was a simple cardboard square, 6 centimeters long on each side and divided into 36 equal squares, each measuring about a centimeter. In the 36 squares disposed in 6 horiontal and vertical lines, as in a Pythagorean table which has been based upon 6 numbers, 27 were filled and 9 were empty; that is, in place of the 9 squares the card was perforated and open in 9 apertures.

One could establish first of all that the 6 first words of the message, composed of 36 letters, had been successively obtained from the 36 squares.

In effect the disposition of the openings was so ingeniously combined in the mechanism of this grille that by making four turns of a quarter turn each (Verne really means three turns after the first placement of the grille), the perforated squares would successively occupy the positions of the unperforated squares without duplication at any place.

*   *   *   *   *   *   *

289

Sarcany wrote on a blank sheet the letters of the 6 first words. This give the following series :

```
i h n a l z
a r n u r o
o d x h n p
a e e e i l
s p e s d r
e e d g n c
```

Then the grille was applied on this set of letters in such a manner that the side marked by a small cross was placed at the top. And then the 9 perforated cells disclosed the 9 following letters while the other 27 remained hidden by the unperforated cells of the cardboard :

```
h a z r x e i r g
```

Sarcany then made a quarter of a turn with the grille from left to right in such a manner that the upper side now became the right. In this second application there were the following letters which appeared through the openings :

```
n o h a l e d e c
```

In the third and fourth applications the visible letters were the following, the writing of which was observed with care :

```
n a d n e p e d n
i l r u o p e s s
```

which signified absolutely nothing. "Let us continue," exclaimed Sarcany. He commenced experimenting on the 6 words forming the second column of the message. Four times he applied the grille on the words, each time making a quarter of a turn. He obtained only the following series of letters, absolutely devoid of meaning :

```
a m n e t n o r e
v e l e s s u o t
e t s e i r t e d
z e r r e v n e s
```

And here are the words which were given by the last 4 applications of the grille :

```
u o n s u o v e u
q l a n g i s r e
i m e r p u a t e
r p t s e t u o t
```

"Well," exclaimed Sarcany, "what are we going to make of this indecipherable logogriph !"

"Now write all the words one after the other," replied the banker very simply, "and then what? Let us see."

Sarcany obeyed and obtained the following sequence of letters :

```
h a z r x e i r g n o h a l e d e c n a d n e p e d
n i l r u o p e s s a m n e t n o r e v e l e s s u
o t e t s e i r t e d z e r r e v n e s u o n s u o
v e u q l a n g i s r e i m e r p u a t e r p t s e
t u o t
```

No sooner had these letters been written when Silas Toronthal wrested the paper from Sarcany's hands, read it and gave vent to a cry, "Don't you see?" he exclaimed, "that before composing the words by means of the grille the correspondents of Count Sandorf had previously written the sentence they had drawn up, backwards!" Sarcany took the paper and here is what he read, going from the last letter to the first:

"Tout est prêt. Au premier signal que vous nous enverrex de Trieste, tous se lèverout en masse pour l'indépendance de la Hongrie. Xrzah."

"And the last 5 letters?" he cried.

"A conventional signature." replied Silas Toronthal.

*   *   *   *   *   *   *

Now Verne does not show the grille which was used in preparing the crytogram, yet a criticism of the cryptographic features of the story involves an attempt to reconstruct the grille from the solution Verne gives. I confess that as I was about to embark upon this experiment I was a prey to certain fears—I was not sure that the cryptogram had been prepared by means of a grille, for it would have been just as easy for Verne to set down the letters of the original cryptogram in some purely random fashion and then merely bring up the letters in their proper order. But it was indeed gratifying to find that the cryptogram is really authentic insofar as its having been prepared by means of a grille is concerned. For the grille shown in fig. 2 is identical with the one Verne used and the sceptical reader may verify the decipherment if he so desires. He will find that every letter which Verne gives as coming successively from each placement of the grille upon the 36-letter squares is correct, and that the entire decipherment, from beginning to end, is correct in every particular.

Of course, Verne might have refrained from including the additional step involving the writing of the original plain text backwards and then inscribing the letters on a checkerboard through the apertures of a grille. The grille alone would have been quite sufficient for the average reader!

There is only one more point which calls for comment. It concerns the reasoning by means of which Verne has Sarcany arrive at the definite conclusion that a grille was employed in enciphering the cryptogram. To have Sarcany say that "in the message an s is an s, a p is a p, but the letters have been rearranged," would really have been valid reasoning only after at least some attempt to demonstrate how he arrives at even this conclusion. He should, of course, have noted that the proportions of vowels, high-frequency and low-frequency consonants in the cryptograms conform to the proportions found in intelligible French, and therefore it is highly probable than an s is an s, a p is a p. But since the letters do not form intelligible sequences, therefore the original letters must have been rearranged so as to destroy the intelligence conveyed by them.

From this point in the reasoning to that wherein Verne has Sarcany reach the conclusion that "the letters have been disposed in a sequence which can only be reconstructed by means of a grille" is quite a jump. An unwarranted elision in logical thought was made by Verne. He could, of course, have remedied this deficiency in exposition had he called attention to the fact that the original cryptogram came in blocks of 36 letters—and 36 is a perfect square. For it is one of the characteristics of grille encipherment that when the sides of the grille are of even dimensions, such as 4 by 4, 6 by 6, 8 by 8, etc., the "capacity" of the grille, that is, the total number of letters that can be enciphered by the four positions the grille may assume, is always a perfect square. When the sides of the grille are of odd dimensions, such as 5 by 5, 7 by 7, 9 by 9, etc., the capacity of the grille is always 1 less than a perfect square. In the case of the cryptogram in Mathias Sandorf, since the 3 blocks of letters contain 36 letters each, there are some grounds for assuming that a revolving grille 6 by 6 was used. Note that I merely say that there are some grounds for assuming that this is the case, for there are literally hundreds of methods of transposition which could be employed, other than that involving the use of a grille, and which might produce blocks of 36 letters. Indeed, there is nothing in the story as it stands to warrant the hypothesis that the arrangement in blocks of 36 letters is anything more than purely an arbitrary selection from among scores of methods of writing out the letters of a cryptogram after a transposition has been effected. However, it is true that the arrangement in groups of 6 letters and in sets of 6 lines, making blocks of 36 letters is today not a usual practice, for 5-letter, not 6-letter groupings are standard today. In Verne's day, however, this practice was just coming into usage and we may readily overlook this small defect in his reasoning. I have by no means made an exhaustive survey of the various types of cryptograms the authors of romances and detective tales have employed, but of the many authors examined Verne is the only one who has employed the interesting device of a grille.

Incidentally, Toronthal's (that is, Verne's) conclusion that the last 5 letters which do not make any sense constitute a conventional signature is unwarranted. For these letters are merely nulls or nonsignificants, necessary to make a complete set of 36 letters in the third section of the message. Indeed, one could readily surmise that since Verne fails to give a plausible explanation of these 5 final letters, he really did not know or understand their function. The evidence might point to the surmise that Verne had aid from some friend who was a cryptographer in the preparation of the grille and the cryptogram. This would hardly be a source of astonishment, for the method of preparing a grille of the sort here involved, while a simple matter, is

292

known to only a very few persons, and even among cryptographers this knowledge is perhaps not common. Further, it is a matter of record that Verne consulted technical experts in various fields and utilized the information they gave him in the interest of accuracy.

3. THE CRYPTOGRAM IN THE GIANT RAFT, OR EIGHT HUNDRED LEAGUES ON THE AMAZON. (FRENCH TITLE: LA JAGANDA)

Although chronologically this tale is the second in which Verne introduces a cryptogram into his work and attempts to weave an account of methods for solution into his story, I have left the cryptogram involved in The Giant Raft to be discussed last for several reasons. First, Verne devotes much more time, thought, and space to its elucidation than he does to the solution of the cryptograms in the two preceding tales. Secondly, the cryptogram in this case is of much more importance as an example of a practical method of secret writing than is either the cryptogram in A Journey to the Center of the Earth or that in Mathias Sandorf. Thirdly, because Verne's novels achieved astonishing success and enjoyed very wide popularity, the type of cryptogram Verne adopted in The Giant Raft became quite well known among laymen and is even sometimes referred to in cryptographic literature as "The Jules Verne Cipher"—although Verne did not "invent" it nor, to be perfectly fair, did he make the slightest pretense at being its inventor. Fourthly, the solution of a cryptogram of this type, that is, its translation without the "key," was, at the time Verne wrote, deemed probably by all laymen and certainly by a few who possessed reputations as cryptographers to be an impossibility. Certainly Verne believed the solution to be impossible; yet he not only undertook to achieve an answer to the enigma without introducing any "tricks" but, what is more, he actually did achieve a solution by having recourse to a method which is perfectly legitimate so far as the professional cryptanalyst is concerned but which strangely enough may be regarded as a "trick solution," by many laymen. This may on first consideration be thought by the reader to redound to Verne's credit, and so it does, as a weaver of interesting romances, but unfortunately it does not redound to his credit as an ingenious thinker, or even as an amateur scientist. For had he really devoted some study to the matter, and had he not accepted blindly the common but erroneous notion that this type of cipher is indecipherable without the key, he might possibly have arrived at the straightforward and really simple method of solution which was devised many years before his time and which is still applicable today.

The hero in The Giant Raft, Joam Dacosta. alias Joam Garral, stands falsely accused of having committed murder. He can only be exonerated and his life saved by solving a cryptogram the key to which was unknown to him or to any of his friends. A certain Judge Jarriquez. before whom Dacosta must establish his innocence, undertakes to solve the cryptogram, the secret of which must be "miraculously divined or revealed" before the end of 8 days. By the time that Jarriquez gets around to trying to solve the cryptogram 4 or 5 days have already gone by, leaving the feat to be accomplished in but 3 days. Verne devotes three entire chapters and parts of two more to the elucidation of the cipher, and in a rather painstaking manner goes into the matter with considerable detail, no doubt in an attempt to interest the reader in the abstruse science of cryptography, just as Poe did in The Gold Bug. But Poe used as his vehicle practically the simplest type of cipher known, that designated technically as monoalphabetic substitution, whereas Verne uses as his vehicle a much more complicated method designated technically as polyalphabetic substitution, or, as the French have it, "substitution by double key." In monoalphabetic substitution, each different letter of the original or intelligible text is replaced by some other character, which is always the same for that letter. Hence in the cryptogram every symbol always represents the same letter in the plain text and conversely, no letter in the plain text has more than one representative in the cipher. But in polyalphabetic substitution this invariant relationship between a plain-text letter and its cipher equivalent no longer holds true: letters which are the same in the plain text may have different equivalents in the cipher text depending upon their position in the text with respect to a key. This key, it is true, may be repeated many times in the course of enciphering the message but if it is unknown it produces varying and (to the uninitiated) quite mystifying results.

In appraising Verne's attempts at unraveling a cryptogram of this sort it will be best to begin by giving an example to show the mechanics of the method, which incidentally is very old.[6]

Let us suppose that the following message is to be enciphered: DACOSTA WAS MY ENEMY BUT HE IS INNOCENT OF THE MURDER. THE PROOF IS IN MY HANDS. A key consisting of a series of digits is agreed upon between the correspondents, say 46548973. This key means merely that the successive letters of the message to be enciphered will be replaced by those standing 4. 6. 5, * * *, places beyond them in the ordinary alphabet. Since the key consists of but eight digits in this case, and

---

[6] In cryptographic literature this method is attributed in Schott's Magia universalis (Nuremberg, 1659) to a Count Gronsfeld, with whom Schott had made a journey from Mayence to Francfort.

the message contains 62 letters, the key is repeated as many times as may be necessary to encipher the entire message. Thus:

```
Message...DACOSTA WAS MY ENEMY BUT HE IS INNOCENT OF THE
Key.......4654897 346 54 89734 654 89 73 46548973 46 548
Cipher....HGHSACH ZEY RC MWLPC HZX PN PV MTSSKNUW SL YLM
Message...MURDER THE PROOF IS IN MY HANDS
Key.......973465 489 73465 48 97 34 65489
Cipher....VBUHKW XPN WUSUK MA RU PC NFRLB
```

The cipher letters are then written out either in an unbroken series of letters (as is the case in Verne's story) or in regular groups (in these days, five letters per group), so as not to disclose the length of the key.

To the reader who is perhaps acquainted only with the most simple types of ciphers this method of cryptography may well appear to be inscrutable without possession of the key, which in this case is a series of 8 digits selected at random. He reasons somewhat as follows: Since there are 10 digits to choose from and repetitions are permissible, such a key of 8 digits may be any one of 10^8 or 100,000,000 different permutations, only one of which will serve to decipher the cryptogram. The chances of guessing the right key is obviously only one in a hundred million—too small to be of practical importance. Moreover, he reasons, if you should try to solve the cryptogram by the well-known principles of frequency, you can't get very far. For note how one and the same letter in the plain text is represented by different letters in the cipher. For example, E, which occurs seven times is represented by M (twice), L, N (three times), and K; N, which occurs six times, is represented by W, T, S, U (twice), and R. On the other hand, look at the cipher letter H; it occurs five times and it stands for the letters D (twice), C, A, and B. How in the name of common sense could anyone not in possession of the key straighten out such inconsistencies and irregularities by any principles of frequency, which in their very nature require some modicum of consistency to mean anything?

This is the sort of reasoning that Verne himself employs, as may be noted in the following extracts, which not only are interesting in themselves but also are quite essential to a criticism of his accomplishments as a cryptographer.

The cryptogram in The Giant Raft was, says Verne, a document

"written in a disguised form in one of the numerous systems used in cryptography. But in which of them? To discover this would require all the ingenuity of which the human brain was capable. [It] contained a hundred lines, which were divided into half a dozen paragraphs."

"Hum" said the judge. after a little reflection; to try every paragraph, one after the other, would be to lose precious time, and be of no use. I had better select one of these paragraphs, and take the one which is likely to prove the most interesting. Which of them would do this better than the last, where the

recital of the whole affair is probably summed up? Proper names might put
me on the track, amongst others that of Joam Dacosta; and if he has anything
to do with this document, his name will evidently not be absent from its concluding paragraph."

Here follows the last paragraph of the document.

Phyjslyddqfdzxgasgzzqqehxgkfndrxujugiocytdxvksbxhhuypohdvyrymhuh
puydkjoxphetozsletnpmvffovpdpajxhyynojyggaymeqynfuqlnmvlyfgsuzmq
iztlbqgyugsqeubvnreredgruzblrmxyuhqhpzdrrgcrohepqxufivvrplphonth
vddqfhqsntzhhhnfepmqkyuuexktogzgkyuumfvijdqdpzjqsykrplxhxqrymvkl
ohhhotozvdksppsuvjhd.

At the outset, Judge Jarriquez noticed that the lines of the document were
not divided either into words or phrases, and that there was a complete absence
of punctuation. This fact could but render the reading of the document more
difficult.

"Let us see, however," he said, "if there is not some assemblage of the letters which appears to form a word—I mean a pronounceable word, whose number of consonants is in proportion to its vowels. And at the beginning I see
the word *phy;* farther on the word *gas.* Hallo! *ujugi.* Does that mean
the African town on the banks of Tanganyika? What has that got to do with
all this? Farther on here is the word *ypo.* Is it *Greek,* then? Close by here
is *rym* and *puy,* and *jox,* and *phetoz,* and *jyggay,* and *mv,* and *qruz.* And before that we have got *red* and *let.* That is good! those are two English words.
Then *ohe—syk;* then *rym* once more, and then the word *oto.*"

Judge Jarriquez let the paper drop, and thought for a few minutes.

"All the words I see in this thing seem queer!" he said. "In fact, there is
nothing to give a clue to their origin. Some look like Greek, some like Dutch;
some have an English twist, and some look like nothing at all! To say nothing
of these series of consonants which are not wanted in any human pronunciation. Most assuredly it will not be very easy to find the key to this cryptogram."

The magistrate's fingers commenced to beat a tattoo on his desk—a kind of
reveille to arouse his dormant faculties.

"Let us see," he said, "how many letters there are in the paragraph."

He counted them, pen in hand.

"Two hundred and seventy-six!" he said. "Well, now let us try what proportion these different letters bear to each other."

This occupied him for some time. The judge took up the document, and,
with his pen in his hand, he noted each letter in alphabetical order.

In a quarter of an hour he had obtained the following table:

a= 3	f=10	k= 9	p=16	u=17
b= 4	g=13	l= 9	q=16	v=13
c= 3	h=23	m= 9	r=12	x=12
d=16	i= 4	n= 9	s=10	y=19
e= 9	j= 8	o=12	t= 8	z=12

Total_____ 276

"Ah, hah!" he exclaimed. "One thing strikes me at once, and that is that
in this paragraph all the letters of the alphabet are used. That is very strange.
If we take up a book and open it by chance it will be very seldom that we
shall hit upon two hundred and seventy-six letters with all the signs of the
alphabet figuring amongst them. After all, it may be chance," and then he

REF ID:A484988

passed to a different train of thought. "One important point is to see if the vowels and consonants are in their normal proportion."

And so he seized his pen, counted up the vowels, and obtained the following result:

```
a =  3
e =  9
i =  4
o = 12
u = 17
y = 19
     ——
Total _____ 64 vowels
```

"And thus there are in this paragraph, after we have done our subtraction, 64 vowels and 212 consonants. Good! that is the normal proportion. That is about a fifth, as in the alphabet, where there are six vowels, amongst 25 letters. It is possible, therefore, that the document is written in the language of our country, that is, in Portuguese, but that only the signification of each letter is changed. If it has been modified in regular order, and a b is always represented by an l, an o by a v, a g by a k, a u by an r, etc., I will give up my judgeship if I do not read it. What can I do better than follow the method of that great analytical genius, Edgar Allan Poe?"

Verne has committed a rather serious error here. It is true that 6 vowels correspond, in an alphabet of 25 elements, to approximately a fifth of the number of letters—a proportion that is true not only of Portuguese but also of French, German, Spanish, English, and in fact of practically all alphabetic languages. Verne was warranted in drawing no conclusions from this fact, least of all that "only the signification of each letter is changed." However, he soon gets on the right track again when he devotes several paragraphs to an explanation of how Poe, in The Gold Bug, solved the cryptogram involved in that "masterpiece,"—this is Verne's own characterization of Poe's great tale. Of course, he brings out quite clearly the basis for Poe's analysis, which is that of frequency.

"What did Edgar Poe do?" he repeated. "First of all he began by finding out the sign—here there are only letters, let us say the letter—which recurred the oftenest. I see that that is h, for it is met with twenty-three times. This enormous proportion shows, to begin with, that h does not stand for h, but, on the contrary, that it represents the letter which recurs most frequently in our language, for I suppose the document is written in Portuguese. In English or French it would certainly be e, in Italian it would be i or a, in Portuguese it will be a or o. Now let us say that h signifies a or o."

After this was done, the judge found out the letter which recurred most frequently after h, and so on, and he formed the following table:

```
h          = 23 times
y          = 19 times
u          = 17 times
d, p, q    = 16 times
g, v       = 13 times
o, r, x, z = 12 times
```

f, s	= 10 times
e, k, l, m, n	= 9 times
j, t	= 8 times
b, i	= 4 times
a, c	= 3 times

"Now the letter *a* occurs thrice!" exclaimed the judge, "and it ought to occur the oftenest. Ah! that clearly proves that the meaning has been changed. And now, after *a* or *o*, what are the letters which figure oftenest in our language? Let us see," and Judge Jarriquez, with truly remarkable sagacity, which denoted a very observant mind, started on this new quest. In this he was only imitating the American romancer, who, great analyst as he was, had, by simple induction, been able to reconstruct an alphabet corresponding to the signs of the cryptogram and by means of it to eventually read the pirate's parchment note with ease.

The magistrate set to work in the same way, and we may affirm that he was no whit inferior to his illustrious master. Thanks to his previous work with logogriphs and squares, rectangular arrangements, and other enigmas, which depend only on an arbitrary disposition of the letters, he was already pretty strong in such mental pastimes. On this occasion he sought to establish the order in which the letters were reproduced—vowels first, consonants afterwards.

After 3 hours' work, in which "he had only to apply successively the letters of his alphabet to those of the paragraph," the judge gives up in disgust. What he did was to assign to each cipher letter a plain-text value in strict accordance with the principles of frequency; that is, since *a* is the most frequently used letter in Portuguese, and *h* is the most frequently appearing letter in the cryptogram, ergo *h=a*. Likewise *y*, the next most frequent letter in the cryptogram, must be *o*, and so on. No wonder that Judge Jarriquez failed! Even had the cryptogram been of the very simple, monoalphabetic type, such procedure would hardly ever result in success. We may be inclined to be charitable and give Verne credit for knowing better than to have his man adhere so slavishly to what is well recognized as only a rather flexible generalization; we might say that he had the judge go through this futile procedure only for the sake of dramatic emphasis. But somehow I feel that Verne actually believed that had the cryptogram been of this simple type, solution must have come by the method indicated—a wholly erroneous notion. No wonder the Judge cries "Confound the thing!"

Next we listen to some dialogue between a young friend, Manoel, and Judge Jarriquez, after the former inquires as to what success has attended the latter's efforts. The judge tells Manoel that he has had no success, but that he is certain that the document is governed by the law of a number.

"Well, sir," answered Manoel, "cannot a document of that kind always be read?"

"Yes," said Jarriquez, "if a letter is invariably represented by the same letter; if an *o*, for example, is always a *p*, and a *p* is always an *x*; if not, it cannot."

"And in this document?"

"In this document the value of the letter changes with the arbitrarily selected number which necessitates it. So a *b*, which will in one place be represented by a *k*, will later on become a *z*, later on a *u*, or an *n*, or an *f*, or any other letter."

"And then?"

"And then, I am sorry to say, the cryptogram is indecipherable."

"Indecipherable!" exclaimed Manoel. "No, sir; we shall end by finding the key of the document on which the man's life depends."

Manoel had risen, a prey to the excitement he could not control; the reply he had received was too hopeless, and he refused to accept it for good.

At a gesture from the judge, however, he sat down again, and in a calmer voice asked, "And in the first place, sir, what makes you think that the basis of this document is a number, or, as you call it, a cipher?"

"Listen to me, young man," replied the judge, "and you will be forced to give in to the evidence."

The magistrate took the document and put it before the eyes of Manoel and showed him what he had done.

"I began," he said, "by treating this document in the proper way, that is to say, logically, leaving nothing to chance. I applied to it an alphabet based on the proportion the letters bear to one another which is usual in our language, and I sought to obtain the meaning by following the precepts of our immortal analyst, Edgar Poe. Well, what succeeded with him collapsed with me."

"Collapsed!" exclaimed Manoel.

"Yes, my dear young man, and I at once saw that success sought in that fashion was impossible. In truth, a stronger man than I might have been deceived."

"But I should like to understand," said Manoel, "and I do not."

"Take the document," continued Judge Jarriquez; "first look at the disposition of the letters, and read it through."

Manoel obeyed.

"Do you not see that the combination of several of the letters is very strange?" asked the magistrate.

"I do not see anything," said Manoel, after having for perhaps the hundredth time read through the document.

"Well! study the last paragraph! There you understand the sense of the whole is bound to be summed up. Do you see anything abnormal?"

"Nothing."

"There is, however, one thing which absolutely proves that the language is subject to the law of a number."

"And that is?"

"That is that you see three *h*'s coming together in two different places."

What Jarriquez said was correct, and it was of a nature to attract attention. The two hundred and fourth, two hundred and fifth, and two hundred and sixth letters of the paragraph, and the two hundred and fifty-eighth, two hundred and fifty-ninth, and two hundred and sixtieth letters of the paragraph were consecutive *h*'s. At first this peculiarity had not struck the magistrate.

"And that proves?" asked Manoel, without divining the deduction that could be drawn from the combination.

"That simply proves that the basis of the document is a number. It shows *a priori* that each letter is modified by virtue of the digits of the number and according to the place which it occupies."

"And why?"

"Because in no language will you find words with three consecutive repetitions of the letter h." [7]

Manoel was struck with the argument; he thought about it, and, in short, had no reply to make.

"And had I made the observation sooner," continued the magistrate, "I might have spared myself a good deal of trouble and a headache which extends from my occiput to my sinciput."

"But, sir," asked Manoel, who felt the little hope vanishing on which he had hitherto rested, "what do you mean by a number?"

"Tell me a number."

"Any number you like."

"Give me an example and you will understand the explanation better."

Judge Jarriquez sat down at the table, took up a sheet of paper and a pencil, and said, "Now, Manoel, let us choose a sentence by chance, the first that comes: for instance—'Judge Jarriquez has an ingenious mind.'"

Then the judge proceeds to encipher this message with the key 234 exactly as we enciphered our example on page 86, with the longer key 46548973. The result he obtains is as follows:

```
j u d g e j a r r i q u e z h a s a n i n g e n i o u s m i n d
2 3 4 2 3 4 2 3 4 2 3 4 2 3 4 2 3 4 2 3 4 2 3 4 2 3 4 2 3 4 2 3
l x h i h n c u v k t y g c t c v e p l r i h r h r y u p m p g
```

The judge concludes his demonstration of the mechanics of the cipher thusly:

"Now you see that if you do not know the number 234 you will never be able to read the lines, and consequently if we do not know the number of the document, it remains undecipherable!

Then he demonstrates with his own example how if one can guess a word in the message one can recover the key, and indeed the demonstration is made with great clarity. But, amazingly, Verne discards this method as unutilizable unless the first digit of the key number should happen to be that which enciphers the very first letter of the word, the presence of which is assumed! This sort of reasoning does little credit to a man of Verne's intelligence. Let us examine the reasoning.

Judge Jarriquez says that he is convinced that the name Joam Dacosta will be found in the paragraph in cipher. He goes on:

"Well, if the lines had been divided into words, in trying the words one after the other—I mean the words composed of seven letters, as the name of Dacosta is—it would not have been impossible to evolve the number which is the key of the document."

"Will you explain to me how you ought to proceed to do that, sir?" asked Manoel, who probably caught a glimpse of one more hope.

"Nothing can be more simple," answered the judge. "Let us take, for example, one of the words in the sentence we have just written—my name, if

---

[7] The reasoning here is quite fallacious. Since the cryptogram is a substitution cipher, even if it were monoalphabetic, h could represent some letter other than h in the plain text. Suppose it represented an l; there are many words which end in double l, which might be followed by a word beginning in l, making three consecutive l's, which would be represented by hhh in the cipher.

you like. It is represented in the cryptogram by this queer succession of letters, *ncuvktygc*. Well, arranging these letters in a column, one under the other, and then placing against them the letters of my name and deducting one from the other the numbers of their places in alphabetical order, I get the following result:

Between *n* and *j* we have 4 letters
Between *c* and *a* we have 2 letters
Between *u* and *r* we have 3 letters
Between *v* and *r* we have 4 letters
Between *k* and *i* we have 2 letters
Between *t* and *q* we have 3 letters
Between *y* and *u* we have 4 letters
Between *g* and *e* we have 2 letters
Between *c* and *z* we have 3 letters

"Now what is the column of digits made up of that we have got by this simple operation? Look here! 423, 423, 423, that is to say, of repetitions of the numbers 423, or 234, or 342."

"Yes, that is it!" answered Manoel.

"You understand, then, by this means, that in calculating the true letter from the false, instead of the false from the true, I have been able to discover the number with ease; and the number I was in search of is really the 234 which I took as the key of my cryptogram."

"Well, sir!" exclaimed Manoel, "if that is so, the name of Dacosta is in the last paragraph; and taking successively each letter of these lines for the first of the seven letters which compose his name, we ought to get—"

"That would be impossible," interrupted the judge. "except on one condition."

"What is that?"

"That the first digit of the number should happen to encipher the first letter of the word Dacosta, and I think you will agree with me that that is not probable."

Now I shall not unduly tax the reader's patience, I hope, but will merely call attention to the fact that "guessing a word"—the "probable-word method," as it is called technically—is a procedure which has been used successfully for at least a couple of centuries. Its mechanics are well known. If the assumed word is present it will yield, in the cipher system under consideration, either the whole key or a portion of it. In either case, the application of this key to other portions of the text will yield good plain text, provided only that the key is applied at the correct point in the cycles or periods into which the cipher may be divided. To make clear just what is meant, let us take the example which was enciphered on page 86, and let us assume that we did not know the plain text but imagine that it contains the words "The murder." If we assume that the message begins with these words, apply them to the cipher letters, and derive the key numbers which will produce H G H S A C H Z E from "The murder" we find the following:

```
If............... H  G  H  S  A  C  H  Z  E
Equals.......... T  H  E  M  U  R  D  E  R
The key is.....14-25—3—6—6-11—4-21-13
```

Since the system is such that the key must be composed of single digits, it is obvious without further investigation that H G H S A C H Z E cannot be the cipher equivalent of "The murder." In fact, if we were making this sort of attempt at finding the key, we would be warranted in stopping with the very first letter, where T is enciphered by H, because the key for this encipherment would be 14, which is impossible since the enciphering key digit can in no case exceed 9. We would then shift the assumed words, "The murder," one space to the right in the cryptogram and try again. Thus:

```
If........................................H G H S A C H Z E Y
Equals....................................  T H E M U R D E R
The key is................................  13  . . . . . . .
```

We stop with the very first encipherment, for the key number exceeds 9. Thus we would shift the assumed words step-by-step until the following point is reached:

```
If........................................Y L M V B U H K W
Equals....................................T H E M U R D E R
The key is................................5-4-8-9-7-3-4-6-5
```

The reader will recognize that we have here the complete key, plus one digit of a second cycle of that key. Had the assumed phrase been longer, the reconstructed key sequence would continue on the second cycle, producing 5-4-8-9-7-3-4-6-5-4-8-9- . . . etc.

Now, of course, we know that the key in this case does not begin with 5-4-8; as a matter of fact it begins with 4-6-5. But since this key is repetitive in character as regards its application in the encipherment, it is not essential that we know what the initial digit in the actual key is, for if we merely apply the reconstructed key to the text at any correct point in the keying cycle, we shall obtain good plain text. Thus, if we take the key reconstructed by assuming that Y L M V B U H K W represents "The murder," *viz*, 5-4-8-9-7-3-4-6, and apply it to our illustrative message not at the very beginning, but at the third letter, we obtain intelligible text. Thus:

```
Cipher....................................H G H S A C H Z E Y R . . .
Key.......................................  5-4-8-9-7-3-4-6-5 . . .
Plain text................................  C O S T A W A S M . . .
```

It is only necessary that we recognize the fact that we have plain text here and divide up the letters properly. Thus: . . . costa was m . . . .

So Verne was decidedly in error when he said that the procedure of assuming the name Dacosta would work only if "the first digit of the key number should happen to encipher the first letter of the word Dacosta." If the assumed word is really there it makes no difference at all with which digit of the key its first letter is enciphered. Incidentally, it is very interesting to note, first, that the very example Verne uses in his attempt to prove that the key can be discovered by "guessing" a word in the cryptogram only if "the first digit of the number should happen to encipher the first letter" of the assumed word, disproves his qualifying condition. For reference to his example shows that the first letter of the name Jarriquez was not enciphered by the first digit of the key, and yet Verne found the correct key or a cyclic permutation of that key by this method. Secondly, it is interesting to note not only that the name Dacosta is really present in the cryptogram which Judge Jarriquez is attempting to solve, but also that the first letter of the name is really enciphered by the first digit of the key! In other words, the very event which the judge says is improbable actually occurred in the cryptogram.

To return once more to the main theme, let us continue with Verne's solution. Manoel suggests that "chance might give us this number."

"This number," exclaimed the magistrate—"this number? But how many digits is it composed of? Of two, or three, or four, or nine, or ten? Is it made up only of different digits, or of digits in different order many times repeated? Do you not know, young man, that with the ordinary ten digits, using all at a time, but without any repetition, you can make 3,268,800 different numbers,[8] and that if you use the same digit more than once in the number, these millions of combinations will be enormously increased? And do you now know that if we employ every one of the 525,600 minutes of which the year is composed to try at each of these numbers, it would take you six years, and that you would want three centuries if each operation took you an hour? No! You ask the impossible!"

After struggling with the matter one whole day fruitlessly, the judge resolves, however,

never to leave the document until he had discovered the cipher. He set to work at it in a fury. He ate no more, he slept no more! All his time was passed in inventing combinations of numbers, in forging a key to force this lock! * * * Suppressed frenzy consumed him, and kept him in a perpetual heat. His whole house trembled; his servants, black or white, dared not come near him * * *. Never had a problem so taken possession of this character, and he had thoroughly made up his mind to get at the solution even if his head exploded like an overheated boiler under the pressure of its steam. * * * It was perfectly clear to the mind of the worthy magistrate that the key to the document was a number, composed of two or more digits, but what this number was all investigation seemed powerless to discover.

The judge decides to try the probable-word method, but because Verne had no clear apprehension of the method this attempt was futile. Here is what the judge does:

"Ah!" he exclaimed, "why did not the scoundrel who wrote this separate the words in this paragraph? We might—we will try—but no! However, if

---

[8] In the edition I have, this number is as given, but it should be 3,628,000. It is the product of the series of numbers from 1 to 10, inclusive. If repetitions are permissible, the total number of permutations is 10^{10}, or 10,000,000,000.

there is anything here about the murder and the robbery, two or three words must be present—'arrayal,' 'diamond,' 'Tijuco,' 'Dacosta,' and others; and in putting down their cryptological equivalents the number could be arrived at. But there is nothing—not a single break!—not one word by itself! One word of 276 letters! I hope the wretch may be blessed 276 times for complicating his system in this way! He ought to be hanged 276 times!"

And a violent thump with his fist on the document emphasized this charitable wish.

"But," continued the magistrate, "if I cannot find one of the words in the body of the document, I might at least try my hand at the beginning and end of each paragraph. There may be a chance there that I ought not to miss."

And impressed with this idea Judge Jarriquez successively tried if the letters which commenced or finished the different paragraphs could be made to correspond with those which formed the most important word, which was sure to be found somewhere, that of *Dacosta.*

He could do nothing of the kind.

In fact, to take only the last paragraph with which he began, the formula was—

$$P = D$$
$$h = a$$
$$y = c$$
$$j = o$$
$$s = s$$
$$l = t$$
$$y = a$$

Now at the very first letter Jarriquez was stopped in his calculations, for the difference in alphabetical position between the *d* and the *p* gave him not one digit but two, namely, 12, and in this kind of cryptogram only one letter can take the place of another.[9]

It was the same for the seven last letters of the paragraph, *p s u v j h d,* of which the series also commences with a *p,* and which could in no case stand for the *d* in *Dacosta,* because these letters were in like manner twelve spaces apart.

So it was not his name that figured here.

The same observation applies to the words *arrayal* and *Tijuco,* which were successively tried, but whose construction did not correspond with the cryptographic series.

After he had got so far, Judge Jarriquez, with his head nearly splitting, arose and paced his office, went for fresh air to the window, and gave utterance to a growl, at the noise of which a flock of humming birds, murmuring amongst the foliage of a mimosa tree, betook themselves to flight. Then he returned to the document.

He picked it up and turned it over and over.

"The humbug! the rascal!" he hissed; "it will end by driving me mad! But steady! Be calm! Don't let our spirits go down! This is not the time!"

And then having refreshed himself by giving his head a thorough sluicing with cold water:

"Let us try another way," he said, "and as I cannot hit upon the number from the arrangement of the letters, let us see what number the author of the docu-

[9] What Verne means to say here is that one letter can take no more than a single digit for its key in encipherment.

ment would have chosen in confessing that he was the author of the crime at Tijuco."

This was another method for the magistrate to enter upon, and maybe he was right, for there was a certain amount of logic about it.

The judge then tries his hand at guessing the key number, assuming dates of various sorts—that of the birth of Dacosta, the year the crime was committed, etc.—but to no avail. "Nothing! All the time nothing!" Then comes an amusing episode highly suggestive of the procedure adopted at times by victims of the unsuppressible game of modern times known as the "numbers racket." Let Verne tell it himself:

Judge Jarriquez had worked himself into such a state of exasperation that there really was some fear that his mental faculties would lose their balance. He jumped about, and twisted about, and wrestled about as if he really had got hold of his enemy's body. Then suddenly he cried, "Now for chance! Heaven help me now, logic is powerless!"

His hand seized a bell pull hanging near his table. The bell rang furiously, and the magistrate strode up to the door, which he opened. "Bobo!" he shouted.

A moment or two elapsed.

Bobo was a freed negro, who was the privileged servant of Jarriquez. He did not appear; it was evident that Bobo was afraid to come into his master's room.

Another ring at the bell; another call to Bobo, who, for his own safety, pretended to be deaf on this occasion. And now a third ring at the bell, which unhitched the crank and broke the cord.

This time Bobo came up. "What is it, sir?" asked Bobo, prudently waiting on the threshold.

"Advance, without uttering a single word!" replied the judge, whose flaming eyes made the negro quake again.

Bobo advanced.

"Bobo," said Jarriquez, "attend to what I say, and answer immediately; do not even take time to think, or I——"

Bobo, with fixed eyes and open mouth, brought his feet together like a soldier and stood at attention.

"Are you ready?" asked his master.

"I am."

"Now, then, tell me, without a moment's thought—you understand—the first number that comes into your head."

"76223," answered Bobo, all in a breath. Bobo thought he would please his master by giving him a pretty large one!

Judge Jarriquez had run to the table, and, pencil in hand, had made out a formula with the number given by Bobo, and which Bobo had in this way only given him at a venture.

It is obvious that it was most unlikely that a number such as 76223 was the key of the document, and it produced no other result than to bring to the lips of Jarriquez such a vigorous ejaculation that Bobo disappeared like a shot!

Verne now interrupts the account of the judge's attempts at the solution of the cryptogram to tell of a plot hatched by Dacosta's relatives to bring about the escape of the prisoner—but the prisoner thwarts these plans by vehemently protesting his innocence and refusing to escape.

Finally, one Fragoso, a trusted servant of Dacosta who had under-taken to do some sleuthing in an attempt to clear his master's name and had gone on a journey into the interior, appears in the nick of time—on the morning of the day on which the condemned man was to be hung. He bursts into Judge Jarriquez's home.

"I come from the province where Torres pursued his calling as captain of the woods!" he gasped. "Mr. Judge, Torres told the truth. Stop—stop the execu-tion!"

"You found the gang?"

"Yes."

"And you have brought me the key to the document?"

Fragoso did not reply.

"Come, leave me alone! leave me alone!" shouted Jarriquez, and, a prey to an outburst of rage, he grasped the document to tear it to atoms.

Fragoso seized his hands and stopped him. "The truth is there!" he said.

"I know," answered Jarriquez: "but it is a truth which will never see the light!"

"It will appear—it must! it must!"

"Once more, have you the cipher."

"No," replied Fragoso, "but, I repeat, Torres has not lied. One of his com-panions, with whom he was very intimate, died a few months ago, and there can be no doubt but that this man gave him the document he came to sell to Joam Dacosta."

"No," answered Jarriquez—"no, there is no doubt about it—as far as we are concerned; but that is not enough for those who dispose of the doomed man's life. Leave me!"

Fragoso, repulsed, would not quit the spot. Again he threw himself at the judge's feet. "Joam Dacosta is innocent!" he cried; "you will not leave him to die! It was not he who committed the crime of Tijuco, it was the comrade of Torres, the author of that document! It was Ortega!"

As he uttered the name the judge bounded backward. A kind of calm swiftly succeeded to the tempest which raged within him. He dropped the document from his clenched hand, smoothed it out on the table, sat down, and, passing his hand over his eyes. "That name?", he said, "Ortega? Let us see," and then he proceeded with the new name brought back by Fragoso as he had done with the other names so vainly tried by himself.

After placing it above the six first letters of the paragraph, he obtained the following formula:

<pre>
        O r t e g a
        P h y j s l
</pre>

"Nothing!" he said. "That gives us—nothing!"

And in fact the *h* placed under the *r* could not be expressed by a single digit, for, in alphabetical order [10] this letter occupies an earlier position to that of the *r*.

The *p*, the *y*, the *j*, arranged beneath the letters *o*, *t*, *e*, disclosed the cipher 1, 4, 5, but as for the *s* and the *l* at the end of the word, the interval which sepa-

---

[10] Verne here again refers to the condition that a keying number for a single letter must not be more than a single digit. The "earlier position" in alphabetical order has nothing to do with the matter, for a plain-text letter such as Y may be enciphered by a keying digit 5, for example, and will then be represented by D. The alphabet in such a cryptographic system is regarded as partaking of the nature of a closed circle of letters.

rated them from the *g* and the *a* was a dozen letters, and hence impossible to express by a single cipher, so that they corresponded to neither *g* nor *a*.

And here appalling shouts arose in the streets; they were the cries of despair.

Fragoso jumped to one of the windows, and opened it before the judge could hinder him.

The people filled the road. The hour had come at which the doomed man was to start from the prison, and the crowd was flowing back to the spot where the gallows had been erected.

Judge Jarriquez, quite frightful to look upon, devoured the lines of the document with a fixed stare.

"The last letters!" he muttered, "Let us try once more the last letters!" It was the last hope.

And then, with a hand whose agitation nearly prevented him from writing at all, he placed the name of Ortega over the six last letters of the paragraph, as he had done over the first.

An exclamation immediately escaped him. He saw, at first glance, that the six last letters were inferior in alphabetical order to those which composed Ortega's name, and that consequently they might yield the number.

And when he reduced the formula, reckoning each later letter from the earlier letter of the word, he obtained

```
O r t e g a
4 3 2 5 1 3
S u v j h d
```

The number thus disclosed was 432513.

But was this number that which had been used in the document? Was it not as erroneous as those he had previously tried?

At this moment the shouts below redoubled—shouts of pity which betrayed the sympathy of the excited crowd. A few minutes more were all that the doomed man had to live!

Fragoso, maddened with grief, darted from the room! He wished to see, for the last time, his benefactor who was on his road to death! He longed to throw himself before the mournful procession and stop it, shouting, "Do not kill this just man! Do not kill him!"

But already Judge Jarriquez had placed the given number above the first letters of the paragraph, repeating them as often as was necessary, as follows:

```
4 3 2 5 1 3 4 3 2 5 1 3 4 3 2 5 1 3 4 3 2 5 1 3
P h y j s l y d d q f d z x g a s g z z q q e h
```

And then, reckoning the true letters according to their alphabetical order, he read:

Le véritable auteur du vol de—

A yell of delight escaped him! This number, 432513, was the number sought for so long! The name of Ortega had enabled him to discover it! At length he held the key of the document, which would incontestably prove the innocence of Joam Dacosta, and without reading any more he flew from his study into the street, shouting,

"Halt! Halt!"

To cleave the crowd, which opened as he ran, to dash to the prison, whence the convict was coming at the moment, with his wife and children clinging to him with the violence of despair, was but the work of a minute for Judge Jarriquez.

Stopping before Joam Dacosta, he could not speak for a second, and then these words escaped his lips:

"Innocent! Innocent!"

    *   *   *   *   *   *   *

Judge Jarriquez sat down on a stone seat, and then, while Minha, Benito, Manoel, and Fragoso stood round him, while Joam Dacosta clasped Yaquita to his heart, he first unravelled the last paragraph of the document by means of the number, and as the words appeared by the substitution of the true letters for the cryptological ones, he divided and punctuated them, and then read it out in a loud voice. And this is what he read in the midst of profound silence:

```
Le véritable auteur du vol des diamants et de
43 251343251 343251 34 325 134 32513432 51 34
Py yjslyddqf dzxgas gz zqq ehx gkfndrxu ju gi

l'assassinat des soldats qui escortaient le convoi.
32513432513 432 5134325 134 32513432513 43 251343
ocytdxvksbx hhu ypohdvy rym huhpuydkjox ph etozsl

commis dans la nuit du vingt-deux janvier mil
251343 2513 43 2513 43 25134 3251 3432513 432
etnpmv ffov pd pajx hy ynojy ggay meqynfu qln

huit cent vingt-six, n'est donc pas Joam Dacosta,
5134 3251 34325 134   3251 3432 513 4325 1343251
mvly fgsu zmquz tlb   qgyu gsqe ubv nror edgruzb

injustement condamné àmort, c'est moi, le misérable
34325134325 13432513 43251  3432 513  43 251343251
lrmxyuhqhpz drrgcroh epqxu  fivv rpl  ph onthvddqf

employé de l'administration du district diamantin,
3432513 43  251343251343251 34 32513432 513432513
hqsntzh hh  nfepmqkyuuexkto gz gkyuumfv ijdqdpzjq

oui, moi seul, qui signe de mon vrai nom, Ortega.
432  513 4325  134 32513 43 251 3432 513  432513
syk  rpl xhxq  rym vkloh hh oto zvdk spp  suvjhd.
```

"The real author of the robbery of the diamonds and of the murder of the soldiers who escorted the convoy, committed during the night of the twenty-second of January, one thousand eight hundred and twenty-six, was thus not Joam Dacosta, unjustly condemned to death; it was I; the wretched servant of the Administration of the diamond district; yes, I alone, who sign this with my true name, Ortega."

And thus the curtain descends with the saving of the hero's life.

By means of the number Judge Jarriquez interpreted the whole cryptogram ... The name Ortega had afforded the means of unravelling the cryptogram, thanks to the sagacity of Judge Jarriquez.

At another point in the story Verne says:

In any case, the situation of Joam Dacosta was most hazardous. If the document were not deciphered, it would be just the same as if it did not exist; and if the secret of the cryptogram were not miraculously divined or revealed *before the end of the* 3 days,[11] the supreme sentence would inevitably be suffered by the doomed man of Tijuco. And this miracle a man attempted to perform!

* * * * * * *

The excitement increased in Manaos as the time ran on; the affair was discussed with unexampled acerbity. In the midst of this enthralment of public opinion, which evoked so much of the mysterious, the document was the principal object of conversation.

At the end of this fourth day not a single person doubted but that it contained the vindication of the doomed man. Every one had been given an opportunity of deciphering its incomprehensible contents, for the "Diario d'o Grand Para" had reproduced it in facsimile. Autograph copies were spread about in great numbers at the suggestion of Manoel, who neglected nothing that might lead to the penetration of the mystery—not even chance, that "nickname of Providence," as some one has called it.

In addition, a reward of 100 contos (or 300,000 francs) was promised to any one who could discover the cipher so fruitlessly sought after—and read the document. This was quite a fortune, and so people of all classes forgot to eat, drink, or sleep to attack this unintelligible cryptogram.

Up to the present, however, all had been useless, and probably the most ingenious analysts in the world would have spent their time in vain. It had been advertised that any solution should be sent, without delay, to Judge Jarriquez, to his house in God-the-Son Street; but the evening of the 29th of August came and none had arrived, nor was any likely to arrive.

We may be certain that Verne thought most highly of his achievement in solving the cryptogram, in the character of Judge Jarriquez. But quite devastating are the words of one commentator,[12] who has looked into the matter and says: "to a modern expert, however, the learned judge appears as a pompous and pedantic ass. Many of his musings and observations would sound shallow even to the most casual reader who took the trouble to follow him carefully." These are pretty strong words, and we shall not accept them without due examination. So let us see how a "modern expert" would proceed to solve a cryptogram of this type.

The solution of a cryptogram of this type, wherein a repeating key is employed, resolves itself into three steps. First, the length of the key must be ascertained; this gives the number of cipher alphabets involved. Second, the letters of the cryptogram must be distributed into individual frequency tables corresponding to the separate cipher alphabets involved. Third, these frequency distributions must be analyzed to find the equivalency between plain-text and cipher-text letters in each alphabet. These steps may sound some-

---

[11] It will be recalled that 4 or 5 days had elapsed between the time Dacosta was arraigned and the time Judge Jarriquez began his attempt to unravel the secret. Verne says:"Joam Dacosta had been arrested on the 24th of August and examined the next day. The judge's report was sent off on the 26th. It was now the 28th. In 3 or 4 days more the minister would have come to a decision regarding the convict, and it was only too certain that justice would take its course."

[12] Hooker, Charles W. R., *The Jules Verne Cipher*, The Police Journal (British), vol. IV. No. 3, January 1931, pp. 107–119.

what complicated and formidable to the reader who has no cryptographic experience, but I assure him that they are really quite
simple. They are especially so in this case.

Let us consider the first step, that of finding the length of the
key. There are various ways of doing this, but only one will be
considered here. If the reader will study the example on page 86
attentively, he will see that despite the fact that a number of different alphabets was employed there are still some repetitions in the
cryptogram, as shown below:

```
h g h s a c h z e y r c m w l p c h z x p n p v m t s s k
n u w s l y l m v b u h k w x p n w u s u k m a r u p c n
f r l b
```

Here we have three repetitions: CHZ occurs twice, XPN occurs
twice, PC occurs twice. Let us refer back to the encipherment of the
example to see how these repeated groups happened to be brought
about. The first CHZ represents the encipherment of TAW by key
numbers 9–7–3; the second CHZ represents the encipherment of YBU
by key numbers 4–6–5. The identity of the cipher letters in these
two cases is a pure accident! It just happened as a result of chance
that two different sets of plain-text letters enciphered by two different
sets of key numbers gave exactly the same set of cipher letters. Repetitions of this sort are called accidental, because that is what they are.
But now note the two groups XPN; the first XPN represents the encipherment of THE by key numbers 4–8–9, and the second XPN
represents the encipherment of another THE by the same key numbers,
4–8–9. In this case, because the same plain-text sequence falls under
the same key numbers twice, the cipher resultants had to be identical.
Of course, if these two THE's had happened to fall under different
key numbers, the cipher resultants would not have been identical—
but then there might have been brought about some other repetition,
for the repetition of single letters, pairs of letters, and sets of three,
four, or more letters is an all-pervading phenomenon in practically
every alphabetic language. Note how the repetition of the pair of
letters PC is brought about: in the first case it represents the MY
of ENEMY, in the second it represents the word MY, and of course,
both MY's were enciphered by the same key numbers. Repetitions
of this sort are called causal repetitions because they are brought about
by a definite cause, viz, the encipherment of similar sequences by
identical keying characters. In such cases the letters must be enciphered by the same cipher alphabets. Now if a message is long
enough, in comparison with the length of the repeating key, there will
be many such cases of causal repetitions—more than sufficient to
overbalance the disturbing element of accidental repetitions, because,

as said before, repetition of sequences of letters in plain language is a characteristic of plain language.

Now if the reader will count the number of letters from the first appearance of XPN to, but not including, the second appearance of this same group, he will see that this number is 24, which is an exact multiple of the length of the key. Also, if the reader will do the same thing with respect to the PC repetition, he will find the number to be 40, which is also an exact multiple of the length of the key. In fact, in the first case the key has passed through three complete cycles between the two occurrences, and in the second case it has passed through five complete cycles. In the case of the CHZ repetition, however, the interval between the two occurrences bears no relation to the length of the key: since the repetition is accidental there can be no relationship. Now in a long message one merely lists the repetitions, finds the length of the intervals between similar repetitions, and sets down the factors of those intervals. That factor which is common to most of the repetitions usually corresponds to the length of the key. The longer the repetition the more weight is to be given to the factors of the interval between its two occurrences, because the less likely is it that such a repetition is of the accidental type. All of this business has been reduced to statistical language, so that in practice the cryptanalyst can estimate pretty closely what the probabilities are that a given repetition is an accident or has been causally produced.

Applying the foregoing procedure to the Verne cryptogram, first we find all the repetitions of two or more letters. This is purely a matter of clerical work and I will not trouble the reader to perform it. Here are all the repetitions of three or more letters in the cryptogram, together with the intervals between them and the factors of those intervals:

From	1st	D D Q F	to 2d	D D Q F	—186 letters.	Factors: 2, 3, 6, 31.
From	1st	K Y U U	to 2d	K Y U U	— 12 letters.	Factors: 2, 3, 4, 6.
From	1st	H H H	to 2d	H H H	— 54 letters.	Factors: 2, 3, 6, 9, 18, 27.
From	1st	R Y M	to 2d	R Y M	—192 letters.	Factors: 2, 3, 4, 6, 8, 12. 16, 24, 32, 48, 64, 96.
From	1st	R P L	to 2d	R P L	— 60 letters.	Factors: 2, 3, 4, 5, 6, 12, 15, 20, 30.
From	1st	T O Z	to 2d	T O Z	—186 letters.	Factors: 2, 3, 6, 31.

The only factor (other than 2 and 3, which are unlikely) which is common to all the intervals between these repetitions is 6, and we may take this to be the length of the key. Great weight may be placed upon the repetition D D Q F, which shows an interval of 186; the factors of this number are 2, 3, 6, and 31. The first two are unlikely and so is the last one, leaving 6 as almost certain.

The letters of the cryptogram are now transcribed into groups of 6 letters, to correspond with the length of the key, and individual frequency distributions for all six positions in these groups are compiled. They are as follows (note that the letter W does not occur in French):

```
PHYJSL   YDDQFD   ZXGASG   ZZQQEH   XGKFNX   RXUJUG
IOCYTD   XVKSBX   HHUYPO   HDVYRY   MHUHPU   YDKJOX
PHETOZ   SLETNP   MVFFOV   PDPAJX   HYYNOJ   YGGAYM
EQYNFU   QLNMVL   YFGSUZ   MQIZTL   EQGYUG   SQEUBV
NRCRED   GRUZBL   RMXYUH   QHPZDR   RGCROH   EPQXUF
IVVRPL   PHONTH   VDDQFH   QSNTZH   HHNFEP   MQKYUU
EXKTOG   ZGKYUU   MFVIJD   QDPZJQ   SYKRPL   XHXQRY
MVKLOH   HHOTOZ   VDKSPP   SUVJHD
```

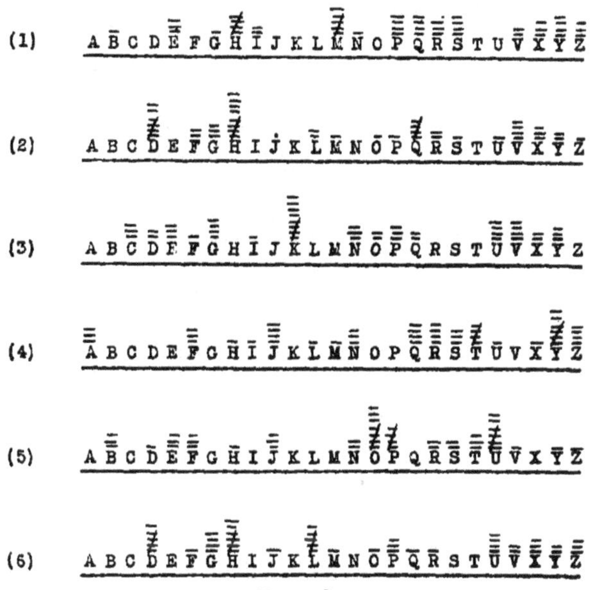

FIGURE 3.

Now in a cipher of this sort, where the digits of a key are added to numbers corresponding to the serial position of the plain-text letters in the ordinary aphabet, the effect is merely to shift all the letters enciphered by the same keying digit forward 1, 2, 3, . . . 9 letters forward, in accordance with the keying digit. For example, in the case under consideration, the key has been found to consist of six digits and hence the cryptogram was transcribed in groups of six letters. The letters occupying position 1 in these groups have all been enciphered by the same keying digit. Suppose the latter were 3; then a D in position 1 in a cipher group would represent plain-text letter A, an E in position 1 would represent plain-text letter B, and so on. This effect can most readily be observed in the distribution labeled alphabet 2 in figure 3. Note the high frequency of D; if it represents A, then the keying digit to produce cipher D from plain-text A would have to be 3. Now how can we prove that 3 is correct? Well, it is easy enough: the high spots and low spots in alphabet 2 should all merely be shifted 3 spaces forward from the places where these high and low spots are normally found if the letters in this frequency distribution were plain-text letters. Now if one were to take 50 letters of ordinary French and distribute them under the normal French alphabet, they would theoretically form the following graph:

A B C D E F G H I J K L M N O P Q R S T U V X Y Z

A comparison of this graph with alphabet 2 quickly tells us that if we will shift the latter three spaces to the left, the sequence of high and low spots will fall just where they should fall if the letters were plain-text letters. Thus:

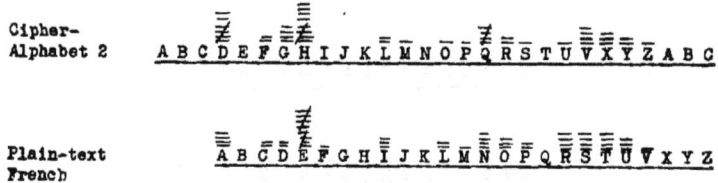

Cipher-
Alphabet 2   A B C D E F G H I J K L M N O P Q R S T U V X Y Z A B C

Plain-text
French   A B C D E F G H I J K L M N O P Q R S T U V X Y Z

FIGURE 4.

Since we have been dealing with alphabet 2, this establishes the digit 3 as the second digit of the key, and the plain-text equivalents may be written under the letters of cipher alphabet 2. Thus:

Cipher   A B C D E F G H I J K L M N O P Q R S T U V X Y Z
Plain   X Y Z A B C D E F G H I J K L M N O P Q R S T U V

FIGURE 5.

This process is termed "fitting the cipher distribution to the normal." By proceeding in the same manner with all the other cipher alphabets, we find that the best "fits" are obtained when the keying digits shown below are assumed:

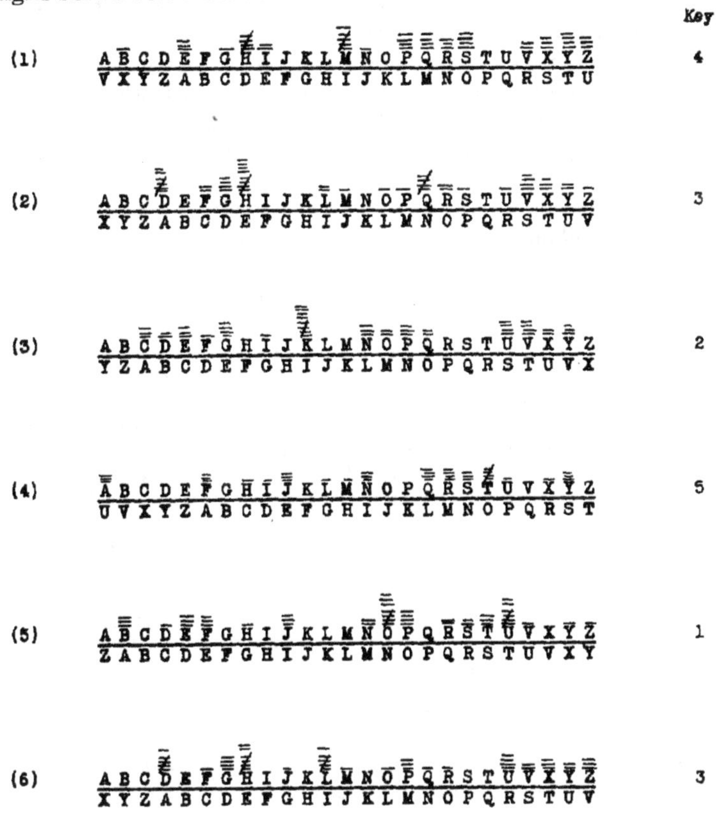

Key

(1)
```
A B C D E F G H I J K L M N O P Q R S T U V X Y Z
V X Y Z A B C D E F G H I J K L M N O P Q R S T U
```
4

(2)
```
A B C D E F G H I J K L M N O P Q R S T U V X Y Z
X Y Z A B C D E F G H I J K L M N O P Q R S T U V
```
3

(3)
```
A B C D E F G H I J K L M N O P Q R S T U V X Y Z
Y Z A B C D E F G H I J K L M N O P Q R S T U V X
```
2

(4)
```
A B C D E F G H I J K L M N O P Q R S T U V X Y Z
U V X Y Z A B C D E F G H I J K L M N O P Q R S T
```
5

(5)
```
A B C D E F G H I J K L M N O P Q R S T U V X Y Z
Z A B C D E F G H I J K L M N O P Q R S T U V X Y
```
1

(6)
```
A B C D E F G H I J K L M N O P Q R S T U V X Y Z
X Y Z A B C D E F G H I J K L M N O P Q R S T U V
```
3

FIGURE 6.

The rest is now a mere matter of clerical work. Applying the key 4-3-2-5-1-3 to the first two or three cipher groups, we obtain plain-text immediately:

```
P H Y J S L   Y D D Q F D   Z X G A S G . . .
4 3 2 5 1 3   4 3 2 5 1 3   4 3 2 5 1 3 . . .
L E V E R I   T A B L E A   U T E U R D . . .
```

The text needs only be divided up into proper word lengths, and the solution is complete: LE VÉRITABLE AUTEUR D . . .

The reader must have noted by this time how simple and straight-forward the solution of a case of this kind can be. Notwithstanding the apparent hopelessness (to the uninitiated) of the problem, it is thus seen to be solvable quite simply, following a procedure and utilizing means known to specialists in cryptography for many years. The present author would indeed welcome an opportunity for earning the round sum of 300,000 francs (even at the current rate of exchange this would buy quite a few books) for solving so easy a cryptogram, for even an amateur cryptanalyst should be able to solve in a couple of hours or so the cryptogram with which Judge Jarriquez struggled for several days. And it is clear that Verne did not purposely exaggerate the difficulty for the sake of heightening the dramatic effect of his story, for he really believed the problem to be beyond the powers of analysis of cryptographic experts. In an interesting volume, Hommes et Choses de Science, the celebrated French engineer, Maurice d'Ocagne, reproduces in facsimile a letter from Verne of which the following is a translation:

28 Oct. 81.

MY DEAR MAURICE: I have received your letter. I believed the document almost indecipherable. If I had known that at the École polytechnique one of your classmates could solve the cryptogram I would have added an interversion of the letters which have guaranteed it against every investigation. But after all Mr. Sommaire took 3 months to find this key. Judge Jarriquez had but 8 days for that. It would not have been astonishing had he not succeeded at all. But let's not tell him; it would make him blow his brains out.[13]

I have not seen your father for a long time. Shake his hand warmly for me. And to you,

Very cordially,

JULES VERNE.

(P. S.) When I see you I want you to tell me how Mr. Sommaire succeeded in that. I vow this intrigues me."[14]

This comment establishes that while Verne had informed himself on the principles of enciphering a message by the so-called Gronsfeld method, he had not acquainted himself with the principles used by experts in solving a cryptogram produced by that scheme. The result

---

[13] The French is "Il se ferait sauter la cervelle," which is rendered in Larousse du XXme Siecle as I have given it. But somehow it fails to fit the context. I can hardly agree with a friend who suggests that the translation by implication is "It will cause his head to swell to the bursting point." Perhaps Verne meant to say that if Sommaire were told what had taken him 3 months to accomplish was done by Judge Jarriquez in 8 days, he (Sommaire) "might blow his brains out."

[14] That Verne was sufficiently intrigued by M. Sommaire's solution to have made an effort to learn more details is established by the following paragraph extracted from an article by d'Ocagne which appeared in Revue Hebdomadaire, Année 37, tom 9, Sept. 1, 1938:

Devoted as he was, as if by a decree of Providence, to the task of spellbinding his contemporaries by his amazing inventions, Jules Verne himself was not lacking in the faculty of being astonished. That was plain to me the day when I communicated to him, before the appearance of vol. II of La Jaganda, a translation made by one of my classmates of the École polytechnique, of the cryptogram given at the beginning of the first volume of this novel, and which he, the author, considered as indecipherable. He purposely even came to the École in order to have my colleague explain to him how he went about successfully executing this feat of divination, and I see him yet, turning my way several times, in the course of this explanation, to exclaim. "What analytical powers! I am literally bewildered by them. What analytical powers!"

315

is that the method employed by Judge Jarriquez depends on a chance suggestion of a "probable word" instead of following the orderly steps of analysis which cryptanalysis shares with chemistry for example. Furthermore, when Verne states in the d'Ocagne letter that if he had known that somebody could solve the cryptogram he "would have added an interversion of the letters which would have guaranteed it against every investigation" one is led to wonder how in that case Judge Jarriquez would have been able to arrive at any solution at all— for by "interversion" Verne can only mean some form of transposition such as he used in the other cryptograms discussed herein, such as reversing the order of the letters, employing a rectangular design or a grille, and so on. Then, indeed, would Judge Jarriquez have struggled in vain and Verne would have had to adopt some other course in extricating his hero from the noose. For according to the method of solution Jarriquez finally adopted, the only way of ascertaining whether the "probable word" ORTEGA was correct was to test the key it yielded on the rest of the cryptogram. Now, if a transposition had been added, this sort of testing, without a complete knowledge of the method that had been followed in effecting the transposition, would be entirely futile.

Despite what may appear to the reader to be quite devastating criticism of Verne as a cryptographer, it is far from my wish to convey the impression that his efforts in this field are unworthy of note. For when we look into the types of cryptograms other writers of romantic tales and detective stories have employed, we must recognize that he stands head and shoulders above them all—not excluding even Poe. The latter used for his vehicle one of the very simplest types of cryptograms known; its analysis was, it is true, an excellent piece of work in The Gold Bug and I hardly think that any writer has surpassed Poe in the lucidity and excellence of the demonstration he gives of the method of solving this type of cryptogram. But Poe never attempted a tale involving anything more difficult than a simple substitution or if he did his efforts came to naught, because Poe's works include only one story involving the solution of a cryptogram. Certainly Poe knew of the type of cryptogram called a multiple-alphabet or repeating-key cipher, but there is reason to believe that he but vaguely grasped the method of solving it. Verne, on the other hand, chose three different types of cryptograms, all more difficult than simple substitution, and wove ingenious stories about them. And when we observe the puerility of the types of cryptograms even modern authors of stories employ, Verne's genius calls for admiration and respect—even on the part of professional cryptographers who know only too well the limitations imposed upon authors who desire to interest casual readers in the fascinating art of solving ciphers.

The Crypt Bug *

By Master Sgt. CHARLES MURRAY

When all good folks are sound asleep,
And all the rest are counting sheep,
He concentrates on cipher text,
And contemplates ways most complex
To render an approved solution
Of some obscure substitution.

While all the world is sleeping, snoring
Loud enough to rip the flooring,
He derives much satisfaction
From the spatial interaction
Of poly-graphic frequencies
And isomorphic sequences,
Of characters on paper slips
Better known as sliding strips.

Slides them West and tries the "Chi" test,
Slides them East and tries the "Phi" test,
Clamps his pipe tight in his mouth,
And grimly slides them North and South,
And if success eludes him then,
Tears them up and starts again.
Meanwhile the clock ticks on and on,
Until at long last comes the dawn.

As the milkman rattles by,
He is heard to heave a sigh,
Slowly piles the work sheets higher,
Calmly throws them on the fire,
Having proved one simple fact;
There can be no doubt of that—
As suspected all along,
Everything he did was wrong.

*(No. 109, July–December, 1940)

316